Crowning the
Nice Girl

Crowning the

Published with the support
of the School of Hawaiian,
Asian, and Pacific Studies,
University of Hawai'i

Nice Girl

Gender, Ethnicity,
and Culture in
Hawai'i's Cherry
Blossom Festival

Christine R. Yano

University of Hawai'i Press | Honolulu

HAWAI

11 10 09 08 07   6 5 4 3 2

Library of Congress Cataloging-in-Publication Data
Yano, Christine Reiko.
Crowning the nice girl : gender, ethnicity, and culture in
Hawaii's Cherry Blossom Festival / Christine R. Yano.
    p. cm.
Includes bibliographical references and index.
ISBN-13: 978-0-8248-3007-6 (cloth : alk. paper)
ISBN-10: 0-8248-3007-5 (cloth : alk. paper)
ISBN-13: 978-0-8248-3059-5 (pbk. : alk. paper)
ISBN-10: 0-8248-3059-8 (pbk. : alk. paper)
1. Cherry Blossom Festival (Honolulu, Hawaii) — History.
2. Beauty contests — Hawaii — Honolulu.   3. Japanese
American women — Hawaii — Honolulu — Ethnic identity.
4. Japanese American women — Hawaii — Honolulu —
Psychology.   5. Japanese American women — Hawaii —
Honolulu — Social conditions.   6. Honolulu (Hawaii)
— Race relations.   7. Honolulu (Hawaii) — Social life and
customs.   I. Title.
HQ1220.U5Y36 2006
305.48'89560969 — dc22   2005037657

University of Hawai'i Press books are printed on
acid-free paper and meet the guidelines for permanence
and durability of the Council on Library Resources.

Designed by April Leidig-Higgins

Printed by Sheridan Books, Inc.

Contents

Acknowledgments

This book is a product of many relationships that come replete with debts, obligations, and heartfelt emotions. As I reread through these pages for the umpteenth time, I am humbled by the webs of friendship and cooperation that produced them. Writing this book was only made possible through the support and help of others, and I feel a tremendous sense of responsibility and gratitude to the many who have contributed to this enterprise.

My first debt is to those directly involved in the Cherry Blossom Festival — the Jaycees, Queens and contestants, and many volunteers. Besides providing me with information and hospitality, they taught me a lot about giving with heart. Jaycee leaders such as Sharene Urakami, Mike Inouye, Leo Asuncion, and Keith Kamisugi showed me by example what it means to bear a sense of responsibility to a community and to give freely and creatively to make things happen. A festival such as this, fueled solely by their labor year after year, is nothing short of miraculous. Knowing that each volunteer is not a paid professional, but gives of her or his time freely while juggling family and career makes the result precious and sometimes fragile. The Queens that I feature in "herstories" deserve my special gratitude, especially Kathy, Gwen, Lenny, Mi, and Cat; but so, too, do the many others whom I interviewed. I only wish that I could have included all of your wonderful stories. A warm *mahalo* goes out to the contestants of the fiftieth Cherry Blossom Festival. They put up with my questions and general presence, convincing me that they all deserve crowns of achievement. Longtime supporter Lillian Yajima warrants special thanks and admiration for her willingness to share memories, newspaper clippings, souvenir books, and general knowledge. She is the grand dame of the Cherry Blossom Festival and I pay tribute to her years of enthusiastic service.

I am indebted to colleagues at the University of Hawai'i, including Jonathan Okamura, Jane Moulin, Karen Jolly, Mire Koikari, Mari Yoshihara, and others. They shared their ideas and thoughts at various stages of this work, and I read their imprint everywhere in these pages. Thanks to Jinzhao Li, Kalindi Vora, Yoko Kurokawa, David LaPorta, and Hirofumi Katsuno for their help. Thanks as well to Lon Kurashige for reading portions of this manuscript and commenting. A special thank you to Jaida Samudra for transcribing tapes and editing, as well as to Masako Ikeda and the anonymous reviewers at the University of Hawai'i Press.

This research was funded in part by a University of Hawai'i Humanities Endowment Fund Grant, for which I am truly grateful. Thanks also go out to Chris Conybeare and Cliff Watson who worked with me on the film and with whom I anticipate future collaborations. *Mahalo* to the board of directors of the Honolulu Japanese Junior Chamber of Commerce for giving me permission to use images from past souvenir books and supplying me with a 2005 poster, as well as to PacificBasin Communications for allowing me to reproduce a cover of *Paradise of the Pacific*.

Families seem to crop up last in acknowledgments, which is backward, because they come first in my mind. My parents have provided tireless support of meals-on-wheels and teen care. My mother seems to have started a beauty-queen chain in my family. My reaction was to turn the spotlight into prose. My daughter Marika has taken wing in her own kind of spotlight as slam poet, graphic artist, and worldly adventurer at the tender age of seventeen. The crowning of her beauty and voice knows no bounds. It is to the men in my family — my father, Scott, and Eli — that I dedicate this book. The spotlight veers past them, and yet this list of acknowledgments is as much about their lives as any. In lieu of a crown, I offer my deeply felt gratitude and love.

Prologue

Sansei Dreams of Beauty Queens and Beyond

J grew up in Hawai'i during the mid-1950s and 1960s, a third-generation (sansei) Japanese American girl from a middle-class family. Every year my family watched the Miss America pageant on TV. We sat in our living room agog at the spectacle of Atlantic City over 5,000 miles away — the glamour, the lights, and most of all, the long-legged beauties. We studied all of them, trying to pick the winner. We were tough critics, scrutinizing teeth that weren't even or legs that weren't long and straight. My mother, aunts, girl cousins, even my grandmother watched the pageant together as part of what we did as females. The men in my family would rather have watched football, but for us this beauty contest was both sporting event and classroom.

We watched as avid students and connoisseurs of (white) female beauty, learning the perfect measurements (36-24-36) and perfect height (five feet, seven inches, or taller). For the most part, these were unattainable for us. Eating all the hamburgers and spinach in the world would not make our breasts grow that big, whittle our waists that small, or stretch our legs that long. Miss America became a source of racial, gendered, geopolitical desire. We were doubly removed: we watched the perfect beauties knowing that we would never be one of them; we watched knowing that even a representative of our state would hardly ever win.[1] We looked upon Miss America as a distant, unattainable ideal, and thus a litany of our deficiencies — too short, too flat-chested, too shy. We would never wear a swimsuit and heels and parade before a crowd. Instead of Miss America, we had the Cherry Blossom Festival (CBF) Queen pageant, a local beauty contest for Japanese Americans.[2] It was the crown made possible for the girls we could find in our mirrors.

We waited every year for the Cherry Blossom Festival poster that showed all fifteen contestants to appear on storefront windows and, when it did, we studied it intently, memorizing the names and faces, silently picking the Queen and runners-up. Most of us would never even attend the Festival pageant, but we would all have seen the poster. That yearly poster became iconic of the entire Festival.

I learned my family's beauty contest vocabulary. "Pretty" meant a natural-born beauty whose good looks and femininity were undeniable.[3] "Attractive" meant one who was eye-catching, but in a slightly nonstandard, even less feminine way. She might have had to work at it. "Cute" meant one who was appealing in a particularly youthful sense, often with round eyes and face. "Pretty" would always win. "Attractive" might be a dark-horse contender. "Cute" would be a runner-up, but a crowd-pleaser, maybe even a Miss Congeniality. I learned a hierarchy of the body, a point system of merits and demerits. Negative points went to small, "single-lidded" (epicanthal fold) eyes, dark skin, crooked teeth, and any height below five feet. High points went to big, "double-lidded" (no epicanthal fold) eyes, fair skin, high cheekbones, high-bridged nose, straight teeth, dimples, and any height over five feet, four inches. Some physical attributes hardly counted at all: legs and breasts mattered little in this contest with no swimsuit portion. Here was our own turf of competition.

This Japanese American beauty contest was simultaneously a boundary of difference and a celebration of our inclusion. We, too, might don a crown, even if that crown distinguished us from other crown-holders. It was not equal footing, but a separate event that pantomimed the moves, gestures, and glory of Miss America. Our Queen would never appear on national television, but she would garner a front-page spread in the local newspapers or a motorcade through downtown Honolulu. This was all the celebrity that a local girl could ever expect or hope to approximate. What's more, the Cherry Blossom Queen could travel — to Los Angeles, where her counterpart in the Miss Nisei Week contest was also crowned, and, even more exciting, to Japan, where she would be treated like quasi-royalty. For a girl in Hawai'i who had hardly left the Islands, this was big stuff.

I have recounted my sansei dreams evoked by the CBF in order to position myself within this research on gender, race/ethnicity, and public culture. My childhood dreams were embedded within a specific geopolitical order that includes the relationship between Japan and the United States, the place of Hawai'i within the United States, the racial politics in Hawai'i, and the role of women within the local Japanese American community. I argue that the CBF must be seen as both product and player of these changing racial and ethnic relations, gender hierarchies, and global flows of people and commerce. In this work I shift between the macroforces of histories, institutions, and communities and the microelements of people's experiences. I place histories in "her-

Fig. 1. 2005 Cherry Blossom Festival Poster

stories," in the words and lives of several women who have worn the Cherry Blossom Queen crown. Conversely, I embed herstories within organizational stories, especially those of the Honolulu Japanese Junior Chamber of Commerce (HJJCC), the volunteer organization that has put on the annual event since 1953. The HJJCC itself must be contextualized within the national and international Jaycee movement of the early twentieth century with its focus on commerce, men, and Christianity. Tacking back and forth between different scales and points of view works toward developing multiple perspectives on a complex event that frames issues of gender within race/ethnicity, community, and culture over time.

Some Conceptual Apparatus: Race/Ethnicity, "Nice Girl," Emplacement, Banality

I have chosen to connect race and ethnicity into a race/ethnicity formulation in this work primarily because the distinctions between the two are typically blurred among those involved in the CBF and the general public in Hawai'i (as well as by many academics). If race is the biologization of group boundaries as "perceived physical differences" and ethnicity is relegated to "putative common descent, claims of shared history, and symbols of peoplehood" (Cornell and Hartmann 1998:35), then in Hawai'i (as elsewhere), the two are often combined. The resultant race/ethnicity category of differences includes physical features of skin color, hair, and shape of eyes, as well as cultural features of values, ethos, language, food, and religion legitimized through assumptions of longstanding, naturalized common ancestry.

Central to this work is the concept of the "nice girl." An event such as the CBF establishes its own related but separate set of standards of judging. While not ignoring physical attributes, I contend that a Japanese American contest such as the CBF places high values upon the "nice girl" — that is, a young, middle-class woman who exemplifies what are often considered Japanese cultural and gendered values of humility, self-effacement, empathy, helpfulness, gratitude, and courtesy in a deeroticized, depoliticized manner. The "nice girl" places others before herself, respects her elders, and, as a representative of the community, presents herself well, especially in terms of public speaking.[4] The CBF incorporates these culturally defined notions of middle-class femininity, some of which stand in contrast to those dominant in Euro-America, but in accord with local values in Hawai'i. The girl-next-door ideal of the CBF rewards humility over ambition, self-effacement over self-aggrandizement, and blending in over standing out. These are ideals that gloss over the modicum of ambition needed of one who would even consider competing in a beauty contest, the willingness to parade on stage, and the outstanding physical attractions of one who would be crowned queen. Even though some of the particulars of the model have changed over the years, including the emphasis upon careers for women in the CBF's later years, the core principles remain the same. The ideal also remains an ideal; not all CBF Queens have necessarily been "nice" by these gendered, cultural definitions. Nevertheless, niceness — more specifically, the performance of niceness — remains, rewarded yearly in the contest's crowning.

The public spectacle of a beauty pageant places a spotlight upon gender, representation, and identity. A beauty pageant by and for a particular racial/ethnic group adds the critical elements of race and ethnicity to the mix. A beauty pageant in Hawai'i further embeds these identity issues within the particular geographies of national-cultural margins and the commercial terrain of global tourism. As Sarah Banet-Weiser points out, participating in a beauty pageant "is a critical element to the production of 'appropriately gendered' women and importantly functions as . . . an introduction to the knowledge and social relations that are expected" of a community icon (1999:64). This leads to the following questions that animate my discussion of niceness: what kinds of idealized citizens are imagined on the beauty pageant stage of the CBF in terms of gender and culture? And if niceness is the broad answer, then how can we embed this idealization and its practices within social and political histories of Japanese Americans in Hawai'i? In fact, niceness is an important part of the model minority myth, and thus a critical component to the public proof of assimilation.

The CBF is a spectacle of what I call "emplacement" — that is, the process of situating oneself within the larger mainstream community. Emplacement overlaps with the concept of assimilation in referencing efforts to blend in, but emphasizes the particularities and strong sense of "place." Whereas the end result of assimilation is an erasure of difference, emplacement acknowledges differences, fitting them into a larger social fabric. Moreover, processes of emplacement never occur in a vacuum, but always within the context of particular "places" that are not only geographical sites, but also rich, shifting sociocultural settings enmeshed within power structures. Emplacement frames the CBF as a case study in social and political processes of race/ethnicity, gender, globalism, culture, and community.

I use "banality" in a number of interrelated ways. For one, banality suggests the ordinary, the quotidian, the everyday, the commonplace. Banality points to things running in perfect working order. It thereby suggests the mainstream, especially in terms of structures and hierarchies. A celebration of banality implies a celebration of the status quo. In the case of the CBF, celebrating banality extols the historical "making it" of Japanese Americans in Hawai'i in the 1950s and 1960s — the achievement of the American dream, the rise to political and economic power, the populating of bureaucracies. Banality is here akin to emplacement. It also speaks to the continuous "making it" of Japanese Americans in contemporary Hawai'i half a century later as they sustain their position as members of the mainstream.

Second, banality suggests routinization. It implies repetition, stasis, things unchanging, looking backward, a general conservative orientation. Banality is part of the tyranny of the "unmarked" (Phelan 1993). More neutrally, banality may be linked to Pierre Bourdieu's concept of habitus — that is, the unreflexive, bodily imprinting of repetition (1990). I am not suggesting that the CBF is a kind of habitus; rather, I argue that it shares with the theoretical concept its own routine habitualness. Routinization arises not only from repetition, but also from doing things in the absence of independent critical thought. In this, Hannah Arendt's work on the "banality of evil" in Nazi Germany shows the normalization of everyday horrific crimes, specifically when critical thought is suspended (1963). The CBF shares little with the "evil" of Nazi Germany, but it does rest on a similar absence of independent critical thought, especially in its later years. As Arendt argues: "Clichés, stock phrases, adherence to conventional, standardized codes of expression and conduct have the socially recognized function of protecting us against reality, that is, against the claim on our thinking attention that all events and facts make by virtue of their existence" (1978:4). Banality in the CBF thus rests in the repetition and redundancy of "protecting us against reality," by self-exoticization, performing the ethnic stereotype in a public setting, and making a cliché of oneself. It rests on people toeing the line, constantly concerned with the eyes of others upon them. It rests on image and image-making and on the superficiality of going through the motions. It rests in pageant themes that dwell in stock phrases.

Third, banality implies critique shared with overlapping concepts of triteness, triviality, and mundaneness. Meaghan Morris points out that the word took a censorious turn only in the late eighteenth century as part of an elitist critique of common taste and value (1996:165). My choice of banality in this analysis is an attempt to broaden its usage while retaining some of the critical lens implied by the term. As Michael Billig is careful to emphasize, "Banal does not imply benign" (1995:6). Thus the politics of banality are embedded within the reproduction of structures of power. Here I want to make clear that my theoretical framework of banality does not mean that I am dismissive of the CBF. Far from it, I am entirely awed by the many individuals who have sincerely devoted countless hours to the event, including generously helping with this research. My inclusion of herstories testifies to the personal achievements enabled by the CBF. I see in these volunteer efforts a poetics of daily life that have helped shape community. But by framing the CBF within banality, I intend to embrace both the politics and poetics laid bare by its commonness.

Lastly, banality suggests a kind of ennui. It accrues in the disconnect between a yearly event and people's lives, as well as sometimes the disconnect within people's lives. The pejorative of banality rests in this break in significance, devolving into the trite, the trivial, and the superficial. This break can come about by locking the event into a form that resists the change of shifting generations, conditions, and contexts, particularly by holding on to old blood-quantum rules long after the community includes persons of mixed ancestry. It can come about as a community's boundaries dissolve over time to the point where the group lacks cohesiveness. It can come about as other identities supersede that which the event is supposed to symbolize.

A 1980 examination of racial/ethnic stereotypes in Hawai'i lists the following as positive attributes that Japanese Americans like to portray about themselves: orderly behavior, stoicism, hard work, thriftiness, group (family, village, country) orientation, loyalty, obedience, personal cleanliness, humility, awareness and acceptance of hierarchy (Rogers and Izutsu 1980:82–83). These positive self-stereotypings correspond directly to the issues that I raise here of niceness, emplacement, and banality.

Female Spectatorship: Gazing at Beauty Pageants

The females in my family were not alone in studying beauty contests so closely. We joined millions of other females gazing upon each other and learning in the process what it means to perform as a woman. Viewing a beauty pageant became for female spectators such as ourselves (and, I might add, male transvestites) a textbook of gendered images, a how-to on the production of those images, and a lesson in hierarchies, rewards, and competition. Jackie Stacey, writing about British female fans of Hollywood stars, asks the same questions that inform this research: "How are feminine identities produced and reproduced in relation to idealised feminine images?" (1994:224) and "What pleasures can they [women] gain from the feminine images produced for the male gaze?" (ibid.:11). Stacey connects issues of gender and power with the pleasures of same-sex looking. In the case of sansei Japanese American females like myself, feminine identities and images were caught up not only in issues of gender, but also in processes of race and ethnicity, as well as our parents' emergence into middle-class life at the geopolitical margins of the United States.

Female spectatorship, sansei or otherwise, must be embedded within the histories of its making as these histories and processes of spectatorship form female subjectivity. As Christine Gledhill argues:

> "Femininity" is not simply an abstract textual position; . . . what women's history tells us about femininity lived as a socio-culturally, as well as a psychically differentiated category, must have consequences for our understanding of the formation of feminine subjectivity, of the feminine textual spectator and the viewing/reading of female audiences. (1988:67)

Spectatorship is part of subject formation — that is, the creation of the self as a self — not as an uncritical acceptance of what one sees, but as a negotiation between what one sees, the active production of that "text," and the equally active meaning-making of viewers. Gledhill continues: "The value of 'negotiation' . . . as an analytical concept is that it allows space to the subjectivities, identities and pleasures of audiences" (ibid.:72). It is the complex nature of this negotiation taking place amid particular sociopolitical contexts that I would like to foreground in my examination of the CBF. This research situates my sansei dreams as well as those of others in the Japanese American community as points deeply embedded within specific cultural and historical locations. One of these locations is the rise to political and economic power of Japanese Americans within Hawai'i that generated the cultural capital of premier events such as the CBF.

In this, I do not want to lose sight of pleasure. Female members of my family and I took obvious and continual pleasure in watching the Miss America pageant on television every year. The pleasure arose in the sociality of watching together. The pleasure also arose in watching the glamorous spectacle of pretty women parading on stage, the drama of competition, and the excitement of crowning a queen, "the most beautiful girl in the world" (Banet-Weiser 1999). We found pleasure in the stunning gowns, immaculate makeup, and perfect hair, not unlike the enjoyment of thumbing through a fashion magazine. At the time we felt a small rush of pleasure: we were coeval participants with the rest of the country in this American ritual, the distance of geography, race, and culture temporarily erased. These were not the guilty pleasures expressed by current feminists, peeking at the soap operas and romance novels of their research subjects. For us, this was the unadulterated pleasure of communally watching a glittery fairy tale.

I am not the same girl who watched the Miss America pageant or stared at the Cherry Blossom poster of contestants several decades ago. And yet, when I see the poster reappear in late January, I take a second look out of habit. I know that changes in judging have theoretically eliminated "beauty" from the competition, yet looking at the poster I automatically rule out the ones that I think could never make it on the basis of appearance. The challenges of feminism have shaped me into a different kind of spectator — one who is even conducting research on the processes of her own earlier spectatorship — and yet I recognize the interpellated self of my earlier undeniable pleasures. I make no apologies for them, as I make no apologies for other former selves that I have inhabited, but I suggest that knowing that former self gives me empathetic insight into the world of the CBF.

This study is based primarily on field research including participant observation and interviews. I acted as a consultant to the fiftieth anniversary CBF pageant in 2002, attending meetings of the pageant committee, observing training sessions of contestants, producing a short film on the CBF that was shown at the Festival ball,[5] and writing an essay for the pageant souvenir book (Yano 2002a, b). I conducted fifty taped interviews, primarily with former Cherry Blossom Queens, as well as past and present organizers, contestants, and the general public. I also analyzed all pageant souvenir books, noting changes in activities, sponsorship, official greetings, and layout. The information from these books was extremely useful in charting the development of the pageant. Archival research included media coverage of the pageant in Japanese and English newspapers, library research on other ethnic beauty pageants in Hawai'i, and web-based research on Jaycee organizations.

As an anthropologist, I looked forward to this project as an opportunity to do fieldwork on my home turf. This is my community of family, friends, and organizations. These are my dreams that I explore. As I conducted the research and wrote this book, I used the dreams as reference points to keep these subjects near. It was not difficult, since the field often drew me in even as I sometimes preferred to keep my distance.

Conducting research on one's own community is, at first glance, easy: I know the shortcuts to resources, people, practices, and emotions. I also know too well the pitfalls of local rivalries, longstanding antagonisms, and competing obligations (cf. Hau'ofa 1982). I maneuver through the community as one of its daughters. What I write has immediate repercussions not only for myself, but for my family and friends. I cannot even pretend to be a detached observer.

The question arises, how to balance celebration and critique? How to assert distance in a community that is not only my own, but that frequently positions me as one of its spokespersons? How to be a true participant and true observer? As I move from interviews to writing, my position becomes less comfortable. I am well aware that the words I write and speak will be read and heard by many of the people to whom I am indebted and who have entrusted their thoughts and memories with me. I am also aware of the privileged position of those words in Hawai'i, given the racial hierarchy that places Japanese Americans numerically at the top in many white-collar professions, especially politics and education.

Shouldering my responsibility to this community while maintaining the integrity of my position as researcher is nothing less than a delicate ethical tightrope. In most cases, where I have debated the inclusion of sensitive material, I have favored the community of my subjects (and myself) and upheld my obligations to them. These are real lives and feelings of people to whom I have longstanding ties. Thus, certain stories that have been told to me will never grace these pages (ethical dilemmas all field researchers face). And yet, I have attempted to carve out sufficient space for critique so that this work does not devolve into congratulatory acclaim of the good deeds of the community. Indeed, I am sympathetic and highly respectful of members of this my community, but these people and their activities are fallible. So, too, am I, both as a participant and as an observer. My solution is to carve a winding path between the celebratory and the critical, between intimacy and distance, between participant and observer.

As anthropology moves increasingly toward native/indigenous anthropology, conducting research on topics close to home, and giving people in communities near and far the tools of research and opportunities for their voices to be heard — toward, in effect, decolonization — my research and ethical dilemmas will become more and more common. It is structured into the positions of empowerment that we advocate for the field of anthropology (Marcus and Fischer 1986). The earlier "dividing practices" of the discipline — hierarchies between outside anthropologists and inside indigenes, between Western self and non-Western others — are being blurred by research such as this (Abu-Lughod 1991:143).

How will others chart their own winding paths? Will anthropology move inevitably closer to uncritical, celebratory renderings? Will native anthropologists feel free to assert a critical stance, moving beyond the us versus them of postcolonial power inequities, to include internal ironies, struggles, conflicts, and hegemonies within the communities of which they are a part? Writing up close and often within the particularities and contradictions "against culture" (Abu-Lughod 1991:138), do we run the risk of shying away not only from critique but also generalization? Does generalization become politicized as another form of essentialization — especially of ourselves? These challenges face those of us who choose to write about our own. They may not be unique: any anthropologist who comes to know the field well, as the field comes to know her well, is to some degree an insider and faces many of these same dilemmas. As Kirin Narayan argues:

> Instead of the paradigm emphasizing a dichotomy between outsider/insider or observer/observed, I propose that at this historical moment we might more profitably view each anthropologist in terms of shifting identifications amid a field of interpenetrating communities and power relations. (1993:671)

The categories of native/insider anthropologist and non-native/outsider anthropologist, according to Narayan, are overblown.

For those of us who are inevitable natives/insiders, however, researching our own comes with an automatic set of responsibilities, obligations, and pitfalls, as well as privileges and pleasures. As we increase in numbers, our challenges and the paths we map will play a part in charting the discipline.

I BEGIN CHAPTER 1 with the subject of beauty pageants in general, interrogating the issues they raise, embedding them within their histories, and in particular examining them as part of global culture that has taken its model from the Miss America contest. I then proceed to the more specific topic of Asian American beauty pageants, looking at ways in which their confluence of race, ethnicity, minority status, and immigration histories makes them a wonderful lens for examining these particular issues within the context of popular culture, media, and gender.

Chapter 2 weaves a complex picture of the specific historical and contemporary contexts of the early days of the Cherry Blossom Festival Queen pageant. I embrace the complexity of multiple subject positions by approaching the CBF from different perspectives. I turn first to the organizers, the HJJCC, recounting the founding of their association. Then I discuss the Jaycee movement in the United States and abroad as part of the organizational context in which this beauty pageant — as many other beauty pageants in the United States — exists. Finally, I look at the context of ethnic beauty pageants in Hawai'i, historically down to the level of high schools and the University of Hawai'i, and contemporaneously with other individual Asian American pageants in the state.

Chapter 3 examines the founding and early development of the CBF in the 1950s and 1960s, its glory years. This account pays close attention to the place of CBF within various contexts: the internal divisions of the Japanese American community, interethnic relations in Hawai'i, tourism, nikkei (persons of Japanese ancestry) communities in the continental United States, and relations with Japan. Each of these contexts provides a different audience for the CBF. While Japanese American women are spotlighted on stage, the focus is simultaneously on the men who have placed them there. Femininity in this way performs a racially deflected lens to showcase the achievements of the American dream for Japanese Americans in Hawai'i in terms of citizenship, class, and masculinity.

I follow the discussion of each time period in Chapters 3, 5, and 7 respectively with a series of CBF Queen herstories — extensive narratives drawn from interviews with CBF Queens — in Chapters 4, 6, and 8.[6] These herstories in-fill personal back stories to the larger processes I discuss in each historical chapter. I precede each Queen's herstory narrative with commentary, pointing up the themes of the interview, focusing on the changing place of Japanese American women and the CBF in terms of race/ethnicity, gender, and identity. I use the herstories as touchstones to comment on ways in which these women's individuated experiences provide the grist for larger, historically situated issues. Within the herstories I let the women speak for themselves, noting that their stories do not exist in a social vacuum, but arise out of the interaction of our conversation.

Chapters 5 and 6 follow the CBF through the 1970s, 1980s, and into the 1990s, addressing the question of its waning audience and disconnect from the lives of many Japanese Americans. By the 1990s, the CBF could be thought of as a beauty pageant in search of an audience, "all dressed up with nowhere to go." What kinds of implications did this have for the Japanese American community in Hawai'i? Was this waning interest in part the result of a waning community? These questions are ones that Jaycees asked themselves as they continued to invest countless hours of effort into an event with a shrinking audience.

Organizers of the 1999 pageant decided to address these questions head-on, radically changing the rules and practices of the CBF in the latter months of 1998. Foremost among these modifications was a change in the blood-quantum rule to allow women of 50 percent Japanese ancestry to compete in the CBF pageant. Chapters 7 and 8 address these changes and their implications. What challenges do mixed-race contestants and Queens pose for the community, especially with the CBF as a metonym for one kind of negotiation of race/ethnicity?

Chapter 9 concludes this book by framing issues of race, ethnicity, spectacle, and community within the intertwined themes of niceness and banality. I examine the specific ways in which banality addresses the ordinariness, routinization, cliché-making, triteness, and ennui that arise from a disconnect between an event and its community. I conclude with a discussion of both the politics and poetics of banality, suggesting ways in which the CBF engages a web of positions and relationships, as well as finds meaning in individuated practices.

Chapter One

Beauty Pageants as Spectacles of Gender, Race/Ethnicity, and Community

Femininity is not a natural, biological phenomenon, but rather an effect which has . . . to be worked hard at to achieve. The work of femininity . . . involves continually producing oneself, indeed one's body, for the pleasure and approval of others.
—Stacey 1994:8

The work of femininity is nowhere better seen than in the spectacle of a beauty pageant, "a large-scale, extravagant cultural production that is replete with striking visual imagery and dramatic action" (Manning 1992:291). Spectacles provide "the principal symbolic context in which contemporary societies enact and communicate their guiding beliefs, values, concerns, and self understandings" (ibid.).[1] Beauty pageants spectacularize not only performances of femininity, but also displays of communities, groups, and selves.[2] Colleen Ballerino Cohen, Richard Wilk, and Beverly Stoeltje argue:

> As universal and diverse as beauty contests are, what they do is remarkably similar. . . . They showcase values, concepts, and behavior that exist at the center of a group's sense of itself and exhibit values of morality, gender, and place. . . . The beauty contest stage is where identities (local, ethnic, regional, national, international) . . . [are] made public and visible. (1996:2)

In showcasing identity as "public and visible," beauty contests borrow commonly recognized idioms of prestige, such as the crown, scepter, and cape. These items enact glittery, feminized signposts of a position devoid of actual power. As Beverly Stoeltje points out, "The beauty pageant creates a role that has no political power, no earning power (though, of course, many pageants have financial awards and lead to future earnings), and no authority to exercise over other people" (1996:15 – 16). The position of beauty queen coincides with that of celebrities in general, which sociologist Fransesco Alberoni calls "powerless elite" "whose institutional power is very limited or non-existent, but whose doings and way of life arouse a considerable and sometimes even maximum degree of interest" (quoted in Marshall 1997:15). Beauty queens, like other contemporary celebrities, hold symbolic prestige in representing the group, but no actual power in controlling that group or shaping its future.

Within this separation from actual power, the beauty queen celebrity is the subject of intense public scrutiny, constituting what Arjun Appadurai calls "tournaments of value":

> complex periodic events that are removed in some culturally well-defined way from the routines of economic life. . . . What is at issue in such tournaments is not just status, rank, fame, or reputation of actors, but the disposition of the central tokens of value in ordinary life. (1986:21)

Beauty pageants thus define and are defined by these "central tokens of value" of the community. The stakes are necessarily high, as Cohen, Wilk, and Stoeltje contend: "By choosing an individual whose deportment, appearance, and style embodies the values and goals of a nation, locality, or group, beauty contests expose these same values and goals to interpretation and challenge" (1996:2). The choice of winner is thus more than about looks; it involves issues of representation and the community itself. The beauty queen and her crowning constitute a story of, by, and for the group, a story open to interpretation, challenge, and conflict.

As much as beauty pageants appear ostensibly to be about women and the groups they represent, in many instances they create a subtext about the men who often wield the power to control the group and stage the event. Nancy Munn's reflections on shells in kula exchange apply as well to women in beauty pageants: "Although men appear to be the agents in defining shell value, in fact, without shells, men cannot define their own value; in this respect, shells and men are reciprocally agents of each other's value definition" (quoted in Appadurai 1986:20). Thus men in control of beauty pageants define women's value, at the same time as women by their display define men's value. There are obvious problems applying this paradigm to beauty pageants today, the foremost of which is the assumption that women, like shells, have no say in defining their value, and that men are the only ones in charge of organizing beauty pageants. Yet, the image remains of women as the interface between male-dominated organizations and the public.

In discussing beauty pageants, one important distinction to be made is between local and pyramidal competitions, although these may coexist in a continuum (Sanders and Pink 1996:48). Local pageants are self-contained; the winner does not proceed to the next level of competition. Pyramidal pageants lead from the local to increasingly wider, linked spheres of competition. Because they ultimately lead to wider spheres of inclusion, pyramidal pageants rely less on local, possibly alternative criteria for judging, and more on general pan-pageant criteria. This inclusiveness gets reproduced at each level of the pyramid, encouraging a choice of queens based on broader appeal and past successes. Local pageants by contrast may adhere to more idiosyncratic criteria and insular standards of beauty.

Beauty pageants intersect with social class in complex, conflicting, and historically shifting ways. For one, they act as a means for women to climb a social ladder, whether furthering a career or marrying up. Theoretically beauty pageants offer democratic access: "It [a beauty pageant] purports to make its judgments on ascribed characteristics. . . . Because these traits are believed to occur randomly with reference to social class, women of any social background may be candidates" (Lavenda 1996:41). However, a number of mitigating factors reproduce social class inequities in pageants. Daughters of beauty queens may share not only the genetic makeup of their mothers, but also the advantage of a family insider knowledgeable in what it takes to win a contest, including dress, makeup, and comportment. If pageants have high fees and require sponsorship, candidates able to pay the fees or with better connections to potential sponsors have an obvious advantage. Contestants able to afford cosmetic surgery may also procure an advantage in a beauty contest. Furthermore, contestants from families who have invested in education or exposed them to social situations mingling with elite may be able to present themselves with greater poise in a public setting. This is part of the finishing-school effect of class differences.

A second issue surrounding social class lies in the complicated relationship between notions of gendered respectability and public spectacle. That is, at least historically according to Victorian standards of decorum, the public arena was not the place for a display of upper-class women in Euro-America, except within the confines of delimited, exclusive events such as a debutante ball.[3] Therefore, the beauty pageant occupies the relatively déclassé space of lower- or middle-class aspirants emulating some of the performance idioms of putatively upper-class debdom.[4] Within the context of American social mobility, however, even debdom, in tandem with beauty pageants, comes with its own yearning edge — what Karal Ann Marling calls the "Debutante's Dream": "a dream of being almost royalty, a paragon of good taste and elegance, a . . . collective family dream in which the pretty daughter is both proof of good breeding and a bid to improve the stock" (2004:7).

The beauty pageant is a status achievement not only for its winners, but also for organizers, including developing countries that regard staging a beauty pageant as a mark of industrial nation status. Robert Foster contends that beauty pageants are among the global activities that simultaneously spell out the distinctiveness of one country from another, and the sharing of a common culture (1991:249). As Katherine Borland argues, "Organizing a beauty pageant now often functions as a badge of civilized, modern status" (1996:75). More specifically, beauty pageants signal a country as coeval with the United States and other industrial nations. According to Candace Savage,

No matter where the idea [of a beauty pageant] traveled around the world, the concept always seemed essentially American. It was as if beauty pageants had all been stamped "Made in the United States." Here, on display for all to see were the quintessentially American values of competition and advancement through merit. (1998:32)

Although Savage ignores other paradigms for beauty pageants that are not necessarily derived from the United States, she is correct in arguing for the global impact of the American model. For example, in Hawai'i local Japanese American organizations such as the HJJCC in the 1950s saw the CBF as a means for demonstrating their Americanness as well as their status within the Hawai'i community. The American model also has an impact overseas through television. According to Borland, small-town residents of Nicaragua avidly watch annual televised broadcasts of the Miss America pageant (1996:75). They are not alone, as paralleled by my own experiences growing up in Hawai'i in the 1950s and 1960s. As Savage avers, "Beauty contests on TV were a magic mirror that, willy-nilly, made every girl and woman into a participant. . . . I was an armchair beauty contestant" (1998:ix).

Not enough scholarly attention has been paid to the economic side of beauty pageants, even though many of the most prominent are produced by large-scale corporations. One may ask, what happens to gender, subjectivity, collective identity, and representation when a beauty pageant and its queen become a brand name, a commodity/image on the marketplace? The most infamous case in point is Donald Trump's ownership of the Miss Universe pageant, as well as his 2005 bid to purchase the Miss America pageant. The celebrity status in this case goes both ways: the beauty pageant gives a particular aura to Trump; Trump makes headlines by way of the pageant.[5]

Corporate sponsorship of contestants can be critical to the pursuit of a major crown. To participate at a competitive level, contestants need a host of expensive support, including trainers and coaches, hair and makeup experts, gown designers, and sometimes cosmetic surgeons. Typically, support personnel specialize in high-level pageants, creating a mini-industry centered on beauty pageants. The products of these mini-industries are subsequently broadcast widely. The fact that Nicaraguans (and others) may watch the Miss America pageant on television indicates further the global impact of the links between mini-industries surrounding beauty contests, media, and corporate sponsors. These links may be highly attractive to contestants hopeful that media exposure will parlay them into careers in the entertainment industry. Even beauty pageants on a smaller, less commercial scale, such as the CBF, rely heavily on corporate sponsors to support events, programs, publicity, and prizes. The inevitable branding of beauty pageants and queens is part and parcel of the event.

What is being branded by this process of spectacularization is, in part, the female body. Susan Bordo writes of the significance of control and containment of the female body:

[Uncontrolled flesh functions as a] metaphor for anxiety about internal processes out of control — uncontained desire, unrestrained hunger, uncontrolled impulse. . . . The ideal here is of a body that is absolutely tight, contained, "bolted down," firm: in other words, a body that is protected against eruption from within, whose internal processes are under control. (1993:189 – 190)

What has been globally codified as the beauty pageant walk, pose, and turn displays female bodies "whose internal processes are under control." These lessons in bodily control are part of the structuring and performance of respectability as "a matter of restraint, a nonexcessive display of the body" (Banet-Weiser 1999:80). The body in this way is trained and coded for the display of not only gender, but also social class.

Medieval historian Ernst Kantorwicz argues that kings in Europe during the Middle Ages possessed two bodies: (1) the body natural, that is physical, corporeal, and transient; and (2) the body politic, that is, positional, representational, and symbolic (1997/1957). Millicent Marcus argues that beauty queens likewise retain two bodies: (1) a concrete, corporeal body; and (2) a transcendent, metaphysical ideal (1992:297; quoted in Robertson 2001:18). What for kings is the body politic becomes for beauty queens the body semiotic. Because of the very visual ways in which many societies engender women — in particular, within the context of a beauty pageant — the tie between the corporeal body and the semiotic body is especially close and fraught with tension. According to people like Donald Trump (see note 5), for example, the corporeal body can only function as a semiotic, representational body if it is appropriately controlled. The beauty queen, unlike the medieval king, must earn the right for her corporeal body to enact the semiotic body. This is why the beauty queen only becomes one through competition — corporeal bodies vying to occupy the semiotic bodily position.

Beauty Pageant Critique

Much has been written critiquing the imposition of Euro-American standards of beauty and femininity through beauty pageants, particularly in international pageants such as Miss Universe, but also in smaller regional and national events (Van Esterik 1996:204; Wilk 1996:226 – 228).[6] Beauty pageants are but one extension of a global network of gendered images proliferating through media, fashion, and celebrity culture. Furthermore, the beauty pageant in the form of the Miss America pageant has become a prototype for beauty contests around the world.

It is not that the Miss America pageant pays no attention to nonphysical attributes. Indeed, as Banet-Weiser explains, by the 1930s, in its bid to elevate its public status, the pageant sought a "certain class of girl" defined by "typicality and respectability" (1999:32). It is that the beauty contest — even one calling itself a scholarship pageant valorizing "typicality and respectability" — is framed by the visuality of Euro-American physical ideals. Naomi Wolf argues that beauty and the industry that surrounds it, including beauty pageants, are part of a larger regime of social control of women: prescriptions for surface appearance actually mask deeper directives for behavior, comportment, and gendered selves (1991:14).

Beauty itself is, of course, a highly contested issue that incorporates issues of race and class distinctions. As Lois Banner makes clear, standards and definitions of beauty vary not only by place, but also over time in conjunction with views on women, trends in art, theater, advertising, and media, developments in medicine, domestic and international politics, and global issues (1983:4–5). Within the context of these differences, the increasingly globalized setting of international beauty contests promotes both a homogenization of beauty standards, as well as an appetite for rewarding exoticized difference within a range of acceptability. Furthermore, beauty culture must be embedded within a history of race relations, class-based politics, and consumerism. Dominant notions of beauty as exemplified in a contest such as the Miss America pageant historically celebrated Anglo, upper-middle-class aesthetics of white skin, blond hair, blue eyes, straight teeth, long legs, full breasts, and a small waist. This was highly circumscribed, racialized, class-based "beauty." The means to achieving that ideal — cosmetics and, for some, plastic surgery — represents the commodification of that aesthetic. "Beauty culture," as Kathy Peiss points out, "should be understood not only as a type of commerce but as a system of meaning that helped women navigate the changing conditions of modern social experience" (1998:6).

At the same time, this gendering of bodily types intersects with local conditions, values, and identities expressed through beauty pageants. For example, Penny Van Esterik writes of "gentleness, silence, and virtue . . . intertwined with the attributes of grace, composure, and beauty to produce a model of Thai femininity" rewarded in Thai beauty pageants (1996:203). Similarly, Jehane Teilhet-Fisk explains a Tongan concept of female beauty that "goes beyond the surface of physical attributes and is deeply entrenched in social and moral values that uphold and emphasize the family, kinship, church, and a nationalist ideology," judged in part through a solo dance event that assesses motions, facial expression, body-foot coordination, and the ability to invoke feeling (1996:186, 193).

The intertwining of the physical and spiritual-moral complex that defines a cultural notion of femininity can be seen as resistant to dominant Euro-American physical ideals and values. Robert Lavenda describes the conflicts surrounding the selection of a community queen in a Minnesota Community queen pageant when judges from the outside selected a queen on the basis of criteria external to the concerns of small towns. In many cases, townspeople disagreed with the judges' choice. "The factors of interest to the community — achievement, family, personality, commitment, and so on — are either difficult to judge over a weekend or are irrelevant to the job of the judges as they understand it" (Lavenda 1996:37). This clash of criteria can have disastrous results when a queen who looks good by classic American beauty standards does not necessarily function well as a representative of the community.

Even longstanding beauty pageants that represent a community's values and identity have been dogged at times by critics. Beauty contests have been the object of moral panic on both sides of the political spectrum, from conservative religious groups to liberal feminists. Erich Goode and Nachman Ben-Yehuda list five characteristics of moral panics: (1) heightened level of concern; (2) increased hostility; (3) some level of consensus that the threat is real; (4) disproportionate concern to actual harm; and (5) volatility of collective behavior (1994:33 – 41). The sense of panic that beauty contests seem to provoke in various segments of the population points to particular practices that are perceived as threatening to society. As Kenneth Thompson argues, "Events are more likely to be perceived as fundamental threats and to give rise to moral panics if the society, or some important part of it, is in crisis or experiencing disturbing changes giving rise to stress" (1998:8).

Much of today's public tends to avoid or dismiss anything labeled "beauty contest" or "beauty pageant." Thus, Miss America is crowned as part of a "scholarship pageant" and the CBF claims that it is a "cultural pageant." For example, Lavenda points out that at various American Midwestern small town pageants, organizers adamantly proclaim:

> "It's not a beauty pageant!" They are quite insistent that the term "beauty pageant" is inappropriately applied to the event that chooses a community queen. To them, to talk of "beauty" is to emphasize physical features when [community] pageants are supposed to find a representative ... who embodies what local people believe to be the best of themselves: talent, friendliness, commitment to the community and its values, upward mobility. (1996:31)

Indeed, this same kind of ambivalence and denial is expressed by contestants and queens, who talk about themselves as "not your typical beauty queen" (see herstories, Chapters 4, 6, and 8).

Asian American beauty pageants raise issues of gender and representation shared with other contests. However, other issues, such as race/ethnicity, culture, and relationship to dominant mainstream society, are specific to the communities they serve and the sociopolitical contexts in which they coexist.

These pageants foreground the connection made between women and minorities as both "muted" categories — that is, subordinated groups "compelled to use the language of the dominators in order to be able to express their interests; neither has the power to define the terms of discourse" (Eriksen 1993:155). Among minority groups, Asian Americans in particular are feminized, producing exotically sexualized, submissive women and emasculated men.

Lisa Lowe points out the heterogeneous nature of "Asian America," since its constituent communities differ by countries of origin, many of which share very little in common. Asian American groups also differ in the length of time in the United States, the generational depth of their stay, the rate of ongoing immigration, the rates of intermarriage and selection of intermarrying partners, socioeconomic class background of original immigrants and subsequent generations, varying degrees and kinds of identification with a "homeland," degree of assimilation to and distinction from mainstream American society, and the particularities of histories within the United States (Lowe 1996:65 – 66). In this, Japanese Americans, the focus of this book, may be exceptional in their generational depth, earlier low rates of intermarriage, relatively low levels of recent immigration, lack of diasporic identification with Japan, and high degrees of assimilation.[7] In the following discussion I address not only the heterogeneity of Asian American communities and their beauty pageants, but also seek the commonalities by which "Asian American beauty pageants" may be fruitfully discussed.

First, the larger society conflates Asian Americans with Asians. Lowe contends that "the Asian is always seen as an immigrant, as the 'foreigner-within,' even when born in the United States and the descendant of generations born here before" (1999:5 – 6). In the case of Japanese Americans, even though they have been part of American society for four to five generations, their media depiction in the United States remains frozen in time as newly arrived foreigners, producing what Darrell Hamamoto dubs a "symbolic containment [that] implies that Japanese Americans still occupy 'probationary' status within the larger society" (1994:11). Second, the larger society fails to differentiate between various national origins, especially within East Asia, treating Japanese, Chinese, and Korean American groups alike. Third, Asian American (qua Asian) women are stereotypically sexualized as submissive geishas or kung-fu practicing dragon ladies.[8] This holds true in spite of media appearances by women such as Margaret Cho, the Korean American stand-up comedienne who works specifically against stereotype. Cho is the anomaly, as Asian American women continue to be represented as expressing a particular brand of orientalized femininity that is both distant and past. They are old-fashioned girls in their submissiveness, with an added exoticized, eroticized twist. Stallybrass and White argue that often in hierarchical contexts, "the top *includes* . . . [the] low symbolically, as a primary eroticized constituent of its own fantasy life. . . . It is for this reason that what is *socially* peripheral is so frequently *symbolically* central" (1986:5). Asian American women have thus become signifiers and objects of desire in mainstream America. Or, as bell hooks contends, "Otherness . . . is offered as a new delight, more intense, more satisfying than normal ways of doing and feeling" (1998:181).

I maintain that Asian American beauty pageants exist within this larger societal and historical framework, but also outside it in a parallel universe of relatively closed communities and ethnic enclaves. Asian American beauty pageants perform both for an insular audience, as well as to a lesser degree the larger society in particularized, circumscribed contexts. According to Lowe, the distancing and exclusion of Asian Americans from national culture in the continental United States has "created the conditions for the emergence of Asian American culture as an alternative cultural site" (1996:x). Hawai'i, however, may be exceptional in incorporating these beauty pageants within its public face, often parading Japanese American and Chinese American queens in performance of its putative multiethnic, multiracial "paradise." The space between American national culture and Asian American culture(s) is one that is brokered in part by gazing; however, the gaze and awareness that follow do not go equally in all directions. Different from the male gaze discussed at length in film theory (Mulvey 1975), this gaze focuses toward power — that is, Asian American communities look to the larger, mainstream, white society far more than the other way around. Furthermore, this is not merely a matter of quantity (who looks at whom more), but content and quality (who looks at whom for what purposes and to what effect).

Asian American beauty pageants form an intersection of gazes, some of which conflict with each other. The most relevant gaze is internal. The beauty queen represents the community to itself as the daughter exemplar. Other gazes, especially the external gaze of the larger society, exert power through tourism or public media. Contestants perform to their notion of the expectations of this larger audience, sometimes reinforcing stereotypes, at other times projecting the effect their performance will have on their everyday lives. For example,

Shilpa Dave explains that contestants in the Miss India Georgia contest "know and perform India in relation to how it impacts their lives in the United States" (2001:345). India — as an Asian "homeland" culture — exists in relation to specific conditions of white American national culture and society for Indian Americans. As Lowe argues, "It is through the terrain of national culture that the individual subject is politically formed as the American citizen, . . . and comes to articulate itself in the domain of language, social hierarchy, law, and ultimately, political representation" (1996:2).

Lateral gazes between Asian American communities of the same ethnicity connect them to each other, especially in pyramidal beauty pageants such as Miss Chinatown U.S.A. or Miss India U.S.A. These lateral gazes also function in pageants that explicitly link up communities by having each other's winners appear at pageant events. For example, the queens and courts of Japanese American beauty pageants in Los Angeles, San Francisco, Seattle, and Hawai'i appear at each other's coronations.

These lateral gazes are no less important than the gazes over one's shoulder, between Asian American communities of different ethnicities, sometimes competing, sometimes cooperating within a larger societal framework. The only intra-Asian American beauty contest that I know of is the Miss Asian America pageant, held annually in California since its inception in 1986. In this pageant, contestants are required to appear in swimsuit, evening gown, and the "ethnic dress" of the Asian culture by which she identifies (Miss Asian America Pageant 2004). The Miss Asian America website depicts five contestants in "ethnic dress" representing groups originally from Japan, China, Korea, Vietnam, and the Philippines. These intra-Asian American gazes come embedded within their own hierarchies, often based on racial/ethnic stereotypes, time of immigration, class differences, and relationships to the larger society. Thus, for example, the CBF Queen and Chinese American Narcissus Queen in Hawai'i often appear at the same civic functions and state of Hawai'i events, as well as at each other's pageants, expressing similar high status, historical longevity, and institutional cooperation. However, neither of the two makes many public appearances with Miss Hawaii Filipina or Miss Korea Hawaii, reinforcing status hierarchies between ethnic groups within Hawai'i.

There are also mutual gazes between communities in the United States and Asia, mediated by organizing bodies such as the Jaycees or Chambers of Commerce in many countries, international pyramidal beauty pageants such as Miss India WorldwidE (sic; see India Festival Committee, Inc. 2004) and Miss Korea International, and the transnational entertainment industry. In the case of the CBF, one of the biggest prizes for the Queen (and one discussed most frequently by former Queens) is a trip to Japan lavishly hosted by sister branches of the

Jaycee International organization. These different and sometimes competing gazes create variable conditions within Asian American beauty pageants, as well as set them apart from mainstream society.

Citizenship, Community, and Family in Asian American Pageants

The multiple gazes of Asian American beauty pageants emerge as part of class- and race-based minority cultures, carving out a separate space even while engaging in mainstream practices. This is not necessarily a separate-but-equal phenomenon, but a separate-and-parallel activity that garners broad recognition. Organizing a beauty pageant does not endow a group with political power, but it does give a group potential public exposure. Asian American beauty pageants, alongside Chambers of Commerce and Jaycee organizations, are ethnic enclave institutions that mimic those of the mainstream while serving their own bounded communities, from within and without. In fact, the ties between beauty pageants and these institutions are not coincidental but deliberate in terms of sponsorship and organization.

The connection between minority cultures and beauty pageants is all the more complex because of the parallel that can be drawn between women and minorities as social groups. Both share a structural position of subordination and subjugation that has been routinized in daily life. As Dru Gladney argues: "Minority is to the majority as female is to male" (1994:93). Stallybrass and White's work on hierarchy and transgression is useful here: "What starts as a *simple* repulsion or rejection of symbolic matter foreign to the self inaugurates a process of introjection and negation which is always *complex* in its effects" (1986:193). In other words, the dominant group both reviles and desires the "other" (e.g., women, minorities); at the same time, through that very revulsion and desire, the "other" becomes part of the dominant group's subjectivity, an "identity-in-difference." Viewing an Asian American beauty pageant produces a double vision of the structures of inequality on a racial stage. In Peggy Phelan's terms, they are multiply "marked" (1993).

Although the mainstream public (as well as members of the ethnic group) might not understand the meaning of a Chinese lion dance or a Buddhist Festival for the Dead, most people recognize and comprehend a beauty pageant. As a result, these pageants may be seen as a locus of ethnic/racial pride and a positioning strategy, especially vis-à-vis minority-majority relations. They are acts of exclusion and inclusion, local "cultural" festivals using the global vernacular of beauty contests. They are also a proving ground of citizenship for both organizers and contestants. What Shirley Lim notes of Asian American beauty pageants during the early Cold War era (1948–1955) holds true today:

"Women of color and Asian American women in particular had differing relations to beauty from European American women. . . . Performing beauty became a strategy for claiming status as citizen-subject" (2003:201). Besides performing beauty, one could also claim citizenship on the basis of organizing public displays of beauty through pageants. Putting on a beauty pageant may be regarded as a quintessentially and performatively American thing to do, not only among nations as discussed earlier, but among minority groups within nations.

Claiming citizenship is particularly important for Asian American communities who share a history of broad racial discrimination, especially for Japanese Americans whose chronicle includes internment and debasement of their culture during World War II. Understanding the social and psychological framework of living in the United States as a presumptive enemy alien provides a critical and ironic base for examining Japanese American beauty pageants as public culture. Although internment was limited in Hawai'i, the closure of all Japanese American cultural institutions from language schools to movie theaters, as well as the voluntary disposal of cultural artifacts such as kimonos, created a climate of fear and intimidation. Within this context, a Japanese American beauty pageant (CBF) held for the first time eight years after the end of World War II may be seen as part of a surge of nisei (second-generation Japanese American) assertion and practice of citizenship. Furthermore, according to Lim, the period of the early Cold War was a time of particular racial tension for Asian Americans throughout the United States, when the "hallmarks of normative Cold War American values included heterosexuality, family life in the suburbs, middle-class propriety, and whiteness" (2003:189). These values are metonymically linked, so that any one — heterosexuality, middle-class economics, morality, and whiteness — could stand for the other. The exclusion of Asian Americans from this set on the basis of race contextualizes many of these beauty pageants.[9] This kind of back story spotlights some of the political tensions inherent in the production of an Asian American spectacle that I discuss in subsequent chapters.

The proving ground of citizenship partly takes place in the arena of judging. The broader the spectrum of judges and the higher their status, the better proof that a beauty pageant is firmly embedded within the larger society, rather than merely part of an ethnic enclave. Lim writes of the Japanese American Nisei Week Queen contest judging of 1952:

By enlisting judges from outside the community, Asian American norms and values could be evaluated against those of mainstream society. . . . Most judges were outsiders to the Japanese American community and were European Americans considered to be experts in the world of business or the world of feminine beauty. . . . This privileged hegemonic values over ethnic community preferences. (2003:196)

An Asian American beauty pageant highlights the constant tensions inherent in its organization and practices vis-à-vis mainstream society even at the level of selecting judges and judging criteria.

Asian American beauty pageants differ to a certain extent from those of the mainstream by the role of families and closeness of their ties to particular communities. In many Asian societies, the family is the most significant social unit, often superseding the individual. This cultural value continues in Asian American contexts, especially those with continuing ties to Asia. In these Asian American groups a contestant represents not only herself, but, sometimes more important, her family. Furthermore, the status of a woman's family within the Asian American community may directly affect her success in the pageant. Therefore, the winner of a pageant may triumph on the basis not only of her own merits, but also those of her family. For example, Dawn Mabalon points out the equal importance of class, race, and family in Filipino American beauty pageants in the 1930s to 1950s in California:

> Victory was a measure of the family's integrity and popularity among certain factions in the community. . . . Light-skinned Filipinas, those with delicate mestiza features such as high Spanish noses, and Filipinas with well-connected families were presumed to be the most likely to win queen contests. (2003:4)

In these Filipino American communities beauty contests were both about the individual as a physical (racialized) ideal and about her family as a social, moral, and class ideal.

Asian American families include restrictive gender roles that are often more patriarchal and conservative than those in mainstream American society. Although these gender roles may have changed in postimmigrant contexts, they often get reinscribed on the Asian American beauty pageant stage, especially where pageant organizers are men. There is often historically a clearly gendered, symbolic divide between paternalistic men and "girls" who are seen as needing protection. The performance of containment/protection of females is part of the bid for respectability on the part of beauty pageants, as well as a specific cultural code of highly proscribed gender roles. The containment of women ties them closely to home and notions of tradition. As Irene Gedalof argues, "Identity narratives repeatedly position 'Woman' as 'place,' as the pure space of 'home' in which tradition is preserved from outside contamination" (2000:339).

Although this may hold true in many cultural groups, within the Asian American context, this inherent conservatism is reinforced by the group's concern to present itself positively within a dominant, mainstream context.

Closely linked to gender roles and Asian American beauty pageants is the gendering of Asian nations as female. Kalindi Vora argues:

> In looking at the discourse of the "Indian Woman" we see that she becomes a point of negotiation in defining Indian-ness both with and against Western-ness. . . . In both post-colonial India and multicultural America, the creation of the Indian woman is inseparable from that of the discourse of Indian-ness in general. (2002:80)

The discursive construct of "Indian Woman" is not isolated, but joins numerous other discourses that conjoin Asian women with their respective nations. Within the context of the feminization of Asia, Asian American beauty pageants place women on stage in affirmation of a geopolitical logic of nationalism and desire.

Race/Ethnicity and Culture in Asian American Pageants

One of the main differences between Asian American and mainstream beauty pageants concerns race/ethnicity as a variable in contestant eligibility rules. Most of these focus on ancestry or blood-quantum definitions of membership. These occur within the context of a national history of blood quantum-based racial categories, such as blackness defined by a "one drop rule." Contestant eligibility rules, therefore, only extend this principle to the beauty pageant stage. For example, who gets to be Japanese American and therefore compete in the CBF depends on rules dictating particular shifting minimum percentages of Japanese "blood." Other permutations combine blood quantum with some other requirements (where X stands for the racial/ethnic group): (1) requiring one parent to be of 100 percent X descent; or (2) requiring the surname of the contestant to be of X ethnicity. Rebecca King addresses the volatile issues raised by the acceptance of mixed-race candidates in Japanese American beauty pageants by the late twentieth century (1997, 1998, 2001, 2002). Using Michael Omi and Howard Winant's racial formation theory (1994), King argues that "racial/ethnic identity is flexible, but . . . is not a choice which is unconstrained" (1997:125). Instead of pan-ethnicity or assimilationism, King contends that groups such as Japanese Americans adopt "transracial ethnic strategies" to selectively include mixed-race individuals of their ethnic group, while excluding others without any Japanese ancestry (2002:121).

Another main difference concerns the (Asian) cultural competence of contestants. Those Asian American communities with active immigration often include a linguistic and/or cultural component in the competition — for example, requiring each contestant to make a speech in the Asian language of her forebears and otherwise demonstrate her ability to retain and perform her ethnic heritage (Lieu 2000:136). Others include cultural practices in the prepageant training of contestants. Therefore, one may compete in terms of cultural knowledge, as well as receive training in order to face the ultimate test of becoming a cultural representative.

In some cases, an Asian cultural component to training accrues over time as the generation of contestants becomes increasingly remote from their immigrant forebears. For contestants such as these, participation in an Asian American beauty pageant is a way to learn about the culture of their ancestors. More accurately, it is a way to learn about an idealized culture as conceptualized in the present that may or may not have been shared by earlier generations in the homeland itself. For example, the CBF includes lessons on Japanese tea ceremony in the training of its contestants, yet tea ceremony is more a part of elite Japanese culture than the working-class culture of Japanese immigrants. What is being taught to contestants at CBF is an upper-middle-class version of aestheticized Japanese culture, something most immigrants themselves never practiced or knew.[10]

In beauty pageants that include a talent portion in the competition, the choice of what to perform itself is an important manipulator and indicator of Asian (American) culture and identity. For example, Shilpa Dave notes of the Miss India Georgia contest:

> [The talent show] represents the most concrete example of the complexities of the imagined ideal "Indian" and how each contestant performs her ideal version of a transplanted Indian identity. . . . It is not how one performs but what one performs and what that represents to the judges and the community. (2001:351)

An Indian American contestant who dances *bharatnatyam* (classical Indian dance) contrasts with others who might belt a Broadway number or perform a hiphop dance. Each contestant makes a calculated decision based both on what she can do and what she thinks the judges want. In Asian American beauty pageants, this decision is enmeshed within issues of culture and identity. Judges' evaluation of the talent portion defines what best represents that Asian American identity.

better to be cultural to homeland than talented in talent portions of pageant

The active performance of Asian culture in Asian American beauty pageants can be seen on stage most clearly in terms of dress. Most Asian American pageants feature women in Asian national costume: for example, Japanese kimono, Chinese *qipao* (Mandarin; the Cantonese word cheongsam is more familiar throughout Chinese America), Vietnamese *ao dai,* and Filipino *terno.*[11] These ethnicized displays are separated from the global beauty pageant displays of women in evening gowns and, in some cases, swimsuits. Asian costumes themselves are overdetermined symbols of upper class, Asian (American) femininity, and diasporic nationhood.[12]

In some cases, the Asian costume is either sufficiently distinct from Euro-American dress or comes with embedded cultural practices that contestants must take lessons in wearing and storing the garment. For example, in the CBF, contestant training includes kimono-wearing; given the restrictiveness of the garment, as well as the length and width of the sleeves, contestants must be taught how to walk, pose, and sit in kimono, as well as how to maneuver the sleeves.[13] Kimono-wearing is considered such an important part of the event that a kimono consultant originally from Japan has long been an important part of pageant personnel (see Chapters 5 and 7).

The coding of Asian American femininity through these costumes nostalgically recuperates a sense of the homeland. As Nhi T. Lieu argues:

> Symbolically, the ao dai invokes nostalgia and timelessness associated with a gendered image of the homeland for which many Vietnamese people throughout the diaspora yearn. . . . The ao dai conjures up romantic images of a Vietnamese past that is pure and untainted by war. (2000:128)

The garment also invokes confusion over the socialized control of Asian American women learning *ao dai* ways of being/performing female in Vietnamese American culture, as shown in the poem "My Pink *Ao Dai*" by Nhien T. Nguyen:

> Breathe in, don't breath [*sic*] out
> hold your gut in
> sit up straight
> take small bites, chew thoroughly (2000:126)

The poem expresses highly gendered, cultural lessons in bodily control and identity centered around the *ao dai.* The same might easily be said for the kimono, *qipao*, and other Asian garments, each in their own respective beauty pageants carrying the weight of symbolic, gendered, group identity.

Another aspect of bodily culture in Asian American beauty pageants is the issue of exposure and modesty. In many Asian societies, a woman is stereotypically expected to display the virtue of modesty. Modesty is more extreme and more strictly policed in the Asian American context than in mainstream (albeit originally puritanical) American society. Furthermore, modesty directly contradicts parading in a swimsuit before a large audience of judges and the public. Some Asian American beauty pageants such as the CBF explicitly do not and have never included a swimsuit portion in the competition. Others, such as Miss Nikkei International, which is dominated by South American organizations whose sense of modesty differs from the more puritanical North American milieu, feature a swimsuit competition. And others began with no swimsuit competition as a point of cultural difference from mainstream America, but introduced it later. Miss Chinatown U.S.A. did not have one when it began in 1958, then added a "playsuit" (short-skirt outfit) portion in 1962, replaced with a swimsuit portion of the competition in 1967. One male organizer of the pageant claimed that the inclusion of swimsuits came at the request of contestants themselves who wanted to "display their beauty" (Wu 1997:23). Note ironically that the introduction of swimsuits into the Miss Chinatown U.S.A. pageant competition came at a time when feminists in the United States were vociferously decrying beauty contests (e.g., the Miss America protest of 1968). This juxtaposition only points up the disparity between many Asian American beauty pageants (and perhaps beauty pageants as a whole) from liberal political movements.

Displaying the body is closely tied to issues of morality in mainstream American society. However, within an Asian American context, the same issue is mapped onto a national/cultural terrain. Participating in and organizing a beauty pageant may be seen as a quintessentially American, and therefore assimilationist, activity. However, displaying one's body Miss America style may be critiqued as going too far, becoming too American, losing sight of one's Asian cultural value of modesty. Ironically, the "separate and parallel" Asian American beauty pageant, sans swimsuit, may be interpreted as both quintessentially American and an antidote to Americanism. For example, Lieu contends that Vietnamese American beauty pageants impose

> a moral code of sexual conduct on young Vietnamese American women who are considered in danger of becoming "too American." . . . Taking part in Vietnamese cultural events such as the ao dai beauty pageant thus steered young women away from the corrupting forces of American culture and kept them "pure" and "Vietnamese." (2000:136, 141)

Purity, here equated with Asian origins, culture, and tradition, is kept intact through the all-American institution of a beauty contest.

The issue of becoming "too American" is one not to be taken lightly in both Asian American (and Asian) contexts. In contrast to the earlier assimilationist paradigmatic Asian American experience, this concern creates a preserve around "homeland" Asian cultures, often resulting in greater conservativism than is found in Asian countries themselves. It is helpful here to recognize many parallel activities taking place in Asia and Asian America vis-à-vis the United States. Globalization emanating from Euro-America and, more recently, from Japan to parts of Asia has generated monumental changes in Asian nations. In many cases the rapidity of change creates generational panic, as youths wholeheartedly embrace what looks like Western goods and practices at the sacrifice of Asian traditions. For example, in Japan, older generations decry the lack of knowledge of cultural practices and values among younger generations. These generational divides in Japan parallel immigrant divides in terms of cultural knowledge: each succeeding generation recedes farther and farther from any Asian cultural origins. At the same time, critics in Japan look to older Japanese American practices as a preserve of past ways and values. The divides go in multiple directions: Japan's youth as ignorant of Japanese culture; Japanese American youth as ignorant of Japanese and Japanese American culture; Japanese American culture as conservative of Japan's past culture; a past assimilationist Japanese American paradigm operating within a nisei cohort that actively embraces American culture. This complicated relationship between tradition, change, generations, and immigrant cultures may be specific to Japanese Americans who have historical depth in the United States, but also influences evolving Asian American beauty pageants.

"Double Eyes": Whose Beauty Is This?

Whose standards of beauty govern judging becomes a critical issue in Asian American pageants enmeshed within larger sociopolitical contexts. For example, Chinese American feminists from the late 1960s through the 1970s protested the Miss Chinatown U.S.A. pageant for its white standards of beauty that reinforced the belief that "the closer you look like the Whites, the prettier you are" (Wu 1997:15). Lim challenges the notion that Asian American beauty pageants only affirm white standards of beauty, arguing that these pageants actually reward "counterhegemonic beauty" (2003:193). King argues, "Japanese American women have either tried to assimilate and fit in with hegemonic models of beauty in the United States or to create a [counterhegemonic] beauty 'difference' that itself has been co-opted by the mainstream as 'exotic'" (2001:163). The resultant competing models of beauty are made all the more complex with the inclusion of mixed-race contestants.

pageant become more complex in judging when it comes to mix-race contestants

One element that both critics and contestants regard as important components of beauty is eyes. The eye and its shape have long been iconic of Asians and Asian Americans, as signified by stereotypic nicknames such as "slant-eyes." Among many women in Asian American communities, the eye — in particular, the eyelid — is a specific focus and concern. This focus and concern rests in the epicanthal fold of many, though not all, East Asians, resulting in what many Asian Americans term "single eye(lid)." Having "single eye(lid)s" sets them apart from whites and other Asian Americans with "double eye(lid)s," and is thus considered undesirable. Many of those with single-lidded eyes either apply thin strips of tape or glue to temporarily create double lids, use considerable eyeliner to effect the look of a larger double-lidded eye, or undergo surgery to permanently alter their lids.

One white, male surgeon in Honolulu who specializes in Asian(American) cosmetic surgery advertises the "double eye" procedure on his website:

> Surgical modification of the upper eyelid (commonly called the double eye operation) has become increasingly popular since 1950. Currently it is by far the most common cosmetic procedure performed in Asia, and is extremely popular in American cities with large Asian populations. In the past, such surgery was considered a "westernization" procedure and as a result, many surgically modified eyelids did not match the patient's face. I have developed techniques that allow individualization of the size and shape of the eye thus achieving an appearance that accentuates and flatters the natural character of the Asian face. (McCurdy 2004)

This doctor and others deny that such surgery "Westernizes" the Asian face. Indeed, because some people of Asian descent have "double-lidded eyes," one might suggest that the ideal is within an Asian frame of reference, rather than white. If this is the case, it is worth noting that it is not necessarily an aesthetic that existed in premodern Asia before the influx of Euro-American goods, media, and people. According to David Palumbo-Liu, "The desire to alter the eyelid is not undertaken necessarily to 'be white,' but to partake of whiteness in a selective fashion. And that whiteness exists precisely in the discourse of social power" (1999:94). The eyelid and its surgical manipulation may therefore be taken as emblematic of postcolonial race relations, power, gender, and class. That is, by achieving a look of what might be interpreted as "whiteness" through surgery, one coordinates one's body with those in power and approximates more closely a mediated feminine ideal.

Eyelid surgery has become an overt part of some Asian American beauty pageants, while remaining a covert part of others. According to Wu, the 1970 Miss Chinatown U.S.A. souvenir book included an advertisement for surgery by a Chinese doctor "who invented a special technique for converting 'oriental eyes' with single eyelids into 'Caucasian eyes' (with double-eyelids)" (1997:29n23). Lieu also reports that a cosmetic surgery center was one of the major sponsors of the 1995 Vietnamese beauty pageant held in Long Beach, California. It even received a five-minute infomercial spot on the commercial videotape of the pageant (2000:145). In these and other examples, the racialized language of double-lidded beauty forms a discursive backdrop for Asian American pageants.

The fact that double-lidded eyes can be considered both ascriptive (inherited trait) as well as achieved (temporarily with tape or glue or permanently through surgery) gives them an ambiguous presence. Double-lidded eyes raise the question much like breast implants: are they real or fake? Some observers contend that one can usually tell a surgically altered eyelid, at least without makeup. And if they are not natural, what are the politics behind their investment? Unlike breast implants, this surgery is particular to Asians and Asian Americans and speaks to specific conditions and contexts of racialized body culture and desire.

Looking to Asia: Diasporas, "Homelands," Transnational Ties

Some Asian American pageants emphasize their difference from Asian pageants. For example, Lieu argues: "Unlike the beauty pageants that take place in Vietnam, Vietnamese Americans celebrate their cultural *difference* as immigrants in a collective effort to preserve 'Vietnamese culture and tradition through beauty pageants'" (2000:129). Apart from the Miss Korea Hawaii pageant, most Asian American beauty pageants have but a distant relationship to those actually taking place in Asia. Other Asian American beauty pageants, especially those organized by communities with ongoing immigration, are tied to Asia and Asian renderings of beauty pageants. I consider these to be diasporic Asian American beauty pageants because of their close and continuing transnational link to a home country. In these cases, the shaping of the pageant is often mediated through the global culture of beauty pageants following an older Miss America mold, including swimsuit and evening gown competitions, a talent portion, and the public display of contestants' measurements. For example, the Miss Korea Hawaii 2002 souvenir pageant booklet included a black-and white-three-quarter length photograph and head-shot portrait of each of the contestants along with information on their height, weight, bust, waist, and hip measurements.[14] The booklet, primarily written in *hangul* (Korean syllabary) rather than English, is clearly geared to an immigrant, diasporic audience. Furthermore, Miss Korea Hawaii goes to Seoul yearly to compete in the Miss Korea

International contest. ~~Participating in this pageant is a way to directly connect with Asia, as well as with other Korean diasporic groups.~~

Several diasporic pageants privilege contestants with the most direct links to their Asian "homelands," expressed as elements of competition in the pageant through required linguistic competence or display of cultural knowledge. Contestants with more distant generational links to immigration or from more distant geographic diasporic outposts are at a distinct disadvantage. For example, Dave relates the awkward experiences of a Miss India Georgia contestant who was generationally more distant than other contestants and whose parents came from Trinidad instead of India: "The isolation of her family from an Indian community [because generationally more distant] and her family's alternate migration pattern [from Trinidad] makes Misty feel even more isolated from Indian culture" (2001:346).

Some diasporic pageants deliberately create links to Asia by dangling lucrative prizes such as travel to the "homeland" through travel and entry into the transnational entertainment industry. For many queens, it will be the first time there. Vora notes these mutually constitutive ties: "Just as the [Indian] film industry has reached out into the diaspora to become a fundamental part of diaspora life, so the pageant has assumed a spot in a now transnational Indian entertainment industry" (2002:3). Several Asian American pageants link directly to Asia through corporate sponsorship. The CBF has long relied on Japanese sponsors such as Japan Airlines and Shiseido cosmetics. The CBF Queen and court travel to Japan, where they visit these corporate sponsors.

Certain political implications surrounding Asian American beauty pageants link to the conditions of the Asian countries with which each is associated. For example, with which Chinese country does a Miss Chinatown U.S.A. ally herself (Wu 1997:24)? Which Korea organizes the Miss Korea International? How does the Miss Vietnam Tet pageant express an attempt to reclaim the *ao dai* as national dress, rescuing its degradation from communist control (Lieu 2000:130)?

The connection of an Asian American pageant to Asia differs in part by the place of beauty pageants within the homeland context. In the case of Japan, for example, beauty pageants receive only limited media coverage and public attention.[15] Japanese American beauty pageants thus do not necessarily build upon a flourishing set of practices in Japan. In the Philippines, by contrast, beauty pageants are a vibrant part of public life. As Dawn Mabalon explains:

> Several years ago, a Philippine tourism secretary told a reporter that "beauty contests are a part of Philippine culture. They say if you want to hold anything in the Philippines, hold a beauty pageant or a cockfight." In the early

decades of Filipina/o American settlement in Stockton [California], these two events — beauty contests and cockfights — remained the most popular events. (2003:3)

The centrality of beauty contests in Philippine culture spills over into Filipino American culture, tying the two in highly diasporic ways. In Hawaiʻi, for example, besides the statewide Miss Hawaii Filipina pageant, there are smaller "hometown" contests organized by local communities tied together by their origins in towns in the Philippines. Each year, a "hometown" queen from Hawaiʻi returns to the Philippines during festival time to celebrate, in part, the overseas diasporic community that she represents (Okamura 2004, personal communication). In the case of India, the success of Indian representatives to international contests (Miss World in 1994, 1997, 1999, 2000; Miss Universe in 1994, 2000; Miss Asia Pacific in 2000) ties beauty pageants closely to notions of modernity and global status (Vora 2002:72). Thus a contest such as Miss India USA draws upon both national and diasporic prominence.

Asian American beauty pageants also intersect with the regionalism of Asian countries in varying ways. As Lieu argues, Vietnamese American pageants enable viewers to occupy multiple subject positions, "as members of the imagined [Vietnamese] nation, as distinct peoples from different regions [in Vietnam], and as Vietnamese refugees" (2000:134). Where emphasis on regional differences is diminished, global diasporic links are strengthened. "The metaphorical erasure and disavowal of regional and local distinctions, in essence, dramatized the organic wholeness of the 'imagined community' [of diasporic Vietnamese Americans]" (ibid.). In some cases, however, the erasure of certain regional differences occurs simultaneously with the reinscription of other regional differences.

Among communities with generational depth in the United States, such as Japanese Americans, Asia is the land of parents, grandparents, great-grandparents, and in some cases even further remote ancestors, not of the contestants themselves. Their relationship to Asia is removed from their everyday lives. Some contestants may speak an Asian language at home, while others have little or no Asian cultural knowledge. Yet, part of the work of the beauty pageant is to perform some version of Asia, as well as Asian America. The simultaneous performance of Asia and Asian America constitutes the schizophrenic cultural split of succeeding generations: one is preserved, distilled, and distorted out of time; the other is dynamic and always changing. This articulation is part of Asian American beauty pageants as they attempt to negotiate the waters between their Asianness and their (Asian) Americanness, producing, in the words of Lieu, "new hybrid, gender and ethnic identities" (2000:129).

What is the work that these Asian American beauty pageants do? Do they challenge national identity? Do they renegotiate transplanted immigrant cultural identities? Most Asian American beauty pageant organizers echo in some way the sentiments of An Vu, a sponsor and advisor to the first Miss Vietnam Tet pageant in San Jose, California: "We don't want girls that are too Americanized but aren't all Vietnamese either" (quoted in Milanese 2002:1). Ien Ang's essay "On Not Speaking Chinese" challenges Asian Americans to develop "a critical diasporic cultural politics [that] should privilege neither host country nor (real or imagined) homeland, but precisely keep a creative tension between 'where you're from' and 'where you're at'" (2001:35). The hybridity of Asian American beauty pageants lies in this shifting tension between "where you're from" and "where you're at," between "all Vietnamese" and "too Americanized," between kimono and evening gown. Each of these choices acts as a stereotypical representation, couching the "creative tension" in simple either-or dichotomies.

In this construct, Asianness (or Japaneseness, Koreanness, Chineseness, Indianness, and so on) — ahistorically conceived, essentialized, and homogenized — has no overlap with Americanness. It matters little that other contrasts, such as Japaneseness versus Koreanness versus Indianness, are overlooked in the process. Asia and its individual countries are signifiers of difference and thus a way of defining America. As Gladney notes, "Minorities, in general, are defined in terms of an accepted majority" (1998:2); but majorities also define themselves in dialogue with minority constructs, as part of their "majoritarian discourse" (ibid.:9). Each is the negation of the other, minimizing and ultimately erasing any overlap. Asian American beauty pageants separate out these threads as metonyms of sociopolitical conditions in the United States.

Part of those sociopolitical conditions lies in the model minority image that haunts so many Asian American communities.[16] When these pageants show "nice girls" doing nice things in slightly exotic ways, then the model minority image is confirmed on gendered grounds. However, when participants threaten to overstep their bounds, imagining themselves beyond the model minority image in places and practices of their own making, then the stereotype begins to crack. The containment of these beauty queens lies directly in the containment of later generations of once-immigrant families whose daily lives are deeply invested in "where they're at," even as they may or may not choose to invest themselves within the confines of "where they're from." Some of these younger generations participate voraciously in the transnational flow of "where they're from," but others live increasingly distant from it, neither knowing nor caring much about it. Nevertheless, both find themselves in surroundings that continue to tie them to an Asian "homeland." Wrangling with model minority status generates some of the "creative tension" of which Ang speaks, finding varying expression in Asian American beauty pageants.

Model minority status is only part of the dynamic of "where they're at." James Clifford argues, "The term 'diaspora' is a signifier not simply of transnationality and movement but of political struggles to define the local, as distinctive community, in historical contexts of displacement" (1997:252). Or more to the point here, in defining oneself as a distinctive community in an American setting, Asian American groups engage in processes of emplacement, asserting and affirming a space within the fabric of sociocultural life in the United States. I contend that beauty contests form part of this emplacement, linking the tensions and conditions of new and old homes, performing the ethnic spectacle within the familiar idiom of beauty pageants. One might argue that part of the goal of many Asian American beauty pageants is to balance difference with blending in, effecting one's own acceptability by the crown of exotica, achieving banality while remaining profound. These processes showcase the tensions of living "where you're at" while made to enact "where you're from."

To what extent are these beauty pageants part of mainstream American society, including its beauty culture? *Pageantry Magazine*, which lists state, national, and international competitions, does not include Asian American beauty pageants (2004). Editor Carl Dunn explains that the magazine can only publish information that pageant organizers send them. Therefore, it is not a matter of excluding Asian American pageants, but of Asian American pageants excluding themselves by not reaching out to the mainstream beauty pageant infrastructure.

The threads of hybridity in these beauty pageants are often taken as historically fixed, as "roots" that circumscribe identity in terms of place, blood/ancestry, heritage, and a desiccated notion of culture. Gedalof suggests that instead of considering identity based upon "roots," it may be more fruitful to think of rhizomes — that is, variable points of connection forming a complex web (2000). I propose to supplant the rhizome analogy with a cybernetic model of extended hyperlinks, forming ever-expanding, changing, and updated configurations. Identity is thus the particular configuration of hyperlinks, generated internally and externally, at any point in time in any given context. Choosing one hyperlink opens up possibilities of other hyperlinks, so that mapping the terrain of identity becomes a multidimensional and historically situated challenge.

Do Asian American pageants foster what Pamela Thoma calls "Asian American transnational feminism" (1999:n.p.)? Do they empower women through "counterhegemonic subjectivities and social formations" (ibid.)? The common insider response is that, yes, contestants and queens do become empowered through their pageant experience. By presenting and manipulating racialized, bourgeois femininity, they gain the power of the spotlight. On the structural level, however, what does each Asian American community achieve by staging beauty pageants? Can we believe in the counterhegemonic efficacy of these events?

I argue that, for the most part, these pageants do not offer counterhegemonic rewards so much as reproduce conservative, gendered expectations, ideals, and practices. Their purpose is not to disrupt, but to coexist in separate-and-parallel fashion. They present an ideal of racialized, ethnicized womanhood, and in the process affirm their own emplacement. The spotlight is framed by contingencies of power relations. Along the way, individuals invested in the pageant often assert their own agency, claiming that they are not "typical beauty queens" or using the runway exposure as a springboard to further careers.

These individuals and the Asian American beauty pageants of which they are a part constitute a "space on the side of the road" — here, a personal, private, lived commentary upon public structures, as well as an alternative, "other-ed" space within America (Stewart 1996:4). Asian American beauty pageants carve out a space in American life that performs against the mainstream in its very carving, as well as affirms it in utilizing a recognizable idiom. In effect, Asian American beauty pageants perform the Asian/American "solidus" that, in the words of Palumbo-Liu "instantiates a choice between two terms, their simultaneous and equal status, and an element of indecidability . . . 'Asian/American' marks *both* the distinction installed between 'Asian' and 'American' *and* a dynamic, unsettled and inclusive movement" (1999:1). Asian American beauty pageants, like Palumbo-Liu's solidus, acknowledge the union and divisibility between Asia and America, between "where you're from" and "where you're at." At the same time, the pageant-as-solidus places this binary within a dynamic, hyperlinked framework of active choices, negotiations, and tensions.

Chapter Two

Historicizing the Cherry Blossom Festival | Engendering the American Way of Life in Postwar Hawai'i

In the propaganda battles that permeated the cold war era, American leaders promoted the American way of life as the triumph of capitalism, allegedly available to all who believed in its values. This way of life was characterized by affluence, located in suburbia, and epitomized by white middle-class nuclear families. Increasing numbers of Americans gained access to this domestic ideal—but not everyone who aspired to it could achieve it.
—May 1988:xviii

his chapter examines ways in which the CBF, born in Hawai'i during the Cold War era of the mid-1950s, mapped onto the "American way of life," with its singular vision of heterosexuality, the nuclear family, middle-class consumerism, and whiteness. The particularities of this mapping undergird critical refractions of race/ethnicity, core-periphery relations, and the regionalism of that vision. The CBF from the outset and variably throughout its subsequent development was both an expression of citizenship — that is, emplacement within the American sphere — as well as a showcase of carefully crafted difference.

In this chapter I provide a historical context for the founding of the CBF and its early years, looking first at the general milieu of postwar Hawai'i, including the place of race relations developed during the prewar and wartime years and dominant representations of Japanese Americans. World War II was but one event in a racialized atmosphere in Hawai'i; it was preceded and followed by others contributing to a nationalist agenda of economic growth and political stewardship. Given the historical context of Japanese Americans in postwar Hawai'i, I examine the founding of the HJJCC, not only in relations with other ethnic groups, but also within the Japanese American community as a particularly nisei organization. I embed the HJJCC within the Jaycee movement in the United States as a gendered, mercantilist, civic institution that speaks directly to the "American way of life" of the 1950s.

In the final section of this chapter, I contextualize the CBF as one of many ethnic beauty pageants in Hawai'i during this period at the high school, university, and community levels. Beauty existed as both a leveling ground and a competitive playing field divided by race/ethnicity in Hawai'i. The contest was not so much about which group had the most beautiful women, but how different groups might participate in the glory of crowning a queen.

Throughout this chapter and book, I examine the role of race in what Omi and Winant term "racialization" — that is, the structuring of everyday experiences and institutions on the basis of the meanings given to race (1994:56). Although race is not the only player on this historical stage — others include gender, class, marginality, globalization (especially tourism), and United States–Japan relations — it is a significant aspect of the period and the discursive practices of the event. Rather than isolate race (as well as race/ethnicity), I embed it within the dynamism of other important factors, events, and institutions of the time. It is this shifting matrix that provides the foundation of the CBF.

Hawai'i of the 1950s: Tropical American Dream for Japanese Americans?

The 1950s was a period during which Japanese Americans — particularly nisei war veterans of the much-decorated 442nd Regimental Combat Team and 100th Infantry Battalion — sought to reap the rewards of their American citizenry from the proving ground of World War II. At 36.9 percent of the population (down from an all-time high of 42.0 percent in 1920), Japanese Americans constituted the largest single ethnic group in Hawai'i.[1] On the political front, Japanese Americans made their mark as central players in the "Democratic Revolution of 1954," the first time that Democrats gained the majority in both houses of the territorial legislature in Hawai'i. The American dream may not have included political advancement, but the election of nisei to office in 1954 proved their emplacement as fully participating citizen leaders within the nation. As early as 1958, the success of Japanese American politicians caused a backlash of resentment with accusations of clannishness. Kotani argues:

> Although the Japanese showed no greater tendency toward ethnic bloc voting than other groups, the growing political and economic influence of Americans of Japanese ancestry became a subject of apprehension for some non-Japanese residents of the islands. . . . By 1958, defeated candidates were blaming their losses on the tendency of Japanese voters to cast their ballots for Nisei candidates. (1985:150)

No sooner had Japanese Americans started to become a political force than their numbers became a threat to other power-wielders in the state.

On the social front, Japanese Americans continued to in-marry (furthering the stereotype of clannishness) and did so until the 1980s, producing families that, race aside, were part of the American dream (Lind 1980:114).[2] This version of the American dream took a slight twist, since many Japanese Americans lived in multigenerational households, due to economic factors as well as a sociocultural emphasis on the extended family. On the economic front, Japanese Americans pursued the middle-class dream of the 1950s, edging them toward prominence in education, business, and politics; however, achievement of that dream was uneven. During this period, they still comprised nearly one-third of all plantation employees, three-fourths of domestic service workers, one-half of small farmers and fishermen, five-eighths of auto mechanics, and over half of proprietors of retail food stores and restaurants (Okamura 2001:75 – 76). At

rise in Japanese-Americans in political possitions as well as

Social Classes. by 1956.

the same time, Japanese Americans aspired to the material accoutrements of the American dream, including owning a home, car, and appliances (the "all-electric home") while attaining financial security to provide for their children (Chinen and Hiura 1997:70).[3] The GI Bill of 1944 and a general push toward higher education helped move this lingering blue-collar demographic into white-collar occupations by 1970 (Kitano 1976:176 – 179).[4] Even if not all veterans benefited equally from the GI Bill, many Japanese Americans in Hawai'i took advantage of this stepping stone to middle-class attainment by gaining educational and income levels comparable to and surpassing those of other ethnic groups.[5]

One critical focus of fulfilling the American dream was language. Speaking English was historically both a litmus test of citizenship, as well as a political weapon of racial discrimination. Beginning in 1924 and continuing in the postwar years to 1960, special public "English standard schools" required admission tests or other proof of mastery of English.[6] These thinly veiled race- and class-based institutions became marks of prestige, citizenship, and assimilation for Japanese Americans and others in Hawai'i.[7] Gender played a significant role in this: "[Nonwhite] girls especially, attempting to live up to their parents' hopes for them, managed to win admission to the English Standard schools. The [nonwhite] boys, frequently blocked by their peer groups from mastering what was accepted as standard English, found the going much rougher" (Fuchs 1961:278). Performing a nonwhite, working-class, "local" masculinity was tied to a machismo indexed by speaking the local vernacular Creole ("pidgin") and not speaking standard English. By contrast, femininity for girls and women from within the same cohort included the aspirations of upward mobility and transcendence of race enabled by standard English. Language thus enacted specific class- and race-based notions of gender.

The proving ground of language was part of the overall performance of citizenship and patriotism.[8] The Japanese American community found no stricter policing than within its own ranks, creating intergenerational cleavages between issei parents who often spoke little English and nisei offspring who spoke standard and Creole English. Lawrence Fuchs explains that during World War II, "the [Japanese American] youngsters from college and high school told their mothers to put away their kimonos, stop eating Japanese food, throw away the small shrines and family swords, preserved for generations; and the old folks had to listen" (ibid.:304). Former parent-child roles and hierarchies were thus reversed.

As part of the generational shift in power and responsibility, and as a flip side to the promotion of standard English, Japanese language facility declined.[9] Kotani explains:

As Nisei businessmen and professionals established firms which served a multi-ethnic clientele, the economic advantages of fluency in the Japanese language declined. When *ojichan* [*sic*] (grandfather) and *obachan* [*sic*] (grandmother) died, use of the Japanese language in the Japanese American family household also died. (1985:155)

This decline in Japanese language in combination with an increasing orientation away from Japan and toward the United States and global culture also precipitated the decline of media institutions established by and geared to issei, such as Japanese-language newspapers, radio, and cinema.[10]

Although Japanese media institutions began their decline during this period, other cultural events in the realm of popular entertainment and sports represented a spike of interest in things Japanese in Hawai'i. Nisei-led orchestras whose repertoire was primarily Japanese popular music and were popular in the 1930s began performing again only three months after the end of World War II in late 1945. By 1950, nisei orchestras were flourishing and performing to enthusiastic Japanese American audiences (Tasaka 1985:50). These orchestras whetted an appetite for Japanese popular entertainment that was cautious at first and then grew with enthusiasm in postwar Hawai'i.

To further satisfy the demand, singers crisscrossed the Pacific in a transnational flow of popular culture between the two countries. One of these was the visit of postwar child star Misora Hibari (1937–1989), whose concert in Hawai'i in 1950 sponsored by Japanese American war veteran groups caused a sensation. Hibari's trip took place only four years after her debut in Japan, demonstrating the closeness of popular culture channels between Japan and Hawai'i.[11] Other Japanese entertainers visited Hawai'i in the postwar period, including some of Japan's most famous singers, composers (e.g., Koga Masao in 1950), dance troupes (e.g., the Takarazuka all-female revue in 1955, 1956, 1957, and 1966 as part of the CBF), and movie stars (e.g., actor-singer Kayama Yūzo in 1969). They were met with tremendous enthusiasm from the Japanese American community. At the same time, a few nisei singers such as George Shimabukuro (b. 1930) made careers performing in Japan after World War II. Japanese record companies deliberately emphasized these nisei singers' Americanness. The companies downplayed their Japanese-language ability or knowledge of Japanese popular songs in order to exoticize them as novelty commodities for Japanese audiences (Waseda 2004:10).[12]

Besides entertainers, athletes participated in this transnational flow between Japan and Hawai'i. College and professional baseball teams from Japan visited Hawai'i during this period.[13] Some nisei baseball players also established careers in Japan. One of the most prominent was Maui-born Wally Yonamine

[handwritten margin note: music crisscrossed themes.]

(b. 1925), who joined Japan's Yomiuri Giants in 1951 as the first American in Japanese professional baseball after World War II, survived the anti-American catcalls of Japanese fans, and eventually became the first American inducted into Japan's Baseball Hall of Fame in 1994. Nisei athletes such as Yonamine and others became a diasporic bridge built upon assumptions that racialized nisei as the "natural" ambassadors of the most popular American sport played on Japanese soil.[14] The appeal of these celebrities and sports teams was not restricted to issei, but extended to nisei fans. Singers, musicians, movie stars, and athletes thus represented a cultural bridge between Japanese American generations in Hawai'i as well as between countries.

The 1950s with its transnational flows of athletes and entertainers between Hawai'i and Japan represented a transitional period during which Japanese popular culture acted as an important link between nations, generations, genders, and classes. Issei and nisei, men and women, middle-class and blue-collar Japanese Americans rallied around these stars and athletes. For many, Japanese popular culture provided an alternative refraction upon the prevailing American dream. For many Japanese Americans in postwar Hawai'i, depoliticized popular culture was a safe arena in which to express and explore their ties to Japan.

Japanese American Gains: Tensions of First-class Citizenship

Ties to Japan were only possible through emplacement within Hawai'i-based American culture, politics, and society. That emplacement in political and economic leadership was uneven and did not come without social cost. The percentage of Japanese American males in white-collar professions tripled between 1930 and 1960, from 3.4 percent to 10.1 percent of the employed Japanese American male population (Kotani 1985:145). At the same time, other Japanese Americans were crowded out by the limited island economy. Both blue-collar and white-collar Japanese Americans outmigrated, typically to the West Coast of the continental United States, especially to established enclaves such as Gardena, California (Beechert 1985:132, Table 9). This postwar exodus suggests the unevenness of economic advancement of nisei.

Japanese Americans strongly supported statehood. In a 1958 survey, 43 percent of Hawai'i's residents favored immediate statehood, but among Japanese Americans the number was as high as 62 percent (Kotani 1985:151). In 1959, when Hawai'i gained statehood, the exuberant words of the time proclaimed, "We all *haoles* (white) now" (quoted in Chinen and Hiura 1997:77). According to Kotani, "For Hawaii's residents of Japanese ancestry, the long journey to first-class citizenship was finally over" (1985:151).

But was it? Racial stereotypes colored first-class citizenship for Japanese Americans. Dominant representations of Japanese Americans became the backdrop against which public performances of niceness such as the establishment of the HJJCC and later the CBF were crucial. These historic representations include images of Japanese men (and other men of color) as violent and deceitful and the association of a certain class of Japanese women with sex and prostitution.[15] These also include longstanding local histories of Japanese Americans as agricultural workers, making their postwar leap into college classrooms and subsequent urban, white-collar jobs significant and timely. Although the heroic acts of nisei soldiers and female civilian workers and volunteers during World War II did much to dispel those earlier images, racial/ethnic stereotypes could not be completely dismissed in the 1950s and 1960s.

Lingering pockets of racial discrimination persisted in postwar Hawai'i. Decorated war veteran and future U.S. Senator Daniel Inouye recalls being refused service at a restaurant in postwar Honolulu because he was nonwhite, in spite of his donning of his soldier's uniform with medals and badges (Okamura 2001:129). The exclusive Oahu Country Club, Pacific Club, Outrigger Canoe Club, Rotary Club, and Waialae Golf Club refused to allow Japanese Americans (and other Asians) membership (Coffman 2003:101; Fuchs 1961:438). This racial discrimination was exacerbated by an influx of outsiders, especially haole from the continental United States to Hawai'i following statehood. In the U.S. Census between 1960 and 1970, the general population of Hawai'i grew by 21.5 percent, but the numbers of whites increased by 50 percent (Lind 1980:13). Part of this was the result of a change in definitions of whites to include Portuguese, Puerto Ricans, and Spanish, but part of this was also a reflection of the influx of 158,000 mostly whites from the continental United States. During this same period, 34,668 immigrants from primarily Asia and the Pacific also took up residence in Hawai'i. This changing mix of peoples in Hawai'i as well as persistent racial exclusions made the "first-class citizenship" of Japanese Americans both more significant as part of the stewardship of the newly dubbed state as well as more complex as part of the unevenness of social equity.

Statehood helped unleash a flood of industry, people, and tourists to the state. In contrast to prewar tourism dependent on the luxury trade of ocean liners, tourism in the 1950s and 1960s to Hawai'i was fueled by the development of relatively affordable airline travel and subsequent expansion of the tourist trade to middle-class travelers (Desmond 1999:134). Tourism grew at an average annual rate of 20 percent throughout the 1950s and 1960s, overtaking agriculture as the largest industry in the 1960s. One of the effects of the growth of mass tourism to Hawai'i was a shift of population and wealth to O'ahu, the destination of direct flights from the continental United States and elsewhere, resulting in a severely lopsided population distribution centered in Honolulu (Fuchs 1961:380–381). Pan American Airways, one of the primary sponsors of the CBF, became a symbol of this new era of air travel. Although mass tourism from Japan had yet to begin, Japan Airlines (another major sponsor of the CBF) began flights to Hawai'i in 1954, furthering a direct link between the two countries. The growth of tourism combined with a postwar economic boom, resulting in the opening of what was dubbed the largest shopping mall in the world, the Ala Moana Center, in 1959.[16]

Among the major stores at Ala Moana Center was Shirokiya, Japan's oldest department store in this, its first branch outside of Japan. The opening of Shirokiya at Ala Moana Center marked a significant moment in the postwar history of Japan, as well as the Japanese American community in Hawai'i. Japan was reconstructing at a phenomenal rate. Only fourteen years after defeat in World War II, it was extending its economic arm into a foreign country, albeit one with a sizeable community of ethnic Japanese who could conceivably support such an endeavor. Although goods from Japan were available in Hawai'i well before 1959, Shirokiya marked the first large-scale, direct marketing and sales from a Japanese department store, providing Japanese Americans and others with goods and a shopping experience considered distinctively Japanese. Given the eagerness with which consumerism was approached in the boom years of the 1950s and 1960s, Shirokiya became an important Japanese foothold in a growing global consumer culture in Hawai'i.[17]

Shirokiya's opening became part of the uneven mix of race-based attitudes in Hawai'i in the 1950s and 1960s. Tamura writes, "As late as the 1960s, a Nisei described a common reaction among Japanese. He said that many were 'afraid to associate with Haoles. It [was] not so much being clannish, but being afraid of Haoles'" (1994:196). The intimidation by decades of English standard schools and Americanization campaigns was not so easily erased by the achievements of statehood, political office, or business success. Language was only part of the problem. So, too, was lingering discrimination in housing, employment, and membership in private clubs. More generally, though, nisei understood too well the ongoing preferential treatment given to haoles in Hawai'i (Tamura 1994:197), as well as the remnants of separate spheres of interaction.

The social pecking order was not a simple haole versus Japanese. Relations between nonwhite minority groups in Hawai'i form a critical and complex part of the postwar backdrop. The 1950 Census gives the following statistics of a population in Hawai'i close to 500,000:[18] Japanese 36.9 percent, Caucasian 23.0 percent, Hawaiian 17.2 percent, Filipino 12.2 percent, Chinese 6.5 percent, others 4.2 percent (adapted from Lind 1980:28). At one level, nonwhites united under the umbrella category of "local," especially with labor strikes linking workers of Japanese and Filipino ancestry, and within the historical context of the notorious race- and class-based 1931 Massie case (see note 15; Okamura 1980:122; Rosa 2000:94; cf. Okamura 1994).

But at another level and in spite of widespread characterization of harmonious relations between racial/ethnic groups in Hawai'i, there existed a persistent hierarchy among nonwhites that denigrated Filipinos, Hawaiians, and Samoans in the pecking order. Japanese Americans — with their large numbers, partial rise to higher socioeconomic status by the 1920s and 1930s, and burgeoning political power beginning in the 1950s — were the target of hostility and resentment from other nonwhite groups. A 1980 list of negative stereotypes of Japanese Americans compiled by the Department of Psychiatry, University of Hawai'i, includes clannishness, ethnic exclusivity, and stubbornness (Rogers and Izutsu 1980:82 – 83). The very successes of Japanese Americans could be interpreted within this negative stereotyping as coming at the expense of other groups.

Japanese Americans form part of what Candace Fujikane has called "Asian settler colonialism" in Hawai'i, generating antipathy among Hawaiians (2000). They incurred animosity from different ethnic groups for some of the misdeeds of Japan: Filipinos for Japan's aggression in Manila, Bataan, and Corregidor during World War II; Koreans for Japan's brutal colonization of Korea from 1910 to 1945 (Fuchs 1961:303 – 304). At the same time, the Chinese American community — the other most successful nonwhite group — cast competitive, sidelong glances at Japanese Americans vying for respectability and acceptance by haole power wielders.

The social pecking order in Hawai'i included many factions and divisions even within the Japanese community: issei versus nisei (and to some extent, versus sansei); kibei (those born in Hawai'i, who were raised and educated in Japan, and subsequently returned to Hawai'i) versus nisei; those from immigrant families versus those more recently arrived, including Japanese war brides; Uchinanchu/Okinawans (Japanese from Okinawan archipelago) versus naichi (Japanese from main islands); those from Honolulu versus neighbor islands; urban versus rural; white-collar versus blue-collar; college-educated versus high school-educated versus elementary school-educated. The CBF — as the product of a nisei, primarily naichi, Honolulu, urban, white-collar, college-educated-led organization — reinforced these animosities and tensions, but provided a healing bridge as a public, civic event.

In many people's minds, the heroics of the nisei war veterans of World War II should have finally proved the Americanization of Japanese Americans; however, decades of longstanding anti-Japanese sentiment and practices in Hawai'i, combined with the racialization of America's World War II, created a state of lingering tension. Japanese Americans walked guardedly through the motions of citizenship, careful to perform their Americanness, even while making large strides in the fields of business, politics, and education. They found it necessary to wave literal and figurative American flags, even while (or perhaps especially when) resuming Japanese cultural practices. The American dream of the 1950s took on an Asia-Pacific tinge for Japanese Americans in Hawai'i, sharing the heady optimism of the postwar era within a racialized context. The CBF performed this version of the American dream, marked with the tensions of first-class citizenship for Japanese Americans in Hawai'i in the 1950s.

social structure of anyone whaving anything to do w/ H.I. ar Japan

Locating Japanese American Women in 1950s Hawai'i

Japanese American women in Hawai'i shared the American dream of others in the 1950s, but did so within economic and sociocultural conditions that altered some of its practices. An important part of the context for the CBF was the place of these women in the decades leading up to and including the 1950s. The CBF Queen of the 1950s emerged from a variable socioeconomic mix, even though her reputation pegged her as coming from the (upper) middle-class strata of Japanese American society. She also arose out of a generational mix of an overlapping nisei and sansei cohort, incorporating the gendered contradictions of transitions in the Japanese American community of Hawai'i in the 1950s. Most important, she arose out of decades of prewar institutionalized Americanization, virulent anti-Japanese wartime sentiment, and a shifting negotiation of American emplacement in postwar Hawai'i.

Women of Japanese ancestry in Hawai'i were notable in the 1950s for the numbers who worked outside the home (Nomura 1989:135–136; Glenn 2002:212). Many worked in domestic services for primarily haole families. There, the quality of their work and quiet demeanor were looked on with favor, as one master states: "They [Japanese domestic workers] are usually quiet, scrupulously neat and clean in appearance, . . . and do not find detail and routine . . . monotonous" (quoted in Nomura 1989:147). Laurie Mengel in her study of issei women in Hawai'i argues: "Domestic service was not demeaning work taken only because racism had left no other alternative. Domestic service instead was emancipation for the women. . . . They became self-reliant and economically self-sufficient" (1997:32).[19] Although Mengel's view may be overly optimistic, many Japanese American domestic servants maintained certain elements of pride about their occupation. Working in haole households became direct lessons in American (upper-class) practices of domestic maintenance: cooking and serving haole food, cleaning with Western implements such as vacuum cleaners, polishing silver, starching and ironing linens, and sewing Western clothing. Working as servants gave Japanese American women firsthand contact and knowledge of the ways of everyday white American life. Some got to know haole as people, even if they were of far different social strata. They also heard and could practice the English language from some of the most respected models available locally. These perquisites of proximity came within an overt structural frame of hierarchy, yet they could also be turned into cultural capital for themselves with direct lessons in assimilation (Glenn 1986:104; cf. Broom and Smith 1963; Smith 1973). In many cases, domestic workers borrowed the prestige of their employers, placing themselves in hierarchies based upon the status of the household within which they worked (Glenn 2002:214). In some cases, long-term domestic service resulted in substantial material rewards for workers, who inherited parcels of land or other goods upon the deaths of their employers.

Besides domestic service, barbering was an important line of work for Japanese American women in the 1950s and 1960s. Barbering was a useful trade, because it was in constant demand by all ages and ethnicities, did not require great linguistic skills, and entailed minimal overhead costs. Best of all, barbering allowed Japanese American women to become independent small business owners. In a 1939 study of barbershops in Hawai'i, 84 percent were run by Japanese women. Barbering, in fact, came to be considered not only a woman's trade in Hawai'i but specifically that of Japanese American women (Nomura 1989:148).

Another common trade was sewing. Japanese American women early on gained a reputation as excellent seamstresses, providing custom tailoring services and opening their own sewing schools.[20] Their numbers dominated the garment manufacture industry in Hawai'i. By 1930, 75 percent of all independent seamstresses in Hawai'i were women of Japanese ancestry, and in 1940 a Japanese dressmakers' association was founded to regularize their trade and increase profits (Nomura 1989:148). The domination of the seamstress profession by Japanese American women continued in the postwar years.

Through the 1950s, Japanese American women, along with most women in the United States, lagged behind men in occupational advancement. This reflected in part an earlier cultural tendency for Japanese American families to invest more in male education than female, as well as the educational advantage that war veterans gained because of the GI Bill. Whereas nisei men moved up the socioeconomic ladder quickly, nisei women advanced slowly and more unevenly (Tamura 1994:221). In the 1950s, many nisei women could still be found working blue-collar jobs at pineapple canneries and other small-scale industries. Furthermore, countless Japanese American women continued to work as unpaid laborers in family businesses such as restaurants and small grocery stores.

Among white-collar jobs, the most common for Japanese American women in the 1950s were teachers, secretaries, nurses, and bookkeepers. Teaching, in particular — a profession highly respected in Japanese and Japanese American society and one with considerable job security — attracted nisei women. They viewed teaching as a stable, relatively well-paying, prestigious escape from plantation and other blue-collar labor (Tamura 1994:230). The University of Hawai'i Normal School, where one could obtain a teaching degree in two years, facilitated entrance into the profession.

In the 1950s, there were marked generational contrasts in the family lives of issei and nisei women. Most issei women acquiesced to the patriarchal, male-dominated system of Meiji-era (1868–1912) Japan. The stereotype of a Japanese woman walking twenty paces behind her husband may or may not always have been literally true, but many issei women maintained at least a publicly submissive relationship to their husbands. Spousal abuse, including wife beating, especially in combination with men's drinking, was not uncommon in issei families (Glenn 1986:213; Mengel 1997:32; Tamura 1994:31; cf. Lebra 1986). These conditions became a model against which many nisei women and some men resisted. The nisei marriage was to be based on an American, rather than Japanese, ideal. Far from the picture bride legacy, the nisei marriage was supposed to be built upon more equal conjugal relations that did not seem as overtly patriarchal and restrictive as the Japanese model of their parents.

Whereas issei weddings were often quick, unceremonious signings of documents, nisei weddings in the 1950s typically included the white bridal gown, veil, bouquet, wedding rings, formal suit or tuxedo, attendants, flower girl, ring bearer, and wedding cake — the American dream on stage. Some nisei weddings added to this American picture the Japanese position of the *nakōdo* (go-between), as a formal nod to past practices of arranged marriages. This kind of cultural mixing extended to photography. Although a portrait of the bride and groom, as well as attendants, captured the important occasion, some nisei couples also took a formal portrait on a separate day dressed in Japanese kimono.[21]

Family life was another part of the American dream that contrasted generationally. It was not uncommon for issei families to have six or more offspring (including one or more that died in infancy), typically born at home with the assistance of a Japanese midwife (Kimura 1988:126). By contrast, nisei women especially in urban Honolulu had only two or three children. They gave birth in hospitals not only because it was now economically feasible, but also following the general emphasis on modern Western medicine. Whereas women seeking the American dream in other places might have imagined themselves as stay-at-home mothers, nisei women in Hawai'i could not afford this luxury. Working outside the home and limiting the number of children seemed to be the only ways to ensure middle-class status for succeeding generations.

A new issei woman arrived on the scene in Hawai'i during the 1950s enabled by the War Brides Act of 1945. The Japanese war bride was met with a certain amount of derision from the local Japanese American community, stemming in part from the "impurity" of her marriage to a non-Japanese (typically white), a lingering suspicion of the circumstances of her marriage, and her limited English. As Glenn points out, "Separation and often estrangement from kin, social isolation, inability to speak English, and restricted employment options placed these women at a considerable disadvantage vis-à-vis their husbands, as well as in relation to the larger society" (1986:232). The fact that many of these marriages ended in divorce exacerbated the negative stereotyping of war brides in Japanese American communities (Togami 2001:408).

The 1950s was a founding period for two elite Japanese American women's organizations, each with informal ties to the CBF. One of these was the mostly Japanese American sorority Wakaba Kai at the University of Hawai'i, established by Lillian Yajima in 1949. The fact that several CBF Queens are members of Wakaba Kai is no accident; during the 1950s and 1960s, the sorority annually selected one member to compete in the CBF and one to compete in the University of Hawai'i multiethnic Ka Palapala beauty pageant. Sorority sisters would help coach and groom these two candidates to victory in their respective contests (see Chapter 4).

Another elite organization was the Japanese Women's Society, founded in 1954 as a primarily nisei organization "to promote the appreciation of Japanese culture in Hawaii" (Japanese Women's Society 2004). Its original membership consisted of wives of politicians, businessmen, and doctors associated with Kuakini Hospital. In fact, as an elite organization, several of its members are former Cherry Blossom contestants and Queens.

The 1950s also saw the exceptional political rising star of a Japanese American woman in the election of firebrand Patsy Takemoto Mink (1927–2002) to the territorial legislature in 1956. The list of her achievements of "firsts" as a Japanese American woman seems far from the anonymity of thousands of blue-collar Japanese American women who lived in the same period and came from similar plantation backgrounds. That Patsy Mink rose from their midst speaks not only to the rapidity of generational changes, but also to the unevenness of that process. Mink acted very much within the spirit of the American dream, here focused not so much on middle-class consumerism, but on full participation in democratic citizenship.

Early History of the HJJCC: Complications of Being American

The public face of the Japanese American community was dominated not by women, but by men in the field of business. The founding of the HJJCC in 1949 by nisei businessmen is a story of the complications of being American in postwar Hawai'i. It is a story of the particular societal problems nisei faced, caught as they were in a double bind of race (vis-à-vis haole power-wielders) and of generation (vis-à-vis issei). It is a story of interchange between Japanese American communities in Honolulu and California, particularly through war veterans. It is a story of citizenship in a transitional period as nisei sought a place within the American dream. The HJJCC became a "separate and equal" organization just as the CBF was a "separate and parallel" event among beauty contests. Here I present the changing narrative of the HJJCC by examining its retrospective telling and retelling in souvenir books of the CBF.

The original impetus for the HJJCC came not from nisei men, but from an issei-led organization, the Honolulu Japanese Chamber of Commerce, headed by President Peter Fukunaga. Originally created in 1900 as the Shonin Doshi-kai (Japanese Merchants Association), the Japanese Chamber focused on concerns of issei businesses, especially trade between Hawai'i and Japan (Honolulu Japanese Chamber of Hawaii 2004).[22] In 1949 Fukunaga suggested forming a Japanese junior chamber organization that would address the double bind of nisei: shut out by both mainstream haole power structures and issei organizations. As Fukunaga tells it:

> [After World War II], a handful of Nisei were members of the Honolulu Junior Chamber of Commerce, the oldest and perhaps the most prestigious young men's organization in Honolulu at that time. The majority of the membership was overwhelmingly young Caucasian men employed by larger companies in supervisory capacities or else young independent professionals. Many of the young Nisei at that time felt they were not yet ready for nor welcome into that group. (Quoted in HJJCC 1985:66)

According to Fukunaga, "Nisei by nature were not aggressive enough to compete with the other young [haole] men of the community" (ibid.). Nisei also felt shut out from issei-led organizations by both language and seniority: "Few Nisei felt comfortable with the Japanese Chamber [of Commerce] because of a problem of fluency in the [Japanese] language, or for the mere fact that the younger men had not yet established themselves in the business world" (ibid.). Although within the larger society issei were at a disadvantage because they lacked fluency in English, within the confines of their own organization issei maintained oligarchic power and control. Nisei war veterans were therefore doubly removed from access to power. Fukunaga "concluded that there was a need for a young Nisei organization in which these young men might feel at home among themselves in developing programs to train future leaders, . . . [and] suggested the formation of a junior division of the Chamber" (ibid.).

The first meeting of the HJJCC took place in November 1949 with forty-five charter members. On January 14, 1950, President Robert Sato delivered his inaugural speech, citing a twofold purpose of the organization: "trying to build good citizenship among our young Japanese-Americans and to provide them with a medium of training for participation in worthwhile community-wide civic projects" (quoted in HJJCC 1999:67). What remains unspoken are the structural impediments to those purposes in postwar Hawai'i.

The formation of the HJJCC met with immediate opposition by both the Honolulu Chamber of Commerce and its junior version, the Honolulu Junior Chamber of Commerce. These two haole-dominated groups thought that forming a new organization along ethnic lines damaged Japanese Americans' bid for acceptance as full-fledged Americans. In a dramatic moment at the inaugural installation banquet of the HJJCC on January 4, 1950, guest speaker Colonel Farrant Turner, former commander of the 100th Infantry Battalion and second vice-president of the Honolulu Chamber of Commerce, criticized the HJJCC as an ethnically separate organization that "would only impede the assimilation process of Japanese Americans in Hawaii" (HJJCC 1985:66).

HJJCC members had to allay fears that they were anything less than fully assimilated Americans. The 1953 program booklet of the first CBF attempted to do just this:

> They [HJJCC] have built a sound position in the community and have done much to promote the American Way of Life, and explain some of the finer aspects of oriental culture to the community. As forward looking, progressive young members of the community, the Japanese Junior Chamber of Commerce hopes to make a definite contribution to the cosmopolitan pattern of our American Way of Life in Hawaii. (HJJCC 1953:5)

The rhetoric speaks directly to the American dream: "American Way of Life," progressive young members of the community. However, it does so in parallel with what Lon Kurashige calls the "biculturalism" of nisei that bestowed upon them a special position as a "bridge of understanding" between the United States and Japan (2002:25). This is expressed as explaining "the finer aspects of oriental culture to the community." Members of the HJJCC were expected to straddle both sides of the Pacific as fully assimilated Americans who had racial/cultural knowledge of Japan. Many of them, however, did not have this knowledge. They had to become quick studies, learning about "oriental culture" in a fast turnaround to present it to the general community.[23]

At the same time, nisei still had to contend with the Americanization demons of previous decades. In 1954, among the events sponsored by the HJJCC were classes entitled "Learn to Speak English for Better Living," echoing prewar and wartime Japanese American endeavors in Hawai'i (HJJCC 1954:5). The newly formed HJJCC was also careful to demonstrate its place in the local community in Hawai'i, as well as the national community of the United States, emphasizing membership in Hawaiian Junior Chamber of Commerce and the U.S. Junior Chamber of Commerce (ibid.). Belonging to such mainstream organizations demonstrated parity within the larger society.

The same man who had harshly criticized the HJJCC at its installation banquet had kinder words for the organization four years later. In the CBF's 1954 souvenir book, Acting Governor Farrant Turner proclaimed:

> The Honolulu Japanese Junior Chamber of Commerce, an affiliate of the United States and Hawaiian Junior Chambers of Commerce, realizes that through the medium of cultural events such as art exhibits, lectures and Japanese folk dance, the people of the Territory will have a better understanding of Japanese culture, . . . the Honolulu Japanese Junior Chamber of Commerce firmly believes that through the above mediums, commerce within the Islands, as well as with the Mainland United States and our foreign countries, will be greatly stimulated to the benefit of this Territory. (HJJCC 1954:2)[24]

The contrast between Turner's criticism of the HJJCC in 1950 and his congratulatory remarks of 1954 demonstrates ways in which the HJJCC was proving itself: (1) in the depoliticized arenas of culture and education; and (2) by contributing to a growing economy vis-à-vis the continental United States and foreign countries, specifically Japan.

Early ambitious talk of pursuing the American dream contrasts with retrospective versions of HJJCC origins. The 1966 CBF pageant book links the HJJCC to Japanese American war-honed masculinity and Japanese culture:

> The end of World War II and the return from the war fronts of many young men whose tireless efforts to restore peace in the world created a need for continued activity in these young men. . . . With this need, 43 [sic; 45] Americans of Japanese Ancestry formed a group to engage in projects beneficial to the community as well as to themselves.

In 1949, with 43 [45] members from all walks of life, the Honolulu Japanese Junior Chamber of Commerce originated with the goal of bringing to Hawaii's people aspects of Japanese culture. In 1952 the organization became affiliated with the United States Junior Chamber of Commerce. The chapter's goals became incorporated with the creed of the U.S. Jaycees ... service to humanity ... free enterprise ... human personality ... government ... God. ... (HJJCC 1966:8)

According to this origin narrative, the seeds of the HJJCC were sown not in 1949, but during World War II when nisei fought to "restore peace in the world." This heroism and "activity" animates the same men through the postwar HJJCC organization and its events, such as the CBF. Rather than an elite, or even middle-class, organization, the HJJCC paints itself as an inclusive, egalitarian group with "members from all walks of life." These members combine the goal of transmitting Japanese culture — contradicting earlier narratives that emphasized performing American culture — with the U.S. Jaycee creed. By 1966 the HJJCC no longer felt the need to prove their Americanness, and could present themselves as arbiters of things Japanese.

Upon the twenty-fifth anniversary of the founding of the HJJCC, first president Robert Sato added another retrospective spin. His account emphasizes "the trials and tribulations of a newly formed organization, especially one established on an ethnic line, trying hard to justify the existence and worthiness to the community" (1975:94). He recounts the Americanization movement of the 1930s, the dilemma of nisei in postwar Hawai'i caught between racial/ethnic lines and generational divisions, and the criticism laid upon the HJJCC by established organizations (ibid.:94 – 96).

More critical retrospectives on the founding of the HJJCC come from the 1980s and 1990s. The histories told in these later retrospectives make World War II the touchstone of the HJJCC, referring to the organization as resolving "the prejudices . . . [of] war [World War II]" (1982:73; 1991:16) and "alleviating some of the ill-feelings brought about by the war" (1983:57). The means to resolving these racial prejudices lay in "asserting themselves in Hawaiian society... [through] a slow, steady process of being accepted by the community" (1982:73). One of the primary activities to win acceptance was in depoliticized events such as the CBF.

The HJJCC's strategies were successful. Membership grew rapidly to more than 130 members in 1954, 200 in 1958, and 250 by 1963. Initially only young men of Japanese ancestry joined. By the late 1950s, with continuing public criticism of ethnic exclusivity, the HJJCC quietly admitted men of other ethnicities. A history of the HJJCC lists several milestones of ethnic inclusiveness: Geminiano Arre, first president of Filipino ancestry in 1969; Richard Bauske, first haole president in 1975; Kenneth Chang, first president of Chinese ancestry in 1979 (see Chapter 3 for further discussion of inclusiveness).

The Jaycee Institution: Raising the American Banner of God, Commerce, and Men

Nisei could not have chosen a better vehicle for emplacement than the national, and eventually international, nonprofit, voluntary, community service-oriented, male Jaycee organization. The Jaycees in the 1950s "stood far above all others as a symbol of fellowship and civic pride . . . the nerve center of the new suburban generation" (Wall 1995:947). The Jaycee organization traces its beginnings to 1910, when Henry Giessenbier formed the Herculaneum Dance Club in St. Louis, which regrouped in 1915 as the Young Men's Progressive Civic Association, and then again in 1916 as the Junior Citizens. These name changes marked a shift from a focus on social activities to personal, professional, and community growth. January 22, 1920, marks the official founding date of the U.S. Junior Chamber of Commerce with twenty-nine charter members in twelve cities. The Jaycee organization grew beyond its national boundaries in 1944 with the first convening of the Junior Chamber International in Mexico City.[25]

The Jaycees in Hawai'i officially began in August 1930, but the seeds for it were sown almost a decade earlier when Hawaii Chamber of Commerce President George P. Denison wrote in his 1921 annual membership report:

> A large number of the larger cities of the Mainland have encouraged the establishment of a Junior Chamber of Commerce. . . . If such a Chamber is organized in Honolulu . . . it should include in its membership the young English-speaking men of other races holding responsible positions or being trained for such positions in the business houses. (Quoted in Hawaii Jaycees 1993:n.p.)

The inclusion of "English-speaking men of other races" may have been more successful in theory than in practice, given the intimidation felt by nisei to the organization. Indeed, all young men listed as charter members in 1930 had haole surnames.

The language of the Jaycees on websites and promotional literature combines secular and spiritual goals targeting young adults at the beginning and middle phases of their careers (within the age limit of thirty-nine years). The Jaycee Creed was adopted by the Junior Chamber International in 1948 and is recited at local, national, and international meetings. As published in the 1955 CBF souvenir book, it states:

We believe:

— that faith in God gives meaning and purpose to human life

— that the brotherhood of man transcends the sovereignty of nations

— that economic justice can best be won by free men through free enterprise

— that government should be of laws rather than of men

— that earth's great treasure lies in human personality

— and that service to humanity is the best work of life. (HJJCC 1955:71)

In connecting Christianity, capitalism, democracy, citizenship, and masculinity, the Creed is no less than the sanctification of the American dream.

By the end of the Cold War, the Jaycees had shifted from national goals to personal, entrepreneurial, and community achievement. This is expressed in another philosophical underpinning of the Jaycees, the "Jaycee Triangle." This equilateral triangle symbolizes equal and interactive tracks for the development of the individual, management/chapter, and community (Hawaii Jaycees 2004). All three parts must develop together and to the same degree; one part of the triangle cannot succeed in isolation from the other two parts. This kind of trilateral development is called the "total Jaycee concept," following the slogan "Develop the whole member through the whole chapter" (ibid.).

Testimonials from individual HJJCC members demonstrate how the Creed and Triangle work in their lives. Wayne Ishihara, a ten-year member, credits his involvement with HJJCC for his growth as a leader in business and as a person:

> I was just out of college and beginning a career when I joined the Jaycees, mainly to participate in the social activities. After a few months I began to realize that the club had more to offer. Before me was a chance to better myself; a chance to meet people; a chance to do something for the community. . . . With each project I gained self confidence and positive mental attitude. . . . With each project was a chance to develop my leadership ability. I began to grow. . . Jaycees has been the catalyst for my personal development and success. (1980:89)

Richard Karamatsu credits the HJJCC with answers to existential questions, providing a sense of fulfillment and meaning:

> From that first day the Jaycees has been the stimuli of my growth, my personal development. It added meaning and challenge to my somewhat routine life. For most of us, life is more than just a career. At the time, I felt a need to serve the community; a need to develop myself beyond what was required of me at work. It's been eleven very satisfying years. . . . I've made

many very close friends through my association with the organization . . . Jaycees has outlined the purpose and goals of my life. I thank Jaycees for that. (1980:89)

These testimonials attribute the Jaycees with providing personal growth, self-confidence, social contacts, friends, and purpose in life.

As a signature project of the HJJCC, the CBF is part of the Jaycee package, including its Creed and Triangle. The CBF of the 1950s acted as a vehicle to realize the Jaycee/American dream and perform members' Americanness. Since then, the CBF is sustained as a community service project that enables the personal growth of HJJCC members. It does so by focusing on individual organizational skills, rather than ties to Japanese American cultural identity. From a Jaycee perspective, the CBF is an exercise in leadership and civic responsibility. With goals and activities generated to develop the individual and the community, the Jaycees create a neat blueprint for citizenship. The Jaycee Triangle linking individual, organization, and community demonstrates the degree to which the HJJCC fortuitously tapped into a network of carefully crafted emplacement.

Crowning Ethnic Beauty Queens in Postwar Hawai'i and Beyond

The public centerpiece of HJJCC's plans to build a profitable civic future was the CBF.[26] In fact, the HJJCC and the CBF are one and the same: not only is the CBF the signature project of the HJJCC, but the two were born at nearly the same time. In 1949, just a few months before the HJJCC was established in November, nisei Akira "Sunshine" Fukunaga traveled to Los Angeles to visit a fellow war veteran. There he witnessed the first revival of the Nisei Week celebration, including its queen pageant, since the end of World War II. The California event spoke to a different set of sociopolitical circumstances from Hawai'i, including large-scale internment and overt racial discrimination (Kurashige 2002).[27] Harry Kitano contrasts the situation for persons of Japanese ancestry in Hawai'i with those in California in four ways: (1) relatively large group vis-à-vis general population; (2) generally more racially tolerant society;[28] (3) one of a large number of different ethnic groups; and (4) proximity to Japan and thereby stronger "homeland" influences (1976:164). Thus, while Los Angeles' Nisei Week remained circumscribed within an ethnic enclave, Honolulu's CBF performed to front-page mainstream media coverage. This is not to say that everyone in Hawai'i paid attention equally, but that the CBF played a major role in the civic life of Honolulu in the 1950s. It was a central part of the Hawai'i version of the "American way of life."

Nisei Week was not the only inspiration for the CBF. In 1950s Hawai'i, other ethnic beauty contests dotted the cultural landscape at the high school, university, and community levels.[29] They provided concrete examples for mixing the American dream with race/ethnicity in idioms of separation borrowed from plantation-era segregation. The pageant that most closely parallels the CBF is the Narcissus Festival, begun in 1950 by the Chinese Chamber of Commerce in Honolulu. The Narcissus event is important to our discussion in four ways: (1) as a forerunner to the CBF; (2) for the overlap between the two events; (3) for the longstanding cooperation between them; and (4) for the sense of competition between them.

Like the CBF, the Narcissus Festival has always been part of a larger festival featuring public events held over two to three months each year. In Hawaiʻi, the queens often appear at each other's events, including their respective coronation balls. The queens also stand side by side representing their communities at statewide appearances. Both contests include similar features, such as cultural demonstrations, cooking shows, fashion shows, and "Western" and "Eastern" components in the pageant itself. Furthermore, both are terminal contests — that is, independent pageants in and of themselves — rather than pyramidal ones. Thus, the queens of these pageants have as their primary focus the local community, rather than the next step in a beauty contest hierarchy.

According to the festival's website, the original purpose of the Narcissus Festival in the 1950s was "to preserve and showcase Chinese art and culture, while promoting commerce at a time when political turmoil in Asia was hindering trade in Hawaii" (Chinese Chamber of Commerce of Hawaii 2004). Part of that political turmoil was the civil war that resulted in the establishment of the communist-led People's Republic of China and the Republic of China (Taiwan). In general, the Chinese business elite in Hawaiʻi sided strongly with Taiwan and felt the need to distance themselves publicly from Communist China, especially during the 1950s Cold War years. Like Japanese Americans during the same period, but for different historical reasons, Chinese Americans had to prove their Americanness. What the CBF and the Narcissus Festival share are not only structures and events, but also a foundation in commerce and a concern for representation vis-à-vis the larger haole-dominated society in Hawaiʻi. They share the contradictions and complexities of the American dream of the 1950s, lived out in the U.S. periphery among people of Asian and Pacific Islander backgrounds.

Precisely because they share so many features and concerns, the two compete with one another for the limelight in Hawaiʻi. According to one CBF Queen from the mid-1950s, the competitiveness between the Japanese American and Chinese American communities at the time was part of the impetus for creating the CBF. This sentiment was expressed in Japanese-language newspapers of the time. For example, a column in the *Hawaii Hochi* in 1953 argued that since the Honolulu Chinese Chamber of Commerce holds its annual Narcissus Festival, the Japanese American community, too, should hold an equally large event (*Hawaii Hochi* 1953b:5). This kind of intergroup competitiveness on the beauty pageant front not only provided a context, but also fueled the event itself.

A closely related type of pageant in the 1950s was what I call "rainbow pageants" that crowned several queens in separate ethnic categories, such as Miss Japanese, Miss Chinese, Miss Korean, Miss Filipino, Miss Caucasian, and Miss "Cosmopolitan." These "rainbow pageants," based on the racial/ethnic separatism of the plantation, supported the image of Hawai'i as a Pacific melting pot. Both McKinley High School in urban Honolulu and the University of Hawai'i held their own "rainbow pageants" in the 1950s. As Banet-Weiser comments:

> Her [Bess Myerson, first Jewish winner of Miss America in 1945] ethnic identity confirms the logic of the melting pot, where different races and ethnic groups supposedly coexist in productive harmony; her difference is precisely the kind needed to sustain the promise of American pluralism, because this difference ironically serves as a point of entry for successful assimilation. (1999:162)

"Rainbow Pageants"

In Hawai'i these "rainbow pageants" suggest the following strands of cultural logic: (1) rather than a single hegemonic ideal of beauty, women can compete through separate and parallel racial/ethnic standards; (2) women provide a nonconfrontational interface to intergroup relations; (3) an apolitical beauty contest is one of the best ways to celebrate differences, even as people share the commonality of the event itself; and (4) the harmony on stage among representatives of these different races/ethnicities purportedly reflects the harmony off stage, contributing to the myth of Hawai'i as a multiracial paradise. These "rainbow pageants," like the CBF, emphasize both the assimilation of its participants, as well as their racialized differences. In these "rainbow pageants" it is important to ask not only how the rainbow is divided, but also what meanings and purposes are attributed to the separate colors.

McKinley High School, the major high school in central Honolulu in the 1940s and 1950s and nicknamed "Tokyo High" for its large population of Japanese Americans, held its own "rainbow pageant" in postwar Hawai'i. In 1949, for example, girls competed to become carnival queens in the following categories: Japanese, Caucasian, Korean, Chinese, Filipino, and Cosmopolitan (a category that included, but was not limited to, being part-Hawaiian). In 1952 the categories changed with the addition of Hawaiian and Portuguese.[30] In the 1940s, the McKinley High School Carnival Queen contest received media coverage in the daily English-language newspapers; Japanese-language newspapers also ran special features on the winner of the Japanese Carnival Queen. Compared to other "rainbow pageants" at the university level, the McKinley High School one was an inclusive, common people's event.[31]

The University of Hawai'i held its own "rainbow pageant" from 1938 to 1971. It also captured media attention from the Honolulu newspapers and the primary monthly magazine of the time, *Paradise of the Pacific*. Starting in 1941, these "rainbow pageants" were officially named the Ka Palapala contest after the school yearbook of the same name. The contest was suspended throughout the war years but renewed in 1946.[32] The 1945–1946 *Ka Palapala* yearbook featured a multipage article on the return of the contest to campus life:

> Supported by enthusiastic veterans who returned to the campus during the second semester, the annual Ka Palapala beauty contest, held for the first time since the outbreak of war, turned out to be one of the biggest events of the year. In the course of the four weeks of the contest, interest overflowed into the community where the campus beauties became a popular topic of conversation. (1945–1946:211).

Holding the Ka Palapala contest was part of the return to normalcy in postwar years.

[handwritten margin note: CBF lead to pageants @ H.S. levels]

The categories of the contest changed in accord with the student body and perceptions of salient units, demonstrating the ways in which the arcs of the purported racial/ethnic rainbow were divided and redivided. This took place at a time when a university education was still an elite phenomenon. In contrast to McKinley High School's racial/ethnic representation, the Ka Palapala categories reflected those groups who had achieved a relatively high socioeconomic status in Hawai'i or were in the process of doing so through higher education. The following categories appeared in most years: Chinese, Japanese, Korean, Caucasian, and Cosmopolitan. "Filipino" appeared for the first time in 1947, indicative of this group's more limited presence at the university.[33]

One of the most fluid aspects of racialization is how mixed-race people were designated.[34] The most common category for mixed-race individuals was "Cosmopolitan," used every year from 1941 on. By default, this typically meant part-Hawaiian, since Hawaiians were the most common group to intermarry. In some years, mixed-race categories were specifically delineated, including "Asiatic-Hawaiian" (typically, Chinese-Hawaiian) and "Caucasian-Hawaiian" in 1939 (a year during which "Cosmopolitan" was not listed), and "Asiatic-Caucasian" in 1951 (both "Cosmopolitan" and "Hawaiian" categories).

Race and culture in the Ka Palapala pageant acted as both dividing lines between categories as well as common grounds for competition. Contestants performed themselves as racially and culturally distinctive. Photo layouts show contestants in ethnic dress, such as Japanese kimono and Chinese cheongsam (*qipao*). Even as the pageant marked these differences, it also provided a common unmarked ground of display, such as appearing in a swimsuit.

What this combination of difference and commonality did was contribute to the notion of Hawai'i as a multiracial paradise. For example, the editors of the 1948 yearbook discussed the "racial/ethnic rainbow" expressed by the beauty pageant:[35]

> If it were at all possible, we would have depicted an ethnic rainbow on our cover design . . . This is not meant to say that we conceive of this university as a "melting pot" in the typical travel brochure sense of the term . . . We are not quite that naive . . . We acknowledge the fact that "racial" fraternities exist in practice. . . . Ka Palapala still sponsors yearly "racial" beauty contests . . . We wanted an ethnic rainbow to illustrate the point that, in spite of all these traditional artifices emphasizing ethnological differences, peoples of different heritages can form as beautiful a harmony as that of the spectrum of the rainbow. The time has come for us not merely to recognize these differences but also to understand them. Cultural diversity need not be cause for conflict. (*Paradise of the Pacific* 1948:28)

This explains some of the racialized practices at the university, as well as the means by which those practices were intended to constitute a "beautiful harmony" through understanding cultural differences. The purported harmony symbolized by the "racial/ethnic rainbow" is a prevalent idea and value in Hawai'i that continues unabated through the 2000s. By 1954, the Ka Palapala contest had become the Ka Palapala Pageant of Nations, echoing postwar institutions such as the United Nations. The yearbook displayed a two-page wide-angle array of all contestants in national costume (*Ka Palapala* 1954:n.p.). The racial/ethnic rainbow was thus translated into a rainbow of nations, even if presumably the great majority of contestants were, in fact, American.

The primarily ethnic sororities at the time played no small part in the operations of the contest. Wakaba Kai was known as the Japanese sorority, Yang Chung Hui (established 1924, later known as Kappa Sigma Chi) and Teh Shih Sheh (date of establishment unknown) as Chinese sororities, Beta Beta Gamma (established 1948) as the Korean sorority, and Ke Anuenue (date of establishment unknown) as the Hawaiian sorority.[36] Each of these sororities selected one of its members to run for the Ka Palapala contest, backed and trained by other members.

The Ka Palapala contest raises the issue of the relationship of racial/ethnic queens to a hegemonic white ideal. On the one hand, according to a former Ka

Palapala queen from the 1960s, ~~the contest emphasized differences between ethnic groups rather than sameness,~~ thereby seeking queens who would be distinct from each other as prototypes of their own groups. Judges might choose a woman who most closely matched their stereotype of each racial/ethnic group, rather than one that more closely approximated a Miss America ideal. Each queen thus represented the ideal for her respective group, and contradicted the notion of a hegemonic white mold.

On the other hand, not all observers agree on the degree to which the Ka Palapala contest celebrated differences among groups. One white male writer in 1955 claimed that the original racial differences of earlier Ka Palapala queens were converging into an "American look" by the 1950s, racializing the model of cultural assimilation prevalent at the time:[37]

> Looking back over the photographs of those earliest [Ka Palapala beauty contest] winners, it is easy to see why contest founders felt the contestants of that period must be judged in several clearly defined categories. Differences between the so-called racial types were easily detected then. Today things are somewhat different.... What strikes an average observer is, when Americans of various ancestries act, talk and think as Americans, any physical characteristics that might indicate a particular background become inconsequential. They have "the American look." (Silverman 1955:22)

Silverman goes on to explain that actually the queens have not so much an "American look" as a "Hawaii look" based on the concept of aloha. As he puts it, "Aloha has a way of rubbing off on all of us" (ibid.:23).

The end of the Ka Palapala contest in 1971 may be seen within the context of the social and political turmoil of the period in the United States. The late 1960s and 1970s signaled a rise of political consciousness, activism, and feminism in Hawai'i as elsewhere. Beauty contests such as Ka Palapala were considered frivolous activities unsuited to a university campus. John Cross, coordinator of student activities at the University of Hawai'i, explained: "There seems to be no place for beauty contests or collegiate-type rah-rah activities any more.... The students and their elected officials are more concerned about social issues and social problems" (quoted in Gereben 1971:B-5). The Ka Palapala contest fell victim to the politics of the era, both from the feminist perspective as an event that places undue emphasis on the physical attributes of women, as well as from the perspective of ethnically based activism. Ethnicity became a site and source of political struggle instead of a source of entertainment on the beauty contest stage. A different kind of pride based in equal rights, empowerment, and social activism was at hand.

Although there was no explicit divide-and-control effort in beauty contests as there was in plantation separatism, these inclusive "rainbow pageants" and events such as Narcissus Festival and CBF symbolically placed queens on stage competing as equals within their own groups. Beauty contests held at McKinley High School and the University of Hawai'i displayed ethnicity as a mythic rainbow of colors, spectacularized through the all-American idiom of a beauty contest. Contests such as the Narcissus Festival and the CBF took one arc of this racial/ethnic rainbow and tied it to community, commerce, and the United States in the 1950s. These arcs — separate and parallel — engendered a version of the American dream that framed the phantasmic solidus of the Japanese American, lived out within the shifting backdrop of 1950s Hawai'i. The backdrop frames the CBF within the possibilities of the era: political power, economic boom, tourist trade, global flows, middle-class luxuries, consumption of Japanese popular culture. But it also frames the CBF within struggle and conflict: racial insecurities, generational transitions, gender inequalities, Americanization/assimilation as proof of citizenship, uneven rise to power and status.

Chapter Three

The Cherry Blossom Festival as Center Stage in Hawai'i |
1950s – 1960s

Whereas, Hawaii is a strategic meeting ground of
Eastern and Western cultures; and

Whereas, Hawaii is deeply interested in the arts and
cultures of Japan; and

Whereas, the Honolulu Japanese Junior Chamber of
Commerce, an affiliate of the United States and
Hawaiian Junior Chambers of Commerce, realizes
that through the medium of cultural events such
as art exhibits, lectures and Japanese folk dance,
the people of the Territory [of Hawai'i] will have a
better understanding of their Eastern friends; and

Whereas, the Honolulu Japanese Junior Chamber
of Commerce, to attain the above ends, has
sponsored a week long of festivities known as the
Cherry Blossom Festival, which will begin with
the crowning of a Queen of American-Japanese
ancestry,

Now, therefore, I, Samuel Wilder King, Governor
of Hawaii, do hereby proclaim the week of April
19 through 25, 1953, as CHERRY BLOSSOM FESTIVAL
WEEK, urging people of all races to attend the
many cultural events that will be offered to this
community.

—Proclamation by Governor Samuel King

(HJJCC 1953:2)

On April 15, 1953, after four years of talk, several months of planning, and $1,000 each from their own pockets, the Jaycees crowned their first Cherry Blossom Queen, Violet Tokie Niimi, from a staggering field of seventy-two candidates before a capacity crowd of 5,000 spectators. (See the Appendix for a chronological list of Queens.) The crowning was only one part of a series of Festival events that had Honolulu abuzz. Two weeks before the start of the Festival, downtown merchants decorated storefronts with paper cherry blossoms to announce the event. Candidates at the media kickoff party posed for photographs in kimono and white carnation lei aboard a Pan American Airways Stratoclipper, symbol of a new era in Hawai'i's fast-growing tourist industry. Contestants rode in a motorcade through downtown Honolulu, ending at 'Iolani Palace, where they were greeted by Governor Samuel King. He proclaimed April 19 through 25, 1953, Cherry Blossom Festival Week. Without doubt, the Cherry Blossom Festival and its Queen — this "separate and parallel" version of the American dream — had arrived.

Performing Selves as American: The "Not Sakura Matsuri"

Calling this community-wide event "Cherry Blossom Festival," rather than using the Japanese equivalent, "Sakura Matsuri," was an indicator of the Jaycees' balancing act as they sought to demonstrate their Americanness. According to a past president of the HJJCC, organizers decided to call the event "Cherry Blossom Festival" instead of "Sakura Matsuri" in strategic positioning vis-à-vis the general Hawai'i community. Although no one was trying to mask the Japanese (American) content of the Festival,[1] organizers believed that the official name should be in English to present a more acceptable public face.

Further evidence of the HJJCC decision to present themselves and the event as American can be seen in the CBF souvenir books. From 1955 through 1960 the covers of these books show CBF Queens wearing evening gowns and crowns and carrying a scepter — all the accoutrements of the Euro-American beauty queen.[2] The regalia of these Queens is meant to simulate that of Miss America, thus legitimizing the event and the organization. From 1954 on, the crown was donated by Pan American Airways and dubbed the "PAA crown." In 1955,

Japan Air Lines donated the scepter, which became known as the "JAL scepter." Souvenir books of this period show photographs of stewardesses from each airline holding the respective items.[3] These physical symbols of faux royalty demonstrated the embeddedness of the HJJCC and its CBF within commercial enterprises that linked Hawai'i to a larger global world.

One other visual idiom of faux royalty, a "fur"-trimmed cape, comes with a humorous back-story that demonstrates some of the makeshift, can-do spirit of the CBF organizers. According to Lillian Yajima, wife of one of the founders of the HJJCC and a central figure in the CBF throughout its entire history to date, the cape worn at the second pageant was a product of her own ingenuity and determination to create a garment befitting her image of a Queen. When she was put in charge of creating the cape, she fashioned a pretty one out of store-bought velvet. The cape, however, did not look "royal" enough to suit her tastes, so she decided to add fur trim. It was not easy to procure fur, real or faux, in Hawai'i in 1954, however. In desperation, she came up with the idea of giving the impression of fur using white feathers.[4] She gathered bags and bags of feathers from chicken vendors, washed them to get rid of the smell, dried them in what became a feather-filled yard, and proceeded to hand-sew them onto the edges of the cape, working late into the night before the coronation. On the night of the coronation ball, Queen Anna Tokumaru proudly wore the cape, but not without some hardship — she was allergic to the chicken feathers and kept sneezing. Few in the audience knew the true source of the faux fur trim. What mattered to the organizers was that the cape, along with the crown and scepter, replicated the idioms of all-American beauty pageants.

The idioms did their job: the impact of the early CBF was immediate and positive.[5] With motorcades through downtown Honolulu, public appearances at shopping centers, and fireworks displays, the CBF secured a major place in the city's urbanscape. In April 1954, *Paradise of the Pacific*, Hawai'i's glossy (haole) mainstream publication, featured the CBF with a three-page article and photo spread (Von Adelung 1954:13 – 15).[6] Within two years of its launch, the CBF was touted by media as a major tourist attraction, second only to Aloha Week.[7] In effect, the members of the HJJCC were fulfilling their role as good citizens by staging a major event that contributed to the economic and social life of Honolulu. Their role was that of the "model minority,"[8] a circumspect position performed with a constant eye upon public reaction.

Through the CBF, nisei in general presented themselves as American citizens. Like other public events during this period, the national anthem was played to kick off the finals of every CBF contest. The early fireworks display of 1953 ended with a sky filled with the stars and stripes.[9] The CBF also displayed patriotism through some of its advertisements, especially during the Vietnam War years (1961–1970). In contradistinction to a national wave of political protest, the HJJCC took a conservative stance in support of the American military:

> The 14th Annual Cherry Blossom Festival and the Honolulu Japanese Junior Chamber of Commerce salute all the men and women of the armed forces of the United States of America serving our great nation in our fight to preserve freedom for all mankind. (HJJCC 1966:54)

The incorporation of events marking elite American culture also enhanced the image of the CBF and the HJJCC. From 1959 and continuing through the 1960s, the Honolulu Symphony performed regularly as one of the Festival events. In 1964, the Cherry Blossom Queen pageant drew 7,100 spectators as the inaugural event of a major civic space in Honolulu, the Honolulu International Center Arena (*Honolulu Advertiser* 1964:A1). In the heady postwar days, this "not-Sakura-Matsuri" event cemented the public emplacement of Japanese Americans in Hawai'i.

Negotiating Japanese (American) Selves in the Balancing Act

Although performing themselves as American was a critical component of the efforts of the HJJCC, from the outset it was clear that the CBF was a Japanese (American) event. The balance of the Festival's American and Japanese components shifted over time in direct response to the general public's stance on Japan and Japanese Americans. As the 1950s and 1960s wore on, overt American aspects were let go as less and less proof was needed to convince the general public of Japanese American emplacement. This shift in attitude was also instigated by a rapidly increasing tourist gaze in Hawai'i that included the CBF. The HJJCC soon recognized the profit to be gained by self-exoticization through the CBF.

From the earliest years, the Festival included Japanese cultural events such as kabuki,[10] flower arrangement, martial arts, bonsai, music, and dance (HJJCC 1953:29–31). Most of these were demonstrated by local practitioners of the Japanese art forms. Although the showcased elements did not particularly relate to the lives of most Japanese Americans in Hawai'i, they linked directly to an aestheticized, exoticized Japan.

These art forms constitute what I call "cultural ambassadors," that is, cultural productions selected for their ties to a sense of the past or an invented conceptualization of "tradition" (Hobsbawm and Ranger 1983). Cultural ambassadors are artistic, portable, visually attractive (photogenic, telegenic), readily appreciated (although not necessarily with the same meanings as in Japan), and distinctive enough to be easily identified as exotic and iconic. Thus, whenever or wherever the occasion arises requiring presentations of "Japan" (here conflated with Japanese Americans), one sees the same kinds of stereotypical performances: women in kimono, koto music, tea ceremony, flower arrangement. This holds true in Japan, as well as in Hawai'i and elsewhere. In the CBF, these displays varied only a little over time and became one source of the community's public presentation of links to Japan.

In the 1950s and 1960s, the CBF held a vital place in the Japanese American community, with full coverage and involvement of Japanese-language newspapers.[11] In the inaugural months of the first Festival from January 21 to April 29, 1953, Japanese-language newspaper *Hawaii Hochi* carried no fewer than 142 articles, photographs, editorials, and announcements of the CBF in its pages. These included articles profiling the different contestants, editorials commenting on the fairness of judging practices, letters from readers opining on the selection of the CBF Queen, and messages from parents of contestants thanking the public for support of their daughters. The newspaper became directly involved in the CBF in 1954, when it sponsored its own guess-the-Queen contest, with a $50 cash prize (*Hawaii Hochi* 1954b:3).

Another *Hawaii Hochi* spin-off from the CBF was the Miss Ohina [Doll] contest begun in 1956 and continuing until 1959 in various forms.[12] In its initial configuration, Miss Ohina was selected by the public from among the Cherry Blossom Festival Queen contestants; however, after the first year, the two contests created separate pools of candidates. Unlike the CBF Queen contest, which included women from seventeen to twenty-six years old, the Miss Ohina contestants were primarily high school students. Most important for the Japanese American community, the Miss Ohina contest allowed those from neighbor islands to participate as fully and equally as those on O'ahu, with contestants and balloting conducted there as well.[13]

In contrast to the Miss Ohina contest, the CBF in the 1950s and 1960s was an O'ahu, and specifically a Honolulu, event.[14] Although from 1954 on, the contest was opened to include contestants from neighbor islands, these contestants had to procure sponsors on O'ahu, as well as face the inconvenience and cost of traveling to O'ahu to participate in events.

[handwritten margin note: early CBF was only for O'ahu islanders. Now open to all H.I. islands.]

In the postwar years, the CBF was important to the Japanese American community in helping bridge the gap between issei and nisei. Although nisei were clearly the organizers and primary participants in the Festival, issei became avid spectators after their initial doubts were dispelled.[15] In fact, the Festival became an arena of cooperation between generations, as proclaimed by a 1954 article: "The biggest reward of the Second Cherry Blossom Festival is that the gap between issei and nisei has narrowed through working together to make this event successful" (*Hawaii Hochi* 1954g:5).

While these cultural events and newspaper coverage overtly linked the CBF to Japanese (American) selves, language became a more covert linkage that shifted with the vagaries of HJJCC leadership and perceptions of public acceptability. Jaycee leadership changed yearly, so many of these shifts may have occurred on individual whim. But the many shifts that did occur suggest the conundrum of language. HJJCC organizers seemed continually at odds within their own ranks trying to gauge how much Japanese and how much English to use in souvenir books. The need to prove one's Americanness through English usage was at its highest in the early 1950s, just when the Japanese-language ability of the HJJCC members was also at its highest because of the high proportion of nisei. In the 1960s as sansei gradually superseded nisei in the HJJCC, performing American through English was taken for granted, and Japanese-language ability among members was waning.

Negotiations of Japanese and English usage in souvenir books peppered the early years of the Festival. The first souvenir books from 1953 through 1955 simply said "Cherry Blossom Festival" in English. But in 1956, the souvenir booklet included "Sakura Matsuri" written in kanji (Japanese ideographs) on the first page, along with "Cherry Blossom Festival" in English (HJJCC 1956:1).[16] In 1957, the souvenir booklet showed a marked increase in the use of Japanese language in captions, names, and advertisements. The names of former Queens and HJJCC organizers were given not only in standard romanization, but also in kanji, with names written surname first, as is the practice in Japan. Furthermore, the Queens were only listed by their Japanese middle names.[17] Thus Queen Anna Keiko Tokumaru became "Tokumaru Keiko" written in kanji. The 1957 souvenir book also included a few advertisements written entirely in Japanese.[18] The 1958 book continued the trend with "Sakura Matsuri" written in Japanese on its cover and a logo that juxtaposed "Cherry Blossom Festival" in English and "Sakura Matsuri" in Japanese on all content pages.[19] By 1959, however, the souvenir book was once again exclusively in English, except for the mixed logo of "Sakura Matsuri" (in Japanese) and "Cherry Blossom Festival" (HJJCC 1959). This schizophrenic mixing of languages in the 1950s provides a linguistic dimension to the CBF's varied audiences, especially issei (who could read Japanese) and nisei (only some of whom could read Japanese), as well as the general acceptability of including Japanese language as part of the Festival's public face.

Another kind of mixing can be seen in the realm of music. The first souvenir book included a song entitled "Hawaii Sakura Matsuri Ondo" (Hawai'i Cherry Blossom Festival Dance). The lyrics were the result of a song contest announced in Japanese-language newspapers in Honolulu, combining themes of Hawai'i and cherry blossoms. The end product was a mixed Japanese and American one: combination of lyrics from five Hawai'i entrants compiled by Japanese lyricist Miyuki Ishimoto, set to music by Japanese composer Uehara Gento, and choreographed in Japan (*Hawaii Hochi* 1953a, c, g). The lyrics sang stereotypically of hula maidens, Honolulu nights, and fragrant ginger blossoms, but the last verse of the song identified Hawai'i as a bridge between East and West: "The West is America, the East is Japan, the islands of Hawai'i act as a go-between" (HJJCC 1953:51).[20]

This contrasts with another song written in English included in CBF souvenir books from 1959 through the 1960s. "Cherry Blossoms" was composed for the CBF by well-known local haole songwriter R. Alex Anderson. This was a contribution outside any ethnic enclave that demonstrated further breakdown of barriers between Japanese Americans and others in Hawai'i. Anderson wrote: "Twirling parasol as she dances / Peeking thru the bars of her fan / Dainty and shy, she's a true butterfly / Of Japan, of Japan" (1959:4).[21] His orientalist lyrics wax poetic about cherry blossoms and beauty queens, conflating Japanese and Japanese American women.

Exotic Women: Gendering the Japanese (American) Stage

Amid culture shows, language shifts, and cherry blossom songs, the main component of performing selves as Japanese (American) was the pageant itself, parading women as both exotic and American. Central to this mixed presentation of women lay the issue of dress, specifically the *furisode* (kimono for a young unmarried woman). From the first pageant in 1953, contestants made several public appearances in kimono — many wearing *furisode* for the first time in their lives. An editorial in 1953 in the *Hawaii Hochi* expressed one reaction:

> Unlike prewar years, I feel that there are fewer people wearing Japanese kimono today. Now we can see the Cherry Blossom Queen candidates in beautiful furisode, recently presented by the Honolulu Japanese Junior Chamber of Commerce. After a long absence, we can again fully appreciate the *obi* [sash] worn high [female-style] and the beauty of gorgeous furisode. (*Hawaii Hochi* 1953d:2)[22]

The 1955 souvenir book showed contestants at the seat of the Territorial government, 'Iolani Palace,[23] with this caption: "This group of Cherry Blossom

Queen candidates were welcomed at 'Iolani Palace by Governor Samuel Wilder King. Clad in colorful kimono, the young women visited the rooms where Hawaiian royalty once trod" (HJJCC 1955:7).

Other photographs from 1955 through the 1960s show HJJCC members (male) in Japanese *happi* (jacket) and *hachimaki* (tied headband), pulling rickshaws through downtown Honolulu, transporting kimono-clad contestants holding *kasa* (Japanese umbrella made of bamboo and painted or plain oiled paper) (e.g., HJJCC 1955:8). In this case, both men and women performed themselves as Japanese (American). Kimono and *kasa* can also be seen in individual portraits of contestants in early souvenir books from 1953 through 1956. Thus, while the covers of these books depicted a Queen in Western gown, the inside pages showed contestants in kimono (and sometimes holding *kasa*). This was part of the cultural mixing and negotiation of the period. In Hawai'i, kimono and *kasa* became emblematic of Japanese femininity drawn from the traditional entertainment/arts world in Japan and reinvented as an idealized, exoticized past.[24]

Kimono were also important in the competition itself. The CBF pageant finals always included a Western evening gown segment in the first half, followed by a kimono segment in the second half. The crowning of the new Queen in the second half made for a highly photogenic, exoticized moment. A key shift took place in 1961, when the cover of the CBF souvenir booklet depicted a Queen in kimono, rather than Western evening gown, for the first time.[25] Since then, nearly all souvenir book covers with Cherry Blossom Queens display them in kimono. As evidence of the cultural mix, the kimono is often paired with crown and scepter.

The kimono that contestants in Hawai'i wore were stereotypically brightly colored, often in pinks and reds. They did not reflect the whole spectrum of kimono actually worn in Japan, which included more subdued and subtle shades and designs selected for particular seasons, social ranks, ages, and occasions.[26] Furthermore, the hairstyles of kimono-clad CBF contestants made no concessions to the highly refined aesthetic of kimono-wearing in Japan that included specifically named hairstyles (Dalby 1993:75–76). In the CBF, by contrast, contestants wore their hair as was fashionable in Hawai'i at the time, even when paired with kimono.

Lessons in wearing kimono became part of contest preparations. These were informal at first, but by the 1960s all contestants attended these lessons. CBF Queen JoAnn Yamada (1961–1962) recalls the cultural lessons she learned through kimono-wearing:

JY: *I think one thing that made me more conscious about being Japanese was my walk. I mean a kimono walk. That's very very different. You know, you just don't walk like you walk normally.*

CY: You mean [you don't] stride around?

JY: *Yeah. Not that I have big steps, because I have very short legs, but it's small in order that the kimono doesn't open, I think. This is my deduction, and that's why you walk kind of pigeon-toed fashion, because you don't want your kimono to open.*

CY: Did you have instructions on how to walk?

JY: *Yeah, I did a little bit. There were two women that supplied kimonos for the contestants and we went two times. One helped to pick colors and one helped me do some of the walking then.*

CY: Did you pick your own kimono or did they pick it for you?

JY: *Well, I almost had a sense that, you know, she [kimono instructor] thought that I had a good chance [of winning], so therefore she was just gonna give me one that she thought matched me. Yeah. I sensed something like that. I'm not too sure. But I had a beautiful kimono, I thought.*

(Personal communication, December 15, 2001)

Learning to walk pigeon-toed in kimono and understanding the manipulations of kimono choice became part of learning how to perform oneself as a Japanese (American) woman.

Indeed, for Yamada, wearing kimono made her feel "Japanese."

CY: How did you feel when you got dressed in kimono?

JY: *Oh, it feels really nice. There's kind of a connection with culture. You know, it's like, I'm Japanese. I look Japanese. So then your whole attitude, your whole thinking goes with the clothing. It's beautiful. The obi was the old-fashioned obi. It's amazing what those women [kimono dressers] can do. They just wrap you and of course, they girdle you really tight. You know, like — [gasps] — breathe for air. But then once it was done, and the product was there, the kimono made you feel very . . . I think Oriental, or very Japanese. It's amazing.*

CY: Did you move any differently?

JY: *Oh yes. Because the kimono is restricting, you know. Then of course you're gonna have to sit up straight. [Chuckles] No slouching. Because it holds you. It's like a board. It just keeps you straight in there. And it just kinda keeps your poise more. It really does! I can see where the kimono is a beautiful piece of clothing, but not very practical. . . . But it's a beautiful feeling to be in a kimono.*

(Personal communication, January 21, 2001)

The kimono itself, then, sends gendered, cultural messages, disciplining the bodily experience of its wearing into what Yamada interprets as "Oriental" or "Japanese" and female.

R. Alex Anderson's Festival song, "Cherry Blossoms," sings of kimono: "Gaily flowered is her silk kimono / Brightly deck'd with blossoms pink and red" (1959:4). The song points up the symbolism of cherry blossom — a benign image of pretty flowers in springtime associated with Japan — for Japanese Americans in Hawai'i. The symbol in Hawai'i has no experiential reference, since for the most part cherry trees do not grow in Hawai'i and local people have little direct knowledge of the trees or blossoms.[27]

In Japan, however, viewing cherry blossoms is an important seasonal practice with national-cultural significance that goes well beyond admiring flower-laden trees. Cherry blossoms in Japan symbolize not only beauty, spring, reproductive power, and the nation itself, but carry the existential significance of ephemerality and transitoriness (Ohnuki-Tierney 2002:32). Cherry blossoms in Japan have even taken on political significance. Kamikaze pilots in World War II were likened to cherry blossoms, ennobled and masculinized by the sacrifice of their young lives for the glory of Japan (ibid.:10). In Hawai'i, however, the namesake cherry blossoms of the pageant represent little more than half the meanings found in Japan: femininity rather than a gendered complex that includes heroic masculinity; beauty alone rather than the preciousness of transitory beauty; blossoming rather than the poignancy of the flowers' demise; and Japan not as lived experience but as distant image. The exoticized women of the CBF draw upon the multivalent symbol of cherry blossoms — differently nuanced from that in Japan, but no less central to the practices of their public gendered imaging.

All-American Debutantes and the American Dream Life

Gendered imaging of the 1950s and 1960s had a critical American dimension as well. After all, these exotic women were supposed to be part of the postwar American dream of modern, middle-class, nuclear-family life. The exotic women of the CBF were thus drawn as symbolic local debutantes, emulating their counterparts in the continental United States.[28] In 1954, for example, CBF contestants were introduced at what was dubbed a "Debutante Dance": "Thousands turned out for the Debutante Dance on March 6 at the Honolulu Armory where the Cherry Blossom Festival Queen contestants were introduced to the public" (HJJCC 1954:64). The *Hawaii Hochi* likewise described the event: "Ronald Fujii, chairman of the ball, said that formal presentation of the beauties will be made in the manner of Mainland coming-out parties. Each contestant in formal gown will be spot-lighted [*sic*] for her entrance on the stage as . . . [the emcee] introduces her to the crowd" (*Hawaii Hochi* 1954a:1). The Euro-American debutante ball, then, was an explicit referential model for the CBF.

Looking the part was important. By 1960, contestants were trained how to move debutante-style as part of the CBF contest preparation. Race and class conjoined during this period. The 1960 souvenir book introduced Mrs. Margo Piper, a haole instructor from the Stenographic Institute of Hawaii, who taught contestants proper sitting and good posture (HJJCC 1960:22). The 1964 book showed contestants going through a prepageant modeling course, with instructions on movement, makeup, and posing for photographers (HJJCC 1964:44). In these ways, the CBF trained its quasi-debutante contestants in the arts of public presentation as American beauties.

As quasi-debutantes, the CBF contestants (and the HJJCC organizers) were supposed to look ahead to a middle-class or upper-middle-class domestic life. Advertisements in souvenir books targeted weddings, new homes, appliances, and other accoutrements of the American dream. Bridal ads such as that for Margo's Bridal Salon occupied a regular space on the back cover of 1950s souvenir books: "Bride-to-be. To be sure: Wear a gown that bears the label of distinction — Margo's — long since acclaimed Hawaii's leading bridal salon" (HJJCC 1958). Advertisements targeted men as well. In both 1956 and 1957, Hale Niu clothing rental company advertised:

> Mr. Bridegroom! YOUR wedding day and what a wonderful day it will be! FULL of happiness and joy! AND you will want that day to be remembered as perfect by you and your beloved. This can only happen if you RENT your Wedding Attire from Hawaii's most complete and economical suit rental house, Hale Niu. (HJJCC 1956:21; 1957:24)

These advertisements went hand in hand with aspects of the Queen's coronation that emulated a wedding. The souvenir book from 1963 showed a girl crown bearer and boy scepter bearer, echoing the flower girl and boy ring bearer of weddings (HJJCC 1963:87). The ceremony also included a "coronation cake" — an elaborate, white, multitiered cake looking much like that for weddings.

Advertisements in souvenir books from the 1950s and 1960s went beyond weddings to a couple's first home. An advertisement for a moving company proclaimed: "Imagine! Moving day and nothing to do! Yes, moving day can be just as easy for YOU!" (HJJCC 1956:29). The Hawaiian Electric Company promoted a modern, all-electric home (HJJCC 1957:34), and made reference to the pageant: "Queen for a day . . . every day when she cooks electrically" (HJJCC

1958:52). Advertisements for the Central Furniture Company boasted the benefits of a Serta bed, while the Honolulu Gas Company talked about cooking at home (HJJCC 1956: 31, 76).

These advertisements filling in the American dream were matched by the prizes given to the Queen. In the 1950s and 1960s they included not only a trip to Japan, but also items for a debutante: hope chest, housewares such as china, vases, and radio, a luggage set, charm course, and makeup. These advertisements and prizes painted a picture of the American dream in which these quasi-debutantes and their husbands would live. Advertisements in CBF souvenir books also acknowledged white-collar, working women, with advertisements for secretarial schools, such as Honolulu Business College and Cannon's School of Business.

These quasi-debutantes of the 1950s and 1960s were defined not by curvaceous bodies, but by cultural values of modesty and humility. In other words, these were "nice girls," rewarded for their interpersonal skills and moral merit. Part of that moral merit lay in not exposing their bodies publicly. Thus, the CBF pageant never had a swimsuit component. In fact, several Queens say that if the pageant had included a swimsuit component, they would never have run. CBF Queen Jayne Kuwata (1958 – 1959) laughingly recalls, "No way! If they did [include swimsuit competition], I wouldn't even run!'" (personal communication, December 20, 2001).

Like other beauty contests of this period, the CBF provided female chaperones and male escorts to and from public appearances for contestants. But what painted contestants as sheltered daughters was not the chaperonage so much as the prominent place given parents in souvenir books. From the 1958 souvenir book on, parents of the Queen and contestants received special mention. For example, the 1958 book showed Queen Carol Saikyo playing the piano, watched by her parents: "Queen Carol demonstrates her multiple talents under the watchful guidance of her folks, Mr. And Mrs. Saikyo" (HJJCC 1958:81). Not only was the Queen depicted as a daughter, but as a middle-class daughter with middle-class musical accomplishments.

Mothers in particular received special mention. The 1960 souvenir book included several photographs of contestants with their mothers, signing up for the contest, and receiving instructions on procedures: "Queen Lorraine [Kirihira] explains her experiences of her reign to the Queen hopefuls and their mothers" (HJJCC 1960:21 – 23). Karal Ann Marling's work on "debdom" — that is, the culture surrounding debutantes in the United States — points to the frequency of an intense level of maternal involvement in these events (2004:170). So, too, the photographs in the souvenir books imply that mothers follow closely behind daughters throughout the events of the CBF. By embedding contestants and Queens as daughters, the HJJCC depicts them as "nice girls" still tied to their families.

Who are those most likely to participate in the CBF? The limitations of the pageant in terms of time and place create structural boundaries on the women who participate. Competing in the CBF automatically excludes young women who move beyond Hawai'i for college, careers, and lives, and stay away at least through the age of twenty-six (maximum age allowed to run in the contest). The contest, in fact, selects the following: (1) those who have chosen or are forced to stay close to home, attending college or working in Honolulu during the critical years of contest eligibility; (2) those who do not marry or have children immediately out of high school, since contestants must be unmarried and childless; and (3) those who go away (to college) but return to Hawai'i before the age of twenty-six. In short, contestants can only arise out of the group of Japanese American women between the ages of eighteen and twenty-six years who are living in Honolulu.

During the 1950s, moving away from Hawai'i for college was not a frequent option for many people, especially women. In subsequent decades, going to college in the continental United States enabled many young people in Hawai'i to develop their personal and professional lives. The CBF is not part of this. Instead, it rewards those who choose to stay close or return home, spending both their childhood and adult years within a bounded radius. Those most likely to run for CBF fall within a contained, conservative milieu: having enough financial resources to withstand the expenses of living in Hawai'i; with enough social prospects for the future not to marry young; but without the impetus to leave Hawai'i for challenges beyond its shores.[29] The contestants and Queens thus represent hometown girls in this most glorified of hometown settings.

Besides beauty contestants and Queens, other women were very much present at the CBF. These were the wives of the HJJCC members who formed an informal support network that officially became the Women's Auxiliary and Women's Advisory Group (HJJCC 1953:10). In the 1955 souvenir book, photographs juxtaposed these two different categories of women — beauty contestants and wives. For example, one photograph showed contestants in kimono and holding *kasa* arrayed next to a swimming pool with the caption, "While the men look after the Queen Contestants...", the adjacent photograph showed wives of the HJJCC busily making decorations for the Festival (HJJCC 1955:72). Both groups of women help masculinize the men, though in different ways: contestants enhance the image of men's paternal/sexual prowess, while wives contribute to their civic productivity.[30]

Whereas Cherry Blossom contestants were both racialized and feminized as exotic, though not necessarily erotic, the men of the HJJCC for the most part were deracialized as intertwined projects of masculinity and Americanization. The processes of Americanizing thus differed by gender: men performed a white masculinity in its production of an entrepreneurial, civic-minded, Jaycee middle class; women performed a racialized femininity through a beauty pageant that borrowed American idioms while highlighting Japanese difference. This gendered difference was particularly important in the early days of the CBF when proving one's Americanness was crucial for the HJJCC. Apart from the few instances of photographs of HJJCC members in Japanese costume pulling Queen contestants in rickshaws (e.g., HJJCC 1955:8), nothing in the way the men dressed or presented themselves tied them to Japan or Japanese Americans.[31] These were first of all men of action and only secondly Japanese Americans.

The Jaycee organization gave them a deracialized purpose for their actions: leadership training through community service. CBF as a civic event of a non-profit organization was viewed as a form of service to the community at large, contributing to the public welfare and to cultural events in Hawai'i. From the first souvenir books of the CBF through the 1960s, the Festival celebrates the efforts of men capable of organizing a large-scale event and thus contributing to the civic culture of Hawai'i. Each book includes photographs of male organizers in formal portraits and/or action shots. According to these visual representations, men make the Queen and contestants possible by planning, organizing, and executing the CBF. Of course, the event requires a female Queen and contestants, but what the souvenir books emphasize are the long hours of manly effort. In the 1956 souvenir book, for example, every aspect of the CBF, from finding contestants to cleanup, was illustrated by photographs and running commentary about the men working to make it happen:

> Many a smoke and conversation-filled session goes on before plans are shaped and completed.... Here are the men who had the job of finding candidates for one of the top honors of the year — Cherry Blossom Queen. (HJJCC 1956:9)
> These are the men who contacted radio and TV stations and did the legwork involved in getting a good "press" for the Festival, the public relations committee. (ibid.:29)
> The committee which produced this directory is shown in session. Many

miles were walked by these men to produce the advertising and editorial material for this publication. (ibid.:59)

Coats and ties were tossed aside for cleanup details. Everyone from the general chairman down joined in the work. (ibid.:58)

The entire CBF, including its Queen, are thus produced specifically through masculine effort.

The CBF, likewise, is positioned not so much as a cultural project, but as a Jaycee project. For example, in 1956, HJJCC President Conrad Akamine wrote:

The Honolulu Japanese Junior Chamber of Commerce, like all the 3,000 Jaycee chapters throughout our country, is a training ground for active young men to become better citizens and leaders in our community.... Our annual Cherry Blossom Festival exemplifies a typical Jaycee project, and we believe it encompasses all of the features that help train an active Jaycee. The Festival involves both local and foreign relations and receives extensive publicity. It invites the participation of all of the people and firms in this community with results mutually beneficial. Most important, planning and successful undertaking of the ten major projects of this Festival ... provides us with a means of training for leadership and "Jayceeism." (Akamine 1956:5)

A message from Governor William F. Quinn in 1958 validated the accomplishments of HJJCC men as organizers of the CBF:

In sponsoring the Cherry Blossom Festival ... the Honolulu Japanese Junior Chamber of Commerce is accomplishing a dual objective. First, it is carrying out one of the basic precepts of its parent organization [Jaycee organization]: "That the brotherhood of man transcends the sovereignty of nations." Secondly, it provides an opportunity for its members to develop teamwork and leadership while performing a community service." (Quinn 1958:7)

These sentiments continued in the 1960s, as echoed by HJJCC President Charles T. Ushijima, who spoke of members' "dedication as Jaycees and devotion to the common cause of individual development through community service, [by which they] have gained valuable training while attaining personal maturity during the crucial years of their lives" (HJJCC 1967:3). None of these narratives mentions Japanese or Japanese American culture. Instead, they focus on men and what they gain from organizing a civic project. The pageant effects nothing less than the masculinization of HJJCC members as all-American, Jaycee men.

The masculinization of HJJCC members is made evident not only by their organizational skills, but also by their scopophilic (i.e., focusing on the visual as erotic) practices. The beauty pageant is an overt institutionalization of the male gaze (even taking into account the female gaze I discuss in the Prologue), objectifying women while sexualizing men as publicly virile (cf. Mulvey 1975). The CBF is thus no exception in this. Stereotypical depictions in 1950s and 1960s souvenir books show male organizers surrounded by a bevy of young female contestants (e.g., HJJCC 1958:15). Age difference reinforces the uneven structure of gender: male organizers, at twenty-one to thirty-nine years of age, are generally older than female contestants, who have to be between eighteen and twenty-six. The male gaze sometimes becomes a violation when it crosses racial lines. An editorial in the *Hawaii Hochi* complained, "I was puzzled at some white men's gaze at the Queen contestants as if they were *'panpan* girls'" [wartime and postwar prostitutes in Japan who cater to white men] (1954c:7). Thus it was alright for Japanese American men to gaze upon Japanese American women, but when white men did so, it became a highly sexualized threat to the community.

When Japanese American men and their organizations sponsored individual contestants, the male gaze — especially that of older men looking upon younger women — can become proprietary. The 1957 souvenir book showed a smiling, young contestant surrounded by older men: "Kapahulu Association presents their queen hopeful" (HJJCC 1957:33). The young contestant acts as the older men's representative, product, and ward. Individual men were sometimes credited with assisting a contestant in her bid to become Queen. For example, a column in the *Hawaii Hochi* compliments businessman Masao Muraoka for the success of Queen Marjorie Nishimura (1955 – 1956):

> The owner of Kalihi Auto Parts and Supply, Mr. Masao Muraoka, also has an artist name, Koshu. It is his good artistic taste that selected the beautiful kimono worn by Miss [Marjorie] Miyoko Nishimura in the Cherry Blossom contest. Muraoka made every effort to ensure Miyoko's victory.... We should say that Muraoka's efforts have been great. (1955c:8)

According to this column, the backstage efforts of one man helped a woman win the crown.

The masculinization of Japanese American men through the scopophilic practices of the CBF included those who usually remained invisible in the souvenir books: male photographers. In Hawai'i during the 1950s and 1960s, amateur photography clubs made up of primarily Japanese American men played a significant role in the visual representation of young women. Many teenage and young adult Japanese American females posed for these amateur photographers, typically dressed in Western clothing with orientalized touches, such as holding a *kasa* or standing in a bamboo grove or Japanese garden. In some instances, amateur photographers provided photographs for the Festival. For example, the 1954 souvenir book included a picture of the officers of the Japanese Photographers Society of Hawaii, whose members took all the photographs for the second CBF (HJJCC 1954:64).

Amateur photographers also sometimes recommended and sponsored a contestant. For example, in the first 1953 CBF, contestant Marjory Emiko Mori was sponsored by the Japanese Photographers Society of Hawaii (*Hawaii Hochi* 1953e:3).[32] And in some cases, amateur photographers not only suggested that certain women run in the CBF pageant, but proceeded to help train them. CBF Queen JoAnn Yamada (1961–1962) recalls:

> There was this amateur photographer friend of mine. He phoned me. He was the one who encouraged me [to run for CBF Queen]. . . . He just liked to take pictures of us girls that were Japanese. And then he somehow encouraged me to try out. . . . He was helping people [run for Cherry Blossom] prior to that. . . . He was interested I think in just trying to help people in Cherry Blossom. (Personal communication, December 15, 2001)

As the eye behind the camera, some of these photographers became experts in judging female beauty. The masculinity of these photographers lay in their visual connoisseurship of women.

The relationship of HJJCC men and others to CBF Queens sometimes went beyond the visual/physical to the spiritual/emotional. The following "love letter" was written to CBF Queen Gwen Nishizawa (1967–1968) and published by the HJJCC in their newsletter *Post Script*:

> Dear Gwen,
>   As a new member I have many Jaycee years ahead of me, and I look forward to each year's Cherry Blossom festivals and personalities.
>   One of the pleasurable anticipations will be the meeting of each crop's contestants and then the working with the new queen for the coming year.
>   As the first Cherry Blossom queen for me you will set the standards by which all who follow you will be measured.
>   I will never forget that first magic moment when the spotlight focused on you dressed in a white gown, crown and scepter and I thought to myself, "We have a queen, indeed." . . . You made me proud to be a member of our chapter for you wore your honor well. . . .
>   I suppose feelings toward Cherry Blossom queens must be like those toward first loves. They can become emotional, but I felt that I had to write

these words so that you and your family know how one member feels, as do many fellow Jaycees.

I just hope that you will remember us as fondly as we will you. Best of luck in all that awaits you, for we wish you only the best.

A New Member (HJJCC 1968:n.p.)

In this rather tenderhearted letter, the male writer openly expressed his admiration for Nishizawa (see Chapter 4 for Nishizawa's herstory). Although some may read this as an individual love letter, I take it — and its publication by the HJJCC — as evidence of a particular relationship between the HJJCC and the CBF Queen marked not only by admiration, but by a certain sense of ownership ("We have a new queen"), objectification ("each crop's contestants"), and implied intimacy. The analogy to first love is not so far off the mark here: the Queen is the star virginal female at the center of attention of an organization of young men. Admiring the Queen, even as benignly as this, places a spotlight on the covertly sexual relationship between Queens and Jaycees.

The Business of Beauty: Intertwining Commerce and Community in the CBF

The masculinity of HJJCC members may be tied closely to their productivity in business. From the start, the CBF aimed to generate revenue. Businesses throughout Honolulu were heavily involved in the CBF in various ways: (1) sponsorship and advertising; (2) balloting; and (3) cherry blossom-themed window displays. Sponsors and advertisers formed a crucial and critical audience for the pageant. Advertisements filled over 65 percent of the first souvenir book in 1953. The companies that advertised in the booklet included those with direct Japanese American ties through ownership or management (e.g., National Mortgage & Finance Co., Nippon Theatre, Honolulu Sake Brewery & Ice Co., Ltd., Hosoi Japanese Mortuary), as well as those without ethnic ties (e.g., Hawaiian Electric, Theo H. Davies & Co., Ltd., American President Lines, Cannon's School of Business).[33]

Balloting was another form of business involvement. In the early contests, participating merchants gave customers one CBF ballot for every dollar spent. Customers then used the ballot to vote for the contestant of their choice or for entrance to CBF events. In 1953, of the seventy-two initial candidates, the fifteen who garnered the most votes through this kind of balloting became finalists. What happened in practice was that often contestants with the most financial backing from family, friends, or sponsors were able to secure their place in the final competition.

By placing the process of narrowing the field of contestants in the hands of the buying public, the CBF Queen contest became a highly participatory event that involved much of the community. According to a comment published in the *Hawaii Hochi*, it took more than simply friends and family supporters to win: "I feel sorry to see one contestant, a granddaughter of a friend of mine, who got eliminated before the finals and is so depressed. I told her that to win a contest like this, one needs an active campaign of supporters ... The Queen is not chosen solely on her beauty and ability" (*Hawaii Hochi* 1956e:6). Indeed, some early Queens talk about contestants actively waging campaigns by creating posters with their photograph and displaying these at public venues. This kind of active public campaign could end up costing contestants' families and sponsors a lot of money, since it required hiring professional photographers, making signs, and purchasing the goods that bought votes. One letter-writer complained: "I hope the way to choose finalists for the Cherry Blossom Queen will change from public voting to official judging, the way the Narcissus Queen is selected. [Signed,] Then, Parents' Burden Will be Less and Capable Candidates Will Remain in the Finals" (*Hawaii Hochi* 1956h:4).

[handwritten margin note: 3rd party supporters heavily influenced outcome of contest]

The 1954 souvenir book talked about the CBF as a boon to business first, and a cultural production second:

> The Cherry Blossom Festival's primary purpose is to stimulate trade. Last year [1953, first year of CBF] approximately two million ballots were distributed to the community and this year twice that number went out. Since a ballot and coupon were handed out with each dollar's worth of purchases, this represents around four million dollars turnover. Although only in its second year, the festival is second only to Aloha Week as a tourist attraction in the Islands. This means thousands of tourist dollars. ... A parallel purpose of the Festival is to develop interest in Japanese culture, which is an important part of the cosmopolitan heritage of the people of Hawaii. (HJJCC 1954:5)

"Japanese culture" gets but a brief mention by the organizers of the CBF at the end of their statement. In this early phase of the CBF, Japanese (American) culture was less important than being a good American citizen by stimulating trade. Ironically, it was by performing Japaneseness — especially through women dressed in kimono — that one proved one's worth as an American.

The success of the CBF could be measured by its growth in sales from year to year. The 1955 souvenir book reported yearly leaps in revenue.

> Last year some 4,600,000 ballots were cast in the Queen Contest, an increase of almost 2,000,000 over the first year's balloting. The HJJCC believes

that there will be a large increase this year as well, especially since the ballots will be used as exchange tender for admission to many festival events. . . . Each ballot passed out will represent a dollar's sale. (HJJCC 1955:66)

The actual number of ballots cast in 1955 numbered around three million, representing $3 million generated for participating merchants. This was a considerable profit for the time, not only for the businesses involved but also for the economy of the territory. By 1956, changes had to be made to rein in a system that was spiraling out of control as a result of its own success. By 1957, the HJJCC did away with the public balloting system, relying instead upon initial screening of contestants by Jaycees. Furthermore, every contestant had to have a sponsor to defray costs.

The CBF retained the position of Miss Popularity, which was awarded to the contestant who garnered the most votes from the public. The HJJCC estimated that over five million votes (500,000 ballots at ten votes per ballot) were cast for Miss Popularity in 1957 (*Hawaii Hochi* 1957b:3). These numbers represent the tremendous interest and involvement of the primarily Japanese American public in the CBF, whether casting ballots, sponsoring contestants, or buying products.

Besides buying and voting for Miss Popularity, the community was drawn into the CBF through recruitment of contestants. In late 1959, the Jaycees offered a reward of a free interisland trip for two on a Matson liner to the person whose recruit ended up winning the crown.[34] Sharing the responsibility of searching for Queen contestants with the public extended the gaze upon eligible women more widely. Although the Jaycees' CBF Queen Search Committee still acted as the arbiter of who could actually compete, asking the public to help recruit candidates broadened the scrutiny of young women for the CBF Queen's position, as well as rewarded the individual who could scrutinize well. Intensifying the gaze of the Japanese American public upon its young women as potential contestants tied the community closer to the event and its Queen.

Parading before the Tourist Gaze

In the 1950s and 1960s, tourism strongly influenced public performances in Hawai'i, and the CBF was no exception. Tourism forced the CBF to "brand" itself — that is, mark itself as distinctive, appealing, and professionally executed. The "brand" that performed best before the tourist gaze was the photogenic, colorful, smiling, demure, kimono-wearing, *kasa*-wielding, rickshaw-riding Japanese (American) beauty queen.

The tie-in with tourism was evident in the strong presence of the relatively new airline industry as advertiser and sponsor in the CBF. The first souvenir booklet in 1953 included advertisements for Pan American Airways, United Airlines, Northwest Airlines, Transocean Air Lines, Philippine Air Lines, Aloha Airlines, and Hawaiian Airlines. The kickoff event for the 1955 CBF was aboard a Pan American Airways flight to Hilo. The contestants' press reception in 1961 was held on a Pan American Airways jet at the just completed Honolulu International Airport. Airlines donated the crown (Pan American Airways), scepter (Japan Airlines), and decorative lanterns (Japan Airlines in 1954). Ocean liners, too, made their way into the CBF. Festival kick-off events were held aboard ships: the *President Wilson* in 1958; the Matson Liner SS *Monterey* in 1962; the SS *President Cleveland* in 1965. Hotels also featured prominently in CBF events. A photograph in the 1957 souvenir book showed contestants at the premier Waikīkī hotel dressed in kimono holding kasa with the caption, "Hundreds of fans and tourists take in the reception at the Royal Hawaiian Hotel" (HJJCC 1957:11). One newspaper article estimated that the reception drew 1,000 spectators to this meeting ground of tourists and residents (*Hawaii Hochi* 1957a:1).

As early as fall 1953, the Hawaii Visitors Bureau became involved. Publicity photographs of "Japanese girls in traditional costumes, athletic events, cultural activities and art exhibits" were distributed to national news syndicates, magazines, and travel editions, promoting the Festival (*Honolulu Advertiser* 1953: B18). This kind of active promotion of the CBF as a tourist attraction continued through the 1960s. By 1964, CBF souvenir books included an insignia indicating the full endorsement of the Hawaii Visitors Bureau.

HJJCC President Teruo Himoto's greeting in the 1959 CBF souvenir book explicitly links the CBF to the tourist economy in Hawai'i: "We hope that our Festival each year will become more and more a tourist attraction to boost the economic conditions of the Territory, especially during the slow tourist months of March and April" (Himoto 1959:3). The CBF, paired with Aloha Week in September and October, boosted tourism during off-peak months. In fact, Cherry Blossom Queens participated actively in Aloha Week, appearing in its parades during the 1950s and 1960s as part of the exotic spectacle.

The CBF also held parades of its own. The first parades in the 1950s wound their way through downtown Honolulu; a decade later the parade venue shifted to Waikīkī. A description in the 1963 CBF souvenir book indicates the scope of the annual lantern parade through Waikīkī:

The colorful and spectacular lantern parade sponsored by the Honolulu Japanese Junior Chamber of Commerce and heartily endorsed by the Hawaii Visitors Bureau annually attracts thousands of tourists as well as kamaaina [resident] families. This year's huge parade will feature the 10th Cherry Blossom Festival Queen and her court, 11 beautiful floats, 7 marching bands, 3 military drill teams, the Aloha Temple Motor Corp, 200 kimono clad lantern carriers and dancers, 20 adorable kokeshi [wooden folk dolls; presumably performed by marchers in the parade] dolls, a colorful daimyo [warrior] procession, a motorcade featuring the 11th Cherry Blossom Festival Beauty Contestants, and many others too numerous to mention. (HJJCC 1963:51)

The lantern parades continued through 1965.

However, by the late 1960s, even though the CBF continued to be endorsed by the Hawaii Visitors Bureau (including a Hawaii Visitors Bureau logo in CBF souvenir books), tourism played a lesser role in its events. Hawai'i by this time had developed a number of competing tourist attractions; thus the CBF was no longer a major event in the burgeoning industry. CBF souvenir books in the late 1960s made little mention of public appearances in tourist areas. The focus shifted instead to shopping malls in Honolulu oriented more toward local residents.[35]

In spite of the importance of tourism in the 1950s and 1960s, the CBF was never strictly and only a tourist attraction. The Festival always performed for local audiences of various ethnicities. The HJJCC also performed for audiences outside Hawai'i, including other Japanese Americans in the continental United States and groups in Japan. But the strength and profitability of the tourist gaze dovetailed neatly with the formative years of the Festival, providing a heady combination that created its own momentum. Tourism provided lessons for the HJJCC on how they could be good Americans by showcasing themselves — or more precisely, the CBF Queen and contestants — as Japanese exotics. With the tourist gaze turned away from the CBF, the Festival refocused upon the local community. Performing oneself as Japanese continued, but for reasons apart from tourism. Increasingly, what had been done in part for profit under the tourist gaze was refocused as a performance of culture and identity.

Bridging Talk: Front Stage versus Back Stage

Before tourist and local gazes alike, the CBF often performed as a bridge: between East and West, "new" and "old," and one part of the "ethnic rainbow" of Hawai'i. For example, in 1958 chairman of the CBF Donald Iwai wrote:

Through pageantry and conviviality, the Jaycees hope to demonstrate that the cultures of the East and the West can mix. Who better to foster a deeper understanding and appreciation of the arts, philosophy and customs of the Orient than our Jaycees who are members of the second and third generations? . . . [The CBF] should bridge the gap between the old and the new worlds. (1958:5)

A statement such as this critically positions nisei and sansei as key figures in spanning East and West. Their bridging relies not on an assimilationist model, but on a hybrid one, mixing cultures of Japan and the United States. Furthermore, Iwai's use of the terms "old" and "new" refers to Japan as the "old" world from which immigrants came, and Hawai'i/America as the "new" world in which they and their offspring now live.

Further discussion of the HJJCC as a bridge can be found in Honolulu Mayor Neal S. Blaisdell's message in 1959:

The members of the Honolulu Japanese Junior Chamber of Commerce are to be congratulated for the excellent job they are doing in presenting a program which not only clearly portrays the culture and entertainment features of Old Japan, but which also reflects the harmonious racial relationships which exist here in Hawaii Nei. (Blaisdell 1959:9)

Here, the bridging of Japan and Hawai'i combines with "harmonious racial relationships," suggesting that combining cultural practices and racial harmony go hand in hand. This is the fundamental "ethnic rainbow" myth: that traversing boundaries with cross-cultural presentations and consumption of music, dance, theater, food, and beauty queens necessarily reflects "harmonious racial relationships" and equal access to resources by racial/ethnic groups.

By the early 1960s, "ethnic rainbow" talk was in full swing. In the 1965 CBF souvenir book, Governor John A. Burns emphasized Hawai'i's uniqueness as a multiracial/cultural paradise:

In our harmonious society, the different cultures represented by the varied ethnic backgrounds of our people are each distinct, yet serve to complement each other and to thus produce the unique blend that is found only in Hawaii. Festivals such as the annual CBF help to preserve the multi-cultural heritage of the people of our Islands. (Burns 1965:4)

According to this kind of bridging talk, the CBF contributes to Hawai'i's multiracial/cultural paradise by showcasing Japanese American distinctiveness, as well as its membership in the rainbow.

Race relations within the multihued rainbow may have looked harmonious at a distance from the front-stage performance, but within the backstage of the Japanese American community there still remained a great deal of boundary-maintenance, especially between haole and those of Japanese ancestry (cf. Goffman 1959). Talk within the Japanese American community expressed concerns about judging, questioning the appropriateness of non-Japanese judges to fairly assess an ethnically Japanese beauty contest. For example, one letter-writer to the *Hawaii Hochi* contended, "I hope that the [CBF] judges will make a decision heeding the fact that ladies who may look beautiful in the eyes of Caucasians are not necessarily beautiful to Japanese. [Signed,] Someone with a different view" (*Hawaii Hochi* 1953h:6). Another editorial demurred, "More than half of the judges for the Cherry Blossom Queen contest final this year were [ethnically] Japanese. That explains the result. I'm happy" (*Hawaii Hochi* 1954e:4). Yet another letter-writer concurred, "Since the Cherry Blossom Queen is to visit Japan, I think it's better to have four or five nikkei [persons of Japanese ancestry] judges out of seven" (*Hawaii Hochi* 1954f:6). And another letter-writer talked about outside criticism of haole judges: "A certain paper criticized the nikkei beauty contests in Honolulu [i.e., CBF Queen contest] as using too many Caucasian judges. [Signed,] Narrow Minded" (*Hawaii Hochi* 1956f:4). Even years later, the same kinds of comments were being made in the *Hawaii Hochi*: "This year's Queen Gwen Naomi Nishizawa is tall for Japanese and has big round eyes — the appearance that Caucasians like. There were only two Japanese out of seven judges this year. Since this is the Cherry Blossom Festival, I think it would be good to have at least 50 percent of the judges to be Japanese" (*Hawaii Hochi* 1967:5). The often racialized gaze of the Japanese American public generated backstage talk that clearly focused on the selection of the CBF Queen.[36]

That gaze and talk also concerned interracial impressions and relations. One letter-writer to the *Hawaii Hochi* praised the CBF kabuki production as one that "impresses Caucasians": "The kabuki shown in the Culture Show was extraordinary. It has big value as English-language theater that demonstrates Japanese theatrical art. [Signed,] It Impresses Caucasians" (*Hawaii Hochi* 1956g:9). Another letter-writer commented snidely, "There are complaints that this year's Cherry Blossom Queen is rather to the liking of whites [*hakujin-gonomi*; preferred by whites]. [Signed,] Too Late" (*Hawaii Hochi* 1956f:4). For these letter-writers — most likely issei, kibei-nisei (raised and educated in Japan), or nisei who could read and write easily in Japanese — haole were power-wielders to be impressed, but kept at a distance from their daughters.

One kind of racial bridging that received only belated and minor mention in souvenir books and Japanese-language newspapers was a change in HJJCC membership to include non-Japanese, as mentioned in Chapter 2. The organization's records give no specific date for this, except to indicate that by the late 1950s the HJJCC extended membership to persons of non-Japanese ancestry as a result of outside criticism of racial exclusivity. Although there may have been some debate about opening up membership, these debates did not surface in

[handwritten margin note:] Complaints that these pageants are too influenced by whites, yet a lot of sponsorship comes from white contributors "PanAm"

either English- or Japanese-language newspapers. The *Hawaii Hochi* made no mention of this major change in the premier Japanese American organization. The other Japanese-language newspaper, *Hawaii Times,* included only one small article within its pages:

> There is a gradual movement within the HJJCC to dispel its racial color. This reveals itself in the fact that four out of 57 new members this year are non-Japanese (three Chinese and one Korean), and that there is a suggestion to remove "Japanese" from the title of the organization. President Sam Okinaga explains . . . "The reason why we allowed non-Japanese is because there is no written rule in our regulations that non-Japanese are not allowed to become a member. . . . Whether we like it or not, the trend [of interracial membership] is going in that direction. It is a good trend. The annual Cherry Blossom Festival will be continued as long as the members of the Japanese Junior Chamber of Commerce are mostly nikkeijin." (*Hawaii Times* 1959a:2)

According to this article, the HJJCC could allow members of non-Japanese ethnicity into the organization because there was no explicit rule keeping them out. Thus this was not a change in policy, but a change in practice.

> CBF souvenir books made no mention of the change in practice until 1962: In an effort to promote the ideals of Americanism and of International goodwill, the HJJCC is truly unique; the membership roster includes names, such as King, Dela Cruz, Kekuna, Kim, Han, Crockett as well as the common Japanese names of Nakamura and Sato. (HJJCC 1962:2)

This after-the-fact disclosure erasing any debate or critique surrounding this major change in membership stands in direct contrast to the highly public debate conducted forty years later concerning the change in blood-quantum requirements for Queen contestants (see Chapter 7).

Japan: Tying and Retying Knots across the Pacific

Older Japanese Americans may have been ambivalent about bridging racial divides in Hawai'i, but these same persons enthusiastically embraced enacting bridges eastward to Japan through the CBF. The evolving relationship between this basically nisei organization and Japan as an overseas audience provides insights as to the role of Japan in the construction and performance of themselves as Japanese American.

Japan's position as an important audience for the CBF was expressed through editorials in the *Hawaii Hochi* in 1953:

We should be aware of how the [CBF] queen is selected. She should be the one whom issei and nisei in Honolulu — or more broadly, all Japanese people in Hawaii — would agree upon. Not only that, she should be the one who can also prove to the Japanese in Japan that the nisei made the right choice. This is the reason that the members of the HJJCC and the judges of the contest should be careful in their selection of the queen. (*Hawaii Hochi* 1953d:2)

At least for this writer, nisei still had to prove themselves to people in Japan. Another editorial expressed similar sentiments: "Since we send the Cherry Blossom Queen to Japan as a representative of the nisei, I hope people will select someone who has characteristics of nisei. She should possess a beauty that is unique to nisei" (*Hawaii Hochi* 1954d:4). Yet another editorial proudly talked about the significance of the CBF Queen in Japan:

> The Japanese Ministry of Transportation invites the Cherry Blossom Queen to Japan, for which the Japan Travel Bureau pays all the expenses. The Queen is treated like a state guest. This demonstrates that the Japanese regard nisei highly and that they consider the Cherry Blossom Queen contest a serious event. [Signed,] The motivating force of the Cherry Blossom Festival. (*Hawaii Hochi* 1955a:4)

Clearly, the CBF was seen as a critical bridge between Hawai'i and Japan, as well as between Japanese Americans and Japanese. The Queen represented this bridge: "The criteria for judging will be charm, beauty, voice, tone, speech, and the ability to represent American life in Hawaii, a melting pot of races" (*Hawaii Hochi* 1953f:3). One of the reasons for the concern over judging lay in the fact that the CBF Queen represented Japanese Americans' worthiness to a Japan that remained a judgmental audience.

Japan occupied an ambiguous position for many nisei: the birthplace of their parents, a foreign land to themselves. Japan was an enemy and source of consternation for the United States, as well as a thorn in the sides of those intent upon proving themselves as patriotic Americans, especially during and immediately after World War II. It was a fount of popular culture consumed enthusiastically by issei and some nisei, even as denigrated by other nisei as unappealingly old-fashioned and distinctly not to their American tastes. Those who chose to become part of the HJJCC and the CBF — whether as members or contestants — self-selected as having a positive and enthusiastic relationship to Japan or a willingness to learn about its culture. Nisei oriented more toward American culture, attitudes, and practices often did not bother with the organization and pageant.

Nisei organizers of the CBF were called upon to stage something called "Japanese culture." They did not necessarily have to create it from scratch: they could consult with elders, dance teachers, and other practitioners of cultural art forms; they could consult with University of Hawai'i professors and Buddhist priests; they could read books on the subject. But the CBF was ultimately the organizers' creation, and the invention of "Japanese culture" was by and large their own. "Japanese culture" as presented in the CBF combined their notion of the culture of their parents with the "cultural ambassadors" of Japan as filtered through a trans-Pacific system of communication based in media, business, institutions, and specific persons who acted as mediators. Some observers praised the HJJCC for introducing "Japanese culture" to audiences. An article in the *Hawaii Hochi* proclaimed, "The Japanese Junior Chamber of Commerce has made the Cherry Blossom Festival a great medium, not only as a stimulus to business and tourism, but also as an introducer of Japanese culture to nisei, sansei, and especially Caucasians" (Iwamoto 1957:2). This "Japanese culture" could only take place outside of Japan in this particular set of historical circumstances as an inevitably Japanese American product.

Direct connection to Japan helped authenticate this creation of "Japanese culture" in the CBF in the 1950s and 1960s. From the first contest on, a visit to Japan was an important prize and obligation for the CBF Queen. In the 1950s, few nisei or sansei had ever traveled to Japan, which made the trip a considerable luxury. For most Queens, it was their first time to visit Japan and was usually the highlight of their reign. CBF Queen Jayne Kuwata (1958–1959) reminisces: "Part of my prize was the Japan trip. Wherever we went, we were greeted by the Governor of Kyoto, everything, with flowers and everything. We really felt like celebrities" (personal communication, December 10, 2001). Especially in this period when travel outside Hawai'i for the average citizen was not common, receiving the red-carpet treatment in a foreign country was held with special regard.

These visits included meeting heads of sponsoring companies and organizations, prominent figures in the entertainment world, mayors of cities, members of the royal family, and even heads of state. In these visits, the CBF Queen gained many of the symbolic privileges of royalty without any of the leadership responsibilities. The fact that a beauty queen could act in any kind of official capacity in the realm of politics demonstrates some of the mixed idioms of royalty/leadership. For example, CBF Queen Ann Suzuki (1965–1966) called upon mayors of various cities in Japan and presented them with official letters of greeting from Honolulu Mayor Neal S. Blaisdell. The CBF Queen thus became an unofficial ambassador of Hawai'i and the United States within this Japanese context.

Tying and retying knots across the Pacific included not only the movement of people between two countries, one year it even included bringing actual cherry blossoms.

> Live Cherry Blossoms were flown in from Japan to be used in the Art Show [in 1962]. Seeing them for the first time, I [Queen Janet Nishino] was fascinated. . . . Touching and smelling the delicate and fragrant blossoms, I began to anticipate my trip to the country from which they were sent. (Nishino 1963:72)

With the airlifting of cherry blossoms from Japan to Hawai'i, the Festival came full circle from symbolic appropriation to importing actual flowers. Few local Japanese Americans had ever seen the actual flowers. Far more important were the symbolic uses to which the flowers were put, suggesting images of Japan, femininity, beauty, and nature. Cherry blossoms constituted the invention and performance of "Japan" in postwar Hawai'i and beyond, replacing memories of Pearl Harbor with that of beauty queens.

Looking Inward: Uchinanchu/Okinawans and the CBF

The spectacle of the CBF glossed over many internal divisions within the community, none more so than that between Naichi and Uchinanchu/Okinawans. There was officially no overt discrimination against persons of Okinawan ancestry within HJJCC: Okinawan Americans were both members and Queen contestants from the early days.[37] The very first contest in 1953 included three Okinawan American contestants out of seventy-two, two of whom were sponsored by the United Okinawan Association. Moreover, they were part of the organization's leadership. In 1955 Conrad Akamine became the first Okinawan American president of the HJJCC; in 1964 George H. Arakaki became the first general chairman of the CBF of Okinawan descent. However, the time lag between backstage organizers and front-stage Queens of Okinawan ancestry was considerable.[38] Although an Okinawan American man headed the HJJCC as early as 1955, it was not until 1967 that an Okinawan American woman was crowned as CBF Queen.

The CBF pageant often included at least one candidate with an Okinawan surname, but in many years there was only one, and in some years there was none.[39] For the years 1953 through 1969, the total numbers of contestants with Okinawan surnames was twenty-five out of 376, or 6.6 percent. By contrast, the Hawaii United Okinawa Association estimates that Uchinanchu constituted approximately 22 percent of Japanese Americans in Hawai'i (HUOA 2000:71).[40] Thus, the 6.6 percent Okinawan American contestants in the 1950s and 1960s indicates woeful underrepresentation. Reasons for this underrepresentation may lie in both the HJJCC not seeking out Okinawan American contestants, as well as these women (and their families) deselecting themselves from the competition.

The first woman of Okinawan descent to be crowned CBF Queen was Gwen Nishizawa (Okinawan by birth, but adopted by her Naichi stepfather; thus without an Okinawan surname) in 1967. The fact that she did not have an Okinawan surname meant that she could easily "pass" as Naichi, even if she did not do so deliberately. As detailed in Nishizawa's herstory in Chapter 4, she did nothing to hide her parentage and in fact spoke openly and movingly about her Okinawan heritage, but this speech came at the very end of her reign, not while she was a contestant or a newly crowned Queen. Her crowning as the first Okinawan American CBF Queen did not get press coverage in English- or regular Japanese-language media. The Okinawan American community had to wait another nine years before a woman with an Okinawan surname would be crowned: CBF Queen Myrah Higa in 1976 (see Chapter 6 for Higa's herstory).

The Okinawan presence in the CBF mostly went unmentioned. Various sansei Queens and contestants profess little knowledge in distinguishing between Naichi and Okinawans. This kind of knowledge was part of their parents' generation, but by the 1950s and 1960s, discrimination against Okinawans by Naichi became an embarrassment to nisei parents. Thus, one sansei CBF Queen recalls that her mother used to say, "We're all Japanese," in a deliberate attempt to deflect any query about the differences between Naichi and Uchinanchu.

The one acceptable arena of difference lay in entertainment/art. Okinawan arts were included fairly early in the CBF as a distinctive subset of Japanese culture. In 1955 the three-day culture show at the Honolulu Academy of Arts included Okinawan dance performed by the Hawaii Ryukyu Ongaku Kyokai. The 1961 lantern parade included an Okinawan lion dance. In spite of Okinawan American underrepresentation among Queens and contestants, and in the presence of Okinawan American male organizers and leaders who had removed any public traces of Okinawan descent from themselves except their names, the CBF relegated Okinawan distinctiveness to the safe and seemingly apolitical zone of the arts.

The 1950s and 1960s heyday of the CBF did not exclude Okinawan Americans. But their inclusion was peripheral — including men within the relative invisibility of membership, only barely including women in the visibility of the contestant circle, finally including a woman in the highly visible front stage of the Queen spotlight, but with no easy public read of her Okinawan background. There was no overt discrimination of Okinawans in the CBF, but there were subtle and continuing ways to keep Okinawans in their place. Okinawans thus occupied the shadows of visibility, waiting in the margins of the public spotlight.

Chapter Four

Herstories I | 1950s – 1960s

Second Cherry Blossom Queen Anna Tokumaru, 1954–1955

Anna Tokumaru stands erectly, moves gracefully, and speaks carefully. When she sits, her hands fold neatly in her lap and unfold only to gesture quietly. Hers is the story of a shy, young, reluctant Queen who never thought she was "pretty" enough — or "Japanese" enough — to run in the CBF pageant. Hers is also the story of a full-blooded Japanese American whose looks, height, and body shape appeared Eurasian, a source of consternation for her mother. Ironically, these very physical qualities made a big hit in Japan and elsewhere precisely because they were atypical. Here was a Queen who fit Japan's image of a Hawai'i/American-born Japanese.[1]

Anna's story paints a vivid picture of 1950s Hawai'i and the place of the CBF.[2] At the time, race was an abiding concern: Anna was criticized by Jaycees for bringing a Chinese American boyfriend to a public event. She talks about being aware of the haole domination of the professions in Hawai'i at the time, and the role of the HJJCC in helping change that imbalance. Class was another important issue. Her mother's main objection to her running in the CBF was that "good girls" did not do such things — that is, expose themselves to public scrutiny, especially in the form of a beauty contest. Anna frequently mentions the image of the *ojōsan* — an upper-class, refined, young Japanese woman — which she felt she was not. She also relates issues of class mobility, which for a woman at the time centered on marrying a professional. The Jaycees played their part in encouraging her to "marry up" as was befitting a CBF Queen by introducing her to college-bound potential suitors. They also encouraged Anna to attend college, but one senses that this was not so much for the sake of education, but to find a high-status husband. Anna's narrative also points up ways in which race and class intertwined: haole had money and clout.

Gender and class intersect in regulating roles for women during this period. Jaycees were up-and-coming professional men, many of them married; contestants were all unmarried young women. The possibility for sexual/romantic relationships between the two groups always existed. However, the HJJCC could scarcely afford scandal, so rules were put in place in later years against fraternizing between HJJCC members and CBF contestants. If contestants felt constrained by the CBF contest, the Queen felt even more straitjacketed by

Fig. 2. Second Cherry Blossom Queen Anna Tokumaru, 1954 – 1955

rules of public decorum. Anna talks about Jaycee members showing up at the nightclub where she was on a date and other kinds of policing of her behavior. Not all of their concern was restrictive, however. Anna also speaks of her close relationship with the Jaycee president and his wife, who acted as surrogate parents during her reign. As part of her queenly duties, Anna consorted with dignitaries, politicians, movie stars — in her words, "Dancing . . . , dancing . . . , dancing. . . ." As Queen, she played the role of the hostess, whose job was to smile, dance, and thus enhance relationships with men in power. With little authority of her own, Anna as CBF Queen thus acted as a liaison between different spheres of male influence.

Anna's narrative raises some issues common to beauty queens in general. One of them is that they often deny that they are the "beauty-contest type." This denial at once invokes the pervasiveness of the stereotyped beauty contest and queen, as well as distances the speaker from that image. I have been struck by the frequency with which CBF Queens of different decades deny their own typicality. Another issue is that of celebrity and living in the public spotlight. In Anna's case, the spotlight included harassment and critique, the impact of which has remained with her for over fifty years. Celebrity raises the public expectations placed upon queens. As the saying goes, "Once a beauty queen, always a beauty queen." Anna talks about living amid these public expectations, having to watch the way she dresses, presents herself, and even conducts some of her private life. One of Anna's strategies for coping with post-Queen life is to hide the fact that she was a CBF Queen from strangers.

I met Anna on December 17, 2001, outside her workplace at a public health center. She had recently moved back to Hawai'i after spending most of her adult life in the continental United States first as a model and later raising show dogs. At the time we spoke, she was engaged to be remarried and was brimming with excitement over the new life she had set before her.

AT: *I was eighteen! A high school student!*

CY: Eighteen. Now, how did a high school girl decide to run [for CBF]?

AT: *I didn't decide to run. What I did was, I was looking for a part-time job. I went to an employment agency, and the man helped me find a job at Ben Franklin department store in Kaimukī at that time. A while later, he called me and said, "You know, I really need your help. I need to sign up ten contestants for this Cherry Blossom contest." I said, "No, no, no, no, no! You know, I'm not pretty. I'm not a beauty contest type. If anything, I'm the exact opposite. I'm awkward, tomboy, the whole thing. My parents will kill me!" Because they're old Japanese style. Ladies don't do things like that. You know, good girls or ladies didn't do that. My parents believed that the only time a woman's name should be in the newspaper was when you're born, you're married, and you died. So I said, "Alright, I'll sign it, but I'm not going to participate, I'm not going to do anything." So he said, "You know, just as long as I have ten names." So I signed the paper, went to work.*

One day my boss called me into his office, and I thought I was going to get fired. And when I got into the office, there were three or four men from the [Japanese]

Chamber dressed in suits, sitting there looking like FBI people. I was frightened to death. Then they told me about signing up for the Cherry Blossom thing and I had not shown up for anything.... And they said, "Well, you know, there's talk that people are saying that you have the contest in the bag, and that's why you don't have to show up." I said, "No, that's hardly the case." I said I had not even mentioned it to my parents. They asked if I would like them to talk to my parents. And I thought, "No waaay!" However, by the time I got home from work, they had visited my parents. And my parents ... I could tell as soon as I got home, something was up. Both my parents said, "How could you do this, bring shame to our family?"

CY: Really?

AT: Yes! "Girls, ladies don't do things like this. They don't enter beauty contests. And they don't go into public or anything. Besides you know you're not pretty enough and you're going to lose and bring shame onto our family." So they didn't talk to me for weeks after that. And my mother talked to her older brother, who's a titular head of the family, and my uncle said, "Let her run. It's good for her. She's too shy and bashful now. It'll be good for her." And I said, "I want to drop out!" And they would not let me drop out.

[handwritten margin note: She didnt want to run, her parents didnt want her to run, her uncle convinced them all she should run.]

CY: Who wouldn't let you? Your family?

AT: My uncle. He gave the decision that it was good for me and I should stay in, so my mother listened to him, and then the whole family agreed. It [CBF] was a popularity contest at that point. You had to buy products and get so many points to apply to whatever girl they wanted to help. So all of my relatives started buying televisions, and my mother bought another television, and I got enough points to qualify for the semifinals, much to my chagrin. And here I was saying, "No, please don't." Once I appeared at a TV station for a Cherry Blossom interview and I was one day late. Here I came in a gown and I was one day late! I had such a mental block to the whole thing. We got into the semifinals and you had to get into a kimono, so all the girls went, and I just sat back and said, "Whatever's left over, just give me that one, I don't care." And when we went to get our gowns, I was the last one that picked a gown. I said, "I don't really care if it's the ugliest one. Give me the one that no one wants."

CY: So you were really reluctant?

AT: I was reluctant. I was afraid of the whole thing. I was afraid of embarrassing myself, my family. I was never considered a beauty. I was always a wallflower when I was in school, so I just thought I didn't have a chance. And as the finals got closer, I started getting anonymous calls saying, "Who do you think you are?" Just nasty things. "Who do you think you are? You're ugly. You shouldn't win." And then people calling and saying, "Oh, we know you're going to win." It was just horrible for an 18-year-old girl to go through those kinds of calls late at night. It *was just everything bad you could say to a girl who's self-conscious, who thought she was ugly. Really started affecting me negatively.*

On the night of the finals, we stood on a platform on the stage, five of us. After they announced, everyone walked off. My gown got caught on a nail, and everyone started walking off and I couldn't walk off. I didn't know what to do, so I just stood there. And then finally a reporter stood up and said, "Her gown's caught! Can't you see that? Somebody's got to help her." I thought, "Oooooh, this is really too much." If I could have melted into the platform, I would have. But . . . someone unhooked my gown and I walked off.

And then we had an interview and you had to come out in a kimono, and everyone had beautiful kimonos and here I was with the last one that no one wanted. And one of the girls, . . . she was the epitome of a Japanese ojōsan. Her kimono came from Japan. She had a beautiful kimono. She walked just like a princess, you know, with her head tilting and moving along, with the pigeon toe [graceful walk with feet turned in]. And here I came, zoom, zoom, zoom [walking quickly with large steps], and that was it. And I don't know whether she placed [in the Court] or not.

But at the end, there were two of us [finalists] backstage, and this girl was older than me. She was sophisticated and confident, and I thought, "Thank goodness, she's gonna win. You know, I have no chance. Please, let it be her." And I was very relieved to see her there. And then when they called her name [as first runner-up], I said, "Oh, but you go on." And she said, "No, I'm the runner-up. You walk [on stage as the Queen]." And all I could say was, "Oh no!" I literally cried, 'cause I thought, "I don't want this, I don't want this."

My mother came on stage, crying, and she said, "I'm so happy for my beautiful daughter!" And I thought, "Mom, how can you say something like that? I know you told me I'm ugly and too tall, no one's gonna marry me, I don't look Japanese. How can you say I'm beautiful now?" . . . After that, I had no real life of my own.

CY: You mean in that year that you were Queen?

AT: *Yes. I was gonna graduate and boys wanted to take me out to a nightclub. We didn't drink. But as soon as we got there, an hour later, somebody from the Chamber found out I was at a nightclub and had to tell the boy, "She has to leave." How embarrassing! After awhile, no one wanted to take me out, because I always had a chaperone.*

CY: That's terrible for a teenage girl. How did you survive?

AT: *I had a lot of guidance from the Chamber president and his wife. They really supported me and helped me along. They tried to give me confidence when I was a little afraid, keep me on a straight line, that type of thing. I think they understood where I was coming from — this shy, meek, inferiority complex kind of person. The only thing that saved me was that I was very good in speech. I used to enter speech contests, and because of that I was able to talk to people and give public speeches.*

It was interesting entertaining older people. Have to dance with everyone. Oh, it was just something! And then I think I was offered a movie contract from Daiei movie studios in Japan. And I didn't want to sign a contract because they would have required me to go to Japanese school. And I'd had a really trying year for me and I didn't want to do that. I didn't want to go to college. Everyone insisted I go to college so I could start at U.H. And then I didn't finish the year. I got married. I moved to the mainland and that ended that.

From what I understand, one of the reasons I was selected was that the people that sponsored it — the Japan Travel Bureau — and some of the other people wanted to have a Cherry Blossom Queen that looked more like a Hawai'i-type Japanese, rather than a Japanese Japanese. So I fit the bill. I didn't know that at the time.

CY: So they [the judges in Hawai'i] picked you because you were atypical?

AT: *Yes, yes. Atypical.*

CY: How tall are you?

AT: *Five [feet] five [inches].*

CY: So at five-five, that was pretty tall. And what else about you was atypical?

AT: *I wasn't flat-chested . . . I was skinny, but I was not flat-chested. I can remember that.*

CY: You mean somebody mentioned that to you?

AT: *A lot of people mentioned that. That was one of those crank calls that I got.*

CY: Oh really? What did they say to you?

AT: *They would say to me things like, I wasn't the prettiest girl. The only thing I had was a chest — or I filled out a bra, let's say. I was just terrified. I dreaded answering the phone. And it would always be later in the evening, after eight o'clock.*

CY: And it was a male voice?

AT: *No. Young women, older women, males, young boys, it ran the gamut. And after the semifinals, it got worse. The night before the finals, the calls were unbelievable.*

CY: Did the Jaycees know about this?

AT: *I told them about it, but there's nothing much they could do about it.*

CY: How did your parents react to these calls?

AT: *I didn't tell them about all of them. I mostly told the Chamber [HJJCC] about it. My father was kind of a shogun [Japanese military leader] father, old Japanese style, distant. My mother felt, "See, when you go into the public eye . . .*

that's what happens, that's what we told you about." So there wasn't much I could do about it.

But it's had a lasting effect on me. And what it's done is, I guard my privacy very carefully. Even now. I have an unlisted phone number, I don't give that number out to anyone. All my friends are told, if they want to remain my friends, they don't tell anyone about the Cherry Blossom [becoming Queen]. I just maintain that as a private part. I only tell people that I get to know. And after I get to know them, then we establish a relationship, it doesn't matter, I tell them. But I also tell them that I like to keep it private.

And I know that it's affected dating men here. It makes a difference. The men would say, "I've never gone out with a Cherry Blossom Queen," as if I'm different. I'm just a person. I want people to accept me as me, not as a Cherry Blossom Queen.

CY: So it still affects the way people look at you?

AT: *Mmm hmm. Yes. How they, not just look at me. How they respond to me. Especially single men. Especially, you know, instead of taking me somewhere that I like, they feel that they have to take me to some fancy place that I'm not necessarily keen on going. 'Cause one fellow I dated, I said, "Oh, you know, I haven't been to a lunch wagon [truck that sells meals and snacks] in so long. I'd like to go get a plate lunch." "Oh, I didn't know Cherry Blossom Queens like to go lunch wagons" [mimicking male companion].*

CY: So they sort of dangle it before you?

AT: *Yeah. They think that they have to be different with me, [rather] than just [being] themselves as a person.*

CY: That is amazing. I had no idea.

AT: *Even the older women that remember [the 1950s] and they know about the Cherry Blossom. They just seem to think that Cherry Blossom Queens should be something, what they think and their ideal, rather than accepting me for what I am.*

You know, after I came back [to Hawai'i], now, I'm not always dressed and all this makeup. I'd like to go around boroboro [dressed informally]. Some people would say, "Well, you're a Cherry Blossom Queen?" or "How come you're dressed like that?" Because I'm not the Cherry Blossom Queen twenty-four hours a day for the rest of my life. I am me. That's why I liked living on the mainland. I could just be myself. And even now I don't put makeup on all the time. . . .

There were a lot of girls I ran with who really wanted to become Queen. They were competitive. They took great care with their looks, their clothing, everything. And I really felt bad that the ones who wanted it the most didn't get it and here someone that wanted it the least, you know, got it. I did feel very bad for them. I also thought, "Maybe the Cherry Blossom people didn't get what they really thought they were gonna get, because I'm not an ojōsan."... But what they wanted was a non-Japanese looking... They wanted, quote, a "Hawai'i looking girl," whatever that is....

It was such a hard year for me. Such a hard year being out in the public light, almost all the time, meeting people constantly. It was draining. But I look back on it now and I would not have given that up for anything.

CY: Really?

AT: *Otherwise I still would have been self-conscious with an inferiority complex....*

CY: When you won in 1954, what kind of attitude was there toward Japanese Americans?

AT: *Right at that time it was starting to change because the war was over. And they had the GI Bill. Most of the 442nd people from here were going to college, and you could see that they were going to enter into the mainstream business.*

As I was growing up, there was still a prejudice against, I would say, in general, immigrants, and the whites controlled almost everything. And I could sense that being a person of yellow skin, you were a little bit less than a person with white skin. And even though I was eighteen years old, I could see that the people in power were whites and there were hardly any professionals that were not white.... So if you wanted to go to a good medical person or a good law person, you'd go to a white person, because they had the background, the connections, and the good school that the nonwhites did not have. I was very conscious of that.

When we moved into our neighborhood up St. Louis Heights [middle-class neighborhood in Honolulu], we were the second nonwhite people that moved into that community. It was all-white and my mother was always reminding me of that — that we shouldn't bring shame to the Japanese people because we were only the second nonwhites to move in here. And the other Japanese family was the sensei [teacher] who taught tea ceremony. And so, you know, it was always where you lived, how much money you had, who your friends were...

CY: And you married...?

AT: *I married a Caucasian and a Chinese. I've been married twice. My first husband was Chinese, which in that day you didn't do. In those days, a Japanese and a Chinese didn't mix. Especially the Cherry Blossom Queen didn't marry a Chinese. So that was a big thing at that time. And my parents always felt, they just said, we would have preferred you to marry a Japanese, but just be happy. So that was that.*

And my second husband was Caucasian. He was an architect. My parents said you should marry a professional. The Chamber [HJJCC] people thought I should marry a professional. So I always looked for a professional. I thought that was the key to happiness.

CY: You said that the Chamber people said that you should marry a professional.

AT: *Yeah. They would introduce me to, like, someone who was going to college, going to Harvard. It was very obvious what they were doing. It wasn't that they would say, "You have to marry such and such." It was much more subtle.*

CY: So they put you in contact with future professionals?

AT: *Yes, yes, yes. I went to an opening of a hotel and I brought as my escort the Chinese fellow that soon became my husband and they were a little bit shocked and tried not to be shocked. And someone said to me, "Is your escort Chinese or Japanese?" I said, "It's obvious he's Chinese." They said, "You know, doesn't it look kind of funny—the Japanese Cherry Blossom Queen brings a Chinese escort?" And I thought, you know, this is my private life. I realize I shouldn't have brought [a person of] that nationality to an opening of a public thing, and I won't do it again, but, it was a learning experience for me. The [racial] lines were still there. Very much drawn.*

CY: Were there ever instances in which Jaycees would date past Cherry Blossom Queens?

AT: *Oh, yes! Even in my year, there were several girls that were dating the Chamber people. Some were married, some were single. I don't know what their reasons were on both sides, but pretty obviously, there was some dating, at the least, if not romance going on. But don't forget that I was the wallflower. I was not skilled at being friendly and outward in those things, and nobody wanted me. Thank goodness. [Laughs]*

CY: During your year as Queen, what kinds of things did you have to do?

AT: *Oh, they were really not too much fun for an eighteen-year-old to do. [Chuckles] For example, I got to go to dinner and dance with many guests from Japan who were established businesspeople and well known in Japan. They were in their forties, maybe in their fifties. And I got to dance with them and dance with them and dance with them.*

I got to take the first Pan American Clipper ride through all the islands. We had breakfast in one island, lunch in another, and dinner in another. And it had a stairwell in the airplane. That was interesting for me.

I got to meet a lot of very kind and nice and helpful Junior Chamber officers. Of course at that time, they were all men. And their wives who took me under their wing. And of course, Mrs. Lillian Yajima, who was Senator's [Tad Yajima's] wife. And she worked so hard to do so much for the contest, including sewing and gluing chicken feathers to the coronation cloak. She was great fun! Even during the rehearsal. She got one of those whoopee cushions. [Chuckles] And she was so anxiously waiting to put it on a seat somewhere. Everyone was so serious about getting the timing right for the coronation. And all of a sudden, someone sat on the cushion and it went, BOOP! And that broke the ice and everyone started relaxing at that time. [Laughs]

I got to be an adopted child of Slim Nakata, who was [HJJCC] president, and his wife who I still keep in touch with every once in a while. She's a wonderful lady. And the Kometanis, they just were so nice. Robert Sato. A lot of these young roosters, as they called themselves, became community leaders and well known businessmen. And the Chamber did a lot to develop that part of the young Japanese. 'Cause remember, this was only ten years after the war then. And the Japanese were just starting to become a force in the community, just moving into the community. . . . So it was an emerging time, then.

CY: So do you see the Cherry Blossom Festival as part of that emergence?

AT: *Yes, I do. Very much so. Because as a group the men learned their leadership techniques. They were a support system to themselves in business and in their developing leadership skills. Their wives supported their husbands in community activities, thereby entering into the community itself. Not just as Japanese, but as a Japanese group in a mixed community.*

CY: Well, yours is an amazing story. Thank you so much, Anna.

AT: *Thank you. I'm so glad to have done this.*

Fifth Cherry Blossom Queen Carol Saikyo, 1957–1958

When I was growing up, the epitome of the Cherry Blossom Queen was Carol Saikyo. Physically, she was tall, fair, with big round eyes, a high-bridged nose, and dimples. She moved gracefully and spoke in a softly modulated voice, pronouncing her words clearly and distinctly. Socially, she married the son of a prominent Japanese American businessman. Carol's hair never looks mussed, even over four decades after her reign. In the 2000s she is a prominent member of the Japanese Women's Society and an active volunteer at Kuakini Hospital.

Carol's narrative points out several aspects of the CBF in the 1950s, including the important role of sponsors in supporting and assisting contestants. In feminist terms, sponsorship meant that contestants were beholden to yet another mediating group of men.[3] Community-based sponsors were primarily male-dominated organizations. Carol's story also illustrates the central role of the male gaze in the CBF. If part of the recruitment of contestants lay in the hands of Jaycee members, they had to be on a continual lookout for potential candidates. As recruiters, the gaze of Jaycee members was intense and constant. The CBF Queen pageant gave Jaycee members not only an excuse for gazing at young women, it also gave them the responsibility to do so. Gazing at women became part of fulfilling the goals of the Jaycee Creed: community service, citizenship, democracy, capitalism, and masculinity.

櫻まつり
6th ANNUAL
Cherry Blossom
FESTIVAL
1958 DIRECTORY
HONOLULU JAPANESE J.C.C.

Fig. 3. Fifth Cherry Blossom Queen Carol Saikyo, 1957 – 1958

Like Anna Tokumaru, Carol was still in high school when she was approached to run for the contest. Unlike Anna's parents, however, Carol's mother was a highly encouraging force. In fact, were it not for her mother's urging, Carol would probably not have entered. Carol's example demonstrates the frequent involvement of mothers in their daughters' participation in a beauty pageant.

The young age of some of the contestants provides justification for the involvement of families and protectiveness of Jaycees as quasi-families. And yet, the conservative role of the Jaycees was not individually decided, but structurally established in the form of rules and chaperones for all contestants. This suggests that it was women's gender and unmarried status that prompted the protectiveness, rather than strictly age.

Carol's story exemplifies the pitfalls and perquisites of life in the public eye. Like Anna, she was shy by nature. Being a beauty queen placed her under constant scrutiny. After one year of this kind of scrutiny, she wanted no more. However, that same public eye paved the way for her eventual marriage to a prominent businessman. Without the crown, the newspaper articles, and living in the public eye for a year, Carol might likely not have met or wed her husband.

I interviewed Carol at her home not far from the Wai'alae Country Club Golf Course. She answered the door dressed impeccably. Hers was the only house I visited where I was invited to leave my shoes on, rather than remove them at the door as is common in Hawai'i (and Japan). Her living room is elegantly decorated with accents of Japanese furniture and art objects. We sat there one late afternoon on December 18, 2001, where Carol served me coffee in bone china cups. She spoke so softly and in such modulated tones that I was afraid my microphone might not pick up her voice. In sum, she is very much the *ojōsan* of which Queen Anna Tokumaru spoke.

CY: So how and why did you decide to enter this contest?

CS: *Actually, I didn't really want to. It was my mom.*

[handwritten: mother wanted her to run, not her]

CY: Your mother?

CS: *Yes. We had several visits from the Japanese Junior Chamber, the Queen Search Committee people came by. I kept refusing, refusing, and finally my mother sat me down and she said, "Why not, just for the fun of it?"*

CY: Now how old were you at the time?

CS: *I was seventeen years old, but by the time the Festival came around, I was eighteen.*

CY: And what was it like to run for Cherry Blossom?

CS: *During those days, we had fourteen contestants, and they were all sponsored by community associations. The format was very different [from today]. You had to have an association represent you, sponsor you. So I was approached by the Kaimuki Community Association. We never lived in Kaimukī. And also the Kalihi Businessmen's Association. So when I decided to run, I felt that since we were living in the Kalihi area, that I should go with the association that I'm living in, so I did. My sponsor was the Kalihi Businessmen's Association.*

CY: Do you have any sense of why your mother wanted you to run?

CS: *During those days, [beauty] contests—it was a form of entertainment.... Now of course they have so many contests and so many other activities. I think this was something that the entire state sort of looked forward to. I don't know, I guess she just thought that it might be a great experience for me. But you know, I was very shy during those days. So I don't even know how I did it.*

CY: Was there any training that the Jaycees offered?

CS: *You know, very little, because in those days, we sort of had to do everything on our own. We had to get our own appearance dresses, we had to get our own kimonos, our own dressers [to help put on kimono]. I think we even had to hire our own person to show us how to walk with our kimonos. And also with our gowns, we had to do it all on our own. The sponsors defrayed the cost of some of our clothing. But that basically is it.*

CY: And how did you go about choosing a kimono?

CS: *I was raised in a very American-type family. And I had no opportunity to wear a kimono. So I think it really made me appreciate the Japanese culture after this. And as you can see [gesturing to her furnishings], I've been collecting Japanese things. I love things Japanese. And I think if not for the contest itself and also going to Japan, which was my first trip to Japan, I probably would not appreciate all of these things.*

CY: What was your reaction to being in Japan?

CS: *Well, it was my first experience. I loved it. Of course, Japan at that time and Japan today are so different. The people in Japan were very hospitable. To them, I guess, during those days, Hawaiʻi was a magic word. That was their dream to come to Hawaiʻi. That was postwar [period], and so many of them had never traveled outside of Japan. And so I was kind of a novelty, I guess. We got to go on various television shows and radio shows and went to a couple of the studios, met actors and actresses.*

CY: Were you considered an American? Were you considered a Japanese?

CS: *Yes, I was considered an American....*

CY: What would you say was your least favorite thing about being Cherry Blossom Queen?

CS: *Well, it was the fact that you no longer have any privacy. I don't know if it's the same today. But you know we were quite visible during those days, and it was always that you had to be on your best behavior because you're representing the Japanese community. I think I never had a period of time when I could just have fun. I was always having to be extremely careful.*

CY: What kinds of things did you feel you couldn't do as either a Queen or a former Queen?

CS: *Some of my girlfriends, the group I ran around with, they were very im-*

pulsive and very spontaneous, and so a lot of times when we were walking home from Roosevelt [High School] going to the bus stop or going to the YMCA for our meetings,[4] they would be singing their hearts out, and here I was, like, "I don't think I can do that." And so they used to get angry with me, you know, they'd say, "Carol, let down your hair and just yell!" And I said, "No, I can't do that." But that's the type of reaction where things were instilled in me that I shouldn't do. I had to be very ladylike, I guess. So I was very mature and very old at my young age. I was more like going on twenty-nine. I think I would have loved to just sing my heart out. And wear grubby clothes. And this is why today I find it very difficult to wear grubby clothes to go out shopping or just to the drugstore or to the market, because I . . . this is me. I mean, I'm always dressed in case I should meet somebody I know.

CY: Now, do you think that's a function of being a past Queen? Or would have that been there anyway?

CS: *Oh, I think it maybe is the upbringing from my mother. . . .*

CY: Did you ever consider running for other beauty contests?

CS: *No, that was it.*

CY: Why not?

CS: *I just didn't like living in a glass bubble. I kind of wanted my own privacy. I really wasn't interested in beauty contests. I was too busy being a student. I worked part-time, too. I worked for Aloha Airlines. First as a stewardess, then I went into reservations.*

CY: In all, how would you say that being the Queen might have changed you?

CS: *Well, I think it did, because it gave me more confidence. I was, as I said, a very shy person. I think I met my husband that way [through the CBF].*

CY: Was he a member of the Jaycees?

CS: *He was not, but he had seen my picture, one of those pictures that came out in the paper. He was in Germany at the time. After college he served two years in the service, and then went to grad school. But during that time, someone had sent him an article on me, the fact that I had won. He saw the picture. He didn't know me at the time, but when he came back, one of his classmates knew me, and so I went to some concert, I think it was the symphony, and we were eating at the same restaurant, and I met him that way. Didn't think anything of it. I guess maybe a couple of months later, we met again at a graduation, and that's when we started going together. I guess if he hadn't seen my picture in the paper, he probably would not have showed any signs of interest to this friend of his. . . . In all, I'm very glad I did it, because it opened up many doors, many opportunities for me. Perhaps my life would have been very different. I don't really know. So I look at it positively. It's made such a positive impact on my life.*

Vivian Honda is another classic Cherry Blossom Queen. Like Carol Saikyo, she is tall, fair, and photogenic. In photographs published in the CBF souvenir book, her smile is unmistakable: she is radiant as she poses newly crowned, as she dances the first dance with Governor John Burns, as she visits the temples of Kyoto, as she waves to the crowds lining the streets in Los Angeles as part of the motorcade for Nisei Week. Her smile lights up every scene.

In person, almost forty years later, the smile has not faded. Vivian graciously ushered me into her newly remodeled home in the luxurious neighborhood of Kāhala on January 25, 2002. We sat in her living room sipping iced tea. As with several of the Queens I spoke with, I could tell that she was a pro at being interviewed. Although she claims not to be a celebrity, she has always lived in the public spotlight of the Japanese American community in Hawai'i: as a daughter of one of its most prominent businessmen and civic leaders; as the Japanese Ka Palapala Queen; as Cherry Blossom Queen; as the wife of a well-known Japanese American dentist; and as a member of the Japanese Women's Society of Honolulu. So not only is Vivian extremely photogenic, her life is a series of snapshots of people's expectations of a Cherry Blossom Queen.

Vivian tells the tale of an insider to the CBF, because of her father's activities and her acquaintance with the first CBF Queen Violet Niimi. Her insider status did not necessarily give her an advantage—although there were those who claimed that was the case—but it did provide her with a certain amount of ease moving in these particular social circles. Vivian's story is one of social class maintenance, reproducing the advantages and perquisites of elite status. This takes nothing away from Vivian: it is easy to see why she won the title of Queen. The persistence of naysayers, however, shows the degree to which beauty contests attract critics and gossip-mongers who question the fairness of judging or express raw jealousy in late-night crank calls.

The job of the CBF Queen, according to Vivian, is to act as hostess. Her narrative is that of a disciplined woman, the consummate Queen who takes hospitality seriously. The role asks women to bridge (men's) groups, providing social lubricant to smooth transactions and help establish, maintain, even advance positive relations. The role often requires that the actor become expert in emotion management (Hochschild 1983), regulating the expression of inner feelings to enhance a performative outer self. Within this context, power—at least publicly recognized forms of public power—resides within those groups she mediates, not in its interstices or in its hostesses. And yet the role borrows idioms of power by mixing this stage queen with actual heads of state, emperors and empresses, and government officials.

Fig. 4. Twelfth Cherry Blossom Queen Vivian Honda, 1964–1965

As was true of most CBF Queens that I spoke with, Vivian never went on to any other beauty contest. The CBF does not typically act as a springboard for further involvement in mainstream beauty contests such as Miss Hawaii, whose winner then competes in the Miss America scholarship pageant. The CBF rewards different, some would say less demanding, components than contests such as Miss Hawaii (or Miss America): rather than curves and legginess, it requires only a modestly proportioned body; rather than performative talents such as singing and dancing, it requires only that one walk gracefully, smile amiably, and speak diplomatically. The CBF rewards graciousness more than flash, crowning the "nice girl" who is humble and modest rather than abrasive, self-promoting, or overly ambitious.

This definition of femininity fits in neatly with the model minority image of Japanese Americans as quiet, diligent, and hardworking. In this way the CBF Queen is an important symbol of and metaphor for the Japanese American community. The model minority "nice girl" Queen plays a critical role for Japanese Americans in Hawai'i by performing racially based, culturally aestheticized, gendered graciousness. Vivian's smile speaks directly to this graciousness.

CY: How and why did you decide to enter the [CBF] contest?

VH: *In the 1950s and 1960s I knew of Violet Niimi [first CBF Queen], because she was very, very close friends with my older sister, who is twelve years older than I am. And I saw this thing [CBF] start with all my father's friends in the Jaycees. During that period, the community was very tight. And this Cherry Blossom Festival was a huge community event, with the lantern parade through Kalākaua Street [Waikīkī]. We had all kinds of events to participate in. It was really huge. And it was very special. And so when they [HJJCC] did come to ask me if I would run, I was very honored actually, to be selected. Why did I run? I guess because I thought it would be a personal challenge, a personal thing I could do to see what I could do, what I could get out of it.*

CY: Was it the kind of thing where when you were growing up, people would tell you, "Vivian, when you get older, you're going to become the next Cherry Blossom Queen"?

VH: *Maybe later on in high school. But not in the beginning. Because actually I might have been about six. I remember going to the first one. I remember it vividly.*

CY: Really? The very first one? When Violet Niimi became Queen?

VH: *I remember because she was the first. My father was active, it was my sister's friend, my family went, and I knew who she was. And in those days even for the president [of the HJJCC] to give them a lei and kiss them . . . I remember them being very embarrassed. His name was Slim Nakata, the first [HJJCC] president that year. I remember that.*

CY: And you remember him?

VH: *Because he was also a family friend and my father had introduced him to his wife. . . .*

CY: What was your reaction to being Queen during that year?

VH: ~~I was overwhelmed at first.~~ *I was very much on a high at first. And then, I think I really wanted to take it seriously and I did. And maybe some people thought, "She shouldn't take it so seriously." But I felt that if you run, and you accept the crown and the position, then you're there for a purpose, and to me it just was so natural to say, "Yes, I'll be able to help." So whatever they asked me to do, if I could, I would do it.*

CY: In your mind, what was the function, in your day, of the Cherry Blossom Queen?

VH: *I think I watched some Queens before me and some were very cooperative and they really attended the functions, although maybe you had many functions, you didn't know a soul. But there are two ways you can do it. If you're there, be there, mentally. You're sort of their hostess for the year. You're mistress of ceremony or hostess to say hello to everybody, ambassador of goodwill. But there were some [CBF Queens] that I notice, you could tell when they were bored. Even those that had the right frame of mind, they also had more discipline, self-discipline. 'Cause when there are people you admire, the little girls are watching them, right? And those that are gracious, when they're very gracious and they show it to each person, I thought that says a lot about the person. And I thought, "Ah, I have to keep that in mind" as something, not only for the Cherry Blossom Festival, but participating in any event. . . .*

CY: Did you ever think of running for Miss Hawaii or any of the other beauty pageants?

VH: *No, it never entered my mind. I really felt like I had done what I wanted to do and it's not my ambition to go on in that area. No, I wanted a normal life. I'm a really boring kind of person because I really like to stay in one place. I like to see my friends. I like to come home every day.*

CY: Do you feel that having that title of Queen gave you any kind of power?

VH: *No, no power whatsoever. It was the first week after the pageant, I was walking around Ala Moana Shopping Center, and that's when I realized that I did have a responsibility. Because I'd be eating an ice cream cone, and I'd see two ladies say, "That's her. She's the Cherry Blossom Queen." 'Cause it was a bigger thing then. And there were a lot of Japanese. So I said, "Wow!"*

People perceive me as being very feminine, and probably thought I took odori [Japanese dance] and all of these ikebana [Japanese flower-arranging] classes, but I wasn't. I was more of a . . . not so much a tomboy, but a free spirit. If you got to know me well, I was, you know . . . I was a klutz. So, I said, "Gee, I probably would have ice cream here," then I said, "Okay, throw it away." And then I'd be happier. So that's the first thing I learned, it comes with the territory. Either you make up your mind to be who you are or you come in-between, you compromise in-between, from being yourself, or being somebody you're not, ~~or you can come~~ ~~*in-between for that one year.*~~

CY: And your solution?

VH: *That's the only solution I think that I was comfortable with.*

CY: To come in-between?

VH: *Right. In other words, I knew what the consequences were for my behavior and there was no one else to blame but myself. If I wanted good feedback, I could, for one year, I think I could do a job and just concentrate on that.*

Fifteenth Cherry Blossom Queen Gwen Nishizawa, 1967–1968

Gwen Nishizawa has a way of walking into a room and making it brighter. It's not so much her dimples, but her eyes and the way she uses them to draw you into her sphere. She engages you by convincing you that you are important. It's a wonderful gift and skill that can only come about because she herself has the kind of confidence that does not require self-promotion. Therefore, she can be and is entirely generous with her warmth.

I met Gwen for the first time on January 31, 2002, at one of the many Starbucks that dot Honolulu. She was between appointments for the consulting firm that she owns and operates. The rapport we established was immediate and continuing, not just because of the interesting stories Gwen had to tell about the CBF, but because of the sincerity and depth with which she spoke. This gift for connecting with people is one that apparently Gwen had early on, judging by the "love letter" that was written to her by a Jaycee member and published in the organization's newsletter (quoted in Chapter 3).

Gwen's crowning is noteworthy for several reasons. ~~She was the first Queen of Okinawan ancestry, one of the few non-Honolulu contestants to win, one of the few blue-collar Queens, and one of the few who was not a student at the University of Hawai'i at the time of crowning~~ (although she was a student earlier and received the help of her sorority sisters). She wears these distinctions proudly, transforming the crown into a badge of effort and luck. According to her, it's not that she was particularly determined to win, but more that given the odds, she was astonished to walk away with the crown. She attributes her winning in part to her confidence—not in victory, but in herself.

Of these various distinctions, the one that Gwen keeps coming back to is the fact that she is, in her words, a "country girl" from Kāne'ohe. Kāne'ohe is a town on the other side of the Ko'olau mountain range from Honolulu on O'ahu; although by the 2000s it has grown into a suburb of Honolulu, at the time of Gwen's crowning, it was considered rural and distant. This kind of place-based identity speaks to the metropolitan (here, Honolulu-centric) na-

16th Annual
CHERRY
BLOSSOM
FESTIVAL

1968 DIRECTORY HONOLULU JAPANESE JUNIOR CHAMBER OF COMMERCE

Fig. 5. Fifteenth Cherry Blossom Queen Gwen Nishizawa, 1967 – 1968

ture of the pageant, as well as more broadly the degree to which Hawai'i by
the late 1960s was dominated by a single urban center. Even on O'ahu, people
from more rural areas felt somewhat left out of the spotlight of the CBF and
other large-scale public events. This kind of peripheral sense was even stronger
on neighbor islands. The fact that Gwen's victory was perceived as a victory for
Kāne'ohe by people of various ethnicities demonstrates the degree to which the

CBF had grown beyond its racial/ethnic boundaries. To people in Kāneʻohe, the CBF was more a Honolulu event than a Japanese American one.

Gwen's victory as the first CBF Queen of Okinawan ancestry is sometimes masked by her Naichi surname. It had taken the HJJCC fifteen years to crown a woman of Okinawan ancestry as their representative, but they did so only obliquely, selecting a Queen who easily "passed" as Naichi. Although many people failed to realize she was of Okinawan ancestry, she made Cherry Blossom history when she traveled to Okinawa as Queen at her own expense (HJJCC 1968:52–64). She also talked about Okinawa in her final speech as Queen. Okinawa thus became a public text, ending years of silence in the CBF.

Gwen raises class issues by describing her family as blue-collar and pointing out that she was not a university student at the time of the contest. She was not necessarily the first blue-collar CBF Queen, but she echoes the widely held perception that this was a contest for *ojōsan*. Perhaps because Gwen comes from a blue-collar background, she is more acutely aware of the bad mix of a Cherry Blossom Queen who works as a cocktail waitress.

The lessons of holding the title of CBF Queen extend in many directions. Gwen has chosen to take one central aspect — self-presentation — and propel that into a career. She herself uses that skill to great advantage, making any person she speaks with feel at ease. In this sense, she is one of the most "queenly" persons I have met by the generosity of her gifts. That very "queenliness" runs tandem with selective Japanese cultural constructions of femininity, not in the sense of being meek and mild, but by showing great empathy.

CY: So how did you get involved in Cherry Blossom?

GN: *Well, how I got involved is actually through my sorority. Those days the sororities were really big and they supported and helped train the girls, and so they were like the cheering section. I was with Beta Beta Gamma. So actually the sorority asked me to go ahead and give it a try. And in these days the guys [Jaycees] came to your house and you know it was like asking your hand in marriage. It was really hilarious when I think back on how it was done. They'd come to the house and they'd sit with you and your parents and they'd explain the whole thing, and "Would it be okay?" and, "We'll take good care of her." And there's an advisor and you're chaperoned and all this stuff. So basically I did it because I just thought it would be something new and different. Never ever thinking I would win. Because of my background, because of my family being blue-collar, being a country girl, those days...*

CY: Country girl? Where were you, growing up?

GN: *Kāneʻohe. In those days, it was big news when I won. Nobody from the country had won before, so if you remember, I was the fifteenth [CBF Queen], so there were only fourteen before me. And they were all either doctors' daughters or very prominent businessmen's daughters, mostly from Honolulu, too. So it was like, "You don't have much of a chance, but you can try," is how I thought, and my friends and my family. I'm sure in my mother's mind, her being Okinawan probably more so, thought, although at that time we never talked about the difference between Japanese and Okinawan or any kind of prejudice or anything like this. But now I'm looking back, I think in her mind she probably never dreamed I would, that I could make it, that I would win.*

CY: She thought that you don't really have a chance?

GN: *Not because of how I looked or anything like that. It was more where I was coming from, blue-collar background. My father was assistant in a kitchen. My mom, I think at the time, I don't know, she was a seamstress at that time or she was still taking in laundry, so we were not of a higher upper class, and when you look at the ones who won before me, they were. So it was very intimidating. So then my mom and dad, actually my mom especially, wondered whether this is something I should do. But if I really wanted to, then of course, she wasn't gonna hold me back. And at that time I felt, well, my sorority sisters were backing me, and they're gonna help me and it sounded like fun.*

CY: What did they do to help you?

GN: *Oh, gosh, we had real training sessions.*

CY: You and your sorority sisters.

GN: *Oh, we had these meetings and we learned to walk and how to smile. We learned those things formally at the Chamber [CBF training] with the modeling person. But it was much more intense with the sorority girls. It's hilarious when I think about it. Oh they were like, okay, walk with a book on your head, ... do the crossover, then [they] asked us questions so that we could practice answering questions. It was really fun, actually, that was the fun part because we got together ... So then the night [of the pageant] came [and] you got this huge cheering section. That's the thing that was also very different I think from today. ... And when you won, you would be on the front page. 'Cause I remember one of the front-page articles said 5,000 watched the Cherry Blossom contest. I mean, thousands of people would go. It was really huge. And then it had the long Miss America ramp and the whole nine yards, the coronation ball. You'd be in the society section. And in those days, the high society section was the front page. And the whole thing was on you.*

CY: How did you feel with your picture on the front page and all of that?

GN: *It was, when I think back, kind of surreal. "That's me? Wow." When you look back at the notable people. See, at the time, I didn't really know who all these people were ... It was just fun and I go out, and I think about it, and there I* am! . . . Same as dancing with the mayor, you know, Mayor Blaisdell, and being crowned by Governor Burns, you know, when you look back you think, what an awesome experience that was!

CY: Can you tell me something about your trip to Japan as Queen?

GN: *That was just incredible, that really was. I mean, here I was, a small-town girl. I remember when I was in Japan I was just so taken by the tall buildings, the subways, and the trains. I was taken by how absolutely pleasant, sweet, and kind everyone was. I just loved the atmosphere in the city, because here I was from Kāneʻohe, Hawaiʻi, small town. I wanted to be in this big city, I wanted to ride a train, I wanted to have the experience of going from one point to another on the train.*

And the other part of it was going to Okinawa for the first time. That was really an experience for me to visit actual blood relatives and people who looked like my grandmother who died when I was six. And they were so poor then, even in 1967 they were still very poor. And I remember being so taken by their home and the way they lived. I remember my old uncle sitting on this floor with this fly buzzing around. And it just didn't bother him at all because that was how he lived.

CY: Can you tell me something about the sort of connection that you made to Japan with this?

GN: *Well, I met some people, you meet a lot of people at banquets and so forth, and I was able to connect with a nice family, a gentleman who worked for Dentsu [largest advertising agency in the world] and he agreed to be my sponsor in Tokyo. So we stayed in touch, corresponded, I worked, I saved $700, I bought a one-way ticket.*

CY: A one-way ticket! You were brave.

GN: *I was brave. I had no other money. I went and managed to get back. Did the same thing to the mainland, did a one-way ticket to San Francisco and $200. I ended up going to San Francisco and living there for five years.*

CY: Doing what kinds of things?

GN: *Oh, different things. First, you'd love this story, I'll never forget this one. Okay, I had no job. Only $200. The only other person I knew was the guy who owned Yamato's restaurant on Grant Avenue in San Francisco. So I went over to say hi to Joe. This is my second day there. I go there and he says, "Oh, you can wear kimono, can't you?" I say, "Yeah." He said, his cocktail waitress had just eloped the night before and he had absolutely nobody to work that night, and he says, "You need work, you have a job." And I say, "No, I don't have a job." So for the first three months I worked from 5 p.m. till 10:30, wore a kimono, served cocktails. But I was so ashamed and I was so, like, "I'm a Cherry Blossom Queen and a cocktail waitress!" I thought, this is really going to be embarrassing, so I didn't tell anybody at home that this is what I was doing. But I won't forget this one night when there* *was this gentleman who was from Hawai'i and he recognized me and I'll never forget how I was carrying a tray full of beer and all this stuff, and he said, "What's a Cherry Blossom Queen doing as a cocktail waitress?" And I tripped over something, dropped everything, splattered the beer! I was so embarrassed!*

CY: Now did you ever get back to Japan?

GN: *I did. And I look forward to going this year in May, actually.*

CY: And will you be going to Okinawa?

GN: *Oh yeah, absolutely. I wouldn't go without going to Okinawa. Very much so. Because you know since that time the whole Okinawan identity and all of that, Okinawa pride, all of that stuff started to come up [in Hawai'i], yet I have not had the opportunity to go back since that time. And I think part of this whole being Queen and everything, I felt very humbled by it, from the fact that God had let me be the winner, you know . . .*

It was time for me to give back, and the only way I could think of was like I joined Japanese Women's Society. So I become as far as an officer for that organization, and that was sort of my way. And the same way, I joined an Okinawan women's group, there's a club for Okinawan women. So I wanted to give back to that heritage as well. Then I joined the Sons and Daughters of 442nd because that was my father's side. So in my fifties, yeah, I thought, now is the time, yeah, I should do it. So that's why I become involved in those groups. Because the idea of giving back never left me, although it's taken this long. Better late than never. It's part of what the culture is too, though, isn't it? Once you start to feel an obligation or feel . . . there's true obligation to give back and to feel real sincere gratitude for what's given to you. I really think it's a cultural thing. I mean maybe in some respects I maybe thought I didn't deserve to be a leader.

CY: You think so?

GN: *Yeah, even if I worked hard, smiling or practicing looking good, my walk, where to put my head and all this stuff, I really . . . I think at that time, and still till today, because there's a lot of insecurities and so, about maybe even being able to do something to give back. Because I was so lucky. It's that feeling. Funny now. . . . But you're really caught between the two cultures, being American, wanting to be very American, and yet you're also Japanese. I think I struggled with that right after being Queen.*

CY: Really? In what way was it a struggle?

GN: *I did. Oh the 1960s was the hippies, right. Long hair and all this stuff. To my mom, that's not a good thing, to grow your hair and wear jeans. And so, but I wanted to, so that was part of who I am, too. I identified with that and I liked rock music, I didn't get into the drugs and pot and stuff, or anything like that, but I did want to have long hair. So after being Cherry Blossom Queen, after living away the whole year was like my first time to grow my hair out, because my mom always wanted me to have short hair. But the time 1970 was around, I had long hair straight down to my back and I remember that one time, my hair had gotten long, and I'd gone back to school, my mom used to scold me all the time because I'd wear jeans with the fringed edges and t-shirts. And I used to wear these dark glasses, because I didn't want anyone to know that I was the former Queen, because Queens always wear their hair up in a bun or really nice and dressed well.*

CY: Even when they're not on stage.

GN: *Oh yeah. . . . I still loved the culture and I still honored it, and I wanted to eventually go back to Japan, but I didn't want to be that Japanese Queen. So I came back with the hair parted in the middle, long, straight. My mom scolded me all the time about it. So actually, that's probably what drove me to want to go to the mainland. I needed to get away from all of that. . . .*

CY: When you were Queen and visiting Japan, did anyone comment that you were Okinawan?

GN: *No. I don't think that whole time anyone really said anything. The first I really thought of it was that article that was sent to me by somebody that was in the* Pacific Press *[Okinawan newspaper in Hawai'i].*

CY: When you signed up as a contestant, did the Jaycees check, are you Okinawan? I mean they wouldn't know by your name.

GN: *They wouldn't have known by my name.*

CY: Not that you were hiding anything. I mean, you did go to Okinawa and visit relatives.

GN: *And in fact I think I was very proud of that by the time I came home, that my speech, you know when you give a speech, when you're all done being Queen, I had a standing ovation and people said it just moved them to tears. When I think back now, I think that was pretty brave to do. But I didn't feel the prejudice, or I didn't feel that, so I just wanted to speak from my heart and say how grateful I was for the whole experience. You know, I didn't think that I had much of a chance of winning. You know, my dad being a blue-collar worker, and being a country girl and also I wasn't a student at that time, at that time I dropped out of UH. I was working, I was a secretary, so more so. In those days, they thought a lot of these kinds of contests were fixed one way or another. Because it seemed like it was always the high society's daughter that would win, you know. . . . Those days that's what they thought. So that's why more so, my opinion, I didn't think I had a chance. . . . There were some really fabulous girls that I thought would have made the final, that didn't. . . .*

CY: Well, I can understand why you won. It's a wonderful story you have.

GN: *[Pause]. . . It was like, maybe five, six, seven, eight years ago, I could be in a grocery store or I could . . . I remember one time, leaving Davies Pacific Center [downtown Honolulu] in a parking garage, ready to pay the attendant, and she [attendant] says, "You, you're the Queen, aren't you?" I mean, I looked at this Hawaiian lady, and she'd gone to Castle High School [in Kāneʻohe] with me, you know. But you see, in that time [late 1960s], they were so proud. All of Kāneʻohe knew! The Kāneʻohe taxi driver came with an orchid plant. Those days there was no bus, right? So you took taxi to town, one dollar taxis. And Sam's taxi, he came with . . . my mom still has that orchid plant. I mean this is how the community in Kāneʻohe was just so thrilled, so proud, this country girl won this contest. But anywhere I would go, if I met somebody from my generation, no matter what, they would stop to make a note about that, they tell you, or they tell their child, "You know this gal, she was Cherry Blossom Queen, you know."*

CY: And so you get it even today.

GN: *Oh yeah, even till today. Even today. Even today.*

Chapter Five

Struggles toward Reform |
1970s – 1990s 30 P9

The Cherry Blossom Festival, while currently in
its 33rd season, is poorly attended by Hawaii's
Japanese-American population and is primarily
attended by friends and family of the queen
contestants, the Issei and older Nisei. The festival,
which still has the distinction of being the only
ethnic pageant that requires contestants to be of a
pure ethnic bloodline, has had problems in recent
years attracting a large number of applicants.
(HJJCC 1985:69)

W
ith the exception of the passage quoted above, the slowly mounting struggles of the CBF from the 1970s on are fairly invisible to a peruser of its souvenir books. One has to read between the lines of the smiling faces and glowing words that fill the pages of these books every year. They typically paint a picture of the Festival proceeding unabated, filled with activities, crowning "nice girl" Queens, staunchly supported by the praise of politicians and community members. One does not see the increasing number of activities in urban Honolulu that splinter the potential audience for the CBF or, more important, get a sense of the public's waning interest in the event. In contrast to the 1950s and 1960s, when the question often arose as to what to perform in the balancing act between Japanese and American cultural identities, the struggles from the 1970s on lay in finding people to watch the performance itself.

Besides lack of audience, the CBF must be contextualized within the political and cultural turmoil of the 1970s in Hawai'i as elsewhere. Vietnam War protests, feminism, the Hawaiian "renaissance" of music and dance leading to the sovereignty movement, and birth of local consciousness as a pan-ethnic source of identity and pride all had repercussions as a context within which the Festival could be seen as a conservative locus, out of touch with the social changes surrounding it. This was also a period of rising backlash specifically against the continuing politico-economic success of Japanese Americans in Hawai'i from the 1950s and 1960s (Kotani 1985:174 – 177). To many people, it seemed that everywhere you turned, there was a Japanese American holding high political office, including state senators and representatives, congressmen and congresswomen, and governor. Japanese Americans also occupied governmental bureaucracies, businesses, and educational and professional positions. The middle-class attainment of the 1950s and 1960s — in other words, success in achieving the American dream — was couched within what was perceived to be clannishness. That attainment was thought to have come at the expense of other ethnic groups, fueling widespread resentment in the 1970s through the 1990s.

The CBF souvenir books show little direct evidence of these events and conditions. The main reason is that a celebratory document such as a souvenir book is far more likely to paint the rosiest of pictures rather than expose the

Festival's problems. Another important reason, however, lies in the fact that the people involved in something like the CBF — that is, the HJJCC members and Queen contestants — tend toward political conservatism, rather than liberal radicalism. In general, they are businessmen, not war protesters, and future secretaries, school teachers, and wives, not bra-burning feminists.

One does see a generational change. By the 1970s and beyond, those in charge of the HJJCC were sansei and then yonsei (fourth-generation Japanese Americans), not the nisei of the 1950s and 1960s. With the shift to sansei and yonsei leadership, combined with membership that by the 1960s included non-Japanese, ties to Japan became less personal and more remote. The generational shift included the passing of issei as an audience for the annual Festival. Ironically, while this shift was occurring, formal institutional ties to Japan were becoming stronger through the establishment of international sister chapters of Jaycees.

In 1984, the Jaycees nationwide, including the HJJCC, opened their doors to women. It took six years for a woman to become president of the organization (Phyllis Yuen in 1990), and eight years for a woman to chair its most public event, the CBF (Lenny Yajima in 1992; see Chapter 6). Although Jaycee members themselves say that the inclusion of women in the organization altered the social dynamic of meetings and activities, the CBF as a public event hardly changed at all.

This chapter takes a sweeping look at the CBF from the 1970s through the late 1990s as a civic event developing its own longstanding traditions. At the same time, it is an event increasingly dealing with the struggles of staying afloat in an ethnic community itself battling the apathy of changing generations and diminishing cohesiveness. Part of this struggle may be viewed as fluctuations between elements of conservatism and progressivism — not as ideological approaches, but as compensatory mechanisms that organizers hatched, one after another, in an attempt to recapture the public attention they once enjoyed. Within this context, I look at the increasing talk of including mixed-race contestants as a means of revitalizing an event that had become less and less relevant to many people's lives. This chapter examines the development and complexity of the CBF, but also the increasing sociocultural warp between the Festival and its milieu, and thus a progressive shift to banality.

Change and its Nemesis in the CBF

The structure of the HJJCC as the organizing body of the CBF invites change. Officers and committee members shift yearly in order to rotate the responsibilities and training of leadership positions. After reaching the age limit of thirty-nine, members must leave the organization; some join the senior Japanese Chamber of Commerce. In theory, this annual turnover of positions, responsibilities, and membership provides a ready avenue for innovation. However, in practice, far more stays the same than changes yearly.

One of the reasons for not changing is inertia: it is far easier to do what has been done in the past than to innovate. Other reasons for nonchange lie in the general conservatism of the Japanese American community, as well as the generational splits that both instigated the formation of the HJJCC (issei versus nisei) and continued, though differently, in the practices of the CBF in the 1970s through 1990s (nisei versus sansei and yonsei). In the 1950s and 1960s, nisei were both intent upon performing their American identities through the CBF, as well as tied to tradition by the watchful eye of issei. Even as issei declined in numbers in the 1970s and 1980s, virtually disappearing by the 1990s, a concern to preserve tradition guided much of the planning of the CBF. The CBF performed a conservative, rather than innovative, function for the community, looking toward Japan as a source of culture and identity. Even as organizers understood the need to develop and retain a broad appeal to the general public, including younger generations of Japanese Americans, this conservatism ran deeply as an assumption of the Festival. The resulting ambivalence played itself out in the CBF: whereas in the 1950s and 1960s, the balancing act was between American and Japanese elements, in the 1970s through the 1990s, the pendulum swung between orienting toward the past and the present/future, between tradition and change, between conservative and progressive bearings.

One may examine some of the pendulum swings between conservative and progressive approaches to the CBF through featured themes of the Festival — a practice that started in 1985. Below I list these themes with my characterization of them as conservative (focused on the past), progressive (focused on the future), or mixed (combining past and future):

1985	Cherry Blossom ... A 100-Year Experience	CONSERVATIVE
1986	The Next Hundred Years: A New Generation	PROGRESSIVE
1987	The Next Generation — Today's Dreams; Tomorrow's Reality	PROGRESSIVE
1988	[no theme]	
1989	Sansei — Bridging the Future	PROGRESSIVE
1990	Pride in Our Heritage	CONSERVATIVE
1991	Commitment to Traditions	CONSERVATIVE
1992	For the Sake of the Children	MIXED
1993	Strength through Cultural Diversity	PROGRESSIVE
1994	Enriching Our Community	MIXED

1995	Celebrating Our Heritage	CONSERVATIVE
1996	Building a New Era	PROGRESSIVE
1997	A Vision for Our Future	PROGRESSIVE
1998	Sharing Our Pride	CONSERVATIVE

The 1985 theme was necessarily retrospective in coordination with the centennial celebration of Japanese contract immigration to Hawai'i (begun in 1885). Subsequent themes in 1986 and 1987 look to the future, followed by a 1989 theme dedicated to sansei as the leaders for the present and future. These form one pendulum swing of progressive themes in the mid- to late 1980s. In the early 1990s, however, the pendulum swung the other way, with twinned themes in 1990 and 1991 focused on the past. The 1993 theme "Strength through Cultural Diversity" demonstrates a remarkably progressive outlook for a Festival that is originally Japanese (American) in content. The theme of cultural diversity fully embraces multiculturalism and the reality of a mixed-race yonsei generation. The rest of the 1990s themes discussed here shift between conservative (1995, 1998) and progressive (1996, 1997) approaches. The yearly shifts, especially through the late 1990s, demonstrate a deep ambivalence on the part of yonsei organizers as they attempt to reinvent the CBF to more closely tie in with their own lives.

Becoming Japanese: Cultural Training
for Organizers and Contestants

Among the conservative elements of the CBF in the 1970s through the 1990s was the presentation of Japanese, not Japanese American, culture as a source of heritage and tradition. Several factors complicated the relationship of Japanese Americans in Hawai'i to Japan during this period. First, an entire generation's distance eased the lingering racial and political tensions of World War II and the postwar years of the 1950s. Second, Japan's meteoric rise to international economic prominence and the aggressiveness of Japanese investors in commercial real estate in Hawai'i during Japan's "bubble economy" of the 1980s instigated considerable anti-Japanese sentiment in Hawai'i. The relationship of Japanese Americans to Japanese national investment in Hawai'i was mixed and ambivalent: on the one hand, a handful of Japanese Americans played an instrumental role in key business transactions; on the other hand, many more joined other locals in their resentment, distancing themselves from this new breed of brash, economically successful Japanese nationals. Third, in conjunction with the anti-Japanese sentiment toward high-profile investors was a mixed reaction to the influx of Japanese tourists to Hawai'i. Waikīkī began to resemble a Japanese colony, with hotels owned by Japanese investors occupied by Japanese tourists on package tours, reading storefront signs written in Japanese. Of course, these Japanese tourists contributed to the local economy tremendously; yet, they were easily ridiculed and regarded with a certain measure of disdain. As local stores gave way to high-end designer stores geared to affluent Japanese tourists, residents of Hawai'i began to feel disenfranchised from parts of their own city. Fourth, at the same time as the Japanese economy was rising to take its place alongside that of the United States, Japanese Americans were becoming more generationally distant from Japan. By the 1980s and 1990s, Japanese American and nonethnic Japanese organizers increasingly shared similar cultural distance from Japan.

CBF souvenir books often featured articles on aspects of Japanese culture written by experts in the field, bestowing prestige to the event and legitimizing links to Japan, but inadvertently demonstrating the distance of those links. These articles attest not to everyday, personal knowledge of the topics, especially by members of the HJJCC, but to esoteric, academic learning of scholars. In contrast with the 1950s and 1960s, when the CBF relied on members and their wives to put on a show of Japanese culture, in the 1970s and beyond, the expertise lay outside the hands of the Jaycees.

Besides the Japanese culture presented in souvenir books and as part of events of the CBF, Queens themselves spoke of their connection to Japan gained through the experiences of their reign. For example, Queen Rae Tanaka (1972 – 1973) wrote:

> In such a short time I developed and became acutely aware of my Japanese heritage after being directly involved with so many activities that dealt with the Japanese culture. Prior to this time, I was constantly exposed to the many and varied cultural aspects of Japan because of my parents' interest, knowledge, and background, but by being an active participant in the festival, my own interest was enhanced and reinforced. (Tanaka 1973:31)

Her recollections of self-discovery and interest in Japan are not unique. Queen LeAnne Higa (1979 – 1980) recalled of her trip, "I am so honored to have been in the presence of my natural heritage and ancestral country" (Higa 1980:33). Likewise, Queen Lisa Nakahodo (1984 – 1985) wrote, "I am thankful for the fact that the HJJCC and its CBF has brought me closer to what I had taken for granted all this time — my Japanese heritage" (Nakahodo 1985:17). What these Queens express is a "natural" connection to Japanese culture based in blood but only realized through the activities of the CBF. This holds true particularly — and ironically — for those women who become CBF Queen, a position publicly upheld as an exemplar (and, some might assume, expert) of Japanese culture.

HJJCC organizers express some of the same sentiment. For example, 1980 General CBF Chairman Dennis Oshiro proclaimed:

> This year, as in the previous years, our main purpose in presenting the festival is to promote a better understanding and appreciation of the Japanese people and culture. Through participation in the various events, our members become very much aware of their heritage. (Oshiro 1980:13)

In other words, Jaycee organizers teach the public about Japanese culture while learning it themselves. The question arises: what about members who are not of Japanese descent? This includes those of Okinawan ancestry, who may choose to claim cultural differences from Naichi Japan, as well as Jaycee members of other ethnicities. What kind of relationship do these nonethnically Japanese leaders have to the Japanese culture presented in the CBF? Are their relationships and experiences different in any way from those organizers of Japanese blood? These questions get to the heart of arguments for and against blood ties, ethnic organizations and their activities, and representation in what I dub a race-culture quagmire (see Chapter 7).

By the late 1980s, Japanese culture became an element formally taught to contestants in preparation for their role as representatives of a community with links to Japan. As in contemporary Japan, so in the CBF: lessons in particular aspects of Japanese culture defined the gender training of a Japanese (American) woman. These lessons included flower arranging, tea ceremony, and classical dance. In the CBF, these cultural lessons were added to standard Euro-American pageant training in makeup and movement. Queen Lisa-Ann Nakano (1988–1989) recalled:

> It's really neat because the whole training process is also a process to get you to know a little bit more about your culture, so we went through ikebana [flower-arranging] classes. . . . We went through Japanese tea ceremony. That was really, really neat because I've never done that. Our family is so Americanized. (Personal communication, January 29, 2002)

For Nakano, as for many others, the CBF training was their introduction to these Japanese cultural elements. As defined by the HJJCC from the late 1980s on, these elements were as important as makeup and stage movement in molding who should represent them.

The 1990 CBF souvenir book was the first to mention this East-West dual training:

From the eastern culture classes of Ikebana, Ochanoyu [tea ceremony], Japanese classical dance by Hanayagi Dance Studio, wearing a furisode kimono provided by Watabe costume; to the western culture classes of cosmetic application and skin care by Shiseido [Japanese cosmetic company; sponsor of the CBF pageant], and pageant training from Barbizon [model agency]. Both eastern and western classes were essential in the preparation for the pageant. (HJJCC 1990:49).

In 1994, the HJJCC added lessons on Japanese business etiquette; this differed from the more typical gender training in contemporary Japan. However, the business etiquette taught to CBF contestants were lessons for secretaries, not executives. By 1997, the number of Japanese culture classes expanded considerably to include Japanese calligraphy, domestic skills such as sushi-making, and nonfeminine practices such as *taiko* (drumming) and *kendō* (martial arts).

What was being taught through these lessons in Japanese cultural practices? On one level, very little. None of these lessons were conducted in great depth over an extended period of time. In most cases, each lesson lasted merely a couple of hours and happened only once during the pageant training period. Contestants were never tested on the content of the lessons, nor did it ever figure in the judging. In sum, these were lessons of very little consequence in the competition; they were merely superficial exposure to aspects of Japanese culture.

[handwritten margin note: Even though some of the lessons were not used, they were still taught.]

The exception was kimono-wearing. Lessons were held over a period of several weeks covering details from folding kimono to walking and bowing. (The actual donning of kimono and tying of obi was left to professional dressers on the night of the competition.) Kimono-clad contestants paraded on the CBF stage before a panel of judges who did not necessarily know anything about kimono or Japanese culture, since they were mainly chosen for their prominence in the general community. What mattered most was not necessarily performing elements of Japanese culture correctly, but performing with grace and confidence. Although kimono-wearing was part of the competition and therefore received more detailed instruction than other cultural lessons, even these could be regarded with less strict adherence because judges typically did not know the difference.

[handwritten margin note: Even judges didn't know anything about the Japanese culture they were judging on.]

What contestants acquired for the most part was a cultural sampler — "Japan lite," if you will — providing a certain minimum familiarity with Japan and Japanese culture to contestants. This "Japan lite" included cultural and gendered training in parallel with what was expected of premarital upper- and middle-class women in Japan and, to a certain extent, among Japanese Americans. The modeling and makeup lessons produced a fair approximation of a beauty queen; the Japanese cultural sampler produced a particular kind of ethnicized queen — the *ojōsan* (see Chapter 4). The HJJCC hoped to create a CBF Queen who could emulate Japanese (American) *ojōsan* before the watchful eye of sponsors and spectators in Japan and Hawai'i.

Ideally, a deeper level of learning would potentially take place. One hope of the HJJCC organizers was that exposure to various aspects of Japanese arts might impart some sense of cultural values to contestants. Queen Kymberly Rae Furuta (1996 – 1997) wrote, "Ikebana class taught me patience; kimono classes taught me about pride in my heritage" (Furuta 1997:31). Thus, even if contestants could not replicate the tea ceremony or reproduce a finely balanced flower arrangement, they could experience firsthand some of the cultural processes such as patience and pride that went into the execution of these.

It is also useful to ponder what was not taught. Japanese language was never a part of the cultural training of contestants. Neither was it ever a part of the formal judging. Realistically, learning Japanese is a long, involved process that requires diligent study. Given the amount of time for training, even if the Jaycees had relegated some of it to Japanese language, the most that a contestant could say if she had no other linguistic background was probably greetings and other formulaic expressions. Furthermore, having to study Japanese as part of pageant training may have been off-putting to contestants, and given an unfair advantage to those who knew some Japanese. Not including Japanese language as part of training (and judging) says something about the expectations of the Jaycees, the conceptualization of the CBF, and the role of the Queen. The Jaycees expect a CBF Queen to act as a symbol of themselves and the Japanese American community, but this is a symbol who does not have to speak — at least in the language of her forebears.

These cultural lessons came about at a time when contestants and organizers were most removed from Japanese culture. By the late 1980s and 1990s, most CBF participants were yonsei.[1] Their sansei parents likely did not speak Japanese or involve themselves in Japanese (American) cultural activities. Their nisei grandparents could speak some Japanese, but not necessarily with their grandchildren. And their issei great-grandparents had, for the most part, passed on. Any direct tie to Japan was tenuous at best. Although a few yonsei contestants may have taken Japanese language at the University of Hawai'i, these same contestants were more likely to have learned hula growing up in Hawai'i than Japanese dance. Japan, then, was a distant, foreign country that few contestants knew either firsthand or even through books. Pageant cultural training became a crash course in how to perform oneself as Japanese (American). Yet the Queen and Court members became public experts in Japanese culture, demonstrating origami-folding as part of community service projects, reading Japanese stories

[margin note, handwritten: HJCC wanted Queens to represent Japan yet none of the girls know anything about Japanese culture nor were they taught to retain any real Japanese culture]

[margin note, handwritten: 1) issei 2) nisei 3) sansei 4) yonsei]

(in English) to schoolchildren, helping with small-scale Japanese crafts for senior citizens. "Japan lite" became the decorative touch to community service projects increasingly demanded of the Queen and Court members.

What Queens gained from their exposure to "Japan lite" was a generalized appreciation for Japan and Japanese culture. Having visited the country of their great-grandparents, they gained firsthand acquaintance with their "homeland" origins. But the Japan they visited in the 1970s through 1990s was a far cry from the Japan that their forebears had left. Instead of rural, poverty-stricken Kumamoto of the 1900s, the Queens visited posh, urban Tokyo of the 1990s. Furthermore, even rural Kumamoto is no longer so rural or poverty-stricken. Thus the acquaintance with Japan through travel that many Queens mention is a Japan that would be as foreign to their immigrant ancestors as to themselves. This Japan — mythologized and iconicized as a homeland — provides an exotic reference point for the past, present, and future in the CBF.

Connections to "Homeland" Japan

Actual connections to Japan by both the HJJCC and its star vehicle, the CBF, increased from the 1970s on and, in fact, became a more formal mix of business, politics, and beauty pageants. From 1974 on, a letter from the consul general from Japan was published in each souvenir book, joining other letters of congratulations from local government officials. Symbolically, these letters gave official recognition of the CBF as a major civic event, acknowledged by the state of Hawai'i, the city of Honolulu, and the Japanese government.[2]

Other kinds of formal exchanges and relationships with organizations in Japan increased during this period as well. One of these was Nihon Sakura no Kai (Japan Cherry Blossom Association, established in 1964), an organization dedicated to promoting the cherry blossom throughout Japan and worldwide.[3] Nihon Sakura no Kai crowns its own Cherry Blossom Queen yearly in Japan. The CBF souvenir book from 1984 mentions Hawai'i's CBF Queen Gayle Koike (1983 – 1984) meeting the Nihon Sakura no Kai Queen Sugako Kogure in Japan (HJJCC 1984:18). Beginning in the 1970s, this organization assisted with arrangements for the CBF Queen, Court members, and accompanying HJJCC members, to gain an audience with a member of the royal family of Japan.

Another formally established relationship was with Jaycee organizations in Japan. In August 1984, HJJCC President Thomas Doi met with mayors, businessmen, and Jaycee members in Japan to invite their participation in the centennial celebration of Japanese contract immigration to Hawai'i and the CBF. The fruits of his labor could be found in the active participation in the CBF in

1985 by Jaycee representatives from Japan and a subsequent call for the establishment of an International Relations Division of the HJJCC. The particular places from which Jaycee relationships with Japan have been established do not necessarily correlate with the places of origin of Japanese immigration to Hawai'i. Rather, they have been established on the basis of institutional and business ties or idiosyncratic personal connections. This disconnect from Japanese American history and experience demonstrates the degree to which the Jaycees were operating independently from older issei-established connections.

The 1985 souvenir book printed congratulatory messages from the Japanese Jaycees of Kojima, Odawara, Kurashiki, Hirosaki, Nagoya, and Tamashima, of which several established continuing long-term formal relationships of exchange. The message from the Hirosaki Junior Chamber of Commerce read:

> Our city, Hirosaki, is known all over Japan for its Sakura Matsuri, which takes place every year in a park with more than 5,000 sakura trees on 120 acres surrounding an ancient castle. I hope this exchange of our Miss Sakura and your Queen will help promote mutual understanding and better relations between the United States and Japan. (Hirosaki Junior Chamber of Commerce 1985:19)

By 1991, the HJJCC had established formal relations ("sister chapters") with Junior Chambers in the cities of Kobe, Kurashiki, and Odawara. The 1993 CBF souvenir book includes a section "Introducing Our Sister Chapter from Japan," with photographs of the presidents of the Jaycee organizations in Kobe, Kojima, Kurashiki, Odawara, and Tamashima (HJJCC 1993:63). These cities continue to be the lynchpins of Jaycee ties to Japan into the 2000s.

While in Japan, the CBF Queen meets with not only other beauty queens, mayors, businessmen, and princesses, but also sometimes heads of state. In 1985, Queen Joanne Hirano (1985–1986) met with Prime Minister Yasuhiro Nakasone, who referred to her as "the Living Sakura from Hawai'i" (HJJCC 1986:19). The CBF Queen has also been part of official entourages from the state of Hawai'i to Japan. In 1988, Queen Lisa-Ann Nakano and Miss Popularity Sharlyn Masaki joined Lieutenant Governor Benjamin Cayetano, Roger Ulveling from the Department of Economic Development, and various Hawaiian entertainers for the opening of the Seto Ohashi Expo (HJJCC 1989:20). In 1989, Queen Lori Matsumura joined state government officials for a celebration of Hawaii Week in Fukuoka City, Kyushu (sister state of Hawai'i). In these examples and many others, the CBF acts as an international ambassador not only for the HJJCC and the Japanese American community, but also for the state of Hawai'i and the United States.

The Authenticity of Princess Michiko

Among the honors bestowed upon CBF Queens from 1972 through 1986 and later was a visit with Japanese royalty. In particular, what impressed many CBF Queens during this period was meeting one of the primary models for the Japanese upper-class woman, Princess Michiko (married Crown Prince Akihito in 1959; from 1989, Empress Michiko). Here was the archetypical *ojōsan*.[4]

Several Queens recalled their meeting with the princess in glowing terms. Queen Deborah Kodama (1977 – 1978) wrote of her visit:

> Princess Michiko is truly a remarkable and admirable woman. Dedicated and devoted to her husband, her family, and her country, she epitomizes the complete combination that so many women strive for today. There is tremendous aura that surrounds her and this may be incomprehensible to people who have never seen her. Her presence touched me. The innermost part of me was numb because of the feelings that I was experiencing. The combination of reverence that the Japanese have for her and the knowledge of my Sansei background made me a distant admirer. It was a unique feeling that will forever remain with me. (Kodama 1978:39)

In our interview, Kodama elaborated on this high point in her reign:

> She [Princess Michiko] has an aura. You know how you hear about people having auras? This is one aura of a person that I have experienced. I mean, it brought me to tears. Honestly. She's just amazing. She is, in the truest sense of the word, she is royalty. The true sense of the word. My mother and I were in the reception area anxiously waiting for Princess Michiko to come in. And her lady-in-waiting announced her arrival, and, oh my gosh, my mother [an issei] started crying . . . I guess for a Japanese national to meet someone from the royal family, it's almost impossible. . . . So just being in the same room with the princess at that time, it drove my mom to tears. I admit, it was a really emotional experience. I think about it now . . . [tears come to her eyes] really . . . she carries herself with such grace. How could you say it? Just grace. I was in awe, totally in awe. Of all the experiences I encountered [as CBF Queen], that meeting with the princess was the highlight.
>
> (Personal communication, December 5, 2001)

For young Japanese American Cherry Blossom Queens, such as Jody-Lee Ige (1982 – 1983), Princess Michiko was a model Japanese woman:

> Out of all my experiences in Japan, there is one occasion that will remain forever vivid in my mind — meeting Japan's Crown Princess Michiko. No

other woman except my own mother has made such a lasting and affecting impression upon me. Princess Michiko was everything I imagined a Japanese woman to be. She emanated graciousness and simple elegance, yet there was a humbleness that spoke of her wisdom of life. I truly believe that her example of a Japanese woman is one that I would like to model myself after. (HJJCC 1983:18)

Graciousness and elegance, combined with humbleness and wisdom, made her a gendered, class ideal. Using overlapping vocabulary, these narratives about Princess Michiko read like a litany of gendered desirability: gracious, soft, gentle, beautiful, radiant, elegant, humble. She represents an ideal to which both Japanese and Japanese American women might aspire. But she goes beyond this ideal by her charisma, possessing a spiritual "aura" capable of moving one to tears. She is the authentic imperial to the faux royal Queens from Hawai'i.

Ironic parallels lie in the meeting of the commoner-cum-faux Queen who changes annually with the commoner-princess who holds the position for life,[5] the Japanese American meeting the Japanese. In photographs of their meeting, one wears a crown (faux Queen), while the other does not (actual princess) (e.g., HJJCC 1974:32). In these CBF narratives, Princess Michiko represents not only true royalty, but also the true Japanese, the true woman. The qualities CBF Queens ascribe to her are those to which the CBF Queens are supposed to strive: beauty, elegance, refinement, gentility, and humility. Furthermore, she is an exemplary wife and mother, fully embedded in institutions of marriage and citizenship. In royal terms, she is the model "nice Japanese girl" elevated to the highest level.

Recruiting "Nice Japanese American Girls"

Vying to be crowned as the ultimate "nice Japanese American girl" requires a field of contestants. The recruitment of contestants by the Jaycees fluctuated over the years, becoming increasingly difficult as public interest dwindled. The Queens from this period I interviewed expressed a range of ways in which they became involved — from media-fed dreams of Miss America (see Prologue) to ethnic sororities at the University of Hawai'i (see Chapter 3) to the solicitation of Jaycee members to stage mothers to acquaintances who participated in the CBF to a simple newspaper ad soliciting applications. Queen Lori Ann Mizumoto (1981–1982) talked of watching beauty pageants on television:

I was one of those little girls who would always watch the pageants on TV. I kind of fantasized about wearing a pretty dress on stage and a crown.... I remember I would always look at the [Cherry Blossom] posters and dream. But I never really said anything to anybody about wanting to run in a pageant. It was just something that was like my private dream, my secret dream.

(Personal communication, February 7, 2002)

Lori Ann, then, was fulfilling a long-held secret dream in running for CBF Queen.

Family members — especially mothers — often played an important role (see Chapter 4, Queen Carol Saikyo). Queen Deborah Kodama (1977 – 1978) recalled:

> DK: *From what I remember, the Jaycees had approached me, I believe, right when I had turned eighteen. At that time I was not interested and I just thought I was a bit too young. So they approached me again a year later, when I was just nineteen. And when they approached me the second time, I said, "Why not?" It was a good time and I became a contestant. But I think primarily it was my mother, at my mom's encouragement.*
>
> CY: Why did you think your mom encouraged you to participate?
>
> DK: *I think it's more a dream that they had for their kids. My mom and dad are from Japan.*
>
> CY: Is there anything that you wanted to get out of it for yourself?
>
> DK: *To make my mom and dad proud.*
>
> (Personal communication, December 5, 2001)

Likewise, Queen LoriJoy Morita (1998 – 1999) needed a nudge from her mother.

> CY: So how did you decide to enter the CBF?
>
> LM: *Well, my mom. She wanted me to do it. We went a couple years before to go watch [the CBF], because I had known a few girls who were running. And we went to go support them and I guess it was kind of a way for my mom to show me what it was all about. She wanted me to do it. She thought it was good, since my college major was Japanese and I had lived in Japan for a year. I was a little hesitant, because I only pictured it as a beauty pageant and I thought, "I would never enter a beauty pageant."*
>
> CY: Why not?
>
> LM: *Just something I never thought I would do or never had an interest in doing. And so I said, "Uhhh, I don't think so." But she told me more about it: it's not necessarily the beauty part, it's more like the cultural aspect, and I would be able to meet more people in the Japanese community here in Hawai'i and hopefully use some of my Japanese language. And meet people in the business community. So, she convinced me. I remember the day my application was*

due, I was at work, and she called me, "Did you turn your application in?" And I said, "Oh, no." I had totally forgotten that there was a due date. "Mail it in today, because today's the last day." And so I mailed it in on the very last day, the postmark date. And I got in. I guess I almost would have let my chance go away, but she was so insistent that I do it, she really wanted me to do it.
(Personal communication, January 14, 2002)

Sisters, female cousins, or friends who had already participated in the CBF have also been influential. Queen Ann Yoshioka (1975 – 1976), for example, says that the idea of running for Cherry Blossom Queen came to her upon the example of her cousin Nancy Yoshioka, who was a Court member in 1971 – 1972 (personal communication, February 25, 2002). Likewise, Queen LeAnne Higa (1979 – 1980) decided to participate after her sister Myrah was crowned Queen (1976 – 1977), becoming the first and only pair of sister Queens (see Chapter 6).

If not family members, then people within a person's social network have been important catalysts for entering the contest. In the case of Queen Marlene Sato (1987 – 1988), a brother's friend played a key role.

MS: *My brother had a friend who heard they [HJJCC] were still looking for contestants, so this was toward the end of their search. They asked my brother, "Is your sister interested in running?" My brother asked me and I asked my Mom, "What do you think?" and she said, "Well, just try, and you know, you might meet a lot of people," and especially if I'm going into business, I can make business contacts. So it was a good opportunity for me to meet a lot of people and learn my Japanese culture and history.*

CY: And your mom said all this?

MS: *My mom kind of encouraged me to, 'cause at first I was, like, "Oh, should I?" and she was, like, "Oh, why don't you try? You can never know what's going to happen." And the main thing was, I would meet a lot of people and make a lot of friends. So I said, "Okay, I'll give it a try." It wasn't that I planned or anything for years to participate or do tryouts.*
(Personal communication, January 26, 2002)

What is common to many of these Queens' narratives is the fact that they express little personal agency in the decision to participate. A few do talk about becoming CBF Queen as a childhood dream or driving ambition. But most relegate agency outside themselves to relatives (especially mothers) or friends who prod them into participation, often submitting their application just before the deadline. Theirs is the nonagency of the passive procrastinator who unwittingly wins. As many of these women tell it, becoming Cherry Blossom

[Handwritten marginalia: "figured at least she could get something out of it for herself instead of doing it for the title & responsibilities it held."]

[Handwritten marginalia: "little interest in participating" "why not" mentality."]

Queen is something that happened to them more than a title they actively sought. Of course, they had to undergo training and compete on stage, but the initial framework of their participation is one that they often narrate as a consequence of forces outside themselves residing within social networks of family and friends. Several of them wanted to satisfy their parents' (especially their mothers') desire for them rather than their own. Others find great satisfaction in pleasing their grandparents.

This deflected ambition fits in well with the balancing act of the "nice Japanese American girl" ideal: assertive, but not aggressive; independent, but always socially embedded; outgoing enough to speak to VIPs in public, but not highly opinionated or controversial in what she actually says. The balance falls along cultural lines, following American ideals of assertiveness and independence, but tempered by Japanese ideals of humility and social embeddedness. It also falls along gendered lines of ideal women who may be public figures, but know their place. Above all, this "nice Japanese American girl" is one who neatly avoids controversy.

Antifeminism and the "Nice Japanese American Girl"

The waves of feminism that swept through the United States beginning in the 1960s barely produced any ripples in the CBF. One ripple, however, was the inclusion of individuated voices of CBF Queens in souvenir books. Whereas previously photographs of the year's events were accompanied by anonymous captions, in 1961 Queen Shirley Fujisaki wrote, "My Trip to Japan," a five-page spread in first-person narrative with photographs (Fujisaki 1961:67 – 71). All subsequent CBF Queens followed suit until 1969, when Queen Janice Teramae wrote far more extensively about her reign, including a poem and reflective essay (Teramae 1969:54). Since then, Queens have regularly contributed their memories of the past year's reign in the CBF souvenir book in the form of a "Letter from the Queen."

This ripple is small when compared to large-scale social changes going on in other parts of the country at the same time. As might be expected with many beauty pageant participants, those who choose to involve themselves in an event such as the CBF tend to be upholders of traditional gender roles. Although this is not exclusively so — and I include contradictions to this (e.g., Chapter 6, Queen Katherine Horio) — a certain amount of self-selection skews the spectrum of women participating in the CBF toward conservatism. This is especially true during a politically contentious period such as the 1970s, when battle lines around gender and other issues are acutely drawn. In fact, beauty pageants were the archetypal site of such battles. Thus, the words of one contestant who wrote about "charm and sophistication that opens doors for her and prepares her for a career in modeling if she chooses, beauty counseling or, the ultimate achievement, *motherhood*" (HJJCC 1970:63), stand in stark contrast to contemporaneous feminist cries. Her words sound not neutral, but reactionary.

Queen Rae Tanaka (1972 – 1973) likewise expressed conservative views in a newspaper interview upon her crowning:

> Asked whether she feared being exploited as a queen, as women's liberationists might charge, she replied that she did not. "You can refuse to be exploited," she said. "You don't have to agree with everything." Of Women's Liberation in general, she said: "It's a good movement in that it opens new fields to women. But I still think men are men and women are women." She said she does "not necessarily" believe in full equality. "I think there're [*sic*] basic differences between the two sexes. I would want to feel secure and protected by a man when I got married." (*Honolulu Advertiser* 1972:A10)

Although some of the conservatism may be performative, especially for media, Tanaka's desire to "feel secure and protected by a man" sounds like a startling admission of 1950s housewifery.

Queen Deborah Kodama (1977 – 1978) was similarly described in a newspaper article as a "traditionalist" who is "apolitical":

> Not surprising, Deborah is a traditionalist. A speech she gave during the pageant was devoted to a celebration of old Japanese values and which was a tribute, she says, to her parents. . . . At the same time, Deborah is apolitical. Although billed as the representative of the Japanese community of Hawaii, her sole observation of recent political and social changes among her people is that "there's a lot more Japanese people in the political arena." (Oshiro 1977:B8)

Deborah, like a number of other contestants and Queens, turned her back on the politics of the time in favor of an older model of femininity.

In spite of the general conservatism of the Jaycees and Queen contestants, that older model of femininity increasingly included careers for women. Queen LoriJoy Morita (1998 – 1999) suggested the following Jaycee version of the ideal Cherry Blossom Queen by the 1990s:

> I think that the [Junior] Chamber has an ideal of what they want in the Cherry Blossom Queen. They want somebody who's very business oriented,

conservative, yet confident. She's got a good head on her shoulders. Someone
who's gonna be committed and disciplined to her reign.
(Personal communication, January 14, 2002)

[handwritten note in left margin: definition of "nice girl" has changed]

This is an update of the "nice girl" model — not the wife/mother so much as
the career woman who can meet the public. This is not a career woman who
occupies the top level of management, however. Rather, she is more likely a low-
or mid-level manager or even executive secretary. This reconfigured "nice girl"
is like "one of the boys": conservative, confident, level-headed, and committed.
In fact, she sounds much like the Jaycees themselves.

"Nice Girl" Bodies: Training, Discipline, and Aesthetics

Although many Queens, contestants, and organizers have long claimed that
the CBF is explicitly not a beauty contest, appearance and bodily discipline have
always been a part of the event. The older model of femininity focused on pageant training, including lessons on makeup, posture, poise, and comportment.
The trainers themselves were women considered experts in the arts of femininity: "It is these women who are responsible for the gradual transformation of
the timid, shy and nervous contestants into princesses with social graces and
confidence" (HJJCC 1974:85). The transformation required effort. The CBF souvenir book explained: "The fantasy of glamour associated with beauty contests
is quickly dispelled. The contest is put into perspective at the onset. Work and
more work is basic and the key to success" (ibid.:26). This refers to the work of
men as well as women. In this way, the CBF provides lessons and performances
on both sides of the stage, from the front-stage performance of women trained
in the arts of female presentation to the backstage performance of men training
themselves to be community leaders through hands-on organizational effort.
Both men and women genderize themselves through the CBF.

This emphasis on training democratizes the contest into one based on effort.
It also dovetails with the self-effacing narratives of many Queens: a disclaimer
that they are not the typical Queen because of shyness, physical clumsiness,
lack of "girlishness" and a concomitant tomboyishness. This distancing of oneself from typicality and stereotype can become an important (and potentially
performative) locus of agency. Queen Lori Ann Mizumoto (1981 – 1982) said
this about herself:

> I'm not like a Grace Kelly [1929 – 1982; Hollywood movie star known for her
> elegance; later became princess of Monaco] — that kind of a person who can
> hold herself very well and carry on her airs and everything. I just can't. I was

more of the shy person too. And I'm so uncoordinated. And I like to play around. One of "You know, you're the most unqueenly Queen we've had, but you're the most fun." [Laughing] 'Cause I'd start pillow fights. I just wasn't girly really. I don't know what it was. I just think that I was probably the most unqueenly Queen.

(Personal communication, February 7, 2002)

Queens from the 50's-60's said the same kind of thing.

The "unqueenly Queen" as a self-deprecatory label distances oneself from the stereotype of beauty queens. Being called an "unqueenly Queen" can be a compliment:[6] it creates a cultural space for the "nice girl" who is common yet manages to be queen, who enables social leveling. The "unqueenly Queen" supposedly lacks natural, ascriptive, "queenly" elements, making training all the more important. A CBF Queen — particularly one labeled an "unqueenly Queen" — represents an achievement based on her efforts and those around her. Thus, CBF (unqueenly) Queens are made, not born.

The notion of a level playing field is important for developing the esprit de corps of the contestants, as well as to address the issue of competition, especially since the CBF — like many beauty pageants — is constantly plagued by rumors of unfair advantage and favoritism. By 1970, Jaycee organizers had tried to level the field with uniform outfits and training:

> The girls are ... outfitted in exact costumes, dress, shoes, and all other accessories provided for by the Jaycees. ... Now you ask, "How does this qualify the statement that any one of these girls could have been the queen?" Simply and truthfully, group-training! The rigorous program designed for the contestants is executed as a group, no girl receiving any more attention than the other. It is said that all our contestants look alike and while this sounds insulting, the opposite is true. It is a compliment that the end result could produce fifteen girls who look like queens. (HJJCC 1970:63)

Elevating sameness to a virtue, the Jaycees quell oft-heard criticism that the CBF creates cookie-cutter contestants and Queens.

The theoretically level playing field deemphasizes bodily differences, with the exception of height.[7] Height is a sensitive issue in Japanese American communities, probably more for men than women. The average height of contestants and Queens has not risen significantly from the 1960s to the 2000s. The heights of contestants have remained fairly steady throughout CBF history at around five feet, two inches.[8] The commonly held belief among many in the Japanese American community is that in the CBF, as in beauty contests in general, a tall woman — in this case, five feet, four inches, or higher — holds advantage over shorter ones. A comparison of heights of Queens does not necessarily bear this out. Overall, less than half the Queens — only twenty out of forty-six for whom height measurements are available — are five feet, four inches, or taller.[9] Being tall, then, has been more of an exception than the norm for both contestants and Queens. Yet, several women I have spoken with talk about the perceived height advantage. Queen Jody-Lee Ige (1982 – 1983, five feet, one inch) spoke about the general advantage of height in a beauty contest:

> CY: How do you feel about the rumored preference for tall Queens?
>
> JI: *I think that it's not specific just to a Japanese pageant. I think it's an overall conception of a tall, regal Queen.*
>
> CY: How tall are you, Jody?
>
> JI: *I'm five-one. I always thought about that as I was going through the process. I would think, "It's difficult to be a Queen. Maybe I'll be lucky if I place [as a runner-up in the Court]."*
>
> CY: So you felt that being short was a handicap?
>
> JI: *Yup. I was prejudiced against my own height.*
>
> (Personal communication, December 6, 2001)

This talk of bodily size says as much about the exceptionality of height in this particular community (even with succeeding generations getting progressively taller) as about the adoption of Euro-American notions of physical stateliness. Although it is true that the average height of Queens is taller than the average height of contestants, I argue that the perception of Queens as tall (or the advantage that height gives a contestant) remains not because of any statistical measure, but because when Queens are tall, they confirm people's image of queenliness. Conversely, when Queens are short, observers take them as exceptions to the rule, rather than challenges to it. Bodies, then, especially on a beauty contest stage, are a confluence of stereotypes, ideals, and perception, rather than statistical measurements.

When I have asked several Queens and contestants from this period about cosmetic surgery, all deny that it played any role in the pageant. Queen Jody-Lee Ige comments:

> CY: Do you remember any contestants having cosmetic surgery?
>
> JI: *I'm trying to think. No, I can't recall that I noticed anything. No eye surgery or whatever. I wouldn't have known if they had their boobs done.*
>
> CY: Right.
>
> JI: *I think I would have been surprised, though. Because of the culture, I would have been surprised. Maybe not the eye surgery because it's kind of com-*

mon, you see a lot of girls with it, but if they had breast augmentation I would have been surprised if they had that, because it's not the culture, the Cherry Blossom culture.

(Personal communication, December 6, 2001)

What Ige refers to as "Cherry Blossom culture" is one that not only deemphasizes breasts, but does so in a moralizing way as an issue of modesty. To be a "nice Japanese American girl," then, means not exposing one's body to public scrutiny or currying unwanted attention through excessive curvaceousness, whether by nature or scalpel.[10]

The one exception to this admonition is eyelid surgery (see Chapter 1), considered common enough among Japanese American women to be acceptable, but still shrouded in discretion. Since the 1950s, eyelid surgeries have steadily increased among the general Asian American female population in Hawai'i, including CBF contestants. However, the subject is still taboo to the extent that I felt I could not ask CBF Queens and contestants, "Have you had eyelid surgery?" Instead, rumors fly concerning who had had the surgery, especially in earlier years when it was not quite so commonplace.

[handwritten margin note: eye lid surgery not suprizing]

Looking the part of the Japanese American "nice girl" in the 1970s to 1990s included fair skin and long hair that could be worn as an up-do. Fair skin had been a more important consideration in the 1950s and 1960s, when issei and nisei clung to Japanese cultural notions of fair-skinned beauty and exposure to sun could be linked to working in the plantation fields. By the 1970s and later, tanning had become a part of beach-going youth culture in Hawai'i, which helped redefine the meaning of darker skin. Nevertheless, Japanese Americans taking part in an event such as the CBF adopted some of the older aesthetics of fair skin, even if temporarily (see Chapter 6 remarks by Queen Kathy Horio). Although untanned skin was exceptional, it marked both an ascriptive light complexion, as well as the achieved skin of one who does not go out in the sun. Therefore, several former contestants and Queens mention instructions from relatives, friends, or kimono instructors to stay out of the sun while preparing for the CBF pageant.

[handwritten margin note: stay out of the sun.]

Hair, too, had to conform as much as possible to a Cherry Blossom norm. Over the decades of the CBF, the meaning of hairstyles changed radically so that the norm of middle-class respectability in one era (e.g., curled, shorter hair in the 1950s and 1960s; see Chapter 4, Queen Gwen Nishizawa) no longer held true for another era. Thus, the long-hair "radicalness" associated negatively with hippies in the late 1960s became important for an up-do in later decades. In several cases during this period, contestants with short hair found themselves growing it long for the contest so that they could wear it in an up-do, and subsequently cutting it short as soon as the contest (or reign) was over.[11] Queen Jody-Lee Ige (1982 – 1983) recalled:

> JI: *For the pageant and for the year, I let my hair grow out. Just because if you're wearing a kimono, you have to have that look, and you have to put the ornaments in your hair. If you don't have any hair [long enough], it's a problem. But as soon as that year was over, I chopped it short. In fact, I showed up at the end-of-the-year party with my short hair.*
>
> CY: And what was the reaction?
>
> JI: *"Wow! That's short!" I said, "Yes!"*
>
> (Personal communication, December 6, 2001)

long black hair was the look if you wanted to be Queen.

Cutting one's hair for at least some Queens and contestants marked a dramatic end to the conformity each felt necessary to fit the Cherry Blossom mold.[12]

The desirable color of hair remained constant through the 1990s. Queen LoriJoy Morita (1998 – 1999) remembered that in the year she was a contestant, brown-highlighted hair was very popular; she and other contestants were nudged to redye their hair black:

> I think our year they [Jaycees] kind of actually, in a subtle way, told us that we shouldn't have highlighted hair. So I think most of us that year had colored our hair trying to get it back to more its normal color. 'Cause I've always liked to highlight my hair. But during my year, no, my hair was black. It was black.
>
> (Personal communication, January 14, 2002)

Black hair in an up-do thus became the norm for this period.

What is important in these bodily modifications enacted as part of pageant preparation is the vagueness of the prompt. Most Queens and former contestants could not recall exactly who said what to them, but remembered very distinctly the effect of such vague communications: stay out of the sun, dye your hair black, let your hair grow long enough to put it up. The finger typically points to the Jaycee organization as a fuzzy target of blame: "The Jaycees told me to . . ." or "The Jaycees let us know . . ." without any specific recall of who said exactly what, when, or where. The repercussions were equally vague: for contestants, perceived less chance of winning; for Queen and Court, voiced and unvoiced disapproval. The Jaycees, in effect, become the faceless, critical public — the amorphous panopticon of bodily discipline (cf. Foucault 1977).

One unambiguous source of bodily discipline was in kimono-dressing. As was the case with CBF Queens and contestants in the 1950s and 1960s, those in the 1970s through 1990s frequently mention kimono-wearing as part of the bodily lessons of their training. From the 1950s through 1985, the kimono instructor was Mrs. Eiko Yorita, an issei from Shikoku, Japan. Several CBF Queens mentioned their gratitude to her and the lessons they learned under her tutelage. Queen LeAnne Higa (1979 – 1980) wrote:

> As I wore my own practice kimonos, I felt quite authentic. I can hardly wait to wear one of Mrs. Yorita's exquisite kimonos. I understand she has many to select from. Also, she knows exactly what style, print and color would be flattering to one's personality and physical attributes. (Higa 1980:19)

Higa's use of "authentic" to imply a deep-seated connection to Japan echoes the words used to describe Princess Michiko. In fact, part of what made Mrs. Yorita special was the authenticity she brought to the kimono-wearing experience, especially as an issei with longstanding knowledge of kimono and its significance. Queen Francene Kondo (1980 – 1981) recalled:

> You wouldn't believe how awkward I felt during our first session. It's not often I have the chance to wear a kimono, especially in the presence of an expert like Mrs. Yorita. But she was very patient and went over the proper way to carry one's self in a kimono. She taught us the correct way to hold the "sensu" or fan and the proper way to bow formally. (Kondo 1981:19)

For Queen Lori Ann Mizumoto (1981 – 1982), wearing a kimono was both physically constricting and emotionally liberating in connecting to her "roots" of Japanese culture.

> I didn't realize that it involved so many layerings and techniques in tying the obi. It's hard to wear! It's so heavy and you can't breathe. It's almost like a corset, I guess. And oh, to use the bathroom — forget it! [Laughing] .... But you feel — I don't know how to explain it . . . you feel really special in it. It's like a connection to your roots or something. It just makes you feel special when you put it on. (Personal communication, February 7, 2002)

The kimono, in effect, molds the Japanese American woman by requiring her to discipline her body to conform to its Japanese aesthetic. The thrill for Mizumoto and others lay in the notion of bodily connecting to their female forebears through wearing kimono.[13]

Although official training of the pageant includes only makeup and comportment, part of what is modeled is niceness — defined here in gendered terms as the ability, proclivity, and responsibility to take care of others. Niceness as emotion work is fundamental to performing the role of hostess (see Chapter 4, Queen Vivian Honda; cf. Hochschild 1983). Because the Queen hosts public functions, the spotlight examines not only her physical appearance, but also her skill in making others feel comfortable. The Queen performs as the gendered mediator of social events, tending to the needs of others, making sure that things go smoothly. The charm-course pageant training ostensibly teaches the visual dimensions of charm; the hope of the Jaycees is that in the process, it also teaches women the emotional and social dimensions of how to be "charming." The ideal Queen is thus the "nice girl" placed on a public stage.

Living in the Spotlight: Once a Queen Always a Queen?

The pageant training of the CBF and experience living in the spotlight lasts beyond the year of a Queen's reign. Many Queens face the relentless public glare throughout their subsequent lives. Violet Niimi (1953 – 1954), as the first Queen, received more than her share of continued publicity. Japanese-language newspapers chronicled her engagement and marriage. Fifteen years after her reign she still garnered a feature newspaper article in the major English-language newspaper complete with photographs of her busy domestic life (Matsuura 1968:C8).

Queen Deborah Kodama (1977–1978), whose reign ended more than twenty-five years ago, reflected on the price of ongoing local fame:

DK: *You know, it never ends.*

CY: Is that right?

DK: *It never ends. Prior to becoming a contestant, if I had to go to Longs [drugstore] or any grocery store, I just put on a pair of jeans and a t-shirt, and go without any makeup. Once as a contestant, people expect you to look a certain way, to act a certain way, to be a certain way because of those labels you bestow upon yourself as a contestant and eventually as Queen or whoever. And that stigma never goes.*

CY: Has anybody ever said anything to you outright?

DK: *No, no. I think it's more the perception that you think people would expect from you and pride in yourself. Even to this day, I've had people coming to the office [where she works] and they would say, "Oh, this is the doctor's wife. And she used to be the Cherry Blossom Queen."*

CY: So you're introduced that way?

DK: *Yes, and I'm thinking, "Oh, don't bring it up. It was a long time ago." I really didn't want people to know.*

CY: Why was that?

DK: *I guess it's mostly privacy. . . . If I don't do anything with the Jaycees for a long time and then they call me, "Can you emcee? Can you be a judge? Can you do this?" and then I do, then somewhere down the line, a patient of my husband or someone will come to me and say, "Hey, I saw you! I didn't know you were Cherry Blossom!" And things like that. So like I said, that stigma never never ends.*

(Personal communication, December 5, 2001)

Deborah considers having been Queen a "stigma" in that she continues to occupy the celebrity spotlight. Even when that light is dim, she has already internalized the public's expectations, so she can never completely turn the spotlight off. Being a CBF Queen means relinquishing the privilege of anonymity. The gender training of the pageant is thus practice for a role that goes on forever, especially for Queens.

Queen Jody-Lee Ige (1982 – 1983) framed the dress and makeup of a Queen within the image of the Jaycees:

During that year, I was conscious that I had to have a certain image, so of course you cannot just go running around. [Laughs] You have to maintain that invention. It's not just myself that I have to think of. It's the Japanese [Junior] Chamber of Commerce, make sure that I'm presenting a good image for them and the pageant and the Japanese community. You're always aware of the fact that people are watching you and thinking, "Gee, is she a good representative of us?"

(Personal communication, December 6, 2001)

Ige speaks enthusiastically of the experience; yet she followed her year as Queen with a move to the continental United States: "After my year [as CBF Queen], I finished up college and I ran away. I went to the mainland and lived there for a couple years to be anonymous" (ibid.). Anonymity, then, becomes a prized condition after more than a year of Queenly celebrity.

Some Queens have even kept their title a secret from their friends and offspring. Queen LeAnne Higa (1979 – 1980) recalled:

CY: Among the people that you encounter, do many know that you are a past Queen?
LH: *[Shaking her head, laughing] No!*
CY: They don't?
LH: *In fact, it's really funny. I don't think my daughter ever knew until she was six or seven years old. She never knew because I never told her. I never showed her any pictures.*
CY: What was her reaction?
LH: *She was shocked. "Mom? My mom?" [Laughing] She was proud, but*

*she was shocked. I never wanted to tell her anything because I wanted her to go
through life making up her own mind, and if she decided one day she wanted
to run in a pageant or whatever, then she should just do it.*
(Personal communication, February 5, 2002)

Mothers such as Higa realize that a beauty queen title can raise unwanted expectations for their daughters. In fact, most Queens whose homes I visited had little visual evidence of their reign on display: no Queen portraits, no photographs, no lingering regalia.

Even Queens from the 1990s, when the CBF did not garner the same kind of attention as previously, feel the glare of the spotlight. Queen Sharon Kadoyama (1991 – 1992) commented ruefully on her prolonged celebrity:

I'm glad I'm now married and have a different last name. Once in a while
people will recognize you, and go, "Hey, I remember you." Or, "Aren't you
… Did I see you run during the year with my cousin or with my friend?" So
you're still in the spotlight, not as much of course, but once a Queen, always
a Queen. People will always watch you.
(Personal communication, January 22, 2002)

The insidious aspect of the public spotlight is its relentlessness. This holds true whether or not someone is actually watching. All it takes to pull a Queen into line is the suspicion or rumor that someone might be watching. For example, Queen Lori Ann Mizumoto (1981 – 1982) related the following:

LM: *I heard somebody called the Jaycees to say they saw some Cherry Blossom Queen after her reign at the swap meet without makeup and just in t-shirt
and shorts.*
CY: And they criticized her for that?
LM: *Yeah, that's what I heard.*
(Personal communication, February 7, 2002)

The disciplinary arm of the spotlight is thus multilayered: Queens critiqued by the public, Queens critiqued by the Jaycees, Jaycees critiqued by the public, Queens and Jaycees self-critiquing by internalizing external critiques, Queens and Jaycees self-critiquing through rumor.

Changing Demographics of Queens and Contestants

The emphasis on pageant training professionalized the competition, taking it out of the hands of younger contestants fresh out of high school as was common in the 1950s and 1960s, and putting it into the hands of older, more mature women in college or recent graduates in the 1970s on. The average age of CBF Queens rose steadily since the start of the contest in 1953 (see Appendix). The average age of Queens is as follows:[14] 1950s — 18.6 years (17 – 22 years); 1960s — 19.3 years (18 – 20 years); 1970s — 21.2 years (19 – 22 years); 1980s — 22.0 years (21 – 24 years); 1990s — 23.1 years (20 – 25 years) (see Chapter 7 for 2000s). The youngest Queens, 17 years old, were in the 1950s, while the oldest Queens, 25 years old, have been in the 1990s and 2000s. These represent nearly the age limits of their respective decades. Queen Jody-Lee Ige (1982 – 1983) comments on the comparative maturity of Queen contestants when she acted as pageant judge in the late 1990s, almost twenty years after her reign as Queen:

> I was very impressed. A lot of them were older and they already had their
> bachelor's [undergraduate degree], which was to me unusual, because when
> we were running, we were in the midst of getting our bachelor's degrees.
> And looking at these women, they already did their bachelor's and maybe
> were working in the industry, they're teachers already, or they're accoun-
> tants. They know where they want to go. And so I guess they were doing the
> pageant to reinforce their culture. Usually, you might think career is more
> important at this point. But to go back and take some time [to do the CBF],
> that was really nice.
>
> (Personal communication, December 6, 2001)

[handwritten margin note: 50-60's Contestants were not allowed to go to school]

This clear trend toward older Queens in a more advanced stage in their lives reflects the different kind of role that the CBF Queen was expected to play from the 1970s on — a role that included more substance and maturity behind the smile — as well as the different kind of training needed to assure that a qualified woman would fill the role.

Although age has been steadily increasing, educational level has remained fairly constant. Although it is true that Queens in recent years have increasingly come from private high schools (see Appendix), this reflects a general trend toward private school education in Hawai'i. Most of the CBF Queens from the pageant's inception were either students at the University of Hawai'i or graduates. The significance of this, however, has changed over the decades. In the 1950s, proportionately fewer Japanese Americans received a university education than in the 1990s; therefore, a university student or graduate in the 1950s occupied more of an elite status among Japanese Americans in Hawai'i. The CBF Queens were indeed culled from what might be considered a local *ojōsan* elite in terms of education. The pageant training that these contestants received in the CBF provided finishing-school gloss to their educational attainment.

By the 1980s, the political and economic forces of the 1950s and 1960s that had spearheaded the HJJCC and the CBF were gone. The public spotlight of 1950s small-town Honolulu had scattered in too many directions. Tourists in the 1980s had numerous attractions from which to choose, making the CBF far less attractive. The HJJCC had to work harder to drum up enthusiasm for the CBF as the event became increasingly remote from people's lives and concerns. The CBF 1988 souvenir book pinpointed some of the concerns of the CBF:

> The yonsei and gosei . . . now blend in alongside their multiethnic peers to face the challenges of Hawaii's future together. . . . These are critical times for such fragile entities as tradition. . . . As the last of our issei forebears pass from us, as the nisei slip into retirement, and as the sansei more firmly shoulder the yoke of social responsibility, the time has come to give serious consideration to the future of our Japanese cultural heritage. (HJJCC 1988:45)

Six years later, HJJCC President Robert S. Morita (1993–1994) expressed similar sentiments:

> Many who are participating in the 42nd CBF are several generations removed from their ethnic roots. The CBF offers many opportunities to experience the tradition and culture of Japan. As one of the generations that will become the future leaders of our community, we are accepting the challenge of maintaining and perpetuating our cultural heritage. (Morita 1994:14)

These narratives, like many others, take Japan and its culture as a heritage to be embraced for the future. The problem with this conceptualization is that neither Japan, culture, nor heritage is immutable or unchanging. Instead, they are dynamic elements, subject to historical transformation and manipulation. They are also subject to internal divisions, especially of class, region, and gender. If a "Japanese cultural heritage" is something to be embraced by Japanese Americans in the rapidly changing context of a globalized Hawai'i, then whose Japan and which culture would constitute that heritage and what form would it take? And, more important, how would these elements intersect with people of different ages, generations, (mixed) ethnicities, and social classes? Linking these shifting sectors to "Japanese cultural heritage" makes for a moving target that repeatedly ties itself down to yesteryears and past generations; thus, the continual return to conservative themes of heritage, tradition, and pride in the CBF.

The question remains, who constitutes the community and how is the CBF

Queen meant to best represent it? The 1994 CBF theme of "Enriching Our Community" provides a good example of the nebulousness of the concepts, as well as the ambiguity over how an organization (and its public representative, the CBF Queen) might "enrich" it.[15] The politicians who provided letters published in the souvenir book each had their own interpretation of the theme. Governor John Waihee interpreted the theme as promoting "activities aimed at sharing the culture, heritage and traditions of Hawaii's Japanese-Americans with all of the people of our state" (Waihee 1994:3). In Waihee's view, the HJJCC and CBF enrich the general community of Hawai'i by presenting Japanese American "culture, heritage and traditions." The conservatism of the CBF, then, like ethnic presentations elsewhere in the United States, finds its value specifically in looking backward to their differences rather than forward to their common milieu. An event such as the CBF is meant to trace the threads of a multicultural society retrogressively to "homelands." This is not so much about emplacement, but about historical displacement to past countries, cultures, and traditions. Performing difference is a civic responsibility, enriching the pluralism of Hawai'i by keeping ethnic threads separate. As Joyce Kono (later Joyce Fasi, wife of Honolulu Mayor Frank Fasi), a participant in the 1957 CBF Queen contest, recalled, "As Hawaii becomes more and more the rainbow of nationalities in the Pacific, we who live here must strive to give each ethnic group its special distinction. It is this quality which gives purpose to our being here" (Fasi 1990:72). The rainbow of ethnicity (Kono's "nationalities"), then, shines most vividly when the separate colors are kept distinct from each other.

Other politicians tied the HJJCC and CBF less to Japanese American culture and more to multiculturalism, a common theme in Hawai'i in the 1980s and 1990s. For example, Lieutenant Governor Benjamin Cayetano wrote, "We should ensure that our children understand and appreciate the cultures of others because they make Hawaii a very special place in which to live" (Cayetano 1994:5). In Cayetano's interpretation, an event such as the CBF makes Hawai'i "a very special place" specifically because of its celebration of difference.

In contrast to these, Japanese Consul General Kensaku Hogen emphasized Japanese cultural values: "This year's theme . . . highlights the Junior Chamber's commitment to providing the community with opportunities for personal growth, cultural awareness and leadership development as well as promoting the traditional values of Japan in Hawaii" (Hogen 1994:9). At the same time, U.S. Representative Neil Abercrombie proclaimed, "Our special sense of community is what makes our island lifestyle unique. It provides a framework for our island values which emphasize our connections and concern for one another. By underlining those values, the 42nd Annual CBF is truly 'enriching our community'" (Abercrombie 1994:13). In contrast with Consul General Hogen's statement, Abercrombie's words reconfigure "traditional values of Japan" into "island values." In this way, Japaneseness becomes part of Hawai'i and Asian culture becomes local.

The Jaycee organizers adopted a different stance, looking forward rather than backward. HJJCC President Robert Morita contended:

> Each successive generation feels a need to prove itself ready to face the challenges that the world presents to it. To successfully meet these challenges, we must do so enthusiastically and aggressively. This year's Junior Chamber theme of "Accepting the Challenge . . . Striving for Community Enrichment" emphasizes this very point.[16] (Morita 1994:14)

To this, CBF Chairman Michael Matsuo added: "It is for . . . two reasons — providing enriching activities for the entire community to enjoy; and personal growth for the contestants and Jaycees — that we have chosen 'Enriching Our Community' as the theme of this year's festival" (Matsuo 1994:15).

What ties many of these statements together is the construction of Hawai'i as a special "multicultural" place, maintained in part by ethnic events such as the CBF. For politicians whose concern is with the overall community of Hawai'i, the CBF can do no better than play a conservative role as a keeper of Japanese (American) tradition. The concerns of the Jaycees — young adults near the beginnings of their careers and starting families — is more on personal growth, organizational development, and community service. Thus, although the Jaycees themselves may want to emphasize progressive elements, those around them expect an event such as the CBF to provide a conservative rejoinder, pulling Japanese Americans back to earlier generations, as well as to Japan.

What is key is that identity for many Queens and organizers alike resides more authentically in Japan than in Hawai'i, even when they speak of their "Japanese American heritage." In this way the locus of identity references Japan and Japanese culture, rather than Japanese American historical and contemporary experiences in Hawai'i. Although immigrant experiences in Hawai'i are not ignored, they are often bypassed in the CBF. Souvenir books and Festival events showcase benign performances of Japanese tea ceremony and shamisen rather than the turbulent Japanese American history of labor strikes, plantation work, and wartime racism. Japanese American identity is thus built on a celebration of the distant and past rather than on controversies found in one's own recent backyard of Hawai'i.

Quietly Revoicing Okinawan (Non)Issues

One area of controversy in the Japanese American backyard of Hawai'i was that of Okinawans/Uchinanchu and the nonissue of their participation and crowning in the CBF. On the one hand, Naichi discrimination against persons of Okinawan ancestry was considered a shameful part of issei history that had lingered in nisei consciousness and practice, and finally evolved into ignorance and mixed feelings for sansei. On the other hand, throughout the 1970s into the 1990s, Okinawans remained as underrepresented among CBF contestants as in the 1950s and 1960s. Typically only one or perhaps two women of Okinawan ancestry participated in any given year. In some years there were none. Within this context, the crowning of Myrah Higa in 1976 as the first CBF Queen with an Okinawan surname, followed three years later by the crowning of her sister, LeAnne Higa, caused only a minor stir (see Chapter 6). Neither of the Higa sisters recalled any negative reactions in either Hawai'i or Japan to their Okinawan ancestry. While some may see the lack of attention paid to crowning a first Okinawan Queen as a positive sign of acceptance, others may see this as part of a practice of ignoring Okinawans. It is a historical contrast between "passing" (and assimilating) as a group and performing cultural difference as a point of pride and politicized identity. Sansei during this period were split between those like the Higa sisters, who considered themselves Japanese foremost and Okinawans secondarily, and a younger (and later) breed who proudly proclaimed their Uchinanchu status as part of a cultural revitalization movement that began in the 1980s.[17] The CBF was not part of this dynamic movement and did little to acknowledge it.

[handwritten margin note: Okinawan ancestory was still an issue in the CBF]

Yet Queens of Okinawan ancestry from this era talked quietly about being Okinawan in a still-naichi dominant world. When the subject of being Okinawan comes up in interviews, the rhythm of conversation skips a beat, the tone of voice drops, and the jaw clenches momentarily. Queen Jody-Lee Ige (1982 – 1983) discussed her experiences:

> CY: Did you feel that there was a consciousness of you being Okinawan?
> JI: *There were some comments made.*
> CY: By whom?
> JI: *Yeah, because there were the Higa girls [Queens Myrah and LeAnne]. So there were the first two Okinawan girls and they were sisters. There was a comment to remind me that, "Oops. We had two before. You're gonna be the third." I thought, "Oh, that's interesting that people even look at that and know that." Because if I were to hear different names, I wouldn't know Okinawan from [not-Okinawan Japanese].*
> (Personal communication, December 6, 2001)

Ige's experiences are a far cry from earlier generations of Okinawan discrimination. Yet, the consciousness of difference remains whispered around the Queen pageant. For example, one person I interviewed revealed a conspiracy rumor that had been circulating. During the 1970s and 1980s, some observers thought they detected a suspicious pattern in regular alternation between Okinawan and Naichi Queens: Myrah Higa in 1975, LeAnne Higa in 1978, Jody-Lee Ige in 1981, Lisa Nakahodo in 1983. What is important is not confirming or denying the deliberateness of the pattern; rather, it is significant that people detect a conspiratorial pattern at all. In other words, a CBF Queen's Okinawan ancestry — even when sansei and yonsei organizers and Queens are theoretically not supposed to care or notice — was noteworthy enough to generate rumor.[18] Such whispers continue even as others loudly proclaim their status as Uchinanchu, embracing music, dance, and other cultural performances of a celebrated, politicized identity.

Scrambling for an Audience: Moving toward Mixing

By these decades, the interest of the general public in the CBF was obviously waning. The Festival no longer made headlines or even front-page news. Crowds no longer thronged shopping centers to view contestants. Attendance at the pageant and other events declined. The waning interest was not due to any laxness on the part of organizers. On the contrary, the HJJCC worked harder than ever to come up with new events that might interest the public.

These new events ran the gamut from song contests to sporting events. From 1969 on, the HJJCC held an amateur song contest called the Kōhaku Uta Gassen (Red and White Song Competition), following the pattern set by a popular televised New Year's Eve music show of the same name in Japan.[19] Although originally limited to Japanese songs and singers, by 1973 the Kōhaku included locally well-known, non-Japanese entertainers and songs. In 1983 organizers of the CBF added sporting events, such as a golf tournament that continues into the 2000s and a six-kilometer fun run, which ended in 1993.

None of these events seemed to work to capture a broad audience for the CBF. The 1985 souvenir book publicly lamented the lack of interest in the CBF (quoted at the beginning of this chapter). The Festival was clearly out of synch with changing times, activities, interests, and demographics. It suffered from a fundamental disconnect with the community. In the framework of this book, it had become banal. As organizers sought solutions in many directions, the possibility of including mixed-race CBF contestants as a way of embracing a larger community touched a particularly raw nerve.

The suggestion to include mixed-race contestants was not new. As far back as 1972, HJJCC President Ronald Nagano remarked: "Each of the 14 contestants is of pure-blooded Japanese descent, a requirement of the contest. This may change in the future . . . if we can't find enough pure-blooded Japanese girls" (quoted by Creamer 1972:A2). Both the pure-blood requirement of contestants and the assumption of their eventual scarcity were part of the discourse surrounding the CBF from the 1970s on. In a 1985 essay entitled "Tomorrow . . . The Future Is Ours," the HJJCC spelled out the issues:

In the future, there will be very few full-blooded Japanese-Americans. . . . The situation may have two different effects upon the lives of the Japanese-American. Primarily, identity as a Japanese-American will be diluted. Efforts to preserve an ethnic identity will be difficult if not almost impossible. . . . Alternatively, on a positive side, intermarriage may cause a great diversity in the ethnic base of Japanese Americans. Possibly in the future, a person who is a quarter Japanese will still identify with his or her Japanese culture. However, this is somewhat contrary to the Japanese concept of purism [sic]. Even today, a person who is not pure Japanese may bear a certain stigma when regarded by the Japanese-American community at large. A prime example of this is the Cherry Blossom Festival. After 33 years, a contestant must still be of full Japanese ancestry in order to enter. Essentially, the message conveyed is that unless a girl is fully Japanese she is not recognized as being Japanese-American and is considered to be unsuitable to represent the community. To keep with this kind of purist thinking could be detrimental to the Cherry Blossom Festival and the Japanese-American community as a whole. . . Intermarriage among Japanese-Americans with other ethnic groups is common. . . . Mixed Japanese should be embraced by the community as being no less Japanese than those of full blood. This will help to ensure that the culture is perpetuated and that there will always be a sense of pride in the legacy that has been left by the Issei and Nisei. (HJJCC 1985:54)

This kind of frank discussion of intermarriage and resultant mixed-race contestants sounds more like backroom talk, rather than front-stage discourse, yet appears in the public forum of the CBF souvenir book. An essay such as this ties together critical elements of ethnic identity, blood, and culture (see discussion of race-culture quagmire in Chapter 7). It also raises the issue of entitlement, asking who has the right to represent the Japanese American community. Finally, it advocates inclusiveness, rather than blood-quantum-based exclusiveness, in its embrace of persons of mixed-blood and its attempt to decouple blood from membership.

The Jaycees continued with a call for mixed-race contestants in order to revitalize the CBF:

to get more contestant participation, CBF opens up to accept part-Japanese women.

By assisting to broaden the foundation of Japanese Americans in Hawaii, the Japanese Jaycees may stimulate additional interest in Japanese culture. A possible method is to encourage more part-Japanese people to participate in the CBF. This can be achieved by opening up the Cherry Blossom Pageant to part-Japanese women. This will add new vitality to an aging event and possibly activate thousands of part-Japanese to become more aware of their ethnic identity. (ibid.:55)

Clearly, the issue of mixed-race contestants would not go away. In fact, it would lead to major, radical reform of the CBF in 1998 in preparation for the 1999 contest. That it was preceded almost fifteen years earlier by statements in the CBF souvenir book shows only that what was backroom talk had attained front-room visibility/audibility.

Chapter Six

Herstories II | 1970s – 1990s

20p9

Eighteenth Cherry Blossom Queen Katherine Horio, 1970–1971

K athy Horio's reputation well precedes her. Different Jaycee members told me I must talk with Kathy, describing her as great, wonderful, fantastic. With each superlative, she became the super Cherry Blossom Queen. So it was with considerable anticipation that I drove to the top of an exclusive urban heights area of Honolulu to interview her on December 17, 2001. I was not disappointed. With one movement she ushered me in, welcomed me warmly, and offered me a seat in her casual but elegant living room. Her hair was short, layered, and highlighted. It was a far cry from the long tresses for which she was known in the 1970s, when this daughter of a doctor was both Polynesian dancer and Cherry Blossom Queen.

Her story is apt for the era. Kathy was never a political activist, nor does she call herself a feminist, but she does label herself a rebel. A high school dropout, she performed Polynesian dance professionally by night and surfed by day. She was the antithesis of the Cherry Blossom Queen. She talks about her own self-reform, of which returning to school and participating in the CBF played a large part. She is someone who can only learn by doing, so she had to do it all. This included running away from the comforts of an upper-middle-class home as well as re-creating herself as a Japanese American beauty queen. In each, she threw herself in it fully and performed to the hilt.

On paper Kathy fit the Cherry Blossom Queen mold: tall (five feet, five inches), university student at the time of her competition, from an upper-middle-class family background. But she was deeply tanned ("purple" in the local slang) from surfing and had long hair for performing Polynesian dance. Even the tiniest scratch below the surface shows many cracks in the mold. It is those cracks that make her story worthwhile. More than the cracks, however, it is the life that she has made for herself before and after her reign as Queen that make her story compelling. The life of a doer, the Cherry Blossom title is only one of her many accomplishments. How she places that title within the rest of her life and how she layers being Japanese American as but one part of her identity as a person, a woman, a wife/mother, a performer, and a volunteer frame her story with significance.

As we spoke, she was sincere and thoughtful in her responses. She paused to

1970
Cherry Blossom
Queen
KATHERINE HORIO

Fig. 6. Eighteenth Cherry Blossom Queen Katherine Horio, 1970 – 1971

consider the answers to some of my questions, and never gushed. My questions took her back over thirty years. During those thirty years she had married a doctor, raised a son, become active in hula (though this time as part of a Christian ministry program), and helped the Jaycees with the CBF. Kathy seems to thrive on a busy schedule. She is the only Queen who has ever e-mailed or phoned me to suggest research-related things to do or other people to interview. I understand why the Jaycees were so eager for me to talk with her: having Kathy on your side is like harnessing an army of energy, resources, contacts, and can-do optimism.

CY: Kathy, how did you get involved in the Cherry Blossom Festival?

KH: *I was actually very nontraditional Japanese. My parents were from San Francisco. We were born here when my father was doing his internship, because he couldn't get an internship in San Francisco. So having parents who were from the mainland was a little different.*

I feel very fortunate to have been raised here. Had a very happy, normal childhood, I would say, quite Japanese [American]. I was the middle child, I was the real rebel, but my older brother and younger sisters were A students. I just ceased to care from eighth grade. A Japanese [American] friend from California came over and taught me how to surf. I got real interested in Polynesian things and then I became totally Hawaiian. Changed my entire group of friends, hung out in Waikīkī, and got very interested in becoming a Tahitian dancer. Which I was fortunate to do. I was so purple [deeply tanned] with long hair and not looking very Japanese anymore. So I started dancing and that led to my being able to dance in Japan for an entire summer.

CY: As a Polynesian dancer?

KH: *As a dancer. For an entire summer. I was about nineteen. That turned me around in terms of realizing the culture and the heritage that I had. Being in Japan and seeing and being exposed to the culture for three solid months. It was such a wonderful experience. I came back and decided I needed to finish high school and go to college. So I got my diploma through the GED [General Education Diploma]. And then I started attending UH [University of Hawai'i] and then I decided, I think it would be a real good way to explore my Japanese heritage by participating in the Cherry Blossom Festival.*

CY: Now did anybody approach you or did you seek them out?

KH: *Nope, nope, I sought them out. And in fact, I sought them out and they were all finished with the recruiting process. So they said, "Just give us a call next year." So I gave them a call the following year. So I literally just signed myself up. [Laughing]*

CY: What did your parents think of it then?

KH: *They thought it was great.*

CY: Can you tell me something about your surfing days?

KH: *I would be surfing when I was supposed to be at school, and . . . I'm very extreme. Very all-or-nothing kind of person. And my father kept saying, "You can surf and go to school, you can dance and go to school." [I was] very hard-headed, very rebellious, and I give them a lot of credit now that I'm a parent for being so* supportive and understanding and never giving up on me. My father even took up surfing — because he'd be standing out there [calling to me], "It's time to come in and go home." And I would never heed his waving his towel, so he took up surfing so he could come out and get me.

CY: And then when you came home from that summer in Japan doing Polynesian dance?

KH: *It was an entire summer in Japan, really fabulous experience getting to dance.*

CY: Did you have a stage name as a Tahitian dancer?

KH: *My name was Tehani, which means My Darling in Tahitian, which is from the* Mutiny on the Bounty.

CY: What did your dancing friends think about you then, doing a 180 [degree switch] in some ways and running for Cherry Blossom?

KH: *They thought it was great. They were totally behind me. I was also attending* UH *at that time, and I would literally just run into class and leave. I was not a real college person. My life was dancing six nights a week for Tavana [Polynesian troupe] and when the pageant came around, that was pretty busy. I continued dancing throughout not only the entire Festival, but the entire year that I was Queen, and kept going to* UH. *So I would literally go from kimono, hair up, and crown, to work every night, hair down, Tahitian dancing mode.*

CY: What did the Jaycees say about that?

KH: *The Jaycees were very understanding, as was Tavana, my boss. He got a kick out of it. We just had to be very careful, because they did not want the show to benefit in any way commercially. And they didn't. They didn't. I think we had a lot of Japanese tourists coming at that time. The tour operators would quietly say, "Oh, she's the Cherry Blossom Queen, Sakura no jōō [Cherry Blossom Queen]." But they didn't capitalize upon it. So it was a very workable thing. And I think it was unique and interesting for everybody, because that had never happened before. And I think I was a very good ambassador, because I was so Hawaiian, but at the same time very Japanese.*

CY: Now, was there a problem, though? I would think that for something like Tahitian dance, you might need to be tanned, but for Cherry Blossom, you might not want that?

KH: *Right. So I was not very tanned that year. That was fine with my boss. They have great stage lights and makeup. My grandmother was very happy. They [Japanese Americans] thought it was horrible to be so purple [deeply tanned] in those days, which is blacker than black. [Chuckles]*

CY: Can you tell me something about what it was like as a contestant?

KH: *I loved the other contestants. You do get to be like sisters. It's a real bonding that happens. It's a wonderful group experience. So it wasn't that I felt better than any of them or more beautiful, by no means, 'cause it's not about physical beauty or the way you look. It was simply that I felt so unique. I felt being raised here, but with parents who had been through internment and war experience, combined with my total immersion and love of Polynesian things and life. I had a Samoan boyfriend at the time.*

CY: I bet the Jaycees loved that.

KH: *I don't think they were really aware of it. So anyway, when I was running, I just felt that what I could bring to represent the community was just really unique and special.*

CY: Had you worn a kimono before?

KH: *No. I had worn yukatas, but that's not the same thing. They had us practice with Mrs. Yorita, who dressed everyone for the CBF pageants for years, but also for every appearance during the year I was Queen. And it was from her entire collection.*

CY: So what was it like to put on a kimono for the first time?

KH: *It was interesting and it felt good. Perhaps part of my ease in experiencing everything that was involved was being an entertainer and being in costume. Although I must say, that's a very unique costume where you can't breathe, eat, bend over.*

CY: So you felt very constricted when you were in a kimono?

KH: *Felt constricted, but felt very nice. It was a very positive experience, and I had a beautiful peach kimono given to me in Tokyo as one of my gifts.*

CY: Now 1970 would have been also a time of bra burning, women's liberation, and all those . . .

KH: *Haight-Ashbury, the height of the hippie flower movement.*

CY: So how did you feel about being a beauty queen in that era?

KH: *Ironically my mother was more the bra-burning, sign-picketing marcher at UH than I was. I had moved from this total Polynesian life, I was still in it, but to this next phase, and I'm sorry to say, not as aware or involved with world politics as I think I should have been. So I don't think beauty pageants are passé and pointless and ridiculous. I don't agree with that because I do think there's a purpose to it and I think a large part of it is just promoting the awareness in the community of the Japanese culture and heritage.*

CY: Is there any event that you can think of that you'd call a highlight as Queen?

KH: *Probably getting to go to Japan. My entire family decided to go with me, except for my brother. I was such a rebellious teen and my dad was so proud. And it was a way that I sort of made up for giving him such a hard time, being such a rebellious teenager. So, I'd have to say that would be one of the highlights. It was a wonderful family trip.*

CY: I understand you've acted as judge for the CBF. What do you look for as a judge?

KH: *I look for someone who has the same qualities that I see in the Jaycees that I treasure and value. And that I think is someone who has great inner beauty, and what I mean by that is, grace and a heart, a really big heart, caring, integrity, not necessarily the outward beauty. Because we've had beautiful girls who are just either really shallow or don't have the right reasons, motivations, for participating in it, which are very obvious and very clear. Someone who just feels like she has a lot to offer not only in terms of wanting to explore their Japanese culture and heritage, but also to give back to the community.*

CY: Is there any kind of advice that you give to contestants?

KH: *I like to tell contestants or Queens to think of yourself as a queen, walk as a queen, and not in a boastful way. But with the true Japanese quality of humility and modesty, but pride in being Japanese, pride that you can have this incredible opportunity to represent the Japanese community of Hawai'i, which is so unique and special.*

Twenty-fourth Cherry Blossom Queen Myrah Higa, 1976–1977

Whenever I asked current Jaycee members about the first CBF Queen of Okinawan ancestry, the name of Myrah Higa inevitably came up. She was the first Queen with an Okinawan surname, and most people assumed that she was thus the first Okinawan Queen. They were wrong, but it made little difference for the value of talking with Myrah.

Myrah is vice-president of an independent aviation company with offices near the Honolulu International Airport. Her company services VIPs who prefer the privacy of a Lear jet to the long waits and security lines at airports. I drove out to her office on the tarmac on December 14, 2001. Mi, as she calls herself, was immaculately groomed in corporate dress, with a ready smile and firm handshake. She credits the CBF with preparing her to become a career woman. It was through pageant training that she learned to conduct herself gracefully, whether standing, walking, or sitting. It was then that she learned the tricks of makeup and the arts of gendered presentation that she carries with her constantly. She exudes an air of confidence common to those accustomed to doing things well. Despite her compact five-foot, one-inch frame, she stands tall, maintains eye contact while speaking, and remembers names. These are some of the lessons of the pageant she has internalized.

At the aviation company, Mi acts as both hostess and executive, making others feel comfortable while ensuring that everything runs smoothly. She is the most public face of the company and one of its senior executives, yet she does

Queen Myrah

Photo by McKINLEY PHOTO STUDIO
Roy Yoshitsugu, Proprietor

Fig. 7. Twenty-fourth Cherry Blossom Queen Myrah Higa, 1976 – 1977

not find it beneath her to pick up the rubbish from the waiting area, rearrange the plastic chairs for guests, or straighten the framed pictures on the walls. She does these things almost unconsciously, without missing a beat in the conversation. Those whom she makes feel comfortable include not only her estimable clients, but also her staff. Many of her employees are attractive females who handle the front office and greet customers with the same style, grooming, and hospitality that have become Mi's trademark. I wondered if they had all gone through pageant training, or if they had learned it on Mi's insistence on polished presentation.

Like many others of Okinawan descent in her generation, Mi refers to Japanese culture as "our" culture. She says that she went to Japanese school and always identified herself as Japanese (American), not necessarily Okinawan. However, during the time when she was growing up in the 1950s and 1960s, the differences between Okinawan and Japanese culture were downplayed in Hawai'i. They existed, but for many people of Okinawan descent the differences were seen as regional rather than cultural. Thus, Mi considers herself Japanese as much as Okinawan.

Mi is impressive in her refusal to take any of her accomplishments for granted. Whether winning the Cherry Blossom crown against odds or becoming vice-president in a male-dominated industry, she has earned her berth. In her current endeavors, she parlays the presentational and hospitality skills she developed in part as CBF Queen into professional smoothness and competence. She wears her accomplishments well. Talking with Mi, one is inevitably motivated to sit up a little straighter, speak more clearly, and arrange one's body into an artful pose.

CY: What made you decide to run in the Cherry Blossom Festival?

MH: *Curiosity. Because you know we're third-generation Japanese and we're so American, so Westernized. It was nice to at least try to get connected back to our roots. And I think more than that it was learning how to wear kimono. I'd never worn them before. And that was part of it. And having a charm course. I thought, well, wouldn't that be fun.*

CY: How old were you at the time?

MH: *Twenty-one. I had just graduated from the university with a bachelor's of education, so I was already teaching, doing some long-term substituting at Wa'anae Elementary [in rural O'ahu]. So that's how I got into the Cherry Blossom Festival, not expecting to win. First of all, I'm vertically challenged.*

CY: How tall are you?

MH: *Five-one. And so all these girls are tall and beautiful. I thought, "Wouldn't it be great to just put a kimono on and have a picture in a kimono?" So that and going to charm course. I thought, wouldn't it be great to learn something new. As well as our culture.*

CY: Did people contact you and say, "Are you interested in running?"

MH: *Yes. They called me and asked if I'd be interested in running.*

CY: Were you surprised?

MH: *Very surprised.*

CY: How did they get your name?

MH: *That's a good question. I think because I was pretty visible at that time. I was also a cheerleader at the University of Hawai'i. I think that's where they probably . . . , "Well, she's Japanese, let's see if she'd be interested." And from what I understand, it was a little difficult to find contestants who'd be willing to run.*

CY: And your reaction when they called you up?

MH: *It's like, "Me?!" Well, first of all, my concern was, because my parents had just put me through college, and still had my sister in college, my brother was in high school, you know, finances were a concern. Because I had heard of all these pageants where the parents would have to do this major outlay of cash. So that was my first concern. They were telling me about all the wonderful things they were going to do for me, makeup classes, charm classes, and I said, "Well, how much is this gonna cost?" They said, "Nothing. The Cherry Blossom organization will sponsor everything. And make an even playing field." So the girls' dresses are from the same designer. You design the dress, but the seamstress will be doing it for you.*

CY: So it's not as if the girl with the most money, who could buy the fanciest gown, has an advantage.

MH: *Exactly. Right. So I thought, "That would be nice." They went down the list: hair and makeup will be taken care of, your dress, your kimono, so they said, "Really, your parents won't be responsible for anything. And you get all these wonderful benefits." And I thought, "Wow. That is really nice. What a nice thing to do." And so for me, I'm very grateful to the organization that they allowed us to be a part of the cultural experience and not burden our parents with that.*

CY: From participating in it, what were the culture elements of it that you found?

MH: *The thing that it reinforced in me was the pride in being Japanese. The pride it took as a group to put this structure [Japanese Chamber of Commerce building] together even after the war. You know, these are our parents still being affected by the war. And they could still gather together, to reflect and watch these people still be a contributing member of society with no bitterness.*

CY: You're talking primarily about the Jaycees?

MH: *The Jaycees. You know wanting to be a part of this organization, having pride in their own heritage, that they'd be willing to sponsor this pageant. Being fair, you know, allowing opportunities for everyone. And it was just a nice reinforcement of all of that. And so, it gave me another opportunity to be proud of being Japanese. I think that was the one nice thing that I saw.*

CY: Had you ever been to Japan before?

MH: *Never.*

CY: Or did you speak Japanese?

MH: *I learned to speak a little bit. But growing up in a home where my parents said, "You're American."*

CY: Did they actually say that to you?

MH: *Yeah. "You're an American." They encouraged us to go to Japanese school, but it wasn't mandatory. "But you need to speak English and learn it well, because you are an American. You're Japanese American. So learn it well."*

CY: Had you done anything like ikebana or Japanese dance, any kind of Japanese arts?

MH: *Never. Nothing. And so to be exposed to it during this time was wonderful.*

CY: What were your parents' reactions when you said, "I'm thinking of running for Cherry Blossom"?

MH: *I think they were like me, a little shocked, like, "Okaaay . . ." And the same thing, you know, "How much is it going to cost us?"*

CY: Why were they shocked, do you think?

MH: *First of all, I had already graduated from college. So they thought I was a little too old for it. And they wanted to know why I would even choose to go through it.*

CY: But I guess the opposite question would be, "Why not?"

MH: *I guess they wanted to let me know that you'd be up there with a lot of people and really only one person can make it. And they said, "What happens if you don't get in?" And I said, "I'm not expecting to. So I won't have any disappointment. It'll be a fun thing to do."*

CY: Was it fun?

MH: *I thought it was wonderful. It was great. I learned to walk like I'm supposed to walk.*

CY: What else did you learn how to do?

MH: *Learned how to put makeup on. And how to do different things with my hair to change the appearance. You know, these are like options in life. It taught me that you don't have to do the same thing every day. And make the best of what you've got. Thank god for makeup and hair dye! [Laughing]*

CY: If someone were to have met you before you did any of this training, and somebody were to have met you after, would they notice a difference, either outside or inside?

MH: *I don't think they would have noticed it immediately. The change I think was very gradual over the years, that I've taken as a result of that. In fact, even this job is really a reflection of what happened when I became Queen. It made me work hard toward something. They helped to motivate each one of us to do our best and be our best, to show our best. Back then, I remember feeling like this timid*

Japanese girl who didn't know how to walk or dress or put makeup on or get my hair done. So what a neat experience. It taught how to make the best of all the potential you have. I think over the years being on top may appear glamorous, but it's hard work and there's a lot that people don't even know about. You're lonely at the top.

CY: As Queen?

MH: *As a Queen. Yes. And people would question, "Why her?" you know. And you get all of those. But I realized from that experience, that if you are on top, you will always get attacked. Because why would someone kick someone who is already on the ground. And so these are really great lessons for me that I've learned. And being the only female in a four-person partnership.*

CY: This company?

MH: *Yes, this. You know it is lonely being the only female in it. Being in charge of my division or my department and having to make the hard calls and being lonely. And so I took a lot of that from that wonderful experience. If you ask me, "Would I do it today?" I don't know if I would.*

CY: Really?

MH: *The reason I guess I wouldn't do it again was, after it was over, and even maybe during the reigning time, because you were now slightly celebrity status or a Cherry Blossom Queen, you got scrutinized a lot. So I couldn't go to the supermarket in rubber slippers with my hair up and no makeup anymore, because, "Oh, my god, is that the Cherry Blossom Queen?" At the beginning it was really difficult to face those . . . because I could hear the whispers.*

CY: You really could sense that?

MH: *Not only sense it. I could hear it. I have great hearing! [Laughing] And so at first I was rather defensive. It's my life now, I'm back to my private life. But you know, that title comes with a responsibility. So you're always being looked at. But I'm kind of glad it did happen, because it made me more aware of "What are we presenting of ourselves?" It is presenting our best every day. And sometimes we do need that little push. Or reminder that, you know, be your best every day.*

CY: I've been told that you're the first Queen of Okinawan ancestry. [This interview was conducted before that with Queen Gwen Nishizawa.]

MH: *Right. So that's another reason why I thought, "There's no way I'm gonna win." My mother would even say, "You know, no Okinawan has won." I said, "It's okay, I'm not here to win. I'm just here to have a good time."*

CY: Did you feel any kind of pressure or criticism, either from the Japanese or Okinawan side?

MH: *Not really. And I went in with a little bit of apprehension because of it. You know, would I be facing that? And it wasn't. I actually felt like I am Japanese.*

CY: Previously, when you've been talking, you've mentioned only being Japanese, and not necessarily being Okinawan.

MH: *I forgot that that was one of my concerns too. But that's a reason why I didn't think I would have a chance. I am vertically challenged and I'm Okinawan!*

CY: You overcame both. [Laughing] During the time of your reign as Queen, did you sense any kind of criticism or did you feel any kind of awkwardness?

MH: *No. And to tell you the truth I was expecting it, but never felt it. And so it was nice to see that maybe in our lifetime, in my mother's lifetime, she could feel that things had gotten better for us. I think in her generation, they did feel it, you know, "the pig farmers" [Okinawan stereotype; lower class] versus "the merchants" [Naichi stereotype; middle class] type of thing. And so it was nice to see that things had changed for the better.*

CY: If you were to judge the CBF pageant, what do you think you would look for?

MH: *I think, because the fact of life is, you have to look at the person's appearance. Who can carry the charisma or the poise of being the Cherry Blossom Queen to represent the Japanese community? I mean, body language says a lot. That's what I teach here with the girls [at the aviation company]. Body language says 70 percent of what you really mean to say. So every month or so, I give them a body language course.*

CY: And when you train your female employees, what do you tell them?

MH: *I tell them that [long pause] how you dress, how you carry yourself, is really a reflection of how you feel about yourself. And it comes through by the choices you make. And I said, "All of those choices are reflected in your body. Your body language, your body choices." Because no one's forcing you to do anything. In our business we're watched by our competitors and our customers. So you're on stage all the time. And maybe that's what I learned most about being Cherry Blossom Queen. You're always on stage until you get home, and you close your own doors at home. And that night of the pageant I said, "Okay, this is it. One opportunity. I've got ten minutes and let's see what happens." You know, be your best, show your best, because you've only got one opportunity.*

Thirty-fourth Cherry Blossom Queen Lenny Yajima, 1986–1987

Lenny Yajima breaks the mold of the stereotypical Cherry Blossom Queen. Although tall and from a "good family," she did not stay in Hawai'i after graduating from high school. Instead, she went to Harvard University, amassing credits at such a rapid pace, she spent a semester in Japan as an undergraduate,

THIRTY-FIFTH ANNUAL
CHERRY BLOSSOM FESTIVAL
HONOLULU JAPANESE JUNIOR CHAMBER OF COMMERCE 1987

Fig. 8. Thirty-fourth Cherry Blossom Queen Lenny Yajima, 1986 – 1987

in effect stalling so that she could graduate with her class. She is by no means a provincial local girl.

If any person has grown up amid high expectations and abundant role models, it is Lenny. Her maternal grandfather, Steere Noda, was a state senator and one of Hawai'i's distinguished athletes. Her maternal grandmother, Alice

Noda, was one of the founding members of the Japanese Women's Society, had her own career as a dental hygiene instructor, and helped professionalize cosmetology in Hawai'i and Japan. Lenny grew up surrounded by CBF planning and activities. Her father, Tad Yajima, was one of the founding members of the HJJCC and acted as CBF general chairman in 1956. Her mother, Lillian Yajima, contributed to the success of the CBF by sewing capes (see Chapter 3), producing plays, and organizing displays of Japanese costumes. That Lenny emerged from this high-powered milieu as a levelheaded, hardworking, unpretentious, and down-to-earth woman is testament to the intelligence, common sense, and strong commitment to public service within which she was raised.

Most people with a similar family background would be accustomed to other people looking past them to their illustrious parents and grandparents. Lenny, however, has accomplished a great deal on her own merit. Aside from becoming Cherry Blossom Queen, she also served as the first female general chair of the CBF in 1992. However, when one meets Lenny, all these accomplishments fade from the picture. She is not one to live in the past, even the not-so-distant one. She lives very much in the present, which is filled with the challenges faced by many working mothers.

She answered my questions thoughtfully, but — like her mother whom I interviewed months earlier — requested to review anything I intended to print to ensure that her words were grammatically correct and coherent. Impression management may run deeply in this high-profile family. Both Lenny and her mother also share attention to detail, high levels of energy, and earnest commitment.

I met Lenny at a suburban Honolulu mall on November 7, 2001. She had come straight from work and wore sensible clothes and little makeup. This former Queen did not capitalize on any kind of studied glamour or glitz. Instead, she looked very much the no-nonsense, working mother that she is.

CY: Lenny, can you tell me how you became interested in things Japanese?

LY: *I became interested in things Japanese when I went to Harvard, believe it or not. I remember watching "Roots" [the television mini-series based upon Alex Haley's novel by the same name]. And all of a sudden, I just felt this urge to go back to my roots. [Chuckles] Up until then, my parents used to speak Japanese at home, and I'd say, "What are you talking about? Please tell me." They'd say, "No, if you want to understand what we're saying, you have to take Japanese." I said, "Okay." But I never did. And so from that point on, I decided I was gonna take Japanese language and go to Japan and visit my relatives. My father was a big help, because he reinitiated correspondence with our relatives in Japan. And I remember getting that letter back from the relatives there and being so excited because they remember us. They felt badly that we all lost touch with each other. And from that time, I made it a point to go over there, stay six months, and get reacquainted with them. Or get acquainted with them.*

CY: So it took going all the way to Harvard for you to want to know more about things Japanese?

LY: *That's right.*

CY: And what about Cherry Blossom Festival? Why did you decide to run?

LY: *I decided to run in the Cherry Blossom Festival because—I'll never forget his name—Dan Morimoto was in charge of the contestant search committee for the Thirty-fourth Festival. And he called me when I was working at Bank of Hawaii—I had just started a new position there—and asked if I was interested. And at first I really said, "No, I couldn't," because I had just started a new position and I knew it would take a lot of time. But he said, "Just give me fifteen minutes and let me talk to you about the Festival." And after those fifteen minutes, I said, "Okay." [Chuckles] He was a good salesperson. And I'm very glad he persuaded me to do that.*

CY: Now, what kinds of things did he tell you that made you decide to go ahead and do it?

LY: *I thought it was going to be a huge time commitment outside or during working hours. And again, I had made a commitment to Bank of Hawai'i in this new position. And I thought I wouldn't be able to ask for so much time off. So that was one big factor. He said, "No, most of the classes are in the evenings, and there are a few public appearances during the day, but they're at lunchtime." And he didn't think it would be such a big commitment during working hours. I thought we would have to go and get our own sponsor. I just don't like asking people to do things for me, so I thought that would be really hard if I had to ask people to sponsor me. But he said, "No, the Honolulu Japanese Junior Chamber of Commerce sponsors each contestant," and the only thing that we would have to do as a contestant would be to get a hairstylist to do our hair for free in exchange for advertising. And that wasn't hard at all.*

CY: Tell me something about becoming Queen and what might be some of the highlights.

LY: *Oh. I'm sure every Queen will tell you that the highlight of their year was the tour of Japan, which included an audience with the crown princess of Japan at that time. And we were very fortunate. It was Crown Princess Michiko, who is now Empress Michiko. She was the dignitary that we were allowed to have an audience with. And that was incredible. You felt yourself like a dignitary, going there to visit her.*

CY: What was it like to visit her?

LY: *Well, very nervous at first. But once you sat down with her—and my mother and father and the general chairperson, Gerald Oyasato, and the president of the Jaycees, Matt Miura — we were all allowed to be there. And once we were there, she is so gracious. She never once made you feel like you were visiting with a crown princess in a palace.*

CY: Do you remember what you talked about?

LY: *She wanted us to talk about Hawai'i. And I remember talking — at that time, Ellison Onizuka [the Japanese American astronaut from Hawai'i who had been killed in the Challenger space shuttle accident in January 1986] was in everyone's minds because of the Challenger tragedy. And we had brought her as gifts — a book about Ellison Onizuka. And then my mother had given her a book about notable women of Hawai'i. And there's a chapter in there about my grandmother. And so she was very interested in that, too. About the history of Japanese women in Hawai'i, and the nikkei, the Americans.*

CY: And have you ever been in any other beauty contests?

LY: *Yes. I was in one other beauty contest, the Miss Nikkei International Pageant in Brazil. And that was another great perk of becoming the Queen of the Festival [CBF]. I don't think every Queen went to the Nikkei International Festival. Because maybe of sponsorship. The* Hawaii Hochi *and* Hawaii Herald *sponsor the representative from Hawai'i to attend the Miss Nikkei International Festival. And it wasn't every year. But that particular year, they were looking for someone, so I said I'd do it, and my parents went with me. And again, we would never have gone to Brazil, I'm sure, if it weren't for this opportunity.*[1]

CY: Now, Lenny, as the Cherry Blossom Queen, you're unusual in being maybe the only one that subsequently served as a general chairperson. Can you talk about becoming the first female and Cherry Blossom Queen chairperson?

LY: *I think it was that my friend, Garrett Toguchi, who was the president of the Jaycees at the time, had asked if I would please consider being the general chairperson, because every year it's very difficult to find someone to chair the whole Festival. You have a lot of people willing to chair individual projects, or just to help with little things, but no one willing to take on the big responsibility. And when he asked he told me that it was already pretty late in the year, and they really needed somebody. I just said, "Okay." I did ask my husband first if it would be okay. [Chuckles] But I think he knew that he couldn't say no. So I have to thank him for supporting me on that, because I wasn't home very much for that whole year.*

CY: Can you tell me something about what it was like to be general chairperson?

LY: *It was very difficult, because there is no handbook on being a general chairperson. Although every year you hope that you're the one that's going to make the handbook. But you just have to go with your feelings as to what to do next. And you do have people who have been involved in past Festivals to help you out, but you're still pretty much on your own when it comes to making the big decisions. So I know we made quite a few changes that year, because I didn't know what else to do, so I said, "Okay, we're gonna just do this." And I'm glad that a lot of those changes can be seen in the book, the commemorative book for that fortieth Festival. And I know we brought on some new sponsors that year. But that was also tough, going out there and trying to get new sponsors for the Festival. People who really didn't know a whole lot about the Festival. And I remember one sponsor, a Japanese national, being kind of antagonistic, maybe because I was a woman and asking him for help. And he shall remain nameless. But anyway, that wasn't a good experience. But it was all part of a growing experience, I would say.*

CY: What are some of the changes that you made as general chairperson?

LY: *Changes to the sponsorship levels and how we categorize the sponsors were some of the changes that I made when I was general chairman. And changes to the commemorative book, some ideas that I had, and thankfully, people who had supported the Festival throughout the past ten years or so were able to help me find one of each of the past Cherry Blossom books so that we could take a photo of the cover of each book, and put those photos, in color, in the book. That had never been done before. And I had always wanted to do that. Because so many people asked, "Does anyone have a complete set of books? We'd like to see, you know, the covers." And nobody had a complete set. So I actually went to Canada to visit a longtime supporter of the Festival, someone named Lenny Lekivetz and his wife Dolly Lekivetz.[2] And he had lots of the old books. Not a whole set. But between the books that he had and the books my parents had, we were able to come up with a full set.*

CY: That's wonderful! Lenny, you've seen the contest from so many perspectives. As a daughter of an organizer, as a contestant, as a Queen, as a chair, et cetera. From all these different perspectives, what do you think is the essence of Cherry Blossom Festival?

LY: *The essence of the Cherry Blossom Festival is people in the Japanese community, including different ethnicities, just coming together, not being paid at all, to see to it that the younger generations, the generations after them, have an idea of the Japanese culture. And that's what it started off as. When my father was very involved in the Jaycees and the Cherry Blossom Festival, that was the idea, to perpetuate Japanese culture, traditions, and I'm just thankful that every year there have been enough volunteers to see it through without an interruption. Because some of the festivals here, I believe, have ended or stopped for a year or two and then started up again. When I was chairman, I was told that the Cherry Blossom Festival is the longest uninterrupted festival in Hawai'i. There may be other festivals that are celebrating longer anniversaries, but there was an interruption somewhere along the way. So we're the longest uninterrupted ethnic festival in Hawai'i.*

CY: Now, Lenny, one thing I forgot to ask you is about the jack-o'-lantern —

LY: *Jack-o'-lantern manjū.*

CY: Can you tell me something about the jack-o'-lantern manjū?

LY: *My mom loves to tell people that it's Lenny Yajima's jack-o'-lantern manjū. I remember before I got married, my mom and I would take some adult education classes. And there was one offered by Mōʻiliʻili Community Center [in Honolulu; includes Japanese craft classes] on manjū making. So we decided to take that class. It might have been during the fall and Halloween was coming up, and I thought, "Oh, that would be kinda neat to dye the dough orange, and then cut out little faces, and maybe make a stem and put green food coloring on it, and make manjū to look like jack o' lanterns." And when we did it, they really turned out cute. And we decided to make dozens of them and take them to Hale Pulama Mau [a nursing home originally for Japanese American elderly] and have the residents there enjoy a little treat that was, you know, kind of American and Japanese combined. So that was a big hit. And from then on, my mom was the one who decided she was gonna teach this to the contestants. And so I go there and I help.*

CY: So since then, it's become part of the Cherry Blossom tradition.

LY: *It has. [Chuckles] Lenny Yajima's jack-o'-lantern manjū. That's right, that's right.*

Forty-fifth Cherry Blossom Queen Cheryl Koide, 1997–1998

Perhaps it was the fact that most of the Queens I had met so far had held the title in much earlier decades, perhaps it was the faded jeans and t-shirt she was wearing on the day that I met her at a suburban Starbucks a mountain pass away from Honolulu, perhaps it was the way the slanting sunlight grazed her hair dyed brown in the style of so many teenagers, perhaps it was a combination of all the above — Cheryl Koide seemed very young as far as CBF Queens go. There was something fragile and even naive in her tendency to gush quietly, as if what she was saying was an intimate confession.

At five feet, seven inches, she is one of the taller CBF Queens. She is not classically pretty and not stately, but her smile is winning and her eyes always look moist with anticipation. There is no sense of mystery to Cheryl. Instead, there is a sense of wonderment, of seeing things for the first time, of discovering herself each day. She invites you to discover her as well, but depending on your own religiosity, that invitation may open new doors or produce an impasse. Cheryl is the born-again Christian Cherry Blossom Queen.[3]

Fig. 9. Forty-fifth Cherry Blossom Queen Cheryl Koide, 1997 – 1998

I include her story because she tells the classic tale of growing up wanting to be a Cherry Blossom Queen. I also include her story because it is an unusual account of simultaneously discovering her Japanese self through the CBF while awakening to Christianity and switching career paths from ophthalmology to ministry as a professional Christian singer. She sees no contradictions in the convergence of Japanese culture and Christianity in her life, all of which occurred over the year-and-a-half during which she was first a CBF contestant and then Queen.

Cheryl seems entirely led by her vision of Christian devotion. That vision kept bubbling to the surface of our conversation. It seeped into her irrepressible smiles and her sparkling eyes that gazed off into the distance. Her devotion led her to move from Hawai'i to Nashville, where she recorded a CD.[4] She was preparing for a tour of Japan at the time we spoke. She said that her manager thought she had real commercial potential in Japan as a Japanese American Christian singer going by "Kumie," her Japanese middle name. The twists and turns of her image made her marketable as a very unusual and attractive commodity.

We first met at a Starbucks on January 16, 2002, but I asked her to return for another interview a few days later on January 21 before the camera. I brought a guitar and requested that she sing one of her songs for me. She was happy to comply. She had composed "Beauty Queen" immediately following her reign and sang it with lilting voice to a quietly plucked guitar. The excerpt that follows is taken from that second interview to which Cheryl showed up relaxed in black knit top and jeans, with a white flower behind one ear. Throughout the interview before the camera, as at Starbucks, her smile never left her face. She always seemed on the verge of saying one thing more.

CY: Can you tell me something about how you decided to run for Cherry Blossom Queen?

CK: *Sure. Gosh, I've always wanted to be the Cherry Blossom Queen since I was a little girl. And I have memories of when I was six or seven, and I would see the [CBF] posters on the wall and I'd ask my aunties about it. And they'd just rave and rave about those girls and what it's like to be a Cherry Blossom Queen. So I think I knew from just a little girl time that it was something that I wanted to do. Just something that I totally looked up to.*

CY: And is it a case where people would say, "You should run for Cherry Blossom Queen"?

CK: *It is. A lot of people I remember telling me that, "Hey, Cheryl, when you grow up one day, you're gonna be the Cherry Blossom Queen." And just putting seeds in my mind about being the Cherry Blossom Queen one day. I think that played a really big part in me, just keeping that in the back of my head, growing up, going to college, and just that desire still being there.*

CY: Now, by the time you did run for Cherry Blossom Queen, the age of feminist critiques of beauty contests were well part of history. Did that kind of criticism play any part for you?

CK: *It really didn't. Even though I think in college, that is something that I became very aware of. The whole feminist movement. And who I am as a woman.*

But when it came down to the Cherry Blossom Festival, because it's not based completely on beauty, a lot is on poise and character and personality. I just saw it as something that I had wanted to do since I was a little girl. And I didn't take it so seriously as to analyze every angle, and what other people might think of it. I definitely don't see myself being in a pageant where it's solely based on beauty. And I think that beauty pageants nowadays mostly aren't. And the Cherry Blossom Festival is definitely on leadership and character, as well as it is physical beauty. So I didn't think too much about that.

CY: And when you thought about running, what did you want to get out of Cherry Blossom?

CK: *When I started running for Cherry Blossom? I think I didn't really know what I was getting into. [Laughs] All I knew was that it was gonna be a great experience to learn about my Japanese culture and get more in touch with my roots, and learn leadership as well as public speaking and interpersonal skills. It really was much more than I had anticipated it to be.*

CY: What was some of that training that you went through?

CK: *The training as a contestant and the training as Queen were both very intense. [Chuckles] And they were awesome experiences. As a contestant, we did a lot of cultural classes. And I got to learn a lot about just my heritage as a Japanese American. And it helped me to understand my family better and it gave me just a deeper appreciation for my culture. And then being the Queen for a year, I just grew so much in just interpersonal skills and public speaking and character and leadership and all those things that make me realize that that was the year that I really grew up.*

CY: Can you give an example of what you really latched onto as far as Japanese culture?

CK: *As far as Japanese culture, I think that the thing that I got the most or that hit me the most was just the appreciation of where I came from and where my ancestors came from. And it really helped me to appreciate my family a lot more, understanding where they came from and where their parents came from. And just understanding how tradition is passed down. That to me was just that understanding of who I am and who my family is in relation to our heritage, that was really the greatest thing I got through the training.*

CY: Now, at the same time that you were doing pageant training, I understand that you became a Christian. Can you tell me something about your becoming a Christian?

CK: *Well, during my time as a contestant, I was praying that, you know, if, God, you're real, please show me a sign. Because even though life was good, it felt like something was really missing in my life. I was doing the Cherry Blossom thing and I had met these two students in one of my English classes. And they were*

Christians. And it was the first time that I met anyone my age who was living a life that was in parallel with what they were saying. You know, they weren't just talking the talk, but they were walking the walk. And just through that, through their relationship with God, I got to understand who Jesus is, and just that prayer that I had been praying for so long, I felt like God was showing me that He really is real. And so I became a Christian when I was running for Cherry Blossom. And just my whole life changed. And that, coupled with Cherry Blossom together, now looking back, it — that was just a huge time in my life. And it was just a time of preparation and a time of training, and a time of really finding out and under-standing who I am.

CY: Can you tell me something about some of those changes?

CK: *Gosh, there were so many changes. I think the greatest change is just my perspective on life. I've always been very ambitious. And I don't think I've lost that ambition, but I've learned how to put it into perspective. My family life has changed as well and my relationship with my friends as well. They've just got-ten deeper relationships and just more meaningful and more real. I was on the road to being a doctor when I became a Christian. [Chuckles] 4.0 [GPA] student in college, you know, Presidential Scholar. I was preparing to be a doctor for so long. And then I became a Christian, and suddenly I start singing, I start writing music, and realized that my passion is music. And that's something that I hadn't realized before. And then just having that perspective of, you know, it's not what anyone else thinks that I should be, or what society is trying to dictate to me on who a successful person is, but really understanding who I was made to be. And who God created me to be. And so that is just a huge change. But more than that, it's just my perspective on life.*

CY: Now what kinds of changes came about as a result of Cherry Blossom Festival?

CK: *Well, the Cherry Blossom Festival was such an important part of the sea-son that I was in. It just helped me understand my culture and my heritage, and just gave me that deep appreciation for Japanese people and Japanese culture, and for what I do now, that just was very important that I got that foundation that wasn't there before. Just singing now and releasing my CD in Japan, and just really having a heart to see the Japanese people come to know who Jesus is and to spread the Gospel there in Japan. Cherry Blossom really helped me to understand the people better and to just really have a heart for them.*

CY: So once you became Queen, were you at the same time a Christian singer?

CK: *Let's see. [Chuckles] When I became Queen, I really wasn't a singer yet. I had started writing music. I'm a saxophone player, and for my speech at the Cherry Blossom Festival at the pageant my speech was all about being a saxophone player. Because that is a big part of who I am. But I never sang. I wasn't a singer, I wasn't a songwriter. I didn't have those gifts. I was a saxophone player. And when the pageant came, I believe I had just started to write music. And what had happened was, I became a Christian, I was taking a creative writing class, and then one of the assignments was to write an original song. And I thought, "Great." I'm not a songwriter, but I remember walking around Ala Moana Shopping Center one day, and just hearing this tune in my head. And I just stopped what I was doing, and I wrote it down on this receipt, just this little piece of paper. And I took it home and I wrote it out. And that was the first song I wrote. It's a testimony on how I came to know the Lord through those two students that I met in my English class in college who showed me who Jesus was. I called them my angels, because I felt like God had sent them to me to show me that He really is real. So I called that song "Angels Walk Among Us." And that song is the first song I wrote, and that's the song that took me to Nashville, Tennessee.*

CY: And did you write songs while you were Queen?

CK: *Right. During my reign, God just kept giving me more songs. And I just kept writing, and then I thought, "Okay, who's gonna sing my songs?" And people would encourage me. "Hey, why don't you try to sing your songs?" And I thought, "No, I'm not a singer." But then I'd have to sing it to them in order for them to hear what it sounds like. And then people would just start encouraging me. "Hey, you should take voice lessons, you know, you're not so bad." [Chuckles] And I started singing and realized that I love singing. And I love worshiping God through my voice. So I picked up the guitar, started taking lessons, started taking voice lessons. And just started singing and kept writing music while I was the reigning Queen.*

CY: What did the Jaycees think of all this? What kind of reaction did you get?

CK: *There were certain instances when they told me it wasn't appropriate to be talking about it [Christianity]. When you visit the princess of Japan you're not supposed to talk about religion, just any religion, you're not to talk about it. Things like that.*

The only thing I do remember is when I ended my reign at the pageant, the Queen's speech, you have the last five minutes to spill your guts, whatever you want to say, and I gave this analogy of myself being like a tree, a cherry blossom tree, and how I started as a little seed, and how I grew and what the different parts of the tree meant for me, like the trunk and my roots are grounded in the foundation of my faith, and who I am and my heritage, and then my grandkids and how they reached out, too. It was so metaphorical you know. And I remember people coming up to me at the end of that, just saying that was the most incredible speech they've heard. 'Cause I spoke a lot about God. And I just gave all the credit to God. And I just told everybody this is it, this is why my life this past year has been so incredible. And I just shared, and it really wasn't a lot, but I guess it was enough that some people were just brought to tears from it. And then some people did say, "Wow, it's kind of religious."

CY: Did the Jaycees know about your involvement with Christian music?

CK: *I think that I wasn't sure yet what really my involvement was gonna be and how big of a part this was gonna play in my life. At the time, I was still discovering these new gifts and just coming into what these new gifts were leading me into, and just discovering this. I think it wasn't until a year or so later after I ended my reign that I really had a strong call or a strong understanding that this is what I'm gonna be doing. So I think a lot of the Jaycees didn't know that I sang until my CD came out a few years later.*

CY: Now, you said Cherry Blossom Festival kind of put you in touch with things Japanese. At the same time, you were becoming a Christian. In your mind, did you see any kind of contradiction between those two? Between being Japanese and being Christian?

CK: *I didn't. I think that God created me just how He wanted me to be. And as I discover more about where I came from in the sense of Japanese culture and heritage, I realize that it's all part of God's plan. And that nothing of who I am is a mistake. That He created me exactly how He wants me to be, and I think I do have some concerns maybe when it comes to [Japanese] good luck charms, things like that, maybe.*

CY: Japanese good luck charms?

CK: *Yeah. Just because, you know, I've learned to put my faith in God, versus any good luck little trinket or anything. That's just my personal conviction.*

CY: Can you tell me about some of the songs you've written?

CK: *I did write a song called "Beauty Queen." And I wrote that song right when I had ended my reign. I think I had just been praying and just reflecting back on my year as the Cherry Blossom Queen, and I just started singing this song to God and it was all about inner beauty. That's one of the greatest lessons that I learned as the Cherry Blossom Queen, and being a Christian, that my value is not about what I look like on the outside, but it's really about what's on the inside.*

Chapter Seven

Controversy and Reform | Finding a Place in the 2089 Twenty-first Century

If we want to have a Festival that reflects the Japanese American community, which is multi-ethnic, the Queen and Court should reflect that multiethnicity. That doesn't mean to say that the Queen and Court will necessarily be multiethnic; they are not judged by their ethnic makeup. But we need to provide opportunities for multiethnic women to participate.

— Keith Kamisugi, president of HJJCC 1998–1999; quoted in Battad 1998:A1

[When questioned about the blood-quantum rule change] It's about time. I know a lot of part-Japanese women who are more Japanese than, like, myself. They're fluent in Japanese, they participate in tea ceremony, they actually know how to do it rather than just watch it. So I don't think it has anything to do with the quantity of Japanese blood. It's really how you feel, what's in your heart.

— Queen Sharon Kadoyama, 1991–1992, personal communication, January 22, 2002

For the most part, changes to the CBF throughout the years have occurred incrementally and without fanfare. As discussed in Chapter 5, the Jaycees sensed dwindling public interest, but did not make any major changes until 1998. It took a maverick individual to break through the general conservatism and complacency of the institution. That individual was Keith Kamisugi, president of the HJJCC in 1998, whose major reforms for the CBF included the acceptance of mixed-race contestants and the deletion of beauty from the criteria of judging.

This chapter discusses these reforms, focusing in particular on the blood-quantum rule. I frame these changes within the public talk and private rumor that preceded them, as well as the absence of discussion only a few years later. The selection of Queens after the rule change broke through the race barrier incrementally. The first postchange Queen, Lori Murayama, is of 100 percent Japanese blood. The second postchange Queen, Vail Matsumoto, has 75 percent Japanese blood and a Japanese surname. The third postchange Queen, Catherine Toth, has 50 percent Japanese blood and a non-Japanese surname. It took three years, but with Toth, the CBF Queen demonstrated the full effect of the rule change.

Blood-quantum rules raise questions about the relationship of CBF participants to Japanese culture. What kind of connections do mixed-race Queens and non-Japanese Jaycee members have to the cultural content of what they present in the CBF? What does race have to do with it? In other words, what are the intersections of race and culture in the CBF? In this chapter I address ways in which race and culture intertwine in discursive juxtapositions in the CBF.

Racing the Stage: Rumor, Gossip, Suspicions of Being *Hapa*

Race talk has hovered over the CBF throughout its history. Rumors of racial impurity have swirled around particular contestants and Queens, questioning their ancestry over a nose that looked improbably tall, hair and skin color too light, facial bone structure too sculpted. They were suspected not merely of being *hapa* (mixed ancestry), but a particular combination — Japanese and haole. The mixture was potent for several reasons. First, any sexual union with non-Japanese was actively discouraged among issei and nisei. This attitude accounts for the characteristically low rate of intermarriage by older generations of Japanese Americans. Second, haole were acknowledged as global and local power wielders. Until the 1950s and 1960s, when Japanese Americans began their rise to power, haole clearly controlled politics and business in Hawai'i as elsewhere. On plantations, haole were typically the *luna* (boss; manager). In large corporations and government, haole were in positions of power. Marrying a haole thus meant marrying a race that represented power, even if the actual marital partner did not necessarily possess particular social, economic, or political capital. Third, sansei and yonsei did intermarry, including with haole, in increasing numbers, creating a generation gap with their parents and grandparents. Although there may have been initial objections to the marriage, the birth of grandchildren tended to ease the conflict. Fourth, this racial mix is one that typically produces visibly distinctive results, in contrast to ethnic mixes such as Japanese-Chinese. Fifth, the visibly distinctive products of this mix are considered by many in Hawai'i to be physically attractive. Japanese-haole contestants in a beauty pageant are thus assumed to have an aesthetic advantage over those of 100 percent Japanese ancestry (see Hara 1998).[1] The irony remains that in an event that focuses on Japanese (American) pride, the aesthetics of a Japanese-haole *hapa* look holds sway, with at least some onlookers.

The stereotypical talk surrounding the appearance of Japanese-haole women addresses only what the Asian face and body have gained by the infusion of haole blood, not the other way around: lighter skin, hair, and eyes, rounded "double" eyes, taller-bridged nose, more sculpted face, greater height, larger breasts, longer legs, smaller head in proportion to overall body (in accord with a Euro-American fashion model ideal). As Kamisugi relates: "To some people, they have this preconceived notion that because they thought beauty was a key component of the Queen contest, and because they thought that generally speaking *hapa* women were more beautiful, that they would have an advantage" (personal communication, October 6, 2003). In short, the whispers surrounding who may or may not be *hapa* (here, Japanese-haole) dug in deeply and persistently because of this purported aesthetic advantage.

[Handwritten margin note: "Crowning the Nice Girl" — not — "Crowning the Pretty girl"]

These whispers were typically faceless — anonymous phone calls made to the Jaycees, rumors circulating behind closed doors — but for some Queens, queries and accusations were made to their faces. Queen Jody-Lee Ige (1982 – 1983) recalled the following incident:

> JI: *When I was running [for CBF], some people would ask me if I was pure Japanese. Actually, I'd even say [jokingly], "Oh yeah, I'm* hapa,*" or "No, I'm not Japanese, I'm half Okinawan," or something.*[2]
> CY: What did they think you were?

JI: *They thought I was mixed [Japanese-haole] because of [gestures to nose].*
CY: Your nose?
JI: *It's my mom's. 'Cause it's just like a Russian nose or something.*
CY: So how did you feel being asked that?
JI: *I just thought that that was interesting. [I'd say,] "No, we all have to be pure Japanese right now, as far as I know."*
(Personal communication, December 6, 2001)

Queen Lori Ann Mizumoto (1981–1982) was also confronted by similar suspicions:

LM: *Well, they questioned my . . . [ancestry]*
CY: Really?
LM: *Yeah, I had to prove it with my birth certificate.*
CY: They thought you were *hapa*, possibly?
LM: *Me and Sheri. She was another one, 'cause she looked* hapa. *Both of us. They questioned that we were pure Japanese.*
CY: When you say "they," who was the "they"?
LM: *Somebody who called the Chamber.*
CY: Oh. You mean, after you were a contestant?
LM: *I think it was after we were contestants. 'Cause when they [Jaycees] came to our house, and we signed the application to become contestants, we had to show our birth certificates. So they [Jaycees] all knew that we were pure Japanese.*
CY: So the Jaycees already knew. But somebody called the Jaycees and said . . .
LM: *Maybe they saw us at the public appearance or saw the [souvenir] book or whatever and questioned it.*
(Personal communication, February 7, 2002)

Suggesting that a contestant or Queen might not be fully Japanese effectively policed race as a requirement for participation in the CBF. Furthermore, the fact that from the beginning of the CBF the Jaycees asked contestants to present their birth certificates, in part as evidence of Japanese ancestry, makes race a constant, historical factor in this "cultural pageant." The fact that the Jaycees had to rely on such a document to verify the purity of a contestant's blood line demonstrates the arbitrary nature of the definitions of race within this context.

very strict on ancestory

The private rumors of mixed blood that hounded particular contestants and Queens combined with some public talk in the mid-1980s of changing the blood-quantum eligibility rule. In 1984, 1985 (in the CBF souvenir book; see Chapter 5), and again in 1993, the HJJCC discussed altering the rules. In each case the HJJCC board of directors nixed reform with an attitude of, "If it's not broken, why fix it?" (Battad 1998:A1). However, Thomas Yamachika, CBF chair in 1993 and of mixed ancestry, supported changing the blood-quantum requirements:

> If you want a true reflection of the culture, you want a Queen to reflect the *times have* culture of the community that she is representing. There are a number of *changed &* people of Japanese ancestry in Hawaii who are not 100 percent. We didn't *ancestry* want our Pageant to stick out as being a sign of racial purity. (Quoted in *majorities* Battad 1998:A1) *have changed*

Embedded within Yamachika's support of the rule change is a concern for the public image of the CBF and the HJJCC. This concern extends as well to consideration of the image of the Japanese American community in Hawai'i. Thus Yamachika's and others' support for the rule change may be for the benefit of the Japanese American community, but it is as much for their image before an audience of the larger local community, as well as Japanese American communities in the continental United States. The larger local audience lay charges of clannishness and exclusivity, accusing Japanese Americans of putting up racial boundaries to keep non-Japanese out. Yamachika and others expressed concern that the Japanese American community in Hawai'i, through an event such as the CBF, lagged behind all other Japanese American communities and other local ethnic beauty pageants in maintaining rules of 100 percent blood-based exclusivity.

In 1998, the public talk surrounding the change began with a front-page article in the daily *Honolulu Advertiser.* Its headline read, "Japanese Pageant Breaks Tradition" (Infante 1999:A1). The article raised numerous issues surrounding the rule change: "clash between the old and new roles of Japanese women, the future of the Cherry Blossom pageant, and the importance traditionally placed on being 'pure Japanese,' which critics in the past have called racist" (ibid.). Despite this public acknowledgment of opposition, Kamisugi felt that criticism against the rule change was not aired as openly as it might because of "the cultural taboo against causing controversy [which] may be keeping some people from opposing the change publicly" (ibid.:A5). Kamisugi may be correct. In contrast with the very public article in the *Honolulu Advertiser* that had been preceded by an earlier front-page article in the English-language *Hawaii Herald* (Battad 1998:A1, A5), the Japanese-language newspaper *Hawaii Hochi* offered no discussion on the issue. The *Hawaii Hochi* only had this to say:

> From this year on the qualifications for Cherry Blossom contestants are changed from 100 percent Japanese to 50 percent. In Hawaii, which is a melting pot of races, interracial marriage is widespread. Therefore it is natural that the Cherry Blossom Festival reflect the nikkei [Japanese American] society which is comprised of many races. (1999:special section)

The *Hawaii Hochi* article treated the change as a simple matter of keeping up with changing demographics. This is not to say that critical discussion did not take place among Japanese-language speakers; only that the newspaper was not considered the forum for airing personal views. Before a public (if Japanese-speaking) face, mixed-race contestants was a nonissue. Instead, heated discussion went on privately behind closed doors. For the most part, the fear of loss of sponsors turned out to be no more than a threat. In reality, according to Kamisugi, there were few economic repercussions from the Jaycees' actions (personal communication, October 6, 2003).

The heated discussions surrounding blood-quantum requirements for Queen contestants contrast with the lack of (public) discussion in the late 1950s, when persons of non-Japanese ancestry were allowed as members in HJJCC (see Chapter 3). The contrast between the handling of the two changes forty years apart points to the difference between the actual body of the organization (i.e., HJJCC members) and its public representation (the CBF Queen). The Japanese American public cared far less about who could join the HJJCC than about who would represent the organization and the community in official settings. The stubborn reluctance to accept a Queen of anything less than 100 percent Japanese blood, even as those putting on the pageant were of different ethnicities, highlights the ironies and contradictions of the process. Within the less public face of the organization, there was greater flexibility far earlier than in the very public face of that organization's Queen.

I argue that the contrast between the virulent debates of 1998 and the non-talk of the late 1950s points to the particularly vital public role given the Queen vis-à-vis the Jaycees and the Japanese American community in Hawai'i. The Queen's front-stage role contrasts with the backstage work of Jaycee members (even if that work is featured in souvenir books). As the foremost public face of this organization and community, the Queen represents Jaycees and Japanese Americans at their most conservative.[3] Like many representations, she need not mirror reality. She must only present the image that Jaycees and Japanese

Americans prefer to the larger general public of onlookers. Thus, the CBF Queen as a position of image, not substance, must meet those conservative expectations as closely as possible. She is the uncontroversial centerpiece — the "nice girl" — for a community that prides itself on toeing the line.

Gender plays a significant role here as well. The organization's president (only men until 1984) is indeed a public figure, but he does not attract as much attention as does the Queen. She — not the HJJCC president — is typically the one who stands alongside mayors and governors at public functions. She may not be a head of state, but she presides as a representation (not a representative) of the organization. She presides by image alone. The importance of preserving that image, therefore, is part of the work of the community, the HJJCC, and the Queen herself. Until 1998, the only figure considered suitable to shoulder that burden was a woman of 100 percent Japanese blood, thus reinscribing the equivalence between race, culture, and identity.

The fact that Jaycees opened their ranks to non-Japanese in the late 1950s with barely a whimper from within their ranks or the Japanese American community shows that racial exclusivity was not the only factor in the long uphill battle to accept non-fully-Japanese CBF contestants. Instead, I argue that the spotlight placed upon the CBF Queen makes her position both fragile and significant, and therefore has made the Jaycees and the Japanese American community in Hawai'i reluctant to change. As long as the CBF Queen was of 100 percent Japanese blood, then race and culture meshed seamlessly. As soon as the Jaycees crowned a Queen with less than 100 percent blood, then the sticky questions of the interrelationships of race, culture, identity, authenticity, and entitlement surface. Who is allowed to be Japanese American? What does Japanese American mean? How does one measure one's Japanese Americanness? What does the CBF Queen represent? And whose Queen is she? Changing the blood-quantum rule for CBF contestants implicates these and other questions for which the Jaycees and the Japanese American community in Hawai'i have only had contradictory answers.[4]

The primary reason given for changing the blood-quantum rule was the reality of intermarriage among sansei and yonsei. What was most often cited was that the CBF should reflect the Japanese American population in Hawai'i, which increasingly includes persons of mixed ancestry. According to the 2000 U.S. Census, Japanese Americans constitute 24.5 percent of the population of Hawai'i (2001). Of these, nearly one-third are of mixed ancestry. In spite of such demographics, the rule change was met with considerable criticism.

In some respects, the rule change suggests a change in focus from Japanese culture to the Japanese American experience in Hawai'i. Kamisugi contended, "We can't afford to focus solely on traditional Japanese culture and arts. We need to bridge the current Japanese culture and the traditional to become a Japanese American heritage of where we came from and who we are today" (quoted in Battad 1998:A5). Kamisugi's statement points up critical distinctions: current Japanese culture versus "traditional" Japanese culture, Japanese culture versus Japanese American heritage, where we came from versus who we are today. Making these distinctions helps the CBF create realistic ties to the Japanese American community of which they are a part.

Interview with Keith Kamisugi

By the time I began this research, Kamisugi had relocated to San Francisco and embarked on a new career in public relations. Fortunately, he agreed to a taped phone interview with me on October 6, 2003. In the interview Kamisugi was articulate and forthright, so much so that I decided to include much of his interview to let him speak to the issues himself. He talked about blatantly engineering the rule change by placing his supporters in decision-making positions on the board of directors and as cochairmen of the CBF. He ran for president on the platform of effecting widespread change in the HJJCC and CBF, including the blood-quantum rule. His election by a wide margin gave him all the validation he felt he needed to proceed full steam ahead. During the course of our conversation, Kamisugi described the resistance and criticisms that were leveled against him and the changes. He disputed the opinion that allowing *hapa* contestants meant that they would enjoy any advantage over women of 100 percent Japanese ancestry. As Kamisugi explained, changing the blood-quantum rule only widened the pool of applicants; all contestants were judged on the same basis. Most important, he spoke with passion about the reasons that he believed such changes were so important for the CBF, the HJJCC, and the Japanese American community in Hawai'i. Kamisugi admitted that the CBF had lost its relevance for the Japanese American community in Hawai'i over the past decades. His commitment to changing the blood-quantum rule was part of his attempt to stem the increasing banality of the event and retrieve what I dub "profundity."

CY: What was your motivation behind pushing for the change in blood-quantum ruling?

KK: *My main motivation was the fact that the Japanese Junior Chamber, an organization that I was actually a relatively new member of, always claimed that the Cherry Blossom Festival and the resulting representatives of that Festival, meaning the Queen and the Court, had some duty to represent the Japanese American community both within Hawai'i and outside of Hawai'i. . . . It was*

very odd to me that in asking the Queen and the Court to represent the Japa-
nese American community, that they had to be full-blooded Japanese American
women.

handwritten margin note: represented Jap-Amer.'s but had to be 100% Jap blood.

CY: Why did that seem odd to you?

KK: *It seemed odd to me because that's not a true representation of the Japanese*
American community today. The Japanese American community today is not
full-blooded Japanese. It's multiethnic. It's hapa. *It's women whose last names are*
not Japanese. And I felt that at its essence, for us to keep out women of multiethnic
background was discriminatory. Now, I also realized that practically speaking I
could not push the Festival to open up to the other end of the spectrum, meaning
allowing women of no Japanese ancestry to come in, because that was the argu-
ment that was posed to me.

CY: So if you're going to let someone with less than 100 percent, where do
you stop?

KK: *I think it's a classic opposition argument. If you're gonna go there, they*
say, why not let anybody in? That's not true to the intent of why we wanted to
open it up. It was to communicate to the community that we believed that the
Japanese American community is multifaceted and multiethnic. That you don't
have to have a Japanese last name, you don't have to have full Japanese ancestry
to be Japanese American. There were questions to me about, "Are you doing this
because the pool of women entering the Festival's Queen contest is getting low and
you want to expand the pool?" And the answer is, "No." It had nothing to do with
the fact that there was a decline. There was a decline in women who were apply-
ing for the Queen contest, but not a dramatic decline. We still had much more
than fifteen women apply for the fifteen spots in the Queen contest. It wasn't about
supply and demand. And there were some people who maybe half jokingly, half
seriously say that if you allow women to enter then hapa *women will win. And I*
didn't really understand that. . . . Number one, part of us changing, part of mak-
ing some of these changes was to as much as possible eliminate the physical beauty
component of the Queen contest. Historically, there were elements of evaluating
Queen contestants that had to do with physical beauty. Most of those were gone by
the time that I got involved. So the conception that Cherry Blossom was a beauty
pageant was mostly mistaken. But as I got more deeply involved in things like
the contestant search process where they do the initial screening, I did find that
there was some wording in there that might make a screening committee member
weigh a contestant's physical beauty. . . . But part of it was to emphasize as much
as possible that there's more to women than physical beauty. Leadership, poise,
charisma, those things should be important. So the whole concept that the change
in the ethnic requirement had anything to do with the misconceived notion of the
Festival being a beauty pageant was out of whack. It was really about the fact that

*if we're gonna continue this contest for Cherry Blossom Queen, that we should
open it up to as many Japanese American women as possible.*

CY: So the change in the blood-quantum ruling and eliminating physical
beauty from the judging were not related?

KK: *The only thing that they were related to was my desire to have the Festival Queen contest reflect us. For one, that it's not, among other things, a beauty contest, and, two, that one of the reasons why we have the Queen and Court is to represent the Japanese American community. And so to be true to that, I think that we needed to set different standards for who these women are, who the Queen and the Court are. And also that if we are asking women to represent the Japanese American community, that we accept the broadest spectrum of women who are Japanese American. And if the definition of Japanese American means more than full-blooded Japanese American women, then that's what we need to strive to. I actually picked 50/50 just because I think at that time that I proposed it, I thought it was a moderate step.*

CY: Did you look to [Japanese American contests in] Los Angeles, San
Francisco, Seattle for any kind of guidance in this?

KK: *I did not.*

CY: You were doing this strictly on your own.

KK: *Yes. Yes. Because I think L.A. and those others would not have been very
good models because the demographics there and the relationship between multi-ethnicity and the JA [Japanese American] community in those areas is different.*

CY: The question is, how do you define the JA community and who gets to
be part of it?

KK: *So I should make clear that my definition of a member of the Japanese
American community and the change in ethnic requirement are different. I mean,
in that case I have to deal with an institution that preceded even me being born. So
my definition of somebody who's a member of the Japanese American community
has only to do with love and respect for the culture and willingness to participate
in it. It has nothing to do with blood. The example I give is, you know I meet
practitioners of Japanese culture who are not a single drop of blood Japanese. You
know you've got haole practitioners of language, of martial arts, of other arts of
Japanese culture who have just this love for perpetuating it and practicing it. And
so to me that person is as much a member of the Japanese American community
as I am, even though I'm 100 percent Japanese [ancestry]. I look Japanese, I have a
Japanese last name, it doesn't matter. It doesn't matter what blood quantum you
have. I think it's your participation, your respect, your practice, and your love for
the culture is what is really the only bar that you need to meet.*

CY: What about taking it from the opposite extreme? What about those
even fully 100 percent Japanese blood who really have no connection to Japa-

nese culture, who don't necessarily love and respect Japanese culture? What do you do with those people?

KK: *Yeah, you know, I didn't mean to exclude people . . . I guess by birth. By birth, if you have ancestral ties to the Japanese —*

CY: Then you're automatically part of it?

KK: *That is also another entry into the community. But if we're talking at a sort of a theoretical level, you're not a member of a community unless you participate in it or somehow you're integrated, not integrated but . . . you have some connection to it. Yeah, I would consider if somebody who's Japanese American and maybe didn't have the privilege of growing up in a community that practiced Japanese American culture, that just the interest alone in their heritage I think to me makes them a member of our community.*

CY: And what about those who aren't interested?

KK: *My only concern with those people who are ancestrally Japanese but are not engaged in the community is that we need to . . . we, meaning the entire community, need to find ways to bring Japanese Americans into the fold. What my emotional energy is focused on is educating the Japanese American community that there are those people who are in our community that don't look Japanese who should be welcomed as members of the Japanese American community. That's sort of the philosophical starting point for the reason why I wanted to have the Chamber and the Festival change the ethnic requirement. But my philosophical starting point and the end result of that change, there was a gap there, but just pragmatically speaking, I can't and it's not really my place to instill my complete philosophy on Japanese American culture and community into an institution that was at the time almost fifty years old.*

CY: So what kind of reaction did you get?

KK: *I got actually a handful of anonymous letters sent to my house that were really disturbing because they used phrases like, "Why am I letting the half-breeds in?" There was one letter that actually used the word "half-breed."*

CY: Did these people sign their names?

KK: *No, no, no, no, but they were clearly from seniors [older adults].*

CY: Now why do you say that?

KK: *Because they were handwritten. I mean you can kind of tell. On lined paper. They were written to me in a way you could tell they weren't written by somebody in my demographic [in their twenties or thirties]. Nobody, at that time, nobody did that. You really had to be a nisei or a sansei I think, you could even kind of tell. I might have been wrong, but that's the impression I got. Unsigned. And what was disturbing to me as much that they used words like "half-breeds" and this wasn't the exact word but essentially they were telling me that I had poisoned the Cherry Blossom Festival.*

Aside from that, I had resistance inside of the organization itself. Not that people didn't agree that the Japanese American community meant more than full-blooded Japanese American women, but that people wanted me to take more time to consider this issue. And my rebuttal to this was that the Junior Chamber had considered this issue for many, many years. As far back as ten years before that time. And we were unwilling to go through the process of making that change. Or even of simply making the change. So my rebuttal was, this has been on the minds of our leaders for many, many years. And the due process involved is the fact that when I ran for the office of president of that organization I made it very clear to people what I intended to do. And I made it very clear to the people that I asked to serve with me on the board of directors that that was the number one thing that I wanted to do. So everybody knew. I didn't do it surreptitiously. I didn't do it in the dark. And there were people who absolutely did not like the matter and the substance of the change.

CY: Was your election to the presidency close?

KK: *No! I don't know the exact number but I won by a pretty significant margin. Now, my detractors at the time would have said that the reason why I got so many votes was I brought a lot of people, a lot of new members, into the organization with me. But why is that wrong? And at the time the Japanese Junior Chamber was facing a process of a decline. And I didn't help that decline, because quite a number of members actually quit.*

CY: Did people quit as a result of your changes?

KK: *Honestly, I think it was as much related to my push to change the ethnic requirement as it was my leadership style. As I reflect now, my style of leadership wasn't very accommodating. Some people felt I ramrodded that thing through. And maybe in their old culture of doing things, I did. But I did it fairly and I did it democratically and I did it above board and I told people what I was gonna do. And some people decided that they weren't going to support me, so they left.*

CY: Now as far as HJJCC goes, what motivated you or what motivates you?

KK: *Well, the first thing was just to do what was right.*

CY: So you felt very strongly this is the right thing to do?

KK: *Yeah. That I think for all the talk of this being a melting pot, there is this hidden discrimination that exists in our community. And part of it was my naiveté. I was only twenty-seven at the time. And I didn't have a long history of interacting with the core establishment of Japanese Americans at that time.*

In fact, let me go back and just say something else. I acquiesced to the first board of directors meeting. Because when I convened the first meeting, there was one item on the agenda and I already told everybody this was gonna be the passage of this change. I was asked not to push that vote through on that first meeting. To survey all of our sponsors, because the rebuttal from the opposition was — or not neces-sarily opposition but the cautious board members — was that if we did the change and we found out that some of our sponsors didn't agree with it, that we would lose some financial support. So I personally went to every single sponsor liaison and let them know that this was what I had wanted to ask the board of directors to do. And I can tell you that of the more than a dozen sponsors of the Cherry Blossom, only one expressed reservations of the change. And the person who expressed his reservations made it clear that it was his personal feeling about the change and that in his position as a corporate sponsor he was fully supportive of it. This person had the wisdom to separate his role as a corporate sponsor versus his personal role as a Japanese American. I totally understood that.... I actually got two or three of them who said, "I thought you guys did this already." So there were actually people who thought that we had opened it up years ago. That to me was a validation.

CY: What about reaction in Japan? I know you talked about the spon-sors, but did you get any sense of how people were feeling in Japan about your change?

KK: *I did not get a single negative comment on it. Now of course I say that realizing that disagreements in Japanese culture are not immediately brought to light, right?*

CY: So they wouldn't necessarily let you know.

KK: *I understood that it wouldn't necessarily be something that I would hear about, or would be told to me. But now that you mention it, that was also one of the arguments of the opposition: our relationships with the five sister chapters, Jaycee chapters in Japan, and our relationship, I guess you could call it, with the Imperial Household 'cause the Cherry Blossom Queen visits the Imperial House-hold, usually with the second or the third princess or whomever. And what would they think? And again, at that time, I was like, "I don't actually care what they think. Our Festival is not beholden to the Imperial Household and we're not be-holden to our sister chapters in Japan. We should consider how our changes affect our relationships, but I think that's the extent of it. And we should be respectful and courteous of that." In the extreme scenario of us no longer being invited to the Imperial Household because we made this change, that's something that I would be 110 percent comfortable to live with.*

CY: Through your change, the blood quantum has been set at 50 percent. Do you foresee a day when it might get down to 25 percent?

KK: *Absolutely. And I'm in favor of that. But bigger than that question is the relevance of the Queen contest to the Japanese American community. I would rather the organizers of the Festival concentrate more on making the Festival and the Queen contest more relevant to our community today than to bring up the question of changing the blood quantum. 'Cause I think that that's [blood quantum is] the lesser of the two issues.*

CY: What do you see as the relevance of Cherry Blossom to the Japanese American community? At least in its current configuration?

KK: *You know, I left Honolulu in 2000, so I haven't been even remotely involved in the last two or three Festivals. But at its very essence I think the Festival as a whole and the Japanese Junior Chamber even outside the Cherry Blossom Festival is a good way for young Japanese Americans to get involved. Not only in the Japanese American community, but just in an organization that does good work in the community. . . .*

But I didn't answer your question very well. The relevance of the Festival today, honestly, I think, is diminishing. And it has been diminishing over the past twenty years. You look at when the Festival started out and it was in many ways a big media event in Hawai'i and it was a big part of the Japanese American community. I cannot truthfully say that the Cherry Blossom Festival is a big part of the Japanese American community today. It is a part of it. And one that everybody knows about. But I think less people today feel any sort of relationship to the Festival like they did before.

Let me leave with you a parting thought. Lori [Murayama] was the first Queen to be selected in the very first Festival that we had the multiethnic requirement. After the Queen and the Court were chosen, I was astounded by criticism that one of the hapa *contestants didn't make the Court. And the criticism went along these lines: "Your change to the 50/50 blood quantum was all shibai [an act] because you've got a full-blooded Japanese American Queen and you've got a Court that except for one person, Alison Tasaka, is full Japanese. And Alison is half Chinese."*

CY: So you're still not crossing the race line.

KK: *The reason why I was astounded by it was that the change in the ethnic requirement does not automatically raise multiethnic contestants to any different level. Meaning that once you're in the door, if you're a multiethnic contestant, you're just like everybody else. So multiethnicity has nothing to do with the Queen and Court. It has to do with the selection of the contestants. And you're given a fair shake like everybody else. . . . But I was just astounded by the fact that people would think that we did it, that we made the change for show, and that the Queen or any member of the Court were not any of the* hapa *contestants, and it took three or four Festivals I think to have a Queen, I think it was Catherine Toth. She wasn't the first multiethnic Queen, but she was the first multiethnic Queen with a non-Japanese last name. And it was at that point, when Cat [Catherine] got selected as Queen, was when the whole issue got revisited again. Not in a negative way, but just as sort of a newsworthy thing. I think by Catherine being selected and the full manifestation of that change actually coming to life was when people realized that if they had any misgivings about it, that they were maybe put to rest.*

Kamisugi's interview brings up critical issues for the CBF, especially regarding change and reform. The formal front-stage reasons given for opposing change were concerns for loss of sponsorship and the possible critique of Jaycee organizations in Japan (including the Imperial Household). These may have been valid concerns, but they were seemingly only a smokescreen for the more informal, backstage reasons for resistance. These came in the form of anonymous letters and private conversations.

In spite of Kamisugi's maverick maneuvering and success, this overall pattern of resistance to change characterizes not only the CBF and the HJJCC, but also the Japanese American community as a whole. Their reluctance to embrace change is evident in the years of talk that led up to major reform in the CBF in 1998. Undoubtedly, Japanese Americans have lived through important historical periods of labor activism and political leadership. They have been at the forefront of liberal politics in Hawai'i, pushing for statehood, initiating legislation for social welfare, abolishing capital punishment, and leading Hawai'i to become the first state to ratify the Equal Rights Amendment and legalize abortion. But as Roland Kotani points out, the liberal politics of the 1950s gave way to conservatism in the 1980s:

> By the eighties, mainstream AJA [Japanese American] Democrats enthusiastically supported corporate tax breaks, an increase in the excise tax rate, and changes in the progressive workers' compensation law. Whereas rebellious Nisei Democrats of the fifties had insisted on greater funding for social services and public education, established Nisei politicians now readily accepted cutbacks in government welfare programs and stagnation in the budget for Hawaii's public schools and university system. (1985:178)

Furthermore, Japanese Americans as a group have shown social conservatism on issues of interethnic/racial relations, as evidenced by the low rate of intermarriage among issei and nisei. The social conservatism continues with sansei and yonsei in their choice of employment, residence, and lifestyle.

In sum, with no political rallying point to galvanize the community, the comforts of middle-class American dream attainment in the 1970s and 1980s reinforced complacency and a concern to present a "nice" public face. Kamisugi broke through that niceness by his leadership fueled by the conviction of the rightness and timeliness of his actions. Had it not been for his personal ambition and drive, who knows whether the CBF would, even in the 2000s, still require its Queen contestants to prove their 100 percent Japanese ancestry.

"Winds of Change": Shaking Things Up

The cover of the 1999 CBF souvenir book looked benign enough. Queen Lori-Joy Morita stood in ochre kimono, tiara gleaming atop her head. In the background, Mrs. Lillian Yajima, lifelong supporter of the CBF, stood in an apricot-colored kimono. Both women were smiling, representing nisei and yonsei generations brought together by the CBF. The theme for that year, "Winds of Change" *[Henka no Kaze]* was written both in English and Japanese. It was only inside the cover that the radical changes were made evident.

Although most of the politicians' greetings published in the souvenir book made no direct mention of the rule change, Japan's Consul General Gotaro Ogawa spelled it out:

> As we approach the turn of the century, this year's theme of the "WINDS OF CHANGE" seems to be leading the Festival toward a new direction. The Japanese-Americans have already been successfully assimilated into the multiethnic community of Hawaii. With the widening scope of participation, the opportunity for an even greater array of contestants to perpetuate their Japanese cultural heritage is a welcome new trend. This change will help contribute toward deepening mutual understanding among the people of a wider range of cultural backgrounds.
> (Ogawa 1999:5)

U.S. Congresswoman Patsy T. Mink also wrote supportively of the change:

> This year's theme — Winds of Change — reflects positive changes that recognize the multiethnic character of our island population. I applaud the Honolulu Japanese Junior Chamber of Commerce for reducing the ethnicity requirement for contestants so that young women of less than 100 percent Japanese ethnicity may vie for the coveted title of Cherry Blossom Queen. This change will allow a broader spectrum of young women with a deep interest in their Japanese heritage to experience the educational and cultural benefits of participating in this competition.
> (Mink 1999:9)

Only these two out of eight other politicians' letters mentioned the blood-quantum rule change.

Congratulatory messages by Kamisugi and CBF General Chairs Pono Chong and Karlton Tomomitsu spoke more directly of the changes. Given the past conservatism of the HJJCC and the Japanese American community in general, Chong and Tomomitsu's letter is nothing short of extraordinary:

Dear Friends:

The saying goes that, "The more things change, the more they stay the same." That may be true for some local Hawaii traditions, but not for the Cherry Blossom Festival this year. The world is definitely changing around us. But "CBF," as we call it, is definitely *not* staying the same. These "winds of change" are not only expressed in this year's Festival theme, but embody the spirit of this last of the 20th century Cherry Blossom Festivals.

We do not make these changes simply for the sake of making change, but for the purposes of adapting and redirecting the Festival to offer the local Japanese community and the community-at-large something more relevant and of interest to them and their families. No longer is the lifestyle and ethnic identity of the local Japanese community like that of the early Festival years. We only seek to change the Festival to again have a strong connection with the community. . . .

Already the "winds of change" have begun to blow as — for the first time ever — we accepted applications for Cherry Blossom Festival Queen contestants from young local women of less than 100 percent Japanese ethnicity (minimum 50 percent). . . . Also, in the Queen area we have removed "physical beauty" as a criterion in the Queen judging. And we have also increased the number of culture classes from 5 to 12, with new classes like genealogy and Japanese history. . . .

We are also assembling — for the first time — professional taiko drum groups from Japan, the Mainland and Hawaii for a major taiko performance in March. These are just some of the exciting changes we are currently overseeing, and we look forward to your support as we execute these and other enhancements to this year's Festival.

(Chong and Tomomitsu 1999:11)

According to Chong and Tomomitsu, changes in the CBF were part of a millennial transition, a self-reflexive assessment of the past and charting of the future. Placing the CBF change within millennial rhetoric gives it not only magnitude, but permanence. Changing the blood-quantum requirement for CBF is thus part of living in the twenty-first century.

Chong and Tomomitsu also spoke of changes as directed by the social environment of Hawai'i rather than engineered by them. They positioned themselves as responders rather than reformers. Framed in this way, organizers of the CBF had no choice but to make changes or risk irrelevance in the sociocultural warp of banality. The change was also framed as restorative rather than innovative. The reforms of 1998 were presented in terms of social awareness and community responsibility rather than sheer innovation. HJJCC members were thus not mavericks, but socially aware, committed community leaders who had the sense to "enhance" the Festival for the sake of its future.[5]

The "enhancement" of the CBF may be seen in part through the changing demographics of the Queen and contestants. The average age of CBF contestants since 1998 is 23.6, continuing the trend of older contestants and Queens discussed in Chapter 5 (see the Appendix). The average age of Queens is even higher at 25.3 years, almost at the upper limit of eligibility of 26 years. By this age, most Queens are out of college and in professional occupations. Contestants and Queens continue to be drawn from a strongly middle-class background. Almost all contestants have graduated or are attending university. Thirty-five percent graduated from private high schools; however, participants from the two most elite private high schools in the state are relatively scarce at only 10 percent.[6] The picture that these statistics paint is one of older women participating in and winning the Cherry Blossom crown, representing primarily middle-class families.

Retrofitting Japan into Performative Identities

In spite of Kamisugi and others' seeming commitment to a Japanese American focus, Japan remains the locus of identity in the CBF. For example, contestants are often asked: "What aspect of the Japanese culture has had the greatest impact on your life and why?" This question assumes, first, that each contestant knows what "the Japanese culture" (singular, essentialized, ahistorical, decontextualized) is, and, second, can retrofit their lives in terms of it. Even those with little knowledge of or interest in Japan have to come up with a "greatest impact" answer.

In their 1999 essays, many contestants invoked what has become a catch-all of "Japanese cultural heritage" in Hawai'i's Japanese American discourse, *kachikan* (cultural values).[7] Thus, one contestant wrote, "The Japanese values of diligence, selflessness, obedience, and honor have been passed on to me by my family" (HJJCC 1999:43). Another alluded to "the importance placed on perpetuating Japanese values, beliefs, and traditions" (ibid.:45). Yet another claimed, "The Japanese value of perseverance has enabled me to achieve my goals" (ibid.:49).

Other contestants took "Japanese culture" to mean cultural practices, particularly in the arts. Some linked themselves to the lessons they learned through Japanese arts: "Playing the koto.... Through its strict discipline, I have learned the importance of hard work, practice and devotion" (ibid.:44); "Taking *odori*

[Japanese dance] classes . . . I learned discipline, team work, to work hard, and most importantly, a very beautiful part of our culture" (ibid.:44); "The Japanese tea ceremony is a metaphor for my life. In *chanoyu* [tea ceremony], a simple act of making tea becomes a spiritual, aesthetic and practical experience" (ibid.:46). However, these practitioners of Japanese arts constitute only a handful within the field of fifteen contestants.

Several women focused their remarks upon family: "Not only has the strength of my familial ties been a source of constant support, but one of inspiration and guidance" (ibid.:45); "Emphasis on the family as the central unit is an aspect of Japanese culture that has the greatest impact on my life. By offering support and stability, and instilling the values of perseverance, sacrifice and harmony, my family provides me with a strong foundation and the necessary tools to succeed" (ibid.:47). The question and contestants' answers recast these primarily yonsei women — many with little prior knowledge of Japan — as ones with strong ties to their "home country."[8]

A high school essay contest begun in 1995 and continuing in the 2000s asks students to write on themes of Japanese culture: "In what ways have the Japanese culture and heritage added to our unique culture here in Hawaii?" (1999), "What single aspect of the Japanese culture do you hope will be passed on to future generations? How can older and younger generations work together to perpetuate this aspect of the Japanese culture?" (2003), and "How has the Japanese culture in Hawaii influenced you as a person, and what one aspect of it would you like to pass on to future generations?" (2004).[9] These exact questions linking Japan and Hawai'i, past and present, have also been used repeatedly as interview questions for contestants. These are the trope queries for younger generations, Jaycee members, and Queen contestants.

The issue remains, why focus on Japan and not Japanese American experience in Hawai'i? Why ignore the culture, history, and experiences that are right under people's noses? Why look to the distant and the past as resources for identity? I argue that Japan offers a source of identity for those casting about without a sure footing in their present time and place. "Japan" as a construct is more easily woven into an identity of one's own making because of its remoteness from everyday life. This holds true even with the proximity of Japan in Hawai'i, including Japanese tourists, students, and business-related residents; people-to-people exchanges at elementary, middle-, and high-school levels, sports teams, and music ensembles; Japanese television- and radio-programming; and the popularity of *manga* [comics], *anime* [cartoons], and J-pop [Japanese pop music]. These incursions of Japan into life in Hawai'i are not typically referenced as elements of "heritage" and "tradition" when Japanese Americans discuss identities

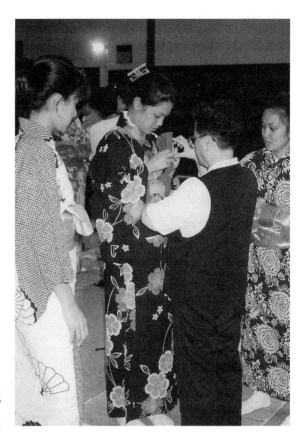

Fig. 10. Sensei Kumiko Sakai teaching contestants the art of kimono-dressing

based in Japan. The Japan of the CBF is a specific one drawn from the past and the distant. This has become truer as "Japan" recedes into a more remote past for succeeding generations of Japanese Americans.

One of the main gatekeepers tying the CBF and its Queens to Japan is the kimono instructor. Since 1972 she has been Kumiko Sakai, born and raised in Japan and trained in the arts of kimono-wearing. For Sakai, wearing kimono is a whole package that includes not only the garment and its wearing, but also body, face, hairdo, movement, facial expression, and character. Each of these components is important in defining and performing the *ojōsan*, the proper Japanese woman. Thus, she teaches contestants how to don the kimono, how to fold it neatly, how to stand, walk, and bow in the garment.

Used to be, we let the girls choose the kimono, and then sometimes the girls cry, because I cannot wear that kimono, so that's why I never win. So I told the judges, it's not the kimono. How they walk in the particular kimono

not a beauty pageant.
"Nice Girl"

they are wearing, judge that instead. That is important. How they bow. And not galloping, not shake the *oshiri* [rump]. Some girls they walk, like real sexy walk, in kimono. And they thought it's elegant, but it's not elegant. (Personal communication, March 8, 2002)

Sakai has her own criteria for assessing the appropriateness of particular contestants, especially in wearing kimono. This appropriateness depends in part on a specific "kimono body type": flat-chested, narrow-hipped, small-footed, with arms that are not too long. This "kimono body" can be easily racialized, especially given the inclusion of mixed-ancestry contestants. Sakai explained:

> KS: *I request the Jaycee people — okay, now, Cherry Blossom is not 100 percent Japanese blood, but you gotta choose and be careful. Not too busty, because if too busty, doesn't match the kimono. And the hip not too wide, because you can't force the kimono. And the feet not too big, because it doesn't look good wearing the zori [Japanese sandal] on the stage. So I just request they [HJJCC] think about this factor. And then it's better to have an Oriental look, not too haole. At least can match the kimono, then no get trouble. It's better they look close to a Japanese.*
> CY: It doesn't match?
> KS: *Yeah. And also too long, around here [gestures to arms].*
> CY: So if their arms are too long, then it wouldn't match the kimono sleeves?
> KS: *Yeah, looks a little bit funny.* (ibid.)

In short, the body that does not match a kimono — large breasts, broad hips, large feet, and long arms — is racialized as non-Japanese. Topped with a face interpreted as non-Japanese, the overall mismatch is an aesthetic and cultural concern for Sakai.

Despite these considerations, Sakai approved the change in blood-quantum requirements.

It's not the blood. It's more about how much of the Japanese heritage they carry. Some [*hapa*] girls are really more traditional Japanese, compared to some pure Japanese who are not traditional at all. I wonder if some of the girls are suitable for Cherry Blossom contestants . . . it's as if they just want to wear the kimono . . . but the thinking is different. If someone like that should win the Cherry Blossom title, it'd be strange. This is what is the most important lesson from this contest . . . Learning about Japanese culture. (ibid.)

[handwritten margin note: didn't see it as a blood issue, but as a way to get more contestants who might know more of what they're doing]

Here Sakai goes beyond bodies and faces to include inner qualities of contestants. She codifies "Japanese culture" in terms of specific values.

People before used to think about others. They had kindness . . . and *omoi-yari* [empathy] but nowadays, they only think of themselves. That's what I would like these Cherry Blossom contestants to learn. Not only for the kimono. Even with the kimono, the obi, the meaning of the design, the bamboo, in the cold of winter, they suffer, so to endure even in the depth of winter, to learn to endure. (ibid.)

She admitted that young Japanese do not necessarily exhibit these values of empathy and endurance any more than Japanese Americans. "No, the Japanese today don't know too much about these things. Parents spoil their children nowadays. But, if they had a strict grandmother, they would be taught properly" (ibid.). Sakai has taken it upon herself to become the "strict grandmother" of the CBF, imparting not only kimono-wearing knowledge, but also Japanese cultural platitudes.

The Race-Culture Quagmire

When Jaycee members, contestants, and Queens were all of 100 percent Japanese ancestry, race and culture could be considered isomorphic. But even this isomorphism was questionable and masked power relations. Whose culture was the standard bearer? Or more to the point, whose culture was erased from the standard? Were persons of Okinawan ancestry considered as Japanese as Naichi? Even within the category of Naichi, there were discrepancies. The dialect and culture of Hiroshima and Yamaguchi prefectures from which many Japanese immigrants came dominated Japanese American life in Hawai'i, but those prefectural practices were not necessarily the national culture codified as mainstream in Japan. "Japanese culture" was even for issei an artificial construct that many had to learn — in the process, sometimes relegating their own regional culture to backwater status. Generations later, defining Japanese culture and its relation to contemporary Japan has become even more problematic, as has relating "Japanese culture" to Japanese American lives.

When one throws in mixed-race/ethnicity contestants and non-Japanese organizers, then the contradictions and ironies of the CBF become even more of a quagmire. The inclusion of mixed-race/ethnicity contestants makes the arbitrariness of linking race and culture more explicit. Regardless of ancestry, most contestants know little about Japanese culture. When I spoke with contestants and Queens, many said that they entered the CBF pageant specifically to learn something about Japanese culture. Furthermore, contestants are not judged on the basis of cultural knowledge.

The blood-quantum ruling allows for situations replete with contradictions: for example, a woman who is of half-Japanese and half-Chinese ancestry ran for Cherry Blossom Festival pageant one year and Narcissus Queen pageant — which requires minimum 50 percent Chinese ancestry and Chinese surname — another year. With this disconnect between race and culture, one woman can apparently compete as the epitome of Japanese American culture one year and the essence of Chinese American culture the next. This example points up the problems inherent in trying to maintain the myth of essentialized identities and representations in ethnic queen pageants.

The apparent distance from Japanese (or Japanese American) culture that non-Japanese organizers bring to the event lays bare some assumptions: (1) that persons of Japanese ancestry know and care about Japanese culture; and (2) that persons of non-Japanese ancestry do not know or care about Japanese culture. Neither of these assumptions is necessarily true. Organizers of non-Japanese ancestry bring an unexpected twist to the HJJCC in their considerable efforts to present Japanese (American) culture. The twist lies not so much in cultural knowledge or lack thereof — regardless of ethnicity, some of the same people who must attend to the cultural details of performance are but one step ahead of the waiting audience, learning the "culture" immediately before presenting it. Rather, the twist lies in the ethnic quandary of, for example, a Filipino American putting on a Japanese American show. This is not the organizers' quandary; it is ours as observers.

A case in point is Leo Asuncion Jr., a second-generation Filipino American, who has been extremely active in the HJJCC. He served as the HJJCC president in 2000 and the CBF general chair in 2003. Asuncion joined the HJJCC not on the basis of ethnicity, but because of personal contacts and particularly because of the Young Business Roundtable program geared to provide Jaycees opportunities for professional development.

>   LA: *What intrigued me about it is just how they run it [CBF]. How they run the Festival, how can they run it better. It was for me more business organizational, like how to run the organization better, how to run programs better, what new things can we do.*
>
>   CY: So it could have been anything — like a carnival or something?
>
>   LA: *Yeah, yeah, whatever activity that the organization was doing at the time.*
>
>   CY: How do you feel as a Filipino helping out in this Japanese American Festival? Do you have any thoughts on that?
>
>   LA: *Not really. [Long pause] I don't really see the focus as an ethnic thing. I*

tend to see the organization [HJJCC] as a business. ~~How can we make it better?~~
It's not a social club, it's not just the Festival, it is everything else. So I've never
seen it as an ethnic thing.

CY: What do you see as the essence of Cherry Blossom Festival?

LA: *For me personally?*

CY: Yeah.

LA: *[Pause] Not so much in terms of what it was meant to be. I think for me,*
I met a lot of great people. A lot of people that we put in charge of the Festival,
we know that's just one project in their lives and it kind of helps define your
capabilities of organization and your knowledge.

CY: So for you the main thing is that it's a big project?

LA: *It's a big project and it's a public project.*

(Personal communication, February 12, 2002)

For someone like Asuncion, helping organize the CBF is worthwhile simply because it is a "big project and . . . a public project." This says less about Asuncion's
individual ethnicity than about the ways in which the event has evolved. For
many organizers of either Japanese and non-Japanese ethnicity, "Japanese" culture may be the theme of the event, but it is not necessarily the goal or actual
substance of it.

Organizing a carnival may be an appropriate analogy. Imagine a school putting on a large-scale carnival yearly and coming up with a different theme each
year. The organizers embrace the theme wholeheartedly, decorating booths,
designing games, even naming rides with the theme in mind. But ultimately,
the event is ineluctably a carnival; the theme is not the event, but gives the event
a focus. In the case of the CBF, for many Jaycee members "Japanese culture" or
even "Japanese American culture" is a theme for what Asuncion calls a "big,
public project." Jaycee members use the CBF as a means to hone their organizational skills, rather than as a soul-searching quest for "heritage."

Race and culture are freely decoupled, at least for this group of organizers
including yonsei and gosei several generations removed from Japan, as well as
those of non-Japanese ancestry. Nevertheless, the CBF clings to an abstract, il-
lusive concept of culture called "Japan" and the necessity of making "Japan" a
locus of performative identity and focus of the Festival. This basic disconnect
characterizes the CBF since the 1970s, paving the way to increased banality of
the event. Any construct of identity within the discursive framework of the
CBF points to a dehistoricized, essentialized, premodern Japan that has little
to do with the lives of the organizers, contestants, or Queens. "Culture" continues to reside in the past and at a distance. "Culture" is a kimono worn as

dress-up — even when carefully selected and clad by an expert from Japan. But in the incongruities and ambiguities of the CBF, the kimono references the wearer as a symbol of the Japanese American community in Hawai'i, perhaps especially when her parentage includes Hawaiian, Chinese, Filipino, and haole forebears.

Chapter Eight

Herstories III | 1999 – 2000s

15p9

Forty-seventh Cherry Blossom Queen Lori Murayama, 1999–2000

The Jaycees were lucky. In the first year of the blood-quantum rule change, they had among contestants a woman of 100 percent Japanese blood who was unquestionably qualified to be Queen. Lori Murayama is pretty, gracious, humble, intelligent, articulate. She is also ambitious. The fact that she is of 100 percent Japanese ancestry is irrelevant given her obvious qualifications. She eased public acceptance of the change in blood-quantum ruling: her winning assured critics that the reform would not affect the kind of Queen they were going to get.

I found Lori busily studying for her medical school exams at the coffee area of the Borders Books, Music, and Cafe in Honolulu on January 10, 2002. Although we had never met, she greeted me warmly and immediately started in on our conversation. Lori impressed me with her combination of humility and drive. She spoke quietly of her year as Queen as grueling and hectic, but it was easy to see how she got through it with such grace. Lori is a hard worker. She lent me a binder detailing all aspects of her year's reign, down to listing those in attendance, the clothes she had to wear, and her overall assessment of each activity. It is this diligence and attention to detail that gives Lori an air of competence. She gets the job done.

Like many Queens and contestants, Lori confessed that public speaking used to make her nervous. This tends to confirm the stereotype of Japanese Americans (perhaps particularly those in Hawai'i) as neither verbally adept nor aggressive. The stereotype is not only cultural, it is also gendered: Japanese American women are often characterized as shy and passive. Public speaking requires the Japanese American female to break out of this mold. Although past Queens may have been seen but not heard, in the contemporary era, Queens and Court members are frequently called upon to make speeches at public events. Lori said that the improvement she made in public speaking helped her get into medical school. In this way, being a CBF Queen enabled her to pursue her profession.

CY: How and why did you decide to enter?
LM: *Actually, when I was small, you know, your parents would bring home*

[handwritten margin note: transition from face of Jap-Amer. culture to actual representative of Jap-Amer. culture.]

伝統の新たなる一ページ

第48回　桜祭り

ホノルル日系人青年会議所

Honolulu Japanese Junior Chamber of Commerce

Forty-Eighth Cherry Blossom Festival

Renewing Our Heritage

Fig. 11. Forty-seventh Cherry Blossom Queen Lori Murayama, 1999–2000

these posters and Cherry Blossom books. I remember back then, there weren't that many Japanese American women who were models. And looking through that, they kind of were like role models to me. I remember one, Lenny Yajima [see Chapter 6]. I remember reading about her and how she goes to Harvard. So these women weren't really beautiful but they were intelligent and had a lot of aspira-

tions. *You know it was kind of nice to identify with Japanese American women. So when I was really small I knew about the Cherry Blossom Festival. I thought maybe it'd be nice for me to run in it, but I was never into public speaking. I mean, if you ask me what's the worst thing you could ever do, it's like stand in front of 100 or 1,000 people and talk about something off the cuff. That was like my worst fear.*

CY: When you decided to run, did anybody criticize you at all?

LM: *No, not really. And the things that I liked about Cherry Blossom contest was the year I ran they changed all the requirements. Before I ran, you only could be [100 percent] Japanese. And they took out beauty completely [from judging]. They replaced that with intelligence—you know, your speaking ability and poise. I thought that was kind of refreshing. So when people said "beauty contest," there's a lot more to it than that.*

CY: In the year that you ran, how many girls were not 100 percent Japanese?

LM: *Three. Alison [Tasaka], she's Chinese Japanese. Cherie [Tanaka] was Chinese Japanese. And Erica [Buder] was, I think she was German mixed.*

CY: How did you feel as contestants with articles in the paper about the change in ruling?

LM: *It's funny, but half the people came up to me, "Oh, that's such a good thing, I'm glad they changed," and a lot of other people were like, "I can't believe they're changing it."*

CY: Did they say, "Okay, You're 100 percent Japanese, you've got to win it for us"?

LM: *No, it was more like, I guess some of the older people, they didn't like the change and they thought all the Japanese girls were not gonna win. Which is kinda strange for me. Just because I'm pure Japanese, I mean, you're saying that* hapa *women have more of an advantage or something like that? I thought that was kind of bizarre.*

CY: If someone were to ask you, what was the high point of that whole year?

LM: *I'd say the community service work.*

CY: What kinds of things did you do?

LM: *Our two major community service projects were, one, we did a blood drive. We had 180 people come to donate blood. So that was a really good thing 'cause not only was it a blood drive, but we had entertainment, a lot of great food. And the other one was we did a reading project. It was an educational project, where we send out letters to different schools seeing if we could talk to the kids. So we'd go to these different schools and we would read to them books and talk to them about our Japanese culture and how important it is to read and to get a good education. So that was really fun.*

CY: What kinds of things did you say about Japanese culture?

LM: *Actually, we did a really cute thing. We were trying to tell them, I know it's important to get a good education, education's more important than appearance. And they're all excited, "Excuse me, is that crown, does it have real diamonds in it? Did you come in a limousine?" It was so cute.*

CY: So they mainly focused on you being a Queen?

LM: *I'm saying ,"Study!" and [the children say], "Is that a real diamond?" [Laughing]*

CY: Now before Cherry Blossom, what kinds of Japanese cultural things had you done?

LM: *Not many. That's why I really wanted to do Cherry Blossom. One of the things I'm really grateful about Cherry Blossom is it gave me a chance to talk about my Japanese heritage. It really did. Even if I haven't been able to do anything like continue taiko.*

CY: Can you think of any specific ways in which that kind of pride manifests itself?

LM: *Not so much real changes; more psychological changes, emotional changes. [I have] more interest when I hear about Japanese issues, Japanese history, like World War II. Before Cherry Blossom I didn't really know much about it. After I read more articles about it. I remember going to Japan and we ended up staying in the same hotel as some of the 100th Battalion [decorated Japanese American troop during World War II]. I remember going up to them and telling them, "Thank you so much for what you guys have done." I'm not that emotional, but I remember starting to cry thinking about the sacrifices that they, Japanese Americans, made. I think, just little things like that, you know. I'm more in touch with Japanese heritage, appreciative and everything.*

CY: If somebody knew you before Cherry Blossom and somebody saw you after, do you think there'd be any significant change that they would notice?

LM: *I'd say my public speaking. Cherry Blossom has really done a lot for me. It gave me a lot more confidence. Especially you get thrown into it, you have to do it, no matter what. So it really increased my confidence in being able to go in front of people and talk. In fact, because of Cherry Blossom I decided to join Toastmasters. I thought it would be good for me to get more comfortable in speaking in front of people. And in fact I think doing that really helped me get into med school.*

CY: Really? How?

LM: *I don't know if you're familiar with our curriculum, but it's called Problem-Based Learning, where basically you don't have a typical format of being lectured to. A lot of it is small group interaction where you're teaching each other. And you have to be comfortable explaining to each other certain things. So presentation is extremely important. In fact, I put that in my entrance for med school: one of my things is I'm more comfortable speaking in front of groups and I think I'll be able to work well because I've had more speaking opportunities.*

I think Cherry Blossom really helped me in that I'm more comfortable in terms of interviews. When I was preparing for our interview for Cherry Blossom, I would have all these practice questions to think about. So in interview time in med school, when he asked me questions, it came out a lot easier, because I had actually thought about a lot of these things for Cherry Blossom. It made my whole interviewing process easier.

CY: Now if you were a judge, what do you think you'd look for?

LM: *What would I look for? I'd look for someone who is committed to improving her community. Being a good role model for young women.*

CY: How would you handle the whole beauty aspect of it?

LM: *I think it's how well they carry themselves, if they're comfortable with who they are, if they're confident. If it was purely on beauty, maybe the outcome would be different.*

CY: But what do you do with someone who is fine in every other way, but . . .

LM: *You mean, is the nicest girl in the crowd, everything about her is just . . .*

CY: I'm just wondering what are the physical limits of acceptability beyond which she wouldn't make a good representative?

LM: *Yeah, I know. Even though we say it's not a beauty pageant, which you know technically the judging criteria is not there, still it seems like an expectation in certain people's minds, especially the older generation. But I would rather have someone who's committed to the community than someone who's just drop-dead gorgeous. I think she would be a great Queen.*

Forty-eighth Cherry Blossom Queen Vail Matsumoto, 2000–2001

Thumbing through the CBF souvenir book for 2001, one comes upon photo after photo of the Cherry Blossom Festival's first Queen of mixed ancestry, Vail Matsumoto. Looking at the photos, one does not scrutinize her face for traces of her 25 percent Italian ancestry. Instead, one cannot help but notice her smile. It is broad and unmistakable, capturing one's attention in every single shot. Her smile radiates ease. It is not necessarily a stately, queenly smile, polished for the stage. Rather, it is a warm, big-hearted smile that draws us in with its generosity.

No article I have read on Vail mentions her smile. Instead, every article dis-

私たち共通の絆
第49回ホノルル日系人青年会議所桜祭り

OUR
COMMON
BOND

HONOLULU
JAPANESE
JUNIOR
CHAMBER
OF COMMERCE

49TH
CHERRY
BLOSSOM
FESTIVAL

Fig. 12. Forty-eighth Cherry Blossom Queen Vail Matsumoto, 2000–2001

cusses her mixed ancestry. The media will not let her simply be a CBF Queen. Instead, she always has to hold the distinction of being the first part-Japanese CBF Queen. That status inevitably becomes her story. There is more to her story, of course. The media found out that Vail's mother is half-Japanese, that Vail was named after a ski resort in Colorado, that she spent some time as a child on the Big Island, that she is an English teacher at a local high school on

Oʻahu. Articles include some or all of these factoids, but her mixed ancestry is always the main story they tell.

Vail smiles with a purpose. She speaks eloquently of voluntarism and community service, including the copious amounts of time and effort the Jaycees put into the CBF. The entire Festival is run on the fumes of their energy. Vail, like many other CBF contestants, Queens, and Court members in recent years, has become a Jaycee member and organizer of the CBF, so she holds multiple perspectives on the CBF.

Vail met me at my office at the University of Hawaiʻi late one afternoon on November 19, 2001. She stopped by after teaching and before her evening class at the university, where she is working on a doctorate degree in educational foundations. In the course of our conversation I could see what lay behind that smile and clearly why Vail had won the crown.

CY: When you decided to run, what did you want to get out of the Festival?

VM: *I didn't know a lot about the Festival. I just knew that they kind of promoted community service and I thought that was important. Even in the application, they asked about community service. So that was one main thing I knew was a part of the Festival and I knew I wanted to get out of it. And learning more about my heritage.*

CY: Or three-quarters of your heritage. [Laughs] What was your training like for the pageant?

VM: *I don't know if I would consider it training for the Festival ball [pageant], which to me is good. Because that wasn't the end-all to everything, or it shouldn't have been for anyone, because the whole idea was to learn about yourself and our culture. So a lot of it was Japanese cultural classes like tea ceremony, taiko, ikebana. We didn't do tea ceremony at Festival Ball. You know, we didn't get up and do a flower arrangement. So those things were just totally gains for ourselves and for us to take with us no matter where we're gonna go or what happened after that night.*

CY: And what do you feel that you learned the most?

VM: *I guess it was the realization that there are people in our community, in the world, who do things purely out of the goodness of their heart. Which is not to say that everything else I learned and gained wasn't valuable, but that to me was something that I did not have before. And I did after. You know, I went in on the first day, and they introduced us to all of these people, these volunteers, and as I went through it, each class, each appearance, there were all these people there. And then I realized "Oh my gosh, these people aren't getting paid, and they're there at every class for us, and they're there doing things behind the scenes, getting things ready, just for us, just for fifteen girls who are getting so much as it is." And then I* think that point was really hammered home once I saw it from the Court perspective. As a contestant, I realized it, and then as a Court member, I saw more of the behind the scenes and I saw a lot of the stress and all this work that goes into it as the contestants are just doing their thing; all these people, you know, supporting them. And now that I'm not on Court and it's a year later, I was persuaded to join the [HJJCC] chapter. Now, I really see and now I really know it because I'm one of them. I completely see the value in it and the worth. Maybe it's easier for me to see because I know what the girls are getting from it. And I'm like, "Why are you doing this?" They are such good people, you know. And that's the biggest thing I've gained.

CY: In your mind, you told me before that you never thought you would ever be a contestant, much less make Queen. So do you have any idea why you think you were chosen?

VM: *Well, on certain days, when I think back on it, I feel like had there been a different judge or different night, the Court could have been totally different. I might not have been on Court. So there are some days when I feel like that. Like maybe someone had a bad night and maybe I had a good night. Then there are other days where I think, you know, I really deserved it. And not in a conceited way, but I try to go in with a pure heart about it and just no expectations. Get as much as I can out of it. And that's what everyone kind of preaches, you know, just don't worry about Festival ball, don't worry about Court. I really tried to do that. Just think to myself, okay, don't worry, don't expect anything, do your best, and that's it. And so there are times when I think, maybe that's why. You know, I'm sure there are people who are bitter about things.*

CY: You mean not having won?

VM: *Yeah. I feel that's one of the hardest things about it: that there have to be winners and losers. That's hard to come to terms with. I can't imagine what it must have been like for other girls who weren't on Court. When I think about Cherry Blossom I feel that it was definitely one of the best parts of my life. No doubt about it, what I got out of it was great. And I like to think even though people will say, "It's because you're Queen." But I like to think that even if I wasn't on Court, I would still be doing the same thing, I'd still be helping, still be a [Jaycee] chapter member, and I'd still feel the same way about it.*

CY: Now can you tell me something about what your Court experience was like?

VM: *Luckily the six of us all got along great. People kept saying, "Wow, you guys get along so well." Luckily we all had this desire to do as many community service projects. We only had a year, so we thought, might as well do as many as we can. And we thought, "Okay, do we want to do something like a big project or do we want to do a lot of little ones?" And we all decided that the little ones might be better. So we just bombarded ourselves with them. Not all of us were there all the time. For example, one of the ones we did over and over but at different schools was we'd go and read Japanese stories to lower-grade students. Sometimes we would teach origami, sing songs, and teach them Japanese phrases. And several we planned during lunch time so that two of our Court members could come during their lunch break. So they would wear kind of a business attire to work, have their sash and crown in their car, zoom over, put that thing [sash and crown] on, read, and then zoom back without eating lunch. And I thought, "What a sacrifice for them." But no complaints, they just said, "Yep, do it during my lunch break and we can be there." And so that was it. Yes we did go on trips, we traveled a lot. But I think we had the most fun doing those projects together.*

CY: And a lot of these things were off stage?

VM: *The community service projects, I'd say five out of the how many we did, maybe we did about sixty, were on stage. Not really on stage but in the spotlight. We were there to just kind of stand there with the sash and crown. But that wasn't the majority of our projects. We bagged rice for HIV/AIDS people down at the church. Just a lot of it was t-shirt, shorts, sometimes with the sash.*

CY: Makeup or no makeup?

VM: *Bagging rice, no makeup. It was early in the morning, and we're all like, "Man, why did we sign up for this?" But we did it.*

CY: Is there anything in your appearance that you had to change over the course of time, between when you first entered and as a contestant and then Queen?

VM: *Yeah, 'cause like now, and before, when I go to work, I don't wear any makeup. And I don't really like wearing makeup. But I just felt that, let's be honest with myself, and I said, "You know what, you look better with makeup, so you might as well . . ." When you're going to be a representative of the HJJCC, why not just for a year —*

CY: When you won the contest, what were you looking forward to the most?

VM: *I remember when we were contestants, the Court at that time had a special little party for us as contestants. And they were promoting at that time their community service project, which was a big blood drive. And so I remember thinking, "Oh, we get to do a big project. And plan a big project like that, as a Court." And I guess that was something contestants remember about them, the forty-seventh Court, they did the blood drive and so I thought, "We need to do something that we'll be remembered for." Something important, something significant. That's something I was looking forward to, to making our little contribution to the whole Cherry Blossom Court timeline.*

CY: Was there anything that made you nervous about becoming Queen?

VM: *I thought that I would have to always be in the spotlight. I wasn't so against that. I was a little nervous about that. Especially since I wasn't sure how the community in general was going to accept the whole idea of me being the first Queen who was of mixed ancestry. Because I had heard about older community members being a little upset or concerned about it when they made the change. So that worried me a little bit, because to me the whole idea of the Cherry Blossom Festival is to bring the Japanese community together. And I was worried. I didn't want that to be something that would divide them. When I think about it now, I think, I shouldn't have been so worried because even those community members who might have seemed against it or were concerned about it or even criticized the president or the members of the Chapter for doing that, really, the fact that they were voicing their opinions or being concerned was a good thing. That means that they were still wanting to be involved and still wanting to have a say. So, even though I might not have agreed with what they were saying, it was still a good thing.*

CY: During that year that you were Queen, did you ever encounter anybody saying anything negative to you?

VM: *Not about my being mixed. Not about that.*

CY: What was the reaction to you in Japan?

VM: *[Long pause] I thought, I worried a little bit about it, because our relationships with our sister Chapters and their presidents, and that's important to the Chapter, and so I worried about that. My mom went out, and she has a haole last name, and so, I thought, is that gonna affect their relationship? But nothing. It was all very positive and no mention of that. I don't know if maybe they're over it and accepted it and saw it as something of a progressive kind of move for the HJJCC. Maybe that's how they saw it. I hope that's how they saw it.*

CY: So in all, how do you feel about being the first Queen of mixed ancestry?

VM: *I'm definitely proud. There's no doubt about that. But I'm also very thankful and grateful to those two contestants who ran the year before who were of mixed ancestry. In fact, one of them helped out the year I ran, and I sent her a thank you card, and I told her, "Thanks for helping out backstage, but my biggest thank you is for laying the groundwork." Because who knows, if they hadn't run and broken the ice for people like me and the First Princess who was also of mixed ancestry, maybe we might not have been on Court or maybe the committee would have been more against it. So I'm very proud, and I'm very grateful.*

Catherine, or "Cat" as she is widely and affectionately known, is a force. Like a magnet, she attracts people to her with her energy, enthusiasm, humor, and down-to-earth confidence. In one bundle, she is the no-nonsense girl-next-door, the vivacious ringleader, the thoughtful writer, the high-flying jokester, the avid surfer. The first *hapa* Queen with a haole last name, Catherine is the kind of Queen the Jaycees love to crown. She is articulate, attractive, motivated, and motivating. Understandably she is also one of the few Queens in CBF history who was voted Miss Congeniality by the other contestants.

Catherine speaks eloquently about her *hapa* experience. She talks about growing up with a *hapa* body ("I was shaped differently") in a world seemingly filled with dainty Japanese American girls. She talks about not necessarily identifying with her "Japanese side," but more with the white side of her family, including studying German instead of Japanese language in school. But she also talks about the commonality between both sides of her cultural background in terms of values. She speaks of being rudely awakened to her Asian American status when she went to Northwestern University and found herself lumped together with other minorities. Race and ethnicity changed from abstract concepts into very real boundaries within people's lives.

Catherine is a ringleader. She viewed the pageant experience as a cooperative arena rather than a competitive one. This kind of ideal was difficult to muster at times during the CBF experience, especially when training changed from a cultural focus to pageant preparation. Catherine admits that the image of the competitive beauty contest remains strong and easily lures people in, even when they have vowed to take a stance against it. Nevertheless, by focusing on empowering the entire group, she says she gained ultimate satisfaction from the event.

She speaks passionately about the CBF as an opportunity to involve herself and others in regular, structured community service. It could be as simple as a volunteer showing up at a certain place at a certain time in order to fill a certain duty, but the rewards of giving in this kind of community setting far outweighed any infringement on free time. In Catherine's words, "the people that we've met, the lives that we've touched, the things that we've done" became their own rewards for herself and other members of the Court.

I interviewed Catherine on March 26, 2002, at her workplace at the *Honolulu Advertiser.* During her reign as Queen she contributed an intermittent column about some of her "royal" experiences. The afternoon of the interview found Catherine chatty, thoughtful, and insightful.

Fig. 13. Forty-ninth Cherry Blossom
Queen Catherine Toth, 2001–2002

CY: First of all, how and why did you decide to enter the competition?

CT: *Well, it wasn't a lifelong dream because I was* hapa *and it was never an option for me, so I didn't grow up wanting to be the Cherry Blossom Queen. When they did open it up, my dad brought it to my attention, and I never really had any interest in running actually. I did it because the opportunity presented itself and*

I thought that this would be a personal challenge for me, being in a situation that I was really uncomfortable in.

Being hapa, *I never fit in with my Japanese side. I never felt comfortable with it, I never looked like the Japanese girls in my class, you know. I was shaped differently. I compared myself a lot physically to them when I was growing up and I had a really hard time with that. And to throw myself in this arena where I would be compared was a struggle for me personally. And I thought, hell, you know, I'm gonna do it. And I'm gonna see how far I can go by being true to myself. I wasn't trained. I was asked to train [by an individual coach], and I turned it down the whole time.*

I wanted to go in there and get the girls to feel really empowered and to get them to work together as a group, to say, "We're gonna represent the Japanese culture, the Japanese American community as a whole, as fifteen contestants and do the best that we can." I mean I wanted them to feel really empowered. This is not a competition on looks, this is really about you finding within yourself this character that we need to develop through these four months. And that was my goal.

I don't know if you heard my speech that night, but it was very much how I'm not Japanese on the outside. And I don't eat with chopsticks and I don't eat sashimi and I can't even speak it and you know, I took German and I identified a lot with my Caucasian side, and yet the values that my grandparents have on both sides are the same. And everything really is the same when it comes down to it. And that was my speech. And I remember when I developed that speech, I had people critiquing me, saying you know, "You should be more pro-Japanese." And I thought, "But that's not me." I mean, I am hapa, *and I'm proud to be* hapa. *And I wanted to get out there and be myself and feel that strength in who I am. It was a challenge for me. It was really a struggle. And I did it. I had no intention of winning. I just wanted to make that statement. And I wanted the girls to feel secure in who they were and not come into this feeling that they had to conform or they had to be this idea of what they thought a Cherry Blossom Queen would be. And I walked away that night feeling that I accomplished what I set out to do.*

It was really a struggle to not fall into the whole idea of, "I need to wear my hair this way. I need to dress this way. I need to behave this way if I wanna win." 'Cause you get caught up in that even if you come into it thinking, "I'm just doing it for the experience, learn more about my culture, yadda yadda yadda..." I mean, you still get into that and it was a challenge for me to not fall into that competition.

CY: How did you feel that you kept a distance from it?

CT: *You know, it's not easy to do that. Because like I said, there's a shift in the Festival. In the first half you're doing culture classes. "Oh, fun!" You're doing origami, you're making sushi, whatever. Then there's this sudden shift and it goes into competition, where you're doing pageant training, you're rehearsing your speech, and there's a change in the attitude because all of a sudden we become contestants; we're not a bunch of girls hanging out after work. We had this thing where every week we would get together and work on impromptu questions and I would have the* Advertiser *reporters write questions and I would of course contribute to that. And my goal was, we're gonna help each other because we have to present this united front that night that we are all smart, intelligent, aggressive, career-oriented, you know, compassionate, sympathetic people. Not one of us stands out over the other. So every week we did this and I think when we would meet we'd all talk about what was going on in our lives, all fifteen of us. A lot of crying went on. We kept telling each other, "You know, it's gonna be okay, we're gonna get through this as long as we all do the best that we can together." We're like, "Steal our answers! If we give a good answer and it's impromptu, and that question comes up that night, take that answer. We're all here to help each other out." And I think for the girls at first, that was uncomfortable for some of them, because some of them were being trained [by outsiders for competitive pageantry]. Some of them were being given advice outside of the Festival.*

We had heard horror stories from years before, you know. And I think because there was this idea that we were going to be together and that night it was gonna be a unified effort to present the best selves that we could, I think people felt comforted in that. I did. That's what helped me get through it. Focusing more on the girls rather than myself and my personal development is what kept the distance for me. I wanted them to do well. I was the fifteenth contestant [to be presented on stage]. I wanted to make sure all fourteen got up in front of me and did the best they could and I would just come on and do my thing. So as long as I kept my focus on them and seeing them through, it was fine. I mean, I edited most of their speeches. I mean, that was how I think I stayed outside of it for the most part.

CY: So what are the elements that you brought to it that you think allowed you to win?

CT: *I feel fairly secure in myself. I mean, everyone's insecure to some extent. And it's not that I don't think that my thighs could be smaller or that my hair could be better or that I wish I could fit size two again. It's not that. I feel secure in the sense that I'm honest. I feel good about the choices that I make. I take responsibility for my actions. I'm pretty okay with failing sometimes, I know that's gonna happen. And I think that's where I think I've fared alright in this, because I know when I get up on stage I'm not thinking, "Suck in. Arms back, shoulders back," or whatever. I'm more thinking about the content of my speech. I want that to be key. I want people to relate to what I'm saying.*

I want my Court to feel comfortable on stage. I want them to have a good experience. My focus has always been on the other girls, always. And that's been the hardest thing. I'm under a lot of scrutiny. I do a lot more than the other girls because I get requests for just the Queen. And I really take the heat because every-thing that's related to the Court through me, I get from someone else.

CY: Can you think of specific examples of where you have had to buffer the girls from a criticism or whatever it is?

CT: *Gosh. Well, you know, we have an advisor. A Queen's advisor. But the advisor will come to me if they have any complaints or if the Chapter has any complaints about the girls' behavior or whatever. Not that we had any, actually, we've been pretty good. We were considered a very laid-back Court. They always say the Queen sets the tone [for the Court]. And you know when I talked to my girls about this, we'd already been close as contestants, I said, "You know, I'm not really into being the real formal Queen, waving and all that kind of stuff. I just want to be able to give something back to the community in a relatable way, have people remember who we are because of our interaction with them, and be real. We're not anything better than anybody else. And I don't feel like wearing a crown means anything to me except that we're ambassadors of the Japanese culture and of the Chapter." That's all we are, really. We're not queens, we're ambassadors. We go to LA and San Francisco and Japan. So, whenever we get criticized for being laid back or a little too informal, it will come to me and I have to tell the girls. And I tell them, "My feeling is that this is who we are. We're not doing anything wrong, we're not doing anything illegal, we're not disobeying our contract, but this is who we are and I feel good about it." And basically that's my stand. And so I let the girls know and I let them know I've defended them. . . .*

CY: Now how does race play into your experiences? You were talking about growing up not looking Japanese. What high school did you go to?

CT: *I went to Roosevelt [High School]. So I'm looking at Mānoa, Makiki [mid-dle-class areas of Honolulu with many Japanese Americans and Chinese Ameri-cans] kids, right? And Papakōlea [government-subsidized Hawaiian homestead] kids. So I had a diversified group of friends. And I've always been that way. And I feel comfortable moving around in different groups. But when I was younger and I went to Catholic school, we didn't have a whole lot of Japanese kids. A lot of Filipino, Hawaiian kids. So that was my group. But when I did baton [twirling], or I did anything outside of that, that had a lot of Japanese . . . and I'm supposed to be Japanese, you know! And I'm supposed to look it. Every time I would see a group of Japanese girls I'd say, "Oh, I want to have straight hair, I want to look like that." Because my cousins look like that. My mom looks like that. And I have hairy arms. I always felt really self-conscious. And I think that's natural for any adolescent. When in high school* hapa *became cool. "Oh, you're* hapa!" *Right, you're not just Japanese. I started to feel a little more secure in being* hapa.

But when I went to Northwestern [University; Chicago], was the first time that I lived outside of Hawai'i. And I always relate this story to everybody I talk to,

the world her around was different from the ways of the past. (50s-60s) *but, [during student] orientation, I'm sitting there, and I'm talking to everybody, didn't realize that I was the only Asian girl in that class and I was. There were only three of us that were minorities. In fact, everybody else was blond hair, blue eyes and I don't notice that kind of stuff. So I'm sitting there talking to everybody. This cute little Midwestern blond girl, pulls me to one side after orientation and says, "What is it like to be a minority?" And I said, "I don't know, ask the black girl. I have no idea." But I have no idea, because growing up in Hawai'i, you're not a minority, you're a majority. We walk around and we don't feel oppression or feel racism. And it wasn't until I went to Northwestern . . . I still didn't feel it when I was there until July 4th, 1999, when that guy [21-year old white suprema-cist Benjamin Nathaniel Smith] went on a shooting spree targeting minorities in Illinois and Indiana. He shot and killed an African American basketball coach about a mile away from where I lived and shot at a Jewish family coming out of church a few blocks away and then a Korean family as well. That was the first time that I thought, when I step out on the street, people look at me as Asian. I never felt that before. And ever since that time, I started to think more and more about it.*

Came home and I ran for the Festival. So this is sort of a series of events that led up to my participating. It's not that I didn't identify with being Japanese growing up, because I did, but it was never that real to me before that day, 4th of July. Which is ironic, day of independence, you know.

CY: Going into it, did you feel that pure Japanese had the advantage?

CT: *Nope. Didn't occur to me. I'm pretty idealistic about everything. I don't normally walk into a situation figuring what's gonna be bad about it yet. I nor-mally just go into it, "Eh, we're gonna have fun! This'll be a great experience. I chose to be here." And if I chose to be here, I will choose for me to be happy while I'm here. That's my feeling. I never thought about it. People have mentioned it to me later, saying things like, "Well, she speaks Japanese, so she definitely has an edge." I know, I guess, but it all depends on what the judges are looking for. It never really bothered me. What am I gonna do? Take like a quick-learning Japanese course? No, it's not me. I can't be pure Japanese. I'm hapa. So why not celebrate my differ-ences? Why not each one of us celebrate our differences? We're not the same. Why try to conform to our assumption of what being Japanese American in Hawai'i is? It's different, everybody you meet is different.*

CY: If you were a judge, what would you look for?

CT: *What would I look for? You know, I look for sincerity in anybody I meet. I think that there are some people who do this for the wrong reasons. And I think that there are people that genuinely believe in the Festival, believe in what it stands for, believe in promoting the culture, and that's what I would look for. Whether they're hapa, whether they're nisei, whether they speak Japanese, whether they don't, I think if that passion is there and it's sincere, I would definitely look for that. What else? I think being personable has its benefits. You don't want somebody that's too aloof or somebody that's too timid, because it's a role that you are in the spotlight, you have to be able to deal with it, you have to be able to take care of your Court.*

And she needs to be a leader, she needs to be a role model. Our contestant pool, people made comments about us because we had a lot of tattoos and piercings. People made comments about that. When they heard people outside our group saying things like, "You better cover up your tattoo because the judges are gonna look." And I think some of them took it too seriously or too personally. It's hard. I mean you're being criticized for what you've done or who you are or what you believe in. And you're worried about the way people judge you. The great fear of everyone, I think, is being judged and here we are putting ourselves in front of judges.

CY: But are there limits to this philosophy of anything goes as long as you're true to yourself?

CT: *Oh, definitely. You are in the spotlight. You have a responsibility to behave a certain way. I feel that's true. I think everything you do, you represent not only your company, your organization, but your family, your friends, yourself. I mean for me, I hold myself up to very very high standards. There's some things I don't do. I don't drink. I don't party. I don't do drugs. I don't smoke. I mean I have a high level of expectations for myself. What I don't do is put that on other people. I don't judge people based on their choices, as long as they understand the consequences of their actions. I know I told my Court this, too, there's some things that we have to do. We have a girl on the Court who's underage. So no drinking. That was a policy. 'Cause some girls can drink, that's fine, you're twenty-one, you can. But when we're together, no alcohol. I don't even want to hear about it.*

CY: You mean, this is a rule you laid down? Not the Jaycees?

CT: *Yeah, well, they can't tell a twenty-one-year-old they can't drink. They don't want you to get drunk. You can have a beer. I think they're pretty okay having a drink, champagne, or whatever. But my thing was, if Jaslyn's [underage First Princess] with us, forget it. If we're a group, we're not doing it. And the girls know that. They know my level of expectations for myself and I think they've all tried to strive toward that.*

CY: So what do you think has been the hardest part of your reign?

CT: *It's actually a lot harder than people think it is. And when the girls saw how much work I have to do and how much crap I have to put up with all the time, they tell me, "Please don't abdicate." You know, because it's a responsibility that I don't think people realize.*

Every year the Court decides how busy they want to be. It's up to you. And we decided in the beginning we wanted to be as busy as possible. My policy was, I would come to every single event whether the girls would show up or not. I knew that not everybody could make it there. So I was at every event regardless. Unless I absolutely couldn't, like I was in the hospital or my mom was in the hospital.

CY: So what do you think is the essence of Cherry Blossom Festival?

CT: *What is it to me . . . The Cherry Blossom Festival to me is a glimpse into our community. And I don't just mean our Japanese American community, but our community in Hawai'i. It is a tradition in our community. And for me to be part of it is in itself rewarding and fulfilling, whether or not I won. Just to have been part of it.*

What I think it does for the community is that it gives young Japanese American women the opportunity to learn a little bit about your culture, to get a taste of it. We're not immersed in it. We are given a class in ikebana. I've done ikebana for two years. And what he showed us in that hour or two hours is just a taste of it. Same with taiko. It's a taste of it and the rest is up to you. It just gives you that opportunity.

It's really strange, but I looked at it when we were on Court, and I think a lot of contestants don't realize this. People always say, "What do you win? Do you win scholarship? Do you win money?" "No." And I always say this, and people say I'm nuts, "You win the opportunity to put together a year long community service program for your area." Whatever you want. That is such a reward! Voluntarism, especially with young people, is not something that we prioritize. And this Festival really promotes that. At least in recent years. And for a lot of these girls, it was such an eye-opening experience. It made them feel good to do something for the community. That was the part of the experience I know every girl walked away with a smile on their face. They will always remember fondly the people that we've met, the lives that we've touched, the things that we've done. And that to me is what makes the Festival so rewarding on a level that people don't see, is that opportunity to give back to the community.

Chapter Nine

Crowning the "Nice Girl" | The Politics and Poetics of Banality

20p9

Smiling was so much a part of the Queen pageant. The contestants were always told to smile, smile, smile—and everybody did.

—CBF Queen Jill Matsui (1973–1974)
   (Quoted in *Honolulu Advertiser* 1973:A12)

Wh
at startles observers of the CBF since the 1998 change in blood-quantum ruling is how little controversy remained only a few short years later. Since Catherine Toth completed the transition to a 50 percent Japanese-haole mixed Queen with a non-Japanese last name, nearly all vestiges of doubt or questions of appropriateness have disappeared. The following year, 2002, when Lisa Okinaga — half-Japanese, three-eighths Chinese, one-eighth Hawaiian — became Queen, newspapers called her "the perfect mix for a Japanese Queen representing the Islands" (Suzuki 2002:A5). Okinaga, a graduate of Kamehameha Schools (private school that gives prefer-ence to students of Hawaiian ancestry) and an active practitioner of hula rather than Japanese dance, seemed to represent the desirable "island blend" of not necessarily Japanese-*haole*, but a nonwhite local mix.[1] By Okinaga's crowning, mixed-ancestry contestants and Queens were not only normalized, but cred-ited with enhancing the CBF. So was the furor over changing blood-quantum requirements much ado about nothing? In this final chapter, I examine the "nothing" of the CBF as a celebration of niceness and banality, an exercise in smooth-running, harmonious relations.

Invoking banality as I am doing here brings within the spotlight its opposite — profundity — and the gradations in between. Profundity implies connec-tions that are deep and meaningful. The profound event arises out of people's lives with an immediacy that draws people to it. Thus the CBF meshed closely with people's lives during the heady decades of its inception during the 1950s and 1960s in the context of pursuing the American dream, dealing with the racial tensions remaining after World War II and rising socioeconomic and political ambitions. The CBF had a point in the postwar years, and the Japanese American community rallied around this big, splashy public event that per-formed and proclaimed their emplacement. The CBF also bridged the gap be-tween issei and nisei/sansei. The general public became caught up in the lavish spectacle that superseded ethnic boundaries. The CBF of the 1950s and 1960s may not have been obviously and indisputably profound, but it did connect with people's lives. In the process of inventing its own traditions — chicken-feather capes and all — the CBF established itself as not trivial, but deeply meaningful. The CBF in the 1950s and 1960s did not garner front-page headlines through publicity agents, but because crowning each year's Queen was considered newsworthy by journalists and the public.

Those front-page days are over. The CBF tropes of heritage and tradition are tied into knots of conservatism. As long as Japan remains its focus, the Festival will bear only an esoteric connection to young people's lives. The local Japanese American context is the exoteric experience for yonsei and gosei organizers, contestants, and audience members. At the same time, contradictions plague this "cultural pageant" that insists upon beauty pageant idioms. When is a beauty pageant not a beauty pageant? The answer for the CBF seems to be, "When it crowns the 'nice girl.'" I take a critical look at the niceness that the CBF crowns, relating it to banality through issues of gender, culture, economics, and politics. And finally, I return to the concept of banality, seeking not only its politics, but also its everyday poetics.

Mixed Shift: From Japan to Japanese American Culture and Experience

Banality had little to do with the 1998 inclusion of mixed-ancestry contestants. In fact, the change in blood-quantum rule turned the attention of the CBF from Japan to embrace more directly the Japanese American experience. Thus, in the 2001 souvenir book, HJJCC President Pono Chong (CBF chairman during the 1998 rule change) wrote:

> As we move into the new millennium, Hawaii will continue to evolve as a multi-ethnic [*sic*]community. For the HJJCC, our future success will rest on not imitating the culture of Japan, but in celebrating American Japanese and local Japanese culture and heritage as it develops through interaction and exchange with other cultures and communities. (Chong 2001:11)

Likewise, CBF cochairs Michael Inouye and Sharene Urakami wrote:

> As we crowned our first Queen of mixed ethnicity last year, we asked ourselves, "What makes us Japanese Americans?" Is it the amount of blood we have, the knowledge of the language, or the traditions we practice in our own home? There must be a common bond we share as a community and it is that bond we must nurture and cherish to perpetuate our unique heritage and culture. (Inouye and Urakami 2001:11).

By focusing on Japanese American culture, history, and social milieu, rather than that of Japan, CBF organizers approximate more closely the "common bond" of which Inouye and Urakami speak.

Nevertheless, the themes set for the CBF after 1999 express conservatism:

2000 Renewing Our Heritage

2001 Our Common Bond

2002 Reflections from the Past . . . Visions for the Future —
50th Anniversary

2003 Future of Our Heritage

2004 Strength in Unity

"Heritage" crops up predictably, pigeonholing Japanese Americans into a sus-pended existence between looking backward and moving forward. The plati-tudinous past remains perceived as a resource for the future. Another com-mon, related theme is that of the group: "our heritage," "our common bond," "strength in unity." Who defines that group? How inclusive is "our"? If the CBF seeks to promote "strength in unity," does this unity eschew controversy and silence divergent voices? These questions point to the very banality of the CBF: its disconnect from people's lives; its willingness to do primarily what has been done before; its claim upon the sediment of conservatism.

I argue that banality crept into the CBF around the time that the Jaycees de-cided they needed themes in the 1980s. In the 1950s and 1960s — when the CBF held a central place in the community life of Hawai'i, when the Jaycees were busy building an organization and an event that celebrated themselves, and when the CBF was part of the emplacement of the HJJCC and Japanese Ameri-cans in Hawai'i and the United States — there was little need for themes. The CBF was a theme unto itself. It was all organizers could do to scramble to meet the needs of a public hungry for spectacle. But in the 1970s, as the CBF be-came an anachronism in the changing sociopolitical climate in Hawai'i and the United States, the event became adrift of its surroundings. Themes intro-duced in the 1980s were an attempt to give coherence to a Festival in search of meaning and relevance.

The CBF became, in effect, merely another Jaycee project. This is not to imply that all Jaycee projects are necessarily banal. Rather, this points to the distance between the CBF and the lives of its organizers. Keith Kamisugi explained: "'Many people still think of the Cherry Blossom Festival as an ethnic (beauty) pageant. It is not.' . . . Instead, Kamisugi sees the festival as a chance to stress character and culture and give Junior Chamber members a chance to run a major event" (Takeuchi 1999:15). This change in conceptualization of the CBF points to the HJJCC as a Jaycee organization whose main function is to "run major events," regardless of any cultural connection. Here several factors coin-cide: (1) the increased professional ambitions of Jaycee members; (2) the grow-ing focus of the Jaycee organization on learning professional skills, including

It started out not needing themes for attention.

community service; and (3) a disconnect between the CBF and any naturalized "ethnic" or "cultural" content. The CBF, according to this interpretation, is only and at most a major event whose themes happen to be linked to Japanese (or Japanese American) culture.

Cherry Blossom Festival Queen Primer for the 2000s

Let me turn now to a basic description of the post-1998 CBF. The requirements to run for Cherry Blossom Festival Queen in the 2000s are as follows:

a. Contestant is of at least 50 percent Japanese ancestry
b. Contestant is a U.S. citizen and resident of Hawai'i
c. Contestant is female by birth
d. Contestant will be not less than nineteen (19) years of age as of January 1 and not older than twenty-six (26) years of age as of June 30 [in the year of competition][2]
e. Contestant has graduated from high school
f. Contestant is of good moral character
g. Contestant is not a member of HJJCC
h. None of Contestant's immediate family member(s) is a member of HJJCC
i. Contestant is not and has never been married
j. Contestant is not pregnant and has never given birth (HJJCC 2001)

The Jaycees do not conduct any check of police records, employment records, school records, or health histories to certify any of the above. Instead, they screen applicants in face-to-face interviews intended to whittle the number down to fifteen official contestants or "semifinalists."[3]

Once the Queen and Court have been chosen, the Queen's advisor plays an important role in guiding their behavior. As a liaison between the Queen and the HJJCC, the advisor gives permission for her to participate in appearances and events, counsels her on her conduct, and schedules her activities. The advisor performs the essential functions of gatekeeper, guardian, and impression manager for the Queen and Court. Because the Queen acts as a public representative, the HJJCC must structurally ensure that her image — as theirs — is carefully crafted. However, the Jaycees are surprisingly lax about certain issues, primarily because these issues have not yet arisen as cause for concern. For example, there is no rule prohibiting posing nude. The only injunction is that if a woman chooses to do so, she should wait until her reign is over so she appears as an individual, not as a Queen or Court member.

The CBF organizers and judges assume no prior knowledge of Japanese (or

Japanese American) culture or history and do not necessarily reward those who possess such knowledge. Taking lessons in tea ceremony, for example, will procure no advantage in winning the CBF crown. Contestants do not have to speak Japanese, so those whose household language is Japanese or who have studied it do not gain any points. There is no talent portion, so perfecting an art form does not find reward here. There is no swimsuit portion, and contestants appear in modest evening gowns and kimono that completely cover their bodies from the base of the neck to their *tabi*-clad toes. Therefore, breast enhancement or other bodily modifications find little place in the CBF.

Given these conditions, what is being judged in the CBF? The answer to which I have alluded throughout this book: niceness. Or at least the stage projection of being nice, defined here as amiable, pleasing, pleasant, tactful, congenial. As one dictionary put it, "The word has come, through overuse, to lack precision and intensity" (Nichols 2001:893). The very blandness of the term suggests its tie to banality. What is important about niceness is that anyone can have it, do it, and be it. Niceness is the democratic, every-person ideal of humility and decency. Not everyone can be beautiful, smart, or rich, but everyone can be or act nice. Furthermore, everyone can remain nice no matter what the conditions of one's existence. What gets crowned on the CBF stage in the 2000s, as in the 1950s, is the "nice-girl" *ojōsan* — the well-bred, middle-class, premarital Japanese American girl-next-door. She is the spectacle of the ordinary in an extraordinary setting.

In representing the Jaycees and Japanese Americans in Hawai'i, the CBF Queen makes of them all "nice girl" *ojōsan*. She epitomizes the model minority, the American dream of middle-class attainment. She may not have been born to the position, but achieves it through hard work, education, personal and family sacrifice, and continually upholding values of human decency — that is, niceness. This is not the upper-class *ojōsan* of Japan, but the immigrant *ojōsan* of Hawai'i, coming from humble roots and never forgetting those beginnings. She is a story of Japanese American achievement that does not celebrate burning ambition so much as a hardworking, family-supported ideal of niceness. The CBF Queen acts as a crystallization of that ideal.

Smiling One's Way to the "Nice Girl" Crown

Mrs. Lillian Yajima, longtime mainstay of the CBF, says that she enjoys watching the transformation that contestants undergo in the process of Festival training and experience. As a teacher of two of the cultural classes (origami boxes and jack-o'-lantern *manjū*) and a faithful attendee at CBF public appearances, she sees the contestants at various stages. She notes that some may initially lack

[handwritten margin note: Even though some rules have changed the competition has not]

Fig. 14. Contestant
Sharry Urada and her
jack-o'-lantern *manjū*

refinement: they may talk and laugh too loudly, move clumsily or exhibit what
Yajima calls "unladylike" behavior. Some may be too shy to speak up in public
settings. By pageant night, however, most of the contestants show greater poise,
self-confidence, stage management, and polish (personal communication, December 12, 2001). The transformation Yajima describes is the finishing-school
polish of the Japanese American "nice girl" *ojōsan*, pulled from her middle-
class ranks and thrust onto a stage where she must learn to mix with mayors,
governors, and CEOs.

In general, the niceness extends to intracontestant relations that the Jaycees
promote (see Chapter 8, Catherine Toth's herstory). Referring to each other as
"Cherry Sisters," contestants use fictive kinship terms to spell out the familial
relationships that are supposed to arise as the result of the intensive period of
CBF training. Contestants are separated from their everyday milieu, undergo
intense training constituting a liminal state, and finally become reincorporated
through their presentation to the public at appearances in shopping malls, cul-

Fig. 15. Contestants posing with drumming teachers after taiko practice

minating in the combined pageant and coronation ball (cf. Van Gennep 1960). In the process, several recent Queens and contestants mention the close friendships that they have formed with one another as "Cherry Sisters." In the 2000s, the HJJCC attempts to build into the structure of the CBF opportunities for bonding, encouraging contestants to help each other, holding informal "talk story" meetings, providing a milieu that is cooperative rather than competitive. The goal of this period of training is to produce as level a playing field as possible, enabling each "Cherry Sister" to put her best foot forward, often with the assistance and support of her fellow contestants.

In 1995, the judging criteria fit the beauty pageant norm of competition, with beauty (30 percent), poise (25 percent), voice and diction (25 percent), and personality (20 percent) all part of the contest. However, in 1999, judging criteria were changed to intelligence (30 percent), poise and presence (20 percent), public speaking (25 percent), personality (20 percent), and participation (5 percent).[4] Given the subjective nature of most of these criteria and the importance of the results, it is no wonder that judging comes under such scrutiny. In the 2000s, the Jaycees attempt to create racial/ethnic and gender balance: half of the judges should be of Japanese ancestry, half non-Japanese, and half should be women, half men.[5] Furthermore, no judge is supposed to have prior close association with any of the contestants. According to the Jaycees, "Ordinary

'95 beauty was a criterin in this "non-beauty" pageant.

people, rather than pageant professionals, serve as judges so that their collective opinion will reflect that of the community" (HJJCC 2002:4). In this way, the Jaycees address criticism of the CBF as elitist. The Queen is a product of the collective wisdom of "ordinary people." Furthermore, since no more than half the judges are Japanese American, the "ordinary" milieu from which the Queen arises is not necessarily racially/ethnically based. The CBF embraces a broader, more inclusive spectrum. The qualities by which these judges select a Queen — "intelligence," speech, poise, personality — have little to do specifically with being Japanese American; they are pan-ethnic, desirable traits.

Several people mention one criterion as particularly important to the CBF: "personality," the very locus of niceness. Queen Myrah Higa (1976 – 1977) says half-jokingly, "I hope I won on my personality. . . . If you took the other angle [her beauty], there was no way I could have won. I think heart and personality are the most important things to judge a person by" (quoted in Tong 1976: A5). But what exactly is "personality" and how is it to be measured? If it is the distinctive character of a person, then that is immeasurable. However, if it is a specific configuration of personal traits, then one may judge an individual by her approximation to that ideal. In local parlance, "personality" means "having personality" — a quality some individuals have (whether by birth or training) and perform, and others do not. Although "having personality" is desirable for females and males, the sanctions against females who do not are greater. I argue that the CBF "personality" ideal rests in the emotional configuration and practices of the hostess: friendly, congenial, outgoing, hospitable.

The physical manifestation of the "nice girl" hostess "with personality" rests in her smile. One newspaper article on Queen Jill Matsui (1973 – 1974) was entitled, "Cherry Blossom Queen Smiles Her Way to Throne" (*Honolulu Advertiser* 1973:A12). Matsui, whose contestant speech was "What Is a Smile?," pontificated:

> Smiling is so much a part of daily living. . . . Sometimes people smile, without giving it a second thought. But it's still so important — and it hardly takes any time and doesn't cost anything. . . . The memory of a smile can last forever. . . . You can be walking down the street, and someone you don't know gives you a warm smile. It's such a good feeling. You might not see that person again, but you can remember the warmth of that smile. (Quoted in ibid.)

The smile as general bedrock of human relations is part of the niceness that CBF celebrates. It is also part of its banality: a smile may mask critique and represent an absence of critical thought by its formulaic habitualness. A smile is the physicalization of social, gendered pleasantry.

The smile is a fundamental part of emotion work in the United States, Japan, and elsewhere, although the quality of the smile and its exact physical dimensions may differ by culture. As Arlie Hochschild argues in describing U.S. flight attendants, "The emotional style of offering the service is part of the service itself" and one of the biggest assets to that style and service is the smile (1983:5). "Service with a smile" defines the emotional labor of the service industry in the United States. It also defines the gendering of service by the very stereotype of girls as being sugar-and-spice nice. As Hochschild explains, "Women are more likely to be presented with the task of mastering anger and aggression in the service of 'being nice'" (ibid.:163). Niceness may be generalized as a cultural value, but within both the United States and Japan, women are more socialized to "be nice" than men and to perform their niceness with a smile. In other words, men more than women in these societies can transgress niceness in socially legitimate ways. Furthermore, the smile becomes the performative symbol of that niceness in everyday life, as well as in the spotlight of the stage.

Contradictions of the Non-Beauty Contest: Bodies and Beyond

Crowning a Queen on the basis of niceness suggests that the CBF is not and has never been a beauty contest, as many of its organizers and Queens adamantly proclaim. This denial has become more vociferous since the 1998 elimination of "beauty" from judging criteria. Even before 1998, however, the CBF was held up as a "cultural pageant," rather than beauty contest, deemphasizing appearance, emphasizing "personality," and focusing on "culture." But to what extent is this possible given its continued use of beauty contest idioms, including crown, tiara, sash, scepter, judging, ramp, labels such as "Queen" and "Princess"? As Queen Gwen Nishizawa (1967 – 1968) says, "It's just like Miss America. You walk down a long ramp like Miss America, and even if you win in your kimono, you give up your crown in an evening gown" (quoted in Battad 1998:A5). If this is not a beauty contest, then why the concern for the fairness of judging, the occasional intense rivalry between Queen and First Princess, rumors of *hapa* contestants before the change in blood-quantum ruling, and reputed advantage of *hapa* contestants in terms of appearance? The contradictions of this non-beauty-contest pageant point repeatedly to the ambiguities of niceness.

The Queen and Court are selected to represent the Jaycees, the Japanese American community, Hawai'i, and sometimes the United States. As representatives, they must concern themselves with physical image as an important public interface. This may justify the significance of bodily aesthetics, even if the details have changed over the course of CBF's history. The 1950s and 1960s quandary over darker complexion gave way to a 1970s and 1980s concern for dyed hair, which shifted in the 1990s and 2000s to covering up tattoos and body piercings. These concerns for physical image beg the question of whether or not a Queen would ever be selected who was fifty pounds overweight, physically handicapped, or even wore glasses onstage.

The beauty pageant aspects of this non-beauty contest are evidenced by the "pageant training" that all contestants undergo. In the 2000s, this is conducted by Pamela Futa-Campbell (CBF First Princess, 1981 – 1982). In the session I observed in 2002, these instructions included posture (the pelvic tuck, shoulders in line with hips, chin parallel to the ground), standing foot positions (right foot at 12 o'clock, left foot at 10 o'clock, weight primarily on back leg, knees slightly bent), arms (elbows slightly bent, hands gently curved and facing the sides of the body, rather than "gorilla style" with the backs of the hands facing front), and walking (men walk heel to ball of foot, women should walk ball to heel; men walk in parallel lines, women should walk with a slight crossover). Futa-Campbell taught contestants how to move and stand to cover up physical imperfections such as bowed legs. She taught specific pageant stage maneuvers, such as facing the audience even when walking in profile. She taught contestants how to smile: "Pick three to four people in the audience and smile directly at them; use your eyes to smile; tilt your head occasionally; smile with different parts of the body." She taught contestants how to work a room: "Know who the major sponsors are; shake hands firmly but not too vigorously; make eye contact; remember names; slow down when speaking to the press." When I observed this training process, one contestant jokingly called out, "I'm becoming like a lady!" to which Futa-Campbell smilingly admonished, "Any time from this point on, you have to take things seriously. Think in your mind, 'This is pageant night.'" If shyness is a problem, Futa-Campbell advised, "Push yourself in uncomfortable situations." One may argue that all of these instructions and admonitions are geared to teaching contestants how to best present themselves, no matter what the situation. (Futa-Campbell also teaches men the art of self-presentation.) Nevertheless, this kind of training only confirms the notion of the CBF as inevitably caught up in beauty pageant practices and values, even when calling itself a "cultural pageant."

The contradictions of the non-beauty pageant are nowhere more evident than in the following frank letter written by Harvard University graduate Dori Takata (First Princess and Miss Congeniality, 1999 – 2000) for the CBF souvenir book:

As a contradiction through and through, I wanted to serve our community in this odd capacity precisely because I am not a likely Queen. Standing at 4-foot-10-inches, I was the shortest contestant, and my passion for food noticeably outweighs any concern over body weight. My acne scars, old college battle wounds, are stubbornly ingrained upon my face. . . . Images are powerful, however, and I sought to provoke a significant evolution in the Cherry Blossom experience. Was it possible to remake the image of the Queen and Court by endorsing a value of culture, education, leadership, and substantive service? The questions which prompted my involvement remain unanswered. Although we and our many predecessors have worked hard, the 47th Court has had mixed results this year. Language and symbols of pageantry and pseudo-royalty — along with the fundamental purpose and structure of the experience — demand close re-evaluation. The answers rest with the leadership of both past and future participants in partnership with the HJJCC board. (Takata 2000:27)

Dori directly addresses the contradictions of holding a non-beauty "cultural" pageant. She herself is intelligent, accomplished, and outspoken. The Jaycees proudly point to Dori's attainment of the title of First Princess to indicate that they crown inner beauty, strength of character, and niceness. The question remains, could she have become Queen?

Crowning Niceness: Japanese Americans in Hawai'i

In crowning the "nice girl," I argue that the Jaycees crown themselves. And taking this one step further, through the Queen and the CBF, the Japanese American community in Hawai'i becomes the "nice girl": feminized, depoliticized, smiling her/their way to a benign place in the local scene. This Cherry Blossom "nice girl" is not presented as a sexy queen (as the Chinese American Narcissus Festival Queen in tight-fitting, thigh-revealing cheongsam often is).[6] Rather, she is the wholesome, sweet, deeroticized, nice, girl-next-door Queen. Feminizing the Japanese American population in this way renders it harmless, presenting an attractive, positive image to the general public. The Japanese American community through the CBF Queen becomes, in effect, banal.

The "nice girl" image has gone through various permutations over the decades of the CBF. In the postwar years of the 1950s and 1960s the Cherry Blossom "nice girl" represented living the all-American dream of emplacement in crown and tiara, albeit switching to kimono as the occasion required. In the 1970s and 1980s, as Japanese Americans occupied positions of the mainstream in politics, business, and education, the "nice girl" image counteracted some of the backlash critique of other ethnic groups. In the 1990s and 2000s, the "nice girl" Queen tapped into Hawai'i's multicultural model of harmonious social relations. Niceness became not only a Japanese American characteristic, but a local virtue sometimes dubbed "aloha spirit." Throughout these years,

Changes in representation over the years.

representing Japanese Americans as a body of niceness has deflected attention away from sociopolitical events and toward a sociocultural virtue of getting along with others.

Niceness is part of the stereotype of Japanese Americans in Hawai'i. They are seen and see themselves as avoiding controversy, promoting social harmony, blending in, and working diligently without complaint. This is the stereotype of the docile plantation worker, the reliable bureaucrat, and the efficient secretary. This stereotype ignores historical incidents of labor strikes led by Japanese workers. It ignores the very deliberate negotiations and maneuvering that resulted in the Democratic Revolution of 1954, which swept Japanese Americans into political office. More recently, it ignores the favoritism and cronyism of Japanese Americans in power who hand out lucrative jobs and contracts to insiders.

Niceness is part of the self-stereotyping of Japanese Americans in Hawai'i. Queen Francene Kondo recalled trying to disrupt her grandmother's belief in the niceness of Japanese Americans:

> I've had many conversations with my grandmother about accepting other races and even accepting the fact that there are some Japanese [Americans] that are very bad. Because she truly believes that just because you're [ethnically] Japanese, you're good. She really did. When I was in high school, there was a classmate of mine who took a butcher knife to another student and killed her. And he was pure Japanese and the student, the girl, was pure Japanese as well. And I still remember having that conversation with her, you know. "He's full Japanese and look what he did; he took that knife and butchered her to death." And I don't remember what she said, but I think that that incident probably opened up her eyes to the possibility that all [ethnic] Japanese are not good.
>
> (Personal communication, February 13, 2002)

Francene's grandmother is not alone. Many older Japanese Americans I have spoken with hold onto the boundaries of them (other ethnic groups) and us (Japanese Americans), defining others in contradistinction to Japanese Americans, who are reputedly trustworthy, reliable, honest, decent, generous with each other, softhearted — in other words, nice.

One can put a Japanese cultural spin on this niceness, invoking terms and values such as *wa* (harmony), *shūdan-shugi* (groupism), *enryo* (self-restraint), *tatemae-honne* (public face-private, true feelings), and *omoiyari* (empathy). Analyzed through a Japanese cultural lens, niceness stems from the social harmony fundamental to group life. Some of the tools of that niceness include self-restraint in not forcing one's wants and needs upon others; understanding and performing the critical distinction between public face and private feelings; and empathy, not only in understanding other people's feelings, but anticipating and meeting their needs before one's own. These cultural attributes of niceness are usually assumed more important for women than men in Japan. Niceness in Japan can also be found in the service culture of *okyakusama* (honored guest), built around placing guests on a pedestal of service and well-being. This hierarchical host-guest relationship of niceness points directly to the CBF Queen as hostess. Although it is true that these Japanese cultural values carry over into Japanese American life, I hesitate to attribute niceness solely to this. Too much can be made of Japan as an originary culture explaining the behavior of Japanese Americans. Not only is the contextual milieu completely different for Japanese Americans in Hawai'i, but the time frame and generational depth of disconnect from Japan is considerable. Furthermore, many of these values are shared by other groups in Hawai'i.

What Japanese Americans in Hawai'i do share with people in Japan is a culture of social conservatism. Here is partly where banality resides. Conservatism rests in the smooth, unbroken surface of the public face, even as small changes take place below the surface. It rests in a concern for that public face, maintaining a positive image. It rests in the nature of change and creativity, often occurring incrementally and over a period of time. It rests in leadership styles that prefer backstage manipulation and maneuvering to front-stage posturing. It rests in consensus, or at least the appearance of it. The Japanese concept of *heibon* — defined as "commonness, commonplaceness; banality; platitude"; and in adjectival form as "common; ordinary; trite; unremarkable" — is important here (Masuda 1974:417). The goal of Japanese socialization is to produce a child who is ordinary and thus able to lead *heibon na seikatsu* (an ordinary life), a life characterized as unremarkable, unproblematic, stable, and predictable. In Japan, people whose lives are *heibon* fill the ranks of white-collar bureaucracies. Similarly, in Hawai'i, *heibon na seikatsu* of Japanese Americans may be found in disproportionate numbers in civil service employment, working for federal or state governments.[7]

Niceness and banality are separate qualities, but they overlap in a shared goal of blending into one's surroundings of emplacement, of becoming "unmarked" and thereby participating as a member of the mainstream. That the HJJCC would choose to blend in by standing out through the spectacle of a beauty pageant is testament to the power and performance of niceness. By acting, doing, and being "nice," the Jaycees and their Queens achieve their own banality — that is, they secure a position in the mainstream that does not threaten others.

The Busyness of Niceness: Community Service

One of the most acceptable ways of "doing nice" is through community service projects. Although the Jaycees have always embraced community service, it is only in recent years that the Queen and Court and even contestants have been equally engaged. Niceness for a CBF Queen is more than a personal trait, but translates into acts of public goodwill. In fact, the busy work of niceness may potentially mask flaws in the system of selecting a Queen and Court, since one does not necessarily have to be nice, but at least be willing and able to "do nice" through acts of public goodwill.[8] Thus in the 2000s, the Queen and Court undertake a mindboggling number of service projects and public appearances despite full-time jobs or university classes. For example, Queen Lori Murayama (1999 – 2000) logged 168 days of CBF-related activities during her year's reign.

Although community service has become a part of many beauty pageants and Jaycee organizations throughout the United States, I argue that CBF community service projects fit in particularly well with the stereotype of Japanese Americans as responsible, industrious, and "quiet but effective." Community service contributes to the image of the niceness of the group as a whole. Since the late 1990s, the Queen and Court have earmarked specific community service projects for their year's reign. Only a small fraction of these are particularly linked to Japanese culture or Japanese American activities. Instead, more often than not, CBF Queen and Court community service projects contribute to the well-being of the pan-ethnic community, linking with organizations such as the American Red Cross, the American Cancer Society, the Salvation Army, and Aloha United Way (umbrella organization of nonprofit organizations in Hawai'i). The CBF Queen has thus been transformed from a smiling, voiceless, crowd-waving ambassador to a hands-on public servant specifically through community service.

Community service has taken the CBF out of the realm of Japanese (American) culture and placed the Queen and Court within the broader local community. At the same time, the CBF Queen and Court must retain their visibility. Queen Lori Murayama reminds future Queen and Court members:

> When doing service projects, find a way to make your Courts visible. That does not necessarily mean wearing sash and crowns, but perhaps with Court T-shirts or something that distinguishes you as the Cherry Blossom Court. Many people only associate the Court with the Pageant and Public Appearances, but by making yourselves visible at community service projects, they might come to realize the Court is more about substance than appearances. (Murayama 2000:2)

Fig. 16. Contestant (and later fiftieth CBF Queen) Lisa Okinaga teaching children origami as part of community service

Murayama acknowledges that projects not only benefit recipients, but also maintain a "nice" public face for the HJJCC and the Japanese American community at large. Community service projects thus enable the performance of niceness for the CBF Court, as well as the HJJCC.

The Politics of Banality: Power and Niceness

The busyness of niceness in the CBF is critical both for embedding the HJJCC within a web of obligations of charitable institutions, as well as affirming its position as first and foremost a service-oriented business organization. The operating language of this niceness is economic; but the story it tells is that of community service. Both language and story come together in a metanarrative of banality.

The politics of banality rests in the ways in which this metanarrative circumscribes a position of power. It attains this position not overtly in an aggressive snatch, but unobtrusively as part of the realm of the status quo. This is the contradiction of representational visibility: those with the most power need the least visibility, because their dominance is assumed. In the 1950s and 1960s, when Japanese Americans were on the rise, the CBF helped their "visibility" as part of their emplacement. However, once they were fairly ensconced within positions of power in the 1970s, the CBF merely performed their banality. Japanese Americans became privileged members of the mainstream, and the CBF's very banality proved that they no longer needed to substantiate their power. Banality, then, may be considered the privilege of the already emplaced.

Banality and the emplacement that it signifies trouble the multicultural model. Those who glorify this model say that Hawai'i is unique in that emplacement is not necessary, there is no majority, only minorities, and all ethnic groups may take pride in their differences. As one headline puts it, "Hawaii's ethnic rainbow: shining colors, side by side" (Yim 1992:B1). The Cherry Blossom Queen thus stands "side by side" with the Narcissus Festival Queen, both flanking the governor of Hawai'i. The problem with this picture, however, is that neither Queen possesses any true power. Their "shining colors, side by side" are decorative rather than substantive. Furthermore, some colors are notably missing from the picture. Why these two Queens and not others? Where is Miss Korea Hawaii or Miss Hawaii Filipina? What about groups who do not publicly crown pageant queens, such as Samoans, Hawaiians, Puerto Ricans, Portuguese, Vietnamese, African Americans, and others? Why is there no Miss Haole? The "shining colors" may coexist "side by side," but their presence and absence speak to different kinds and expressions of representational visibility and power. In short, some colors of the ethnic rainbow "shine" more "equally" and to greater purpose than others.

In the mid-1980s Franklin Odo criticized the multicultural model of racial/ethnic harmony and characterized the Japanese American community in terms of what I dub banality:

Fuzziness is considered a virtue and has been distorted into a basic Japanese or "local" value which discourages controversy and open disagreement. Worse, this superficial harmony is said to reflect Japanese or Japanese American culture or heritage. AJAS [Japanese Americans] who do not conform run the risk of being considered "unlocal" or "unJapanese." The result is a large and important ethnic community which has nothing to debate and no ideas to argue, whether internally among regional, generational or social-class lines or relative to other groups in Hawaii. (1984:xx)

It is exactly in the avoidance of controversy, disagreement, and therefore lack of debate or meaningful discussion that banality resides. Banality is the "superficial harmony" that has been culturalized as Japanese, Japanese American, and/or local. It is a benign "be nice" ethos, sometimes called the "aloha spirit," taken not only at the individual level, but extended to embrace the group and thus political level.

Banality pauses at the blip that mixed-ancestry Queens and members provoke, opening up the rupture between race and culture. But it pauses only briefly before returning to the busyness of its enterprise. That busyness devolves into a basic Japanese or "local" virtue of niceness that discourages controversy and open disagreement. But what is wrong with niceness? What does niceness obscure? Niceness, like banality, silences critique. It erases unpleasantness. It places interaction (social, political) on an individual level, obscuring the place and inequalities of groups. Niceness suggests simplistic solutions to complex situations; it sidesteps the complications and ambiguities of daily life in a global setting. Niceness is emotion work for those under pressure to perform. It is also the political work of surface harmony.

The Poetics of Banality: Enriching Individual Lives

One may be hard put to find poetics in banality, but it may be found in the blossoming confidence of a shy girl, or the continuing friendship between fifteen "Cherry Sisters," or the pride of a father hugging his newly crowned daughter. It may be found in the growing maturity of young women, developing poise on stage and responsibility and consideration for others off stage. As one parent explained to me: "We notice a big change [in our daughter]. She's more appreciative. Like when I do small things for her. Now she always says, 'Thank you.' They [Jaycees] must teach them [contestants] filial piety or something like that." This parent places a Japanese cultural spin on the blossoming of his daughter through participation in the CBF. He, like several others I spoke with, notes the transformative power of the experience for many women.

Poetics is also found in the herstories of Queens and contestants, embedded in their individual lives, meanings, and emotions. Each Queen shares a crown invested with symbolic obligations to represent the organization, the group, the state, and the nation. How each has managed to don the crown of niceness is part of the individuated story she has to tell. It lies in the busyness of Jaycee organizers launching a full-scale practicum in organization, follow-through, and leadership. Their volunteer efforts conducted over several months find their own rewards and frustrations, even if before a public that in the 2000s seems not to pay much attention. The poetics lie at the individual level of investment made by each of the CBF's many participants.

One may also find poetry at the group level, in the achievements of genera-

Fig. 17. Supporters cheering on contestants at a shopping mall appearance

tions of immigrants and their offspring, who have played it safe, toed the line, and presented a good face to the public. This may be considered the lived poetics of immigrant groups. Is banality thus endemic to the practices and achievements of immigrant groups? Perhaps, inasmuch as banality may be framed in terms of assimilation. But increasingly there is greater acceptance of other cultures and less willingness to accept the assimilation model passively. Indeed, the banality of the CBF may occur as a predictable outcome of historical circumstances and sociopolitical contexts. Nevertheless, this banality merits our attention because of its gendered dimensions, cultural logic, political implications, and economic outcomes.

Are all beauty pageants banal? Perhaps, if they all only focus on the most superficial aspects of a woman. However, if in the process of crowning a Queen, a beauty pageant galvanizes an ethnic group's sense of itself, if the Queen becomes a rallying point of group pride, if having a Queen proves a group's worthiness to themselves and to others, then I suggest that a beauty pageant under these particular historical circumstances rises above its own inherent banality and approaches profundity. This was the CBF of the 1950s and 1960s. The poetics of banality may rest in a smile — not so much the practiced ones on stage, but those of onlookers who see the spotlight as a measure of their worth.

In the end it is the busyness of the CBF that generates part of its overall poetics. It is busyness that does not come with long pauses for reflection, but speaks primarily in the doing. The public helping hand has become the focus of the event. More important, this helping hand deliberately transcends race/ethnicity and culture. The CBF is part of the struggling poetics of a community attempting to redefine itself beyond race/ethnicity and establish a broader base and relevance. The "Japanese" (American) label hovers above the CBF and the HJJCC. In the 2000s, organizers often wonder what to do with it. The challenge for them is not to hold onto it as an albatross from the past, but use it to prod them into a future where the creative poetics of race/ethnicity and culture reside.

NOTES

Prologue

1. As of 2004, Hawai'i had two Miss Americas, Carolyn Sapp in 1992 and Angela Perez Baraquio in 2001. (In 1997, Hawai'i's Brooke Lee won the Miss USA pageant and then went on to win Miss Universe.) The first Miss Hawaii of 100 percent Japanese ancestry was Tracy Toguchi in 1995.

2. Hawai'i's Cherry Blossom Festival is not the first in the United States. The first Cherry Blossom Festival was begun in 1935 in Washington, D.C., in commemoration of the planting of cherry trees from Japan in 1912. In 1940, a queen pageant was added to the Washington, D.C., festival (National Park Service 2004). Contestants include representatives from all states and territories, are not necessarily of Japanese ancestry, and, according to a 1958 newspaper article, are selected by "the spinning of a wheel" (*Honolulu Advertiser* 1958:B3).

3. Here I freely employ the terms of beauty that my family used. In Chapter 1 I problematize these same notions of "beauty" and "good looks" as embedded within issues of race and class.

4. Fear of public speaking was one of the most frequently mentioned obstacles among contestants and Queens that I interviewed.

5. The nine-minute film is entitled *Cherry Blossoms on Parade* (Yano 2002a), with executive producer Chris Conybeare and cameraman Cliff Watson. It is not available for sale.

6. Note that here and elsewhere, I refer to each Queen by her maiden name for several reasons: (1) this is the name by which they won the crown, and by which the general public remembers them; and (2) using maiden names protects their current privacy.

Chapter One. Beauty Pageants as Spectacles of Gender, Race/Ethnicity, and Community

1. Guy Debord argues that in contemporary society, media spectacles replace experience and meaning with image, commodity, and representation to the extent that we become spectators to our own lives (1995).

2. I use the words "contest" and "pageant" interchangeably to refer to events that judge women and crown a queen. The two have slightly different connotations, however: "contest" is strict competition; "pageant" suggests some of the performative aspects of spectacle, as well as references the faux royalty imagery of its practices. Although

catalyzing events such as the Miss America pageant originally called themselves "contests," increasingly "pageant" is the preferred label. One good example is the Florida-based magazine and website called *Pageantry Magazine*, which provides information and listings of beauty pageants at the state, national, and international levels (2004).

3. For example, see Chapter 4, Anna Tokumaru's explanation of her parents' reluctance to allow her to compete in the CBF pageant. In Tokumaru's case, both social class and Japanese (American) culture combine to provide rationale for her parents' objections.

4. Even the notion of debutante balls as the purview of upper classes must be couched within American fantasies of Horatio Alger-like upward mobility for daughters and their families. As Karal Ann Marling points out, "Debbing is a ritual grounded in aspiration, retrospection, and legitimization. America's would-be aristocrats want to reaffirm their blood ties to greatness" (2004:6). The class lines surrounding debdom in the United States blurred even further in the late 1920s and 1930s when debutante heiresses acquired their own press agents, appeared in gossip columns, and sometimes ventured into show business and advertising (ibid.:9–11).

5. Trump's infamous beauty pageant incident occurred in 1996, when the expanding waistline of the reigning Miss Universe, Alicia Machado from Venezuela, became headline fodder. When she went from 112 pounds at the time of her crowning to 160 pounds some months later, Trump publicly insisted that Machado lose weight, in part to protect his investment. She is quoted as saying, "When I get to New York thinking they [pageant organizers] were going to help me, I find myself in a gym with eighty photographers all taking pictures and watching the little pig exercise" (quoted in Perlmutter 2000:159).

6. Euro-American definitions of facial beauty were made explicit in 1940, when American cosmetics company Max Factor Jr. developed a prototype of the All-American face. It was model Mary Parker—blond, fair-skinned, with balanced proportions (Savage 1998:63).

7. See Barringer, Gardner, and Levin (1993:24–26) for comparisons of immigration from Japan, China, Korea, Philippines, and Vietnam to the United States; summarized in King 2002:122, Table 7-2.

8. The question of how to designate the sociopolitical conditions of Asian American women semiotically has been broached by different theorists. Laura Hyun Yi Kang uses "Asian/American women" to express tensions between these designations, as well as "the shifting separations and crossings" between Asia and the United States (1997:405). Lisa Lowe uses "Asian immigrant women" and "Asian American women" to differentiate the two in terms of birth, but she joins them in her expression "Asian 'American' women" to "signal the ambivalent and multidirectional sets of identifications that both . . . have to the nationalist construction of 'American'" (1997:273).

9. "The growth and consolidation of American ethnic beauty pageants during the Cold War era was accompanied by the development of local and regional pageants in South America, Asia, and the Caribbean. In the 1930s and 1940s, these pageants had grown in popularity as newly decolonizing nations attempted to perform modernity and nationhood. . . . Thus overseas competitions existed for reasons similar to Asian American ones" (Lim 2003:195).

10. In Japan, too, lessons in tea ceremony are part of gendered, bodily training that marks social class. Although the top-ranking masters of tea schools are men, the vast majority of students are women. Lessons in tea ceremony are regarded as suitable training in particular for middle- and upper-middle-class marriageable women who are expected to gain elegance and a refined sense of aesthetics through such instruction. Immigrant women of days past did not have the time or money to indulge in such leisure activities.

11. The stepping-stone pageants held in various locations of the Korean diaspora proceeding to the Miss Korea International contest are a notable exception. However, the lack of ethnic dress in these contests may be understood within the context of their direct, pyramidal connection to the Miss Korea International contest held in Seoul. In other words, the diasporic Korean contests held in the United States are actually part of an Asian contest in which women of Korean ethnicity from many parts of the world compete. Since most Asian beauty contests do not include competition in ethnic dress, the Asian American components of Miss Korea International follow suit.

12. The *ao dai* was originally a unisex outfit worn by both elite men and women. As Vietnamese men adopted Western styles of dress, the *ao dai* increasingly became a women's garment, with regional distinctions and stylistic changes (Lieu 2000:131).

The Chinese *qipao* was originally an upper-class man's garment adopted by young, urban, middle-class women in the mid-1920s in Shanghai. By the 1930s, the garment had become sexualized and eroticized with a form-fitting shape and high side slits (Clark 1999:158). The *qipao* was associated in China with urban modernity, rather than with tradition (Li 2002:18 – 19).

The Japanese kimono is also in some sense a unisex garment, but kimono for men and women are distinguished by fabric pattern, *obi* (sash), and mode of wrapping.

13. In Japan there are formal schools of kimono-dressing with codified names for different ways of tying sashes, draping kimono, and styling hair. There are also professional kimono-dressers.

14. Unlike the Miss America model, however, they were shown in casual clothes, such as jeans or mini-skirts. This also contrasts with the image of CBF contestants, presented in recent souvenir books in professional attire such as suits or tailored dresses.

15. Beauty contests in Japan may not gain great media attention, but the idiom of beauty contests pervades many aspects of daily life. Many universities annually crown a queen (e.g., Miss Waseda University); women representing regional products may be dubbed, for example "Miss Peach."

16. The phrase "model minority" was first coined in print in the *New York Times Magazine* in 1966 by William Petersen in an article, "Success Story, Japanese American Style" (1966). Petersen praised Japanese Americans for their high educational levels, median family income, and low crime rates. The "model minority" appellation extended to Chinese Americans in an article published in the *U.S. News and World Report* in the same year (reprinted in Tachiki, Wong, and Odo 1971:6 – 13), and eventually characterized Asian Americans in general. Critics of the "model minority" imaging of Asian Americans point out the many fallacies with the model, as well as its divisiveness vis-à-vis other ethnic groups, such as African Americans (e.g., Suzuki 1977).

Chapter Two. Historicizing the Cherry Blossom Festival

1. According to the U.S. Census of 1950, the population of just under 500,000 in Hawai'i included the following ethnic mix: 36.9 percent Japanese, 23.0 percent Caucasian (including Spanish and Portuguese), 17.3 percent Hawaiian and part-Hawaiian, 12.2 percent Filipino, 6.5 percent Chinese, 1.9 percent Puerto Rican, 1.4 percent Korean, and 0.8 percent others (quoted in Lind 1980:34).

2. Marriage patterns among Japanese Americans in Hawai'i contrast with those in the continental United States, where significant outmarriage was occurring by the mid-1960s. Japanese rates of outmarriage in Los Angeles County rose from 23 percent in 1959 to 49 percent in 1972 (Kitano 1976:106–107).

3. The dream of a single-family dwelling remains elusive for many in Hawai'i in the 2000s due to the prohibitive cost of housing within a limited land base.

4. The GI Bill, also known as the Servicemen's Readjustment Act, signed into law by President Franklin Roosevelt, provided any veteran who had served a minimum ninety days, regardless of color or financial need, up to $500 per term for postsecondary education. By 1947, veterans constituted nearly half of college enrollment in the United States (May 1988:68). The bill also provided low-interest home mortgages, sparking a demand for new homes and contributing to the spread of suburbia, another ingredient in the American dream.

5. The GI Bill has been called a "Magic Carpet to the Middle Class" (Lehrer 2000), but it did not bring all veterans of color and region on equal footing to their white counterparts. According to Sarah Turner and John Bound, the GI Bill had markedly different effects on black and white veterans in the South: "For those black veterans more likely to be limited to the South in their collegiate choices [segregated postsecondary institutions designated for blacks did not offer education beyond the baccalaureate degree], the GI Bill exacerbated rather than narrowed the economic and educational differences between blacks and whites" (2002).

6. In some elementary schools, students were placed in high or low tracks based upon teacher assessments of classroom performance, especially in English-language fluency. Those in the high track automatically entered English-standard intermediate or high schools.

7. According to the website of one of the former English standard schools, in 1955 these schools were "abolished because the State Central Committee of the Democratic Party of Hawai'i declared them as segregating the children by socioeconomic and ethnic lines" (Ali'iōlani Elementary School 2004). The last class graduated from Roosevelt High School as an English standard school on O'ahu in 1960.

8. Lessons for Japanese Americans in American patriotism and citizenship had begun even before the war in the 1920s and 1930s. The Americanization campaign of the 1920s and 1930s intended to promote assimilation of Japanese Americans, developed out of fear and suspicion on the part of haole (white) society. It also arose amid the reputation of Japanese as "unassimilable," too wedded politically and culturally to Japan as a home country to relearn new ways of speaking, acting, and developing affiliations. As one white commentator wrote expressing the fears of the period, "The Japanese, to a number of onlookers, seemed mysteriously clannish and prone to stick

to their own kind, and their ties to the homeland seemed especially strong" (Brown 1989:14). The goal of prewar Americanization/assimilation was to reeducate those of Japanese ancestry into Anglo-conformity, while keeping them on the lower rungs of the socioeconomic ladder. Middle-class attainment was explicitly not a part of the agenda.

9. Attendance at Japanese-language schools dropped by nearly 60 percent between 1947 and 1980; in a 1971 survey of Japanese Americans in Honolulu, only 3 percent of sansei claimed to be fluent in Japanese (Kotani 1985:155).

10. In the 1950s, there were still several Japanese movie theaters in Honolulu, but by 1984 all had closed (Kotani 1985:156). There were also six Japanese-language radio stations in Honolulu in the 1950s, of which only one remains in the 2000s (ibid.). Instead, families eagerly bought television sets and gathered around to watch a combination of national and local programming, mostly in English. In the 1950s, Japanese-language shows were offered on three television stations (KGMB-TV, KONA-TV, and KULA-TV), which also offered English-language programming.

11. The singer returned to Hawai‘i in 1975 to perform as part of the CBF.

12. The postwar nisei singers were preceded by several Japanese American singers in the 1930s who were frustrated by the racial barriers they found in the continental United States and fled to Japan, where they enjoyed successful careers performing jazz (Atkins 2001:82). In postwar Japan, nisei singers from Hawai‘i were made to sing "GI songs." These mostly English-language songs, typically written and originally performed by GIs stationed in Japan, employed orientalist musical idioms, and sprinklings of what was dubbed "Bamboo English," a crude mixture of English with simple Japanese words and phrases sung with Anglicized mispronunciation (Waseda 2004:4 – 6). Japanese record companies had nisei singers deliberately mispronounce Japanese words in accord with the "Bamboo English" developed by American GIs (ibid.:12).

13. Visits by Japanese university baseball teams to Hawai‘i began as early as 1905 with a visit by the team from Waseda University and 1908 with a visit by the team from Keio University (Tasaka 1985:18).

14. Whereas nisei athletes were assumed to compete on Japanese terms, nisei singers were asked to perform as Americans for Japanese consumption. The two fields of sports and popular music in Japan used different aspects of the dual nature of Japanese and American — the figurative solidus of Hawai‘i's Japanese Americans — for their own purposes during the postwar period.

15. Incidents that contributed to the racial stereotype of nonwhite (including Japanese Americans) male violence include the infamous 1931 Massie case in which the wife of a U.S. Navy officer accused five "local" men of raping her. The men included two of Japanese ancestry, two of Hawaiian ancestry, and one of Chinese ancestry. While the jury was deadlocked and the defendants were out on bail, the Navy wife's family took revenge and killed one of the men. Although the family was found guilty, the governor of Hawai‘i commuted their sentence to one hour spent in his office.

16. According to promotional literature from the management offices of Ala Moana Center, it is still the world's largest open-air mall and was the first to achieve over $1 billion in gross sales (Ala Moana Center n.d.).

17. Interestingly, other marks of U.S.-based globalization did not arrive in Hawai‘i

until considerably later. McDonald's, for example, opened its first outlet in Hawai'i in November 1968.

18. These numbers combine those that self-identify as mixed and unmixed in each category except Caucasian. The following are percentages of mixed for each category: Hawaiian 85.8, Chinese 8.9, Filipino 12.6, Japanese 2.2, Other races 27.3 (U.S. Census Bureau 2001).

19. In contrast with this view is Glenn's work on Japanese American maids in northern California. She writes of their "triple oppression": "trapped in work that is widely regarded as the most menial employment in our society, subjected to institutional racism of the most virulent sort, and subordinated at home by a patriarchal family system" (1986:xi).

20. Issei women arrived in Hawai'i without knowing Western-style sewing, but quickly learned how to use sewing machines, draft patterns, and piece together Western garments, often with the help of Portuguese and Spanish women in the neighborhood (Kawakami 1993:97–98).

21. In these formal portraits, naichi women wore *montsuki*, the black five-crested formal kimono, while Okinawan women wore colorful dressy kimono. Men either wore kimono, *hakama* (formal divided-skirt attire), or more typically a Western suit (Kawakami 1993:14–15).

22. In 1968 it joined the Chamber of Commerce in Hawai'i as an associate member with broad interests in the furthering of economic activity in the state as a whole. In 2004, the other ethnic organizations listed as associate members of the Chamber of Commerce of Hawai'i were (alphabetically listed): African American Chamber of Commerce, Chinese Chamber of Commerce, Filipino Chamber of Commerce, Hawaii Hispanic Chamber of Commerce, Hawaii Island Portuguese Chamber of Commerce, Hawaii Korean Chamber of Commerce, Native Hawaiian Chamber of Commerce, Portuguese Chamber of Commerce of Hawaii, Vietnamese American Chamber of Commerce, and WUB Hawaii–Okinawa Chamber of Commerce (Chamber of Commerce of Hawaii 2004).

23. California-based Japanese Americans organizing the Nisei Week celebration in 1930s Los Angeles faced the same problem: "The festival was never an attempt to replicate Japanese folk traditions . . . because they [Japanese American leaders] had no real conception of Japanese festivities. They had to be taught the basic steps of the ondo [Japanese dance] . . . and schooled in the customs, folklore, and history of their ancestral homeland" (Kurashige 2002:42–43).

24. Turner's proclamation follows the pattern of the previous proclamation by Governor Samuel King, with the addition of the paragraph on economic objectives, as well as a mention of the previous year's festival (HJJCC 1953:2).

25. In 2004, Junior Chamber International had more than 6,000 chapters in 101 countries throughout the world (Junior Chamber International 2004).

26. Other projects in the early years included a nurse scholarship dance, Hawaii-Japan student conference, and drives for the Aloha Week Festival, Community Chest, Red Cross, and Christmas Seals (HJJCC 1999:67).

27. Although nearly 120,000 Japanese Americans living in the continental United States were interned during World War II, only approximately 3,300 Japanese Ameri-

cans from Hawai'i were (Okamura 2001:67). This may have been in part because they were a necessary labor force during the war.

28. Kitano's characterization of Hawai'i as a racially tolerant society is one echoed by a number of sociologists such as Romanzo Adams, Andrew Lind, and Bernard Hormann. However, Jonathan Okamura paints the sociological picture differently, arguing that this benign, assimilationist portrait obscures more rancorous race relations in Hawai'i (2001). Furthermore, Gary Okihiro details systematic anti-Japanese (including Japanese American) sentiment in Hawai'i from the time of contract labor through the end of World War II (1991).

29. Other ethnic beauty pageants in Hawai'i in the 2000s include the Miss Korea Hawaii pageant begun in 1992 (the winner goes on to the Miss Korea International contest); and the Miss Hawaii Filipina pageant, begun in 1959 as Miss Philippines Hawaii. The Miss Hawaii Filipina pageant is the only pyramidal contest that takes place within Hawai'i; contestants are those who have won their respective island's contest — Miss Oahu Filipina, Miss Maui Filipina, Miss Kauai Filipina, Miss Molokai Filipina, Miss Hawaii Island Filipina, and Miss Lanai Filipina.

Within the Chinese American community, the Miss Chinatown Hawaii Scholarship Pageant is a pyramidal competition, whose winner goes on to vie for the Miss Chinatown USA crown in San Francisco. In 1990 the Miss Chinatown Hawaii Scholarship Pageant, Inc. — a joint organization of both the Chinatown Merchants Association and the Honolulu Chinese Jaycees — was created to organize the contest.

A related type of beauty pageant is implicitly ethnic because of the sponsoring organization. For example, the Chrysanthemum Ball Queen on Maui is sponsored by Maui AJA (Americans of Japanese Ancestry) Veterans, Inc. (organized in 1947) and the County of Maui. The contest has been held since 1953 with a queen crowned on the basis of the amount of money she raises for Japanese American veteran groups.

30. These shifting categories do not exactly correspond to the population distribution in Honolulu in 1950 (per U.S. Census): Japanese (36.9 percent), Caucasian (including Portuguese, 23.6 percent), "Part Hawaiian" (15.0 percent), Chinese (10.7 percent), Filipino (7.0 percent), Hawaiian (2.0 percent), Korean (1.9 percent), and Puerto Rican (1.6 percent) (U.S. Census Bureau; quoted in Lind 1980:57). However, the population of Honolulu was not necessarily reflected in the population of McKinley High School at the time. Although these statistics are not available, I suggest that in the Carnival Queen categories, there was a relative overrepresentation of Asians (including Koreans as a separate category) and underrepresentation of part-Hawaiians/Hawaiians and Puerto Ricans since they were lumped together in the category "Cosmopolitan."

31. In Hawai'i, high school is considered a common denominator and marker of experience. As part of a legacy of low rates of postsecondary education, one of the questions two locals ask when meeting for the first time is, "What high school did you attend?" A high school "rainbow pageant" in postwar Hawai'i thus garnered considerable media attention.

32. During the war, the Ka Palapala contest was replaced by the queen and court of the Pineapple Bowl, a football game held in January at the old Honolulu Stadium. The queen and court of the Pineapple Bowl were not always selected from among University of Hawai'i coeds; neither were they chosen to represent different ethnici-

ties. The 1942 queen and court include a haole queen, and eight attendants (five with haole surnames, and one each with Japanese, Hawaiian, and Chinese surname) (*Ka Palapala* 1942:73).

33. The categories do not always reflect campus demographics. For example, in the 1968 contest, the category of "Negro" was included; however, this did not necessarily reflect a large number of African American students at the time.

34. In the Ka Palapala contest, the category in which one chose to run was a matter of self-identification and possible strategy. Single-race categories apparently did not require any specific minimum blood quantum. For example, in 1954, twin sisters competed in two different categories, Hawaiian and Japanese (Silverman 1955:22).

35. During this period and for decades afterward, the rainbow was the symbol of the university.

36. Some of these sororities changed their ethnic composition, especially during the 1960s. For example, Beta Beta Gamma became known as more of a "cosmopolitan" sorority, admitting women of different ethnicities. There were also corresponding "brother" fraternities. Among the ethnic fraternities in the 1960s were Tu Chiang She and Peng Hui (Chinese), Phi Kappa Pi (Korean, but later Japanese as well), and Hui Lōkahi (Hawaiian).

37. Palumbo-Liu notes the use of anthropologist Franz Boas' work on the physical plasticity of immigrants from Eastern Europe to the United States who, after a generation or two of life in America began to more closely resemble other Americans: "Assimilation was both a psychic *and* a somatic phenomenon, the latter now presenting in concrete form the actuality of Americanization (and, conversely, if certain bodies *won't* change, or do so only recalcitrantly, then it is taken as an index to their resistance or inability to assimilate)" (1999:85). This placed Asian immigrants at a distance since they were considered far less easily assimilable, both physically and psychically. However, here the Ka Palapala observer notes the physical assimilation of Asians and others into a convergent "American" or "Hawaii" look.

Chapter Three. The Cherry Blossom Festival as Center Stage in Hawai'i

1. Here I deliberately use the phrase "Japanese (American)" to suggest that although organizers may have called this a "Japanese" event, it is in fact a Japanese American practice.

2. The first souvenir book in 1953 featured a line drawing of a woman in kimono; the second book in 1954 showed a head shot of Queen Violet Niimi wearing a crown and kimono, but very little of the kimono can be seen. The next six books all show Queens in Western gown.

3. The presence of stewardesses in the CBF souvenir books echoes the desirability of the profession at the time for women who might want to travel.

4. Using feathers in a cape also had a local precedent in feathered capes for Hawaiian royalty.

5. Success, of course, provides easy fodder for a rumor mill built on jealousy. Thus, a *Hawaii Hochi* columnist commented: "The Cherry Blossom Queen Contest is a serious occasion that the haole community supports as a big spring event in Honolulu.

The event also brings several million dollars to our businesses. People who spread malicious rumors about the contest are jealous of other people's success" (*Hawaii Hochi* 1955b:5).

6. Nine years later, in February 1963, the CBF made the cover of *Paradise of the Pacific* with a photo of two kimono-clad contestants (see cover).

7. Begun in 1946 by a group of former Jaycees known as the Jaycee Oldtimers, Aloha Week was organized to attract tourists to Hawai'i during the off-peak season (typically September and October). Although the emphasis in Aloha Week was on Hawaiian music and dance, it always included traditions from other cultures in what was called a "public celebration to honor Hawaii's cosmopolitan heritage" (Aloha Festivals 2004).

8. Although these events predate the phrase "model minority" by a decade, I argue that the concept and image hold true in mid-1950s Hawai'i.

9. The fireworks display also included a depiction of Mount Fuji, a national symbol of Japan, but the finale displayed the American flag (HJJCC 1953:31).

10. Kabuki has played a consistent, if minor, role in the CBF since its inception in 1953. At lower amateur levels, kabuki productions were a part of Japanese American culture in Hawai'i as prewar entertainment. The first CBF in 1953 featured a kabuki production (in English, performed primarily by local university students) at the University of Hawai'i. The souvenir book from that year included an article entitled "What Kabuki Means," explaining aspects of the theatrical form (HJJCC 1953:14). The Grand Kabuki performed in Hawai'i in 1964 and 1965 at the prestigious Honolulu International Center Concert Hall (Tasaka 1985:130–131). Hosting the Grand Kabuki theater in Honolulu as part of the CBF showcased the ability of the HJJCC to put on a large-scale show, authenticating themselves as having direct access to Japan.

11. In the 1950s Japanese-language newspapers were read primarily by issei and older nisei, especially kibei-nisei (Japanese Americans born outside Japan such as in Hawai'i, raised in Japan, and then returned to their place of birth; kibei-nisei are culturally closer to Japan than the United States). *Hawaii Hochi* attempted to bridge the linguistic generation gap by including an English-language section in their newspaper. The nisei organizers of the CBF were not necessarily readers of Japanese-language newspapers. Therefore, the linguistic gap persisted, as reflected in the following editorial in *Hawaii Hochi*: "Why does the Japanese Junior Chamber of Commerce advertise the Cherry Blossom Festival only in English-language newspapers? Why not in Japanese-language newspapers?" (*Hawaii Hochi* 1953c:6).

12. The contest was sponsored initially by Mills Laboratories of California, makers of the popular One-A-Day Multiple Vitamins. By sending in an empty box of the vitamins with the name of a Queen contestant written on it (worth twenty points) or a ballot printed in the *Hawaii Hochi* (worth two points), senders could vote for their favorite contestant. The winner of the Miss Ohina contest won a round-trip ticket to the continental United States and other prizes (*Hawaii Hochi* 1956a:3). Because of the tie-in to Mills Laboratories and vitamin supplements, the Miss Ohina contest enlisted the support of local pharmacies. A crowd of 2,000 people attended the reception at one drugstore in Honolulu in 1956 (*Hawaii Hochi* 1956b:1). As an indication of the popularity of the contest, the first winner, Hilda Mikami, won with 12,000 votes (*Hawaii Hochi* 1956c:Special Edition 2).

13. For example, the Miss Ohina contestants of 1957 included four from Honolulu, six from rural Oʻahu, one from Maui, two from Kauaʻi, and six from the island of Hawaiʻi.

14. According to a 1955 article in the *Hawaii Hochi*, the island of Kauaʻi had its own Cherry Blossom Queen in a contest held independently from the CBF (*Hawaii Hochi* 1955d:3). The Kauaʻi Cherry Blossom Queen and runner-up attended the CBF coronation ceremony in Honolulu in 1955.

15. A 1956 columnist for the *Hawaii Hochi* writes, "In the beginning, the older generation [issei] was half dubious about the young people's [nisei] idea of putting on the Cherry Blossom Festival as too bold. But now that everyone sees the success of the Festival, all those worries seem to be swept away" (*Hawaii Hochi* 1956d:1).

16. Hiragana is considered an indigenous syllabary, in contrast with kanji, which was imported from China. In the local Japanese-language press, "sakura" and "matsuri" are variously rendered in kanji and hiragana. Although the Chinese character for "sakura" exists, the word is more typically written in hiragana in Japan. One possible explanation for the choice of hiragana in writing "sakura" in Japan is the use of cherry blossoms as a national symbol. Therefore, the use of hiragana in writing "sakura" can suggest a nativist nuance. The 1953 souvenir book's publication of "Hawaii Sakura Matsuri Ondo" spells out "sakura" in hiragana (HJJCC 1953:51). In other instances, "sakura" is written in kanji and "matsuri" in hiragana (e.g., Tasaka 1985:84). Quibbling over the particular writing system may seem like academic hair-splitting, but in Japan the choice of writing system can carry important nuances.

17. Many issei families adopted the practice of naming their nisei children with English personal name and Japanese middle name. This practice has continued with sansei offspring as well, but has declined with succeeding generations.

18. The advertisements in Japanese were not for Japanese American–owned or –related companies or Japanese products. One was for Finance Factors, Ltd. (HJJCC 1957:20), and the other was for Hawaiian Telephone (HJJCC 1957:41).

19. This is also the first souvenir book that displayed contestants in Western dress, rather than kimono (HJJCC 1958).

20. Translation is by the author.

21. R. Alex Anderson (1894 – 1995) is considered one of Hawaiʻi's foremost composers of *hapa-haole* songs (Hawaiian songs with English lyrics) (see Stone 2001).

22. That return, however, was not without critique. Only a few short years later, one columnist for the *Hawaii Hochi* remarked, "Why do all the contestants wear the same kind of gaudy furisode kimono? This does not demonstrate any individual characteristics. I hope the contestants next year will show us revolutionary, modern, chic aesthetics in kimono" (*Hawaii Hochi* 1957c:6).

23. ʻIolani Palace is the only royal residence in the United States. The appearance of Queen contestants at the palace was part of the legitimizing process of the HJJCC, the CBF, and Japanese Americans in general.

24. In other contexts, the *kasa* itself became emblematic of exoticized Japanese femininity. The *kasa* alone was even more accessible as a traveling signifier of exotica without the bother of procuring and dressing women in kimono. Thus photographs of young Japanese American women taken by amateur male photographers in Hawaiʻi

during this period often posed them in Western dress, but placed them in Japanese gardens and with the added touch of holding a kasa. The kasa, with bamboo spokes arrayed in back of a model's head framing her face, became a stereotypical visual backdrop to the exoticized female.

The paper umbrella as an icon of exotica can be linked to tiki bar culture in the United States. The decorative paper umbrella that comes in exotic drinks has been a part of tiki bar culture since the 1930s, when the well-known Polynesian-themed restaurant-bar Trader Vic's adopted the idea of exotic drinks and cocktail umbrellas in them from Don the Beachcomber restaurants, which had pioneered "Polynesian"-style dining. Moreover, tiki lore suggests that the decorative umbrellas "were available in Chinese restaurants [in the United States], which coincides with the view . . . that the parasol (or at least the idea of putting it in a drink) was a Chinese-American invention" (Adams 2004). The CBF of the 1950s and 1960s was explicitly not part of tiki bar culture. Yet I contend that the Festival shares in some of the meanings symbolized by the umbrella, ironically enacting both marginal and mainstream statuses.

25. This was also the first year that the Queen was shown wearing a kimono rather than Western dress when meeting the governor (HJJCC 1961:7).

26. Dalby argues that color was the one sphere in which an individual of the Heian period (ninth through late twelfth centuries in Japan) could express herself: "Even though the robes [kimono] were of standard cut, changed by rigid rule of season, and made of fabrics assigned by rank, an irreducible element of personal choice was involved in the combining of colors" (1993:223).

27. Several people from Japan that I have spoken with express surprise that Hawai'i has a Cherry Blossom Festival without actual cherry blossoms.

28. In her work on debutante culture, Karal Ann Marling contrasts the separate ethnic debutante balls of African Americans, in which the emphasis is on education and upward mobility, with the equivalent quinceanera gala celebrations of a girl's fifteenth birthday in Latin communities in the United States which aim to "legitimate and control the sexuality of the pubescent girl" (2004:168). These parallel "debutante balls," like the CBF, bring to the fore issues of race, class, sexuality, and community within gendered idioms of celebrity.

29. There are exceptions, of course, and I include some of these Queens and their herstories (e.g., Chapter 6, Queen Lenny Yajima).

30. Female support of men's activities received brief mention in early souvenir books (e.g., HJJCC 1953:10, HJJCC 1954:66). General chairman of the CBF Kenneth Hasegawa remarked: "I wish to take this opportunity to thank the present membership of the HJJCC and their wives who have been diligently planning and working these past few months preparing" (1967:5).

31. The contrast between women and men in the CBF parallels the historical disjuncture in early twentieth-century Japan when women continued to dress in kimono, while men switched to Western clothing (even as they returned to Japanese clothing in the privacy of their homes). This clothing divide expresses a symbolic split that links women to tradition and men to modernity.

32. Mori was not listed in the CBF souvenir book as a contestant in the 1953 pageant, but is profiled and photographed in the *Hawaii Hochi* article.

33. Subsequent souvenir books in this period displayed far less advertising, ranging from a low of 36.2 percent of available page space in 1966 to a high of 53.3 percent in 1969, with an average of 43.6 percent (excluding 1953).

34. An article in the Japanese-language *Hawaii Times* announces the recruitment drive:

> This year, the Cherry Blossom Festival invites the public to participate in the search for the girl who will become Queen of the Festival next spring. A free trip for two to Hilo on the Matson liner Lurline is the prize offered to the person who submits the names of the candidate who is chosen Queen of the 1960 Cherry Blossom Festival. (*Hawaii Times* 1959b:1)

35. For example, the 1968 CBF souvenir book lists public appearances by CBF Queen contestants at Ala Moana Center, GEM department store, Windward Shopping Center, Gibsons discount store, Arakawa's plantation department store, and Holiday Mart discount store. Except for Ala Moana Center, none of these are tourist destinations.

36. It is not only Japanese Americans who took a racialized stance toward the CBF Queen contest. When asked their impressions of the CBF, "One [Japanese entertainer] said that in Japanese beauty contests, winners tend to be a Japanese-type beauty like actress Yamamoto Fujiko, but in Hawaii the winners have a Caucasian type of face. She thinks that it may be because the Japanese in Hawaii put on make-up in a Caucasian style, dress like Caucasians, and behave like Caucasians" (*Hawaii Hochi* 1957d:1).

37. I am determining Okinawan HJJCC membership and CBF contestants by surname alone, assisted by the list of Okinawan issei (and therefore their names) published in Hawaii United Okinawa Association 2000. Some names are ambiguous, in part because of name modifications that took place in Hawai'i and elsewhere; I do not include these. Identifying Okinawans by surname may obscure those who are half-Okinawan or others whose surnames do not belie their Okinawan background.

Using surnames to identify Okinawan Americans is important because they are not necessarily phenotypically distinguishable from Naichi. Okinawans are stereotyped as short, hairy, and dark-complected, but in reality the stereotype is confounded as often as confirmed. Because of the reliance on surnames (and the ambiguity of some names), identifying Okinawans is not shared equally in the Japanese American population. In fact, each passing generation of Naichi retains less and less knowledge about the implied ancestry of these names.

38. This parallels the time lag and contrasting public discourse surrounding HJJCC organizers of non-Japanese ancestry and Queen contestants of less than 100 percent Japanese blood.

39. Based on unambiguous surnames, I calculate the following for this time period: 1953 — 3 Okinawan contestants/72 total; 1954 — 6/53; 1955 — 0/32; 1956 — 3/24; 1957 — 0/14; 1958 — 1/15; 1959 — 2/18; 1960 — 0/14; 1961 — 3/15; 1962 — 1/15; 1963 — 2/15; 1964 — 1/15; 1965 — 1/15; 1966 — 1/15; 1967 (year that Gwen Nishizawa was crowned Queen) — 1/15 (does not include Nishizawa); 1968 — 0/14; 1969 — 0/15.

40. Exact figures for the Okinawan American population in Hawai'i are difficult to come by, since the U.S. Census counts them as "Japanese." The HUOA figure is

estimated for the late 1990s; however, the ratio of Naichi and Okinawans in Hawai'i has not changed considerably from the postwar period to the present.

Chapter Four. Herstories I

1. According to Anna, she felt she was chosen because Japanese sponsors wanted a CBF Queen who looked more American than Japanese. Anna's looks certainly confirm this. But, so, too, does the appearance of the first runner-up, Jean Sera.

2. In these and other herstory chapters, I refer to Queens by their personal name, rather than (maiden) surname. My use of personal names in the introductory narrative reflects the friendships I developed with them.

3. One notable exception to community organizations as being male-dominated was a group of women called "Haha no kai" (Mother's Society) from the Mānoa Valley area of Honolulu. Seventh CBF Queen Jayne Kuwata recalls being recruited to run and gaining the sponsorship of Haha no kai (personal communication, December 20, 2001).

4. Roosevelt High School was the only English standard high school on O'ahu, graduating its last such class in 1960. Carol's attendance at Roosevelt gives her a certain amount of prestige at the time.

Chapter Five. Struggles toward Reform

1. Carrie Takahata's poem "Making Yonsei" expresses the cultural bind of yonsei in Hawai'i caught between generational and cultural worlds (2002:73 – 74).

2. Although a Consulate General of Japan had been established in Hawai'i since 1885 (the beginning of contract immigration to Hawai'i from Japan) and a consul general from Japan headed its operations from 1886, the CBF did not gain this kind of full recognition until 1974.

3. Nihon Sakura no Kai has been responsible for planting over 2,400,000 trees in Japan and in over fifty countries overseas. Mr. Minoru Shinagawa (b. 1925), executive director and founding member of Nihon Sakura no Kai, was the 2000 recipient of the CBF Community Service Award. Shinagawa is responsible for arranging the annual gift of a furisode kimono for the CBF Queen yearly. See HJJCC 2002:82 – 83 for more on Shinagawa and the organization.

4. The idea of a Japanese model for the middle-/upper-class Japanese American woman is not new or unique to the CBF. In an essay entitled "Onna — Onnarashii (Woman — Womanly, Ladylike)" published in the 1984 CBF souvenir book, Ethel Aiko Oda discussed the socialization of Japanese American women in Hawai'i: "Issei women tried to rear their daughters exactly the way they had been brought up in Japan. In many families, the oldest daughters in the family were usually held more closely to the Japanese ideals of female behavior than were the younger daughters. . . . If the family could afford to, daughters were sent to Japan for their schooling. . . . Often the minister's wife, female Japanese school teachers and other women in the community, particularly those who had been educated in Japan were pointed out to us as models of exemplary behavior" (1984:38). Although she does not use the term, what Oda re-

fers to is the inculcation of *ojōsan* ideals through these class-based, cultural models of Japanese femininity.

5. Princess Michiko is a commoner by birth who married into the royal family. However, she comes from an extremely wealthy elite family that is far from common.

6. Of course being an "unqueenly Queen" can be a critical comment on one who does not live up to the public's expectations of queenliness.

7. The fact that most contestants in the CBF are relatively short compared to those of, for example, the Miss America scholarship pageant, is part of what many of them say makes this a do-able competition for them.

8. The average height of contestants fluctuated from a low of five feet, one inch, in 1985 and 1987 to a high of five feet, three inches, in 1993 and 1998.

9. Among Queens in the 1950s and 1960s, eight out of the first seventeen were over five feet, four inches. In the 1970s and 1980s, that ratio dropped to seven out of twenty. Then in the 1990s (through 1998), five out of nine were over five feet, four inches.

10. This notion of the "nice Japanese American girl" may be changing, especially with breast augmentation and other kinds of cosmetic surgery on the rise in Hawai'i in the 2000s.

11. This concern for hair long enough to be worn in an up-do was not a part of the 1950s and 1960s aesthetic.

12. This connection between long hair and fitting a kimono-derived mold did not hold true in earlier years. A glance at the portraits of CBF Queens in the 1950s and 1960s shows that few, if any, had long hair. Each wore their hair short in the style of the day with kimono.

13. From 1986 on, kimono training and dressing for the CBF has been handled by a Japanese company, Watabe (Saison des Brides for Watabe). The shift in kimono-dressing in the CBF from an individual (Mrs. Yorita) to a company (Watabe) in the mid-1980s reflected the inevitable passing of the issei generation. However, it also marked connections to a different kind of Japan — not so much the homeland of immigrants and their descendants in the 1950s and 1960s, but a postwar global presence in the 1970s and beyond.

14. The average age of contestants likewise has risen over the decades: 1960s — 19.7; 1970s — 20.4; 1980s — 22.3; 1990s — 23.4 years. See the Appendix for year-by-year average age of contestants.

15. In Japanese, the theme reads *"Yutaka na shakai no tame ni,"* which may be translated rather ambiguously as, "For the betterment of our nation/society."

16. At the time, the CBF and the HJJCC each had themes for the year.

17. In 1980, thirty-eight sansei embarked on a "Leadership Tour" to Okinawa. Inspired by what they found, they created a club for young adults that led to the establishment of Young Okinawans of Hawaii. The club's goals were "to stimulate interest in and promote learning about the history of Okinawa and its people, to promote the preservation and perpetuation of the cultural heritage of Okinawa, and to provide social activities that will foster goodwill and friendship among its members" (Hawaii United Okinawa Association 2000:back cover).

18. This example also points to the ways in which a beauty contest (including one

that calls itself a "cultural pageant") inevitably generates rumors of unfair practices and judging by a faceless, nameless public.

19. Amateur song contests had long been part of popular entertainment and social occasions in Japan and Japanese American communities. The CBF was no exception. A talent contest was part of the 1964 CBF. An All-Hawaii Amateur Song Contest (called *"Nodojiman,"* literally "boasting of the throat," after a popular radio and television program in Japan) was begun in 1965 and continued for several years. The Kōhaku was only the latest iteration of amateur song contests included in the CBF.

Chapter Six. Herstories II

1. Lenny placed as Miss Simpatico (akin to Miss Congeniality).

2. Lekivetz is a longtime supporter and fan of the CBF since he visited Hawai'i in 1960 from his home in Saskatchewan, Canada. On his yearly visits to Hawai'i, he volunteered to help with CBF events by putting up posters and chauffeuring contestants, Queens, and Court members, as well as purchasing souvenir books and distributing them free of charge. He became known in local circles as "Mr. Cherry Blossom." In 1986 ill health prevented Lekivetz from traveling to Hawai'i. Nevertheless, he maintains contact with the CBF by donating Canadian silver dollars each year to be distributed to all CBF contestants. He and Lenny have kept up a Lenny-to-Lenny correspondence through recent years; in fact, Queen Lenny is the distribution point of the silver dollars Canadian Lenny sends yearly.

3. Some other Cherry Blossom Queens also publicly proclaim their ties to Christianity, including Kathy Horio.

4. "Awaken the Dawn," 2000, AwakenFire Music CK1215. Produced by Jon Basebase and Kumie.

Chapter Seven. Controversy and Reform

1. This does not take into account those typically older Japanese Americans who may prefer the aesthetics of a purely Asian face.

2. It is not uncommon for persons of Okinawan ancestry to be thought of as possessing more Euro-American facial features than Naichi Japanese. This may have to do in part with their tendency toward rounded "double" eyes, as well as darker lashes and eyebrows.

3. The time lag and different levels of public discourse surrounding Queens of less than 100 percent Japanese ancestry in contrast with organizers of non-Japanese ancestry parallels that of organizers and Queens of Okinawan ancestry (see Chapter 3). Thus, the race-talk of 1998 parallels some of the unspoken fears and ethnic boundary maintenance that may have prevented a woman of Okinawan ancestry from being crowned Queen no earlier than 1967.

4. Blood-quantum rules have long been a part of American policies of race-based entitlement. Frequently, they were instigated by governmental policy and then made to compete with more indigenous tracings of descent or internalized by the people

themselves. At one extreme and unique to the United States and to African Americans is the one-drop rule that defines persons as "black" if they have any known African black ancestry. This hypo-descent rule assigns racially mixed persons status on the basis of the subordinate group (Davis 1991:5). The Hawaiian Homes Commission Act of 1920 provided a definition of "Hawaiian" as based minimally on 50 percent Hawaiian ancestry, a legal definition of "native Hawaiian" used by the state of Hawai'i in the 2000s. This definition of "native Hawaiian" competes with more inclusive, indigenous genealogical rules that "connect people to one another, to place, and to landscape" (Kauanui 1999:138). Blood quantum has also been used in American Indian identity politics to define, for example, membership in the Cherokee Nation of Oklahoma in which "the significance of blood quantum was internalized and then codified by tribes themselves ... in the wake of the 1934 Indian Reorganization Act" (Sturm 2002:87). These varying blood-based definitions of group membership form a critical context within which CBF organizers' practices must be examined.

5. Other reforms of the year dotted the CBF. In an attempt to deemphasize physical attributes, contestants' heights were not given in souvenir books. (Two years later, neither would their ages.) Public appearances at shopping malls included "mini-matsuri" (festival) of contestants publicly demonstrating simple Japanese-related crafts such as stamped bookmarks and origami to children. In conjunction with the CBF, the HJJCC designated two new awards: (1) the Outstanding Young American of Japanese Ancestry Award for "one male and one female American of Japanese Ancestry who have been devoted to promoting the Japanese culture and heritage in Hawaii"; and (2) Cherry Blossom Festival Community Service Award to "an individual who has shown dedication to the perpetuation and success of the Cherry Blossom Festival over the years" (HJJCC 1999:53). In addition, the Jaycees instituted a "Cultural Outreach Program" of teams of volunteers visiting public elementary schools and after-school care programs to "promote the Japanese culture and heritage to young children" (ibid).

6. These figures must be further contextualized by a steadily increasing and unusually high rate of private school attendance in the state of Hawai'i, including among Japanese Americans. In other words, girls of full- or part-Japanese ancestry fill the rosters of private schools in Hawai'i, including the two elite ones. However, only a relatively small percentage of them are represented by CBF contestants. Students at elite private schools are more likely than most to leave Hawai'i to attend college. This does not preclude graduates from returning to Hawai'i to participate in the CBF, but their numbers are relatively few.

7. A good example of this can be found at the permanent gallery of the Japanese Cultural Center of Hawai'i. The first thing a visitor to the gallery finds is a set of *kachikan*, values, carved as symbolic pillars of the Japanese American experience in Hawai'i.

8. The only contestant that did not provide such predictable answers was a *hapa* contestant who wrote: "The opportunity to participate as a part Japanese contestant ... emphasizes this year's theme 'winds of change.' This theme holds a personal meaning of appreciating cultural diversity and change within the communities" (ibid.:42). Hers was the only answer to directly address the hubbub surrounding the CBF in this year of reform.

9. The contest is open to all students in grades nine through twelve who attend

school in Hawaiʻi. Informational packets soliciting entries are mailed to all high school English teachers, Japanese-language teachers, and school newspapers. Judges have been educators, writers, and community leaders. The HJJCC awards prizes of first $100, second $75, and runner-up $30, and publishes prize-winning essays in the CBF souvenir books.

Chapter Nine. Crowning the "Nice Girl"

1. Okinaga credits hula training with teaching values and stage know-how: "Since I have been dancing [hula] . . . since I was in seventh grade, I have learned not only hula steps, but also many different values that are important to succeed in life. . . . Some of these values are respect, discipline, responsibility, and appreciation. These are values that can span across culture and are important . . . [to] people of every ethnic descent" (quoted in Suzuki 2002:A-5).

2. There has been discussion by the Jaycees to raise the age limit to 27 years.

3. Unlike other beauty contests, a CBF contestant cannot run more than once. By contrast, women competing multiple times in contests leading to the Miss America scholarship pageant is so commonplace that it becomes part of their resume. For example, a newspaper article on 2004 Miss Hawaii Olena Rubin entitled "Fourth Try was the Charm" detailed her repeated attempts at the Miss Hawaii title before finally winning in 2004 (Ting 2004:34).

4. As set forth in the 2002 Contestants' Agreement, contestants are judged twice by a team of five to seven judges. Individual interviews are held one week prior to the Festival ball, where intelligence and speech (15 percent), personality (15 percent), and poise and appearance (10 percent) are assessed. Contestants are finally judged at the Festival Ball for public speaking (20 percent), personality (15 percent), and poise and presence (15 percent). This off- and on-stage judging combine speech (35 percent), personality (30 percent), poise and appearance/presence (25 percent), and attendance (10 percent) (HJJCC 2001).

5. The concern for the ethnic makeup of judges stems from the 1950s, when there were disagreements over the ability of non-Japanese judges to fairly and competently assess an ethnically Japanese Queen. See Chapter 3 for further discussion. This ideal formula was not actually followed in 2002: of the six judges, only two were of Japanese ancestry (at least by their surnames), and two were female.

6. Other kinds of contrasts between the CBF and Narcissus Festival imaging of women can be seen in events and their advertising in which both Queens and Courts appear. For example, in 1999 both were involved in community service for the Blood Bank of Hawaiʻi. The poster advertising this event provides visual contrast between the CBF and the Narcissus Festival Queen pageant. Although both Queens and Courts wore tiaras and sashes, the rest of their attire imaged them differently. The CBF Queen and Court members were dressed in solid black suits, giving them a professional business look. The Narcissus Queen and Court, by contrast, were dressed in exotic, close-fitting white embroidered cheongsam. I argue that a pageant such as the Narcissus Festival continues to exoticize Asian women, while one such as the CBF emplaces them within middle-class America, deemphasizing racial-cultural differences.

7. Terence Rogers and Satoru Izutsu link the high numbers of Japanese Americans in civil service in Hawai'i to two factors: (1) civil service jobs were the first white-collar jobs open to racially unbiased competition; and (2) "the structured hierarchy of such occupation . . . attractive in the Japanese cultural tradition, especially when coupled with a perceived upward social mobility" (1980:80).

8. Furthermore, "doing nice" involves not only the Queen, but all members of the Court, as well as contestants. At a public event, Queen and Court members dress alike and wear crowns and sashes; the Queen can only be distinguished by the size of her crown and identification on her sash. The busy work of "doing nice" thus defuses the hierarchy of the Queen's position since Queen and Court members participate and present themselves similarly.

ABBREVIATIONS

HPU   Hawai'i Pacific University
JAIMS   Japan-America Institute of Management Science
KCC   Kapi'olani Community College
LCC   Leeward Community College
UH   University of Hawai'i
USC   University of Southern California

Year	Name	Age	(ave.)*	Occupation/education**
1. 1953 – 1954	Violet Niimi	22	(–)	UH student
2. 1954 – 1955	Anna Tokumaru	17	(–)	high school student
3. 1955 – 1956	Marjorie Nishimura	19	(–)	UH student
4. 1956 – 1957	Molly Ishida	19	(–)	UH student
5. 1957 – 1958	Carol Saikyo	18	(–)	UH student
6. 1958 – 1959	Jayne Kuwata	18	(–)	UH student
7. 1959 – 1960	Lorraine Kirihara	18	(–)	UH student
8. 1960 – 1961	Shirley Fujisaki	17	(–)	high school student
9. 1961 – 1962	JoAnn Yamada	19	(–)	UH student
10. 1962 – 1963	Janet Nishino	18	(–)	UH student
11. 1963 – 1964	Joyce Mizuo	21	(–)	UH student
12. 1964 – 1965	Vivian Honda	19	(–)	UH student
13. 1965 – 1966	Ann Suzuki	20	(–)	UH student
14. 1966 – 1967	Sandra Shimokawa	19	(–)	UH student
15. 1967 – 1968	Gwen Nishizawa	20	(–)	secretary
16. 1968 – 1969	Janice Teramae	21	(19.5)	UH student
17. 1969 – 1970	Amy Fukuda	18	(19.8)	UH student
18. 1970 – 1971	Katherine Horio	21	(19.1)	UH student
19. 1971 – 1972	Gail Kobata	21	(19.5)	UH student
20. 1972 – 1973	Rae Tanaka	21	(20.1)	practice teacher (UH)
21. 1973 – 1974	Jill Matsui	22	(20.0)	sales clerk (Pacific University)
22. 1974 – 1975	JoAnn Noborikawa	22	(20.9)	UH student
23. 1975 – 1976	Ann Yoshioka	22	(20.9)	UH student/flight attendant [**Punahou School**]

Year	Name	Age	(ave.)*	Occupation/education**
24. 1976 – 1977	Myrah Higa	21	(20.5)	teacher (UH)
25. 1977 – 1978	Deborah Kodama	19	(20.7)	UH student
26. 1978 – 1979	Sharon Tomasa	21	(20.5)	UH student [St. Andrew's Priory]
27. 1979 – 1980	LeAnne Higa	22	(21.7)	UH student
28. 1980 – 1981	Francene Kondo	22	(21.7)	executive secretary (KCC)
29. 1981 – 1982	Lori Ann Mizumoto	21	(21.3)	legal secretary (KCC, UH)
30. 1982 – 1983	Jody-Lee Ige	21	(21.6)	UH student
31. 1983 – 1984	Gayle Koike	23	(21.8)	head cashier of accounting, Mitsukoshi Hawaii (UH)
32. 1984 – 1985	Lisa Nakahodo	21	(21.9)	UH student
33. 1985 – 1986	Joanne Hirano	23	(22.5)	UH student
34. 1986 – 1987	Lenny Yajima	24	(22.6)	community relations assistant director, Bank of Hawaii (Harvard) [Punahou School]
35. 1987 – 1988	Marlene Sato	22	(23.0)	UH student
36. 1988 – 1989	Lisa-Ann Nakano	21	(23.1)	HPU student [Sacred Hearts Academy]
37. 1989 – 1990	Lori Matsumura	22	(23.1)	UH student [Mid-Pacific Institute]
38. 1990 – 1991	Lani Sakamoto	24	(22.6)	sales clerk (UH)
39. 1991 – 1992	Sharon Kadoyama	24	(24.1)	executive secretary (UH)
40. 1992 – 1993	Lesli Yoshida	25	(23.5)	flight attendant/part-time teacher (UH-Hilo)
41. 1993 – 1994	Dori Lyn Hirata	25	(24.1)	public relations, JAIMS (UH)
42. 1994 – 1995	Kendelle Yamamoto	22	(23.5)	LCC student/customer service, Hawaiian Airlines
43. 1995 – 1996	Laurie Toma	25	(23.2)	teacher/part-time counselor (UH, U. of Maryland)
44. 1996 – 1997	Kymberly Rae Furuta	20	(23.0)	UH student [Iolani School]
45. 1997 – 1998	Cheryl Koide	20	(23.7)	UH student
46. 1998 – 1999	LoriJoy Morita	23	(23.0)	UH medical student [Iolani School]

Year	Name	Age	(ave.)*	Occupation/education**
47. 1999 – 2000	Lori Murayama	24	(23.6)	UH student [**Mid-Pacific Institute**]
48. 2000 – 2001	Vail Matsumoto	25	(23.5)	teacher; UH graduate student [**Mid-Pacific Institute**]
49. 2001 – 2002	Catherine Toth	26	(23.8)***	journalist (Northwestern)
50. 2002 – 2003	Lisa Okinaga	26	(23.3)	accountant (Loyola Marymount) [**Kamehameha School**]
51. 2003 – 2004	Heather Suehiro	26	(23.5)	teacher (UH)
52. 2004 – 2005	Meredith Kuba	26	(23.6)	UH graduate student (Bowdoin College) [**Punahou School**]
53. 2005 – 2006	Brooke Hasegawa	23	(24.2)	UH graduate student (USC) [**Punahou School**]

* Average age of contestants; 1953 – 1967 contestants' ages not given in souvenir books.

** Occupation at time of crowning; university in parentheses in cases of working women with degree (where known) or undergraduate degree; if private high school, name of school noted in brackets, boldface. All of the above information as it appears in souvenir books or in newspapers.

*** In 2001 the Jaycees discontinued providing contestants' ages. Therefore, I estimated contestants' ages by their year of high school graduation, calculating an age of 18 years upon graduation. I also took into consideration the age limit of 26 for participation.

REFERENCES

Abercrombie, Neil. 1994 [Letter]. *Honolulu Japanese Junior Chamber of Commerce Forty-Second Cherry Blossom Festival*. Honolulu: Honolulu Japanese Junior Chamber of Commerce. P. 13.

Abu-Lughod, Lila. 1991. Writing Against Culture. In Richard G. Fox, ed. *Recapturing Anthropology*. Santa Fe: School of American Research Press. Pp. 137–162.

Adams, Cecil. 2004. Who Invented the Cocktail Umbrella and Why? http://www.straightdope.com/columns/pp1117.html (Accessed May 4, 2004).

Akamine, Conrad. 1956 [Letter]. *Honolulu Japanese Junior Chamber of Commerce Fourth Cherry Blossom Festival*. Honolulu: Honolulu Japanese Junior Chamber of Commerce. P. 5.

Ala Moana Center. n.d. [circa 2002]. *Ala Moana: Hawai'i's Center*. Promotional brochure.

Ali'iōlani Elementary School. 2004. http://www.k12.hi.us/~aliiolan/html/chronology.htm (Accessed March 10, 2004).

Aloha Festivals. 2004. http://www.alohafestivals.com (Accessed May 2, 2004).

Anderson, R. Alex. 1959. Cherry Blossoms. *Honolulu Japanese Junior Chamber of Commerce Seventh Cherry Blossom Festival*. Honolulu: Honolulu Japanese Junior Chamber of Commerce. P. 4.

Ang, Ien. 2001. *On Not Speaking Chinese: Living Between Asia and the West*. London and New York: Routledge.

Appadurai, Arjun. 1986. Introduction: Commodities and the Politics of Value. In A. Appadurai, ed. *The Social Life of Things: Commodities in Cultural Perspective*. Cambridge: Cambridge University Press. Pp. 3–63.

Arendt, Hannah. 1963. *Eichmann in Jerusalem: A Report on the Banality of Evil*. New York: Viking Press.

———. 1978. *The Life of the Mind: The Groundbreaking Investigation on How We Think*. New York: Harcourt.

Atkins, E. Taylor. 2001. *Blue Nippon: Authenticating Jazz in Japan*. Durham: Duke University Press.

Banet-Weiser, Sarah. 1999. *The Most Beautiful Girl in the World: Beauty Pageants and National Identity*. Berkeley: University of California Press.

Banner, Lois W. 1983. *American Beauty*. Chicago: University of Chicago Press.

Barringer, Herbert, Robert W. Gardner, and Michael J. Levin. 1993. *Asians and Pacific Islanders in the United States*. New York: Russell Sage Foundation.

Battad, Gwen. 1998. Too Little, Too Late? *The Hawaii Herald*. August 21, 19(16):A1, A5.

Beechert, Edward. 1985. *Working in Hawaii: A Labor History*. Honolulu: University of Hawai'i Press.

Billig, Michael. 1995. *Banal Nationalism*. London: Sage Publications.

Blaisdell, Neal S. 1959 [Letter]. *Honolulu Japanese Junior Chamber of Commerce Seventh Cherry Blossom Festival*. Honolulu: Honolulu Japanese Junior Chamber of Commerce. P. 9.

Bordo, Susan. 1993. *Unbearable Weight: Feminism, Western Culture, and the Body*. Berkeley: University of California Press.

Borland, Katherine. 1996. The India Bonita of Monimbo: The Politics of Ethnic Identity in the New Nicaragua. In Colleen Ballerino Cohen, Richard Wilk, and Beverly Stoeltje, eds. *Beauty Queens on the Global Stage: Gender, Contests, and Power*. New York: Routledge. Pp. 75 – 88.

Bourdieu, Pierre. 1990. *The Logic of Practice*. Stanford: Stanford University Press.

Broom, Leonard, and S. H. Smith. 1963. Bridging Occupations. *British Journal of Sociology* 14:321 – 334.

Brown, DeSoto. 1989. *Hawaii Goes to War: Life in Hawaii from Pearl Harbor to Peace*. Honolulu: Editions Limited.

Burns, John A. 1964 [Letter]. *Honolulu Japanese Junior Chamber of Commerce Twelfth Cherry Blossom Festival*. Honolulu: Honolulu Japanese Junior Chamber of Commerce. P. 4.

———. 1965 [Letter]. *Honolulu Japanese Junior Chamber of Commerce Thirteenth Cherry Blossom Festival*. Honolulu: Honolulu Japanese Junior Chamber of Commerce. P. 4.

Butler, Judith. 1990. Performative Acts and Gender Constitution: An Essay in Phenomenology and Feminist Theory. In Sue-Ellen Case, ed. *Performing Feminism: Feminist Critical Theory and Theatre*. Baltimore: Johns Hopkins University Press. Pp. 270 – 283.

Cayetano, Benjamin. 1994 [Letter]. *Honolulu Japanese Junior Chamber of Commerce Forty-Second Cherry Blossom Festival*. Honolulu: Honolulu Japanese Junior Chamber of Commerce. P. 5.

Central Pacific Bank. 2004. http://www.cpbi.com (Accessed March, 1, 2004).

Chamber of Commerce of Hawaii. 2004. http://www.cochawaii.com (Accessed April 13, 2004).

Chikasuye, Clesson. 1971 [Letter]. *Honolulu Japanese Junior Chamber of Commerce Nineteenth Cherry Blossom Festival*. Honolulu: Honolulu Japanese Junior Chamber of Commerce. P. 57.

Chinen, Karleen, and Arnold Hiura. 1997. *From Bentō to Mixed Plate: Americans of Japanese Ancestry in Multicultural Hawai'i*. Los Angeles: Japanese American National Museum.

Chinese Chamber of Commerce of Hawaii. 2004 http://www.chinesechamber.com/narcissus/about/history (Accessed April 18, 2004).

Chinese Pageant Page. 2004. http://www.geocities.com/misshk73/ (Accessed April 19, 2004).

Chong, Pono. 2001 [Letter]. *Honolulu Japanese Junior Chamber of Commerce Forty-*

Ninth Cherry Blossom Festival. Honolulu: Honolulu Japanese Junior Chamber of Commerce. P. 11.

Chong, Pono, and Karlton Tomomitsu. 1999 [Letter]. *Honolulu Japanese Junior Chamber of Commerce Forty-Seventh Cherry Blossom Festival.* Honolulu: Honolulu Japanese Junior Chamber of Commerce. P. 11.

Clark, Hazel. 1999. The *Cheongsam*: Issues of Fashion and Cultural Identity. In Valerie Steele and John S. Major, eds. *China Chic: East Meets West.* New Haven: Yale University Press. Pp. 155–166.

Clifford, James. 1997. *Routes: Travel and Translation in the Late Twentieth Century.* Cambridge, Mass.: Harvard University Press.

Coffman, Tom. 2003. *The Island Edge of America: A Political History of Hawai'i.* Honolulu: University of Hawai'i Press.

Cohen, Colleen Ballerino, Richard Wilk, with Beverly Stoeltje. 1996. Introduction. In Colleen Ballerino Cohen, Richard Wilk, and Beverly Stoeltje, eds. *Beauty Queens on the Global Stage: Gender, Contests, and Power.* New York: Routledge. Pp. 1–11.

Cornell, Stephen, and Douglas Hartmann. 1998. *Ethnicity and Race: Making Identities in a Changing World.* Thousand Oaks: Pine Forge Press.

Creamer, Beverly. 1972. 14 Begin Their Journey to Cherry Blossom Fame. *Honolulu Star-Bulletin.* February 2:A2.

Cruz, Tania, and Eric K. Yamamoto. 2003. A Tribute to Patsy Takemoto Mink. Introduction. *Asian-Pacific Law and Policy Journal* 4(2):569–571.

Dalby, Liza. 1993. *Kimono: Fashioning Culture.* New Haven: Yale University Press.

Dave, Shilpa. 2001. "Community Beauty": Transnational Performances and Cultural Citizenship in "Miss India Georgia." *Literature Interpretation Theory* 12(3):335–358.

Davis, F. James. 1991. *Who is Black? One Nation's Definition.* University Park: Penn State University Press.

Debord, Guy. 1995. *The Society of the Spectacle.* New York: Zone Books. Translated by Donald Nicholson-Smith. Originally published in France as *La Société du Spectacle,* 1967, by Buchet-Chastel.

Deford, Frank. 1978. *There She Is: The Life and Times of Miss America.* New York: Penguin Books. Originally published 1971.

Desmond, Jane. 1999. *Staging Tourism: Bodies on Display from Waikiki to Sea World.* Chicago: University of Chicago Press.

Dower, John. 2001. *Embracing Defeat: Japan in the Wake of World War II.* New York: W. W. Norton.

Eriksen, Thomas Hyllund. 1993. *Ethnicity and Nationalism: Anthropological Perspectives.* London and Boulder, Colo.: Pluto Press.

Ethnic Studies Oral History Project. 1981. *Uchinanchu: A History of Okinawans in Hawaii.* In conjunction with United Okinawan Association of Hawaii. Honolulu: Ethnic Studies Program, University of Hawai'i at Mānoa.

Fasi, Joyce. 1990. Reflections. *Honolulu Japanese Junior Chamber of Commerce Thirty-Eighth Cherry Blossom Festival.* Honolulu: Honolulu Japanese Junior Chamber of Commerce. P. 72.

Foster, Robert. 1991. Making National Culture in the Global Ecumene. *Annual Review of Anthropology* 20:235 – 260.

Foucault, Michel. 1977. *Discipline and Punish: The Birth of the Prison.* New York: Pantheon Books.

Fuchs, Lawrence H. 1961. *Hawaii Pono: A Social History.* New York: Harcourt, Brace & World.

Fujikane, Candace. 2000. Asian Settler Colonialism in Hawaiʻi. *Amerasia Journal* 26(2):xv – xxii.

Fujisaki, Shirley. 1961. My Trip to Japan. *Honolulu Japanese Junior Chamber of Commerce Ninth Cherry Blossom Festival.* Honolulu: Honolulu Japanese Junior Chamber of Commerce. Pp. 67 – 71.

Furuta, Kymberly. 1997 [Queen's Letter]. *Honolulu Japanese Junior Chamber of Commerce Forty-Fifth Cherry Blossom Festival.* Honolulu: Honolulu Japanese Junior Chamber of Commerce. Pp. 31, 33, 35.

Gedalof, Irene. 2000. Identity in Transit: Nomads, Cyborgs and Women. *The European Journal of Women's Studies* 7(3):337 – 354.

Gereben, Janos. 1971. A Farewell to Rah-Rah and All That. *Honolulu Star-Bulletin.* October 14:B5.

Gladney, Dru. 1994. Representing Nationality in China: Refiguring Majority/Minority Identities. *Journal of Asian Studies* 35(1):92 – 124.

———. 1998. Introduction: Making and Marking Majorities. In Dru Gladney, ed. *Making Majorities: Constituting the Nation in Japan, Korea, China, Malaysia, Fiji, Turkey, and the United States.* Stanford: Stanford University Press. Pp. 1 – 9.

Gledhill, Christine. 1988. Pleasurable Negotiations. In E. Deidre Pripham, ed. *Female Spectators: Looking at Film and Television.* London: Verso. Pp. 64 – 89.

Glenn, Evelyn Nakano. 1986. *Issei, Nisei, War Bride: Three Generations of Japanese American Women in Domestic Service.* Philadelphia: Temple University Press.

———. 2002. *Unequal Freedom: How Race and Gender Shaped American Citizenship and Labor.* Cambridge, Mass.: Harvard University Press.

Goffman, Erving. 1959. *The Presentation of Self in Everyday Life.* Garden City, N.Y.: Doubleday.

Goode, Erich, and Nachman Ben-Yehuda. 1994. *Moral Panics: The Social Construction of Deviance.* Oxford: Blackwell.

Hamamoto, Darrell. 1994. *Monitored Peril: Asian Americans and the Politics of TV Representation.* Minneapolis: University of Minneapolis Press.

Hara, Marvis. 1998. Carnival Queen. In Erick Chock, James R. Harstad, Darrell H. Y. Lum, and Bill Teter, eds. *Growing Up Local: An Anthology of Poetry and Prose from Hawaiʻi.* Honolulu: Bamboo Ridge Press. Pp. 196 – 207.

Hasegawa, Kenneth. 1967 [Letter]. *Honolulu Japanese Junior Chamber of Commerce Fifteenth Cherry Blossom Festival.* Honolulu: Honolulu Japanese Junior Chamber of Commerce. P. 5.

Hauʻofa, Epeli. 1982. Anthropology at Home: A South Pacific Islands Experience. In Hussein Fahim, ed. *Indigenous Anthropology in Non-Western Countries.* Durham: Carolina Academic Press. Pp. 213 – 222.

Hawaii Hochi

———. 1953a. Sakura Matsuri Ondo no Kashi Kenshō Boshū [Cherry Blossom Festival Song Lyrics Wanted, Prizes to be Awarded]. February 5:3.

———. 1953b. Sakura Matsuri o Mainen no Gyōji ni Shitai [Make Cherry Blossom Festival an Annual Event]. February 11:5.

———. 1953c. Kabachi [Editorial]. February 26:3.

———. 1953d. Nansen Hokuba [Editorial]. February 28:2.

———. 1953e. Sakura Matsuri Joō Kōho [Cherry Blossom Queen Nomination]. March 6:3.

———. 1953f. Sakura Matsuri Joō: Chiji ga Taikan [Governor Crowns Cherry Blossom Queen]. March 24:3.

———. 1953g. Sakura Matsuri Ondo Naru: Chikaku Odori no Keiko ni Shakushu ["Sakura Matsuri Ondo" Completed. Dance Practice Starting Soon]. April 2:3.

———. 1953h. Kabachi [Letters]. April 15:6.

———. 1954a. Cherry Queen Contestants Ball to Be Like Coming Out Party. March 5:1.

———. 1954b. Joō Ate Kontesuto [Guess-the-Queen Contest]. March 10:3.

———. 1954c. Kabachi [Letters]. April 15:7.

———. 1954d. Kabachi [Letters]. April 21:4.

———. 1954e. Kabachi [Letters]. April 22:4.

———. 1954f. Densha Nisshi [Editorial]. April 23:6.

———. 1954g. "Sakura Matsuri" no Seikō wa Itchi Kyōryoku no Tamamono [The Success of the Cherry Blossom Festival Is the Result of Cooperation]. May 1:5.

———. 1955a. Kabachi [Letters]. January 28:4.

———. 1955b. Ano Mimi Kono Mimi [That Ear, This Ear]. January 29:5.

———. 1955c. Densha Nisshi [Editorial]. April 1:8.

———. 1955d. Kauai no Sakura Joō [Kauai's Cherry Blossom Queen]. April 4:3.

———. 1956a. Miss Ohina-san Contest Winner Will Be Given Mainland Trip. February 14:3.

———. 1956b. Thousands See Cherry Blossom Queen Candidates at Thrifty Drug. February 24:1.

———. 1956c. Hilda Mikami Polls 12,000 Votes. March 3: Cherry Blossom Special Edition 2.

———. 1956d. Nansen Hokuba [Editorial]. March 22:1.

———. 1956e. Holo Holo Cho [Editorial]. March 23:6.

———. 1956f. Kabachi [Letters]. March 28:4.

———. 1956g. Kabachi [Letters]. March 29:9.

———. 1956h. Kabachi [Letters]. April 2:4.

———. 1957a. Joō Kōho Shōkai-kai [Reception for Queen Contestants]. February 18:1.

———. 1957b. Total of Miss Popularity Ballots 5 Million. April 4:3.

———. 1957c. Holo Holo Cho [Editorial]. April 10:6.

———. 1957d. Kobore-Dane [Scatterings; Miscellaneous]. April 13:1.

———. 1967. Fujin to Seikatsu [Women and Life]. April 5:5.

————. 1999. Sakura Matsuri Tokushū-gō [Cherry Blossom Festival Special Edition]. March 13:special section.

Hawaii Jaycees. 1993. History of the Hawaii Jaycees. The Fiftieth Anniversary Banquet of the Hawaii Jaycees. n.p.

————. 2004. http://www.hawaiijaycees.org (Accessed April 26, 2004).

Hawaii Times. 1959a. Honoruru Nikkei Shonen Shōkō ga Jinshuteki na Shikisai Issō [Honolulu Japanese Junior Chamber of Commerce Wipes Out Its Racial Color]. November 2:2.

————. 1959b. Free Hilo Trip on Lurline for Cherry Queen Guesser. November 3:1.

Hawaii United Okinawa Association. 2000. *To Our Issei . . . Our Heartfelt Gratitude* [Booklet commemorating centennial of Okinawan immigration to Hawai'i]. Honolulu: Hawaii United Okinawa Association.

Higa, LeAnne. 1980 [Queen's Diary]. *Honolulu Japanese Junior Chamber of Commerce Twenty-Eighth Cherry Blossom Festival.* Honolulu: Honolulu Japanese Junior Chamber of Commerce. Pp. 31, 33.

Himoto, Teruo. 1959 [Letter]. *Honolulu Japanese Junior Chamber of Commerce Seventh Cherry Blossom Festival.* Honolulu: Honolulu Japanese Junior Chamber of Commerce. P. 3.

Hirata, Dori Lynn. 1994 [Queen's Letter]. *Honolulu Japanese Junior Chamber of Commerce Twenty-Third Cherry Blossom Festival.* Honolulu: Honolulu Japanese Junior Chamber of Commerce. Pp. 20 – 23.

Hirosaki Junior Chamber of Commerce. 1985 [Letter]. *Honolulu Japanese Junior Chamber of Commerce Thirty-Third Cherry Blossom Festival.* Honolulu: Honolulu Japanese Junior Chamber of Commerce. P. 19.

HJJCC (Honolulu Japanese Junior Chamber of Commerce)

————. 1953. *Honolulu Japanese Junior Chamber of Commerce First Cherry Blossom Festival.* Honolulu: Honolulu Japanese Junior Chamber of Commerce.

————. 1955. *Honolulu Japanese Junior Chamber of Commerce Third Cherry Blossom Festival.* Honolulu: Honolulu Japanese Junior Chamber of Commerce.

————. 1956. *Honolulu Japanese Junior Chamber of Commerce Fourth Cherry Blossom Festival.* Honolulu: Honolulu Japanese Junior Chamber of Commerce.

————. 1957. *Honolulu Japanese Junior Chamber of Commerce Fifth Cherry Blossom Festival.* Honolulu: Honolulu Japanese Junior Chamber of Commerce.

————. 1958. *Honolulu Japanese Junior Chamber of Commerce Sixth Cherry Blossom Festival.* Honolulu: Honolulu Japanese Junior Chamber of Commerce.

————. 1959. *Honolulu Japanese Junior Chamber of Commerce Seventh Cherry Blossom Festival.* Honolulu: Honolulu Japanese Junior Chamber of Commerce.

————. 1960. *Honolulu Japanese Junior Chamber of Commerce Eighth Cherry Blossom Festival.* Honolulu: Honolulu Japanese Junior Chamber of Commerce.

————. 1961. *Honolulu Japanese Junior Chamber of Commerce Ninth Cherry Blossom Festival.* Honolulu: Honolulu Japanese Junior Chamber of Commerce.

————. 1963. *Honolulu Japanese Junior Chamber of Commerce Eleventh Cherry Blossom Festival.* Honolulu: Honolulu Japanese Junior Chamber of Commerce.

————. 1964. *Honolulu Japanese Junior Chamber of Commerce Twelfth Cherry Blossom Festival.* Honolulu: Honolulu Japanese Junior Chamber of Commerce.

———. 1966. *Honolulu Japanese Junior Chamber of Commerce Fourteenth Cherry Blossom Festival*. Honolulu: Honolulu Japanese Junior Chamber of Commerce.

———. 1968. An Open Letter from a New Member to 15th Cherry Blossom Festival Queen Gwen Nishizawa. *Post Script* VII(15). N.p. Honolulu: Honolulu Japanese Junior Chamber of Commerce.

———. 1975. *Honolulu Japanese Junior Chamber of Commerce Twenty-Third Cherry Blossom Festival*. Honolulu: Honolulu Japanese Junior Chamber of Commerce.

———. 1982. *Honolulu Japanese Junior Chamber of Commerce Thirtieth Cherry Blossom Festival*. Honolulu: Honolulu Japanese Junior Chamber of Commerce.

———. 1983. *Honolulu Japanese Junior Chamber of Commerce Thirty-First Cherry Blossom Festival*. Honolulu: Honolulu Japanese Junior Chamber of Commerce.

———. 1985. The HJJCC in Retrospect: Yesterday — Dreaming of a Better Tomorrow. *Honolulu Japanese Junior Chamber of Commerce Thirty-Third Cherry Blossom Festival*. Honolulu: Honolulu Japanese Junior Chamber of Commerce. Pp. 66 – 69.

———. 1991. *Honolulu Japanese Junior Chamber of Commerce Thirty-Ninth Cherry Blossom Festival*. Honolulu: Honolulu Japanese Junior Chamber of Commerce.

———. 1994. *Honolulu Japanese Junior Chamber of Commerce Forty-Second Cherry Blossom Festival*. Honolulu: Honolulu Japanese Junior Chamber of Commerce.

———. 2001 [Unpublished Handout]. Fiftieth Cherry Blossom Festival Queen Contestant Agreement. Honolulu: Honolulu Japanese Junior Chamber of Commerce.

———. 2002 [Unpublished Handout]. How to Utilize the CPG. Honolulu: Honolulu Japanese Junior Chamber of Commerce.

———. 2003. *Japanese Women of Hawaii: A Legacy of Strength and Leadership*. Honolulu: Honolulu Japanese Junior Chamber of Commerce.

———. 2004. http://www.cbfhawaii.com (Accessed February 2002 through May 2004).

Hobsbawm, Eric, and Terence Ranger, eds. 1983. *The Invention of Tradition*. New York: Cambridge University Press.

Hochschild, Arlie. 1983. *The Managed Heart: Commercialization of Human Feeling*. Berkeley: University of California Press.

Hogen Kensaku. 1994 [Letter]. *Honolulu Japanese Junior Chamber of Commerce Forty-Second Cherry Blossom Festival*. Honolulu: Honolulu Japanese Junior Chamber of Commerce. P. 9.

Honolulu Advertiser

———. 1953. Plans Developed to Promote Cherry Festival. September 16:B18.

———. 1958. Miss Ann Kai Represents Hawaii in D.C. Festival. March 12:B3.

———. 1964. Cherry Blossom Pageant Shines in New Arena. March 9:A1.

———. 1972. Training Pays Off for Rae. April 10:A10.

———. 1973. Cherry Blossom Queen Smiles Her Way to Throne. April 2:A12.

Honolulu Japanese Chamber of Hawaii. 2004. http://www.honolulujapanesechamber .org (Accessed April 30, 2004).

Honolulu Star-Bulletin. 1946. Bon Dance Revival Squelched. July 10:A1.

hooks, bell. 1998. Eating the Other: Desire and Resistance. In Ron Scapp and Brian Seitz, eds. *Eating Culture*. Albany: State University of New York Press. Pp. 181 – 200.

Hunter, Pat. 1980. Best Contest of All, Says New Queen of Cherry Blossoms. *Honolulu Advertiser*. April 9:A14.

Ige, Jody-Lee. 1983 [Queen's Letter]. *Honolulu Japanese Junior Chamber of Commerce Thirty-First Cherry Blossom Festival*. Honolulu: Honolulu Japanese Junior Chamber of Commerce. Pp. 15–19.

India Festival Committee, Inc. 2004. http://www.worldwidepageants.com/ (Accessed January 25, 2004).

Infante, Esme. 1999. Japanese Pageant Breaks Tradition. *Honolulu Advertiser*. March 18:A1, A5.

Inouye, Mike, and Sharene Urakami. 2001 [Letter]. *Honolulu Japanese Junior Chamber of Commerce Forty-Ninth Cherry Blossom Festival*. Honolulu: Honolulu Japanese Junior Chamber of Commerce. P. 11.

Ishihara, Wayne. 1980 [No title]. *Honolulu Japanese Junior Chamber of Commerce Twenty-Eighth Cherry Blossom Festival*. Honolulu: Honolulu Japanese Junior Chamber of Commerce. P. 89.

Iwai, Donald. 1958 [Letter]. *Honolulu Japanese Junior Chamber of Commerce Sixth Cherry Blossom Festival*. Honolulu: Honolulu Japanese Junior Chamber of Commerce. P. 5.

Iwamoto, [no personal name given]. 1957. Takarazuka Are Kore [Takarazuka This and That]. *Hawaii Hochi*. April 22:2.

Japanese Women's Society. 2004. http://www.jwsonline.org/index.php?page-aboutjws (Accessed April 20, 2004).

Junior Chamber International. 2004. http://www.jci.cc (Accessed April 18, 2004).

Ka Leo o Hawaii

———. 1938. Six Beauties Win Campus Queen Titles. March 19:1.

———. 1939. Beauty Contest Winners Retain Girlish Modesty. April 15:2.

Ka Palapala

———. 1945–1946 [Yearbook]. Honolulu: University of Hawai'i. Pp. 209–217.

———. 1954 [Yearbook]. Honolulu: University of Hawai'i. [No pagination given; nine pages].

Kang, Laura Hyun Yi. 1997. Si(gh)ting Asian/American Women as Transnational Labor. *positions* 5(2):403–437.

Kantorwicz, Ernst H. 1997. *The King's Two Bodies: A Study in Mediaeval Political Theology*. Princeton: Princeton University Press. Reprinted from 1957 edition.

Karamatsu, Richard. 1980 [No title]. *Honolulu Japanese Junior Chamber of Commerce Twenty-Eighth Cherry Blossom Festival*. Honolulu: Honolulu Japanese Junior Chamber of Commerce. P. 89.

Kauanui, J. Kehaulani. 1999. "For Get" Hawaiian Entitlement: Configurations of Land, "Blood," and Americanization in the Hawaiian Homes Commission Act of 1920. *Social Text* 59:123–144.

Kawakami, Barbara. 1993. *Japanese Immigrant Clothing in Hawaii 1885–1941*. Honolulu: University of Hawai'i Press.

Kimura, Yukiko. 1988. *Issei: Japanese Immigrants to Hawaii*. Honolulu: University of Hawai'i Press.

King, Rebecca Chiyoko. 1997. Multiraciality Reigns Supreme? Mixed-race Japanese Americans and the Cherry Blossom Queen Pageant. *Amerasia Journal* 23(1):113 – 128.

———. 1998. The Changing Face of Japanese America: The Making and Remaking of Race in the Japanese American Community. Unpublished Ph.D. dissertation, University of California, Berkeley.

———. 2001. Mirror, Mirror, on the Wall: Mapping Discussions of Feminism, Race, and Beauty in Japanese American Beauty Pageants. In Teresa Williams-Leon and Cynthia L. Nakashima, eds. *The Sum of Our Parts: Mixed-Heritage Asian Americans*. Philadelphia: Temple University Press. Pp. 163 – 172.

———. 2002. "Eligible" to be Japanese American: Multiraciality in Basketball Leagues and Beauty Pageants. In Linda Trinh Vo and Rick Bonus, eds. *Contemporary Asian American Communities: Interventions and Divergences*. Philadelphia: Temple University Press. Pp. 120 – 133.

Kitano, Harry. 1976. *Japanese Americans: The Evolution of a Subculture*. Englewood Cliffs, N.J.: Prentice-Hall.

Kodama, Deborah. 1978. A Letter from Queen Deborah. *Honolulu Japanese Junior Chamber of Commerce Twenty-Sixth Cherry Blossom Festival*. Honolulu: Honolulu Japanese Junior Chamber of Commerce. Pp. 37, 39.

Kondo, Francene. 1981 [Queen's Diary]. *Honolulu Japanese Junior Chamber of Commerce Twenty-Ninth Cherry Blossom Festival*. Honolulu: Honolulu Japanese Junior Chamber of Commerce. Pp. 19, 21, 23, 25, 27, 29, 31, 33.

Kotani, Roland. 1985. *The Japanese in Hawaii: A Century of Struggle*. Honolulu: The Hawaii Hochi, Ltd.

Kuakini Health System. 2004. http://www.kuakini.org/roots/history.html (Accessed March 5, 2004).

Kumie [Koide, Cheryl]. 2000. Awaken the Dawn. CK1215. Kāneʻohe, Hawaiʻi: AwakenFire Music. Compact disc audiorecording.

Kunitsugu, Kango. 1979. Shoyu — 1200 Years Older Than Catsup. *Honolulu Japanese Junior Chamber of Commerce Twenty-Seventh Cherry Blossom Festival*. Honolulu: Honolulu Japanese Junior Chamber of Commerce. Pp. 69 – 71.

Kurashige, Lon. 2002. *Japanese American Celebration and Conflict: A History of Ethnic Identity and Festival in Los Angeles, 1934 – 1990*. Berkeley: University of California Press.

Lavenda, Robert H. 1996. "It's Not a Beauty Pageant!" Hybrid Ideology in Minnesota Community Queen Pageants. In Colleen Ballerino Cohen, Richard Wilk, and Beverly Stoeltje, eds. *Beauty Queens on the Global Stage: Gender, Contests, and Power*. New York: Routledge. Pp. 31 – 46.

Lebra, Takie Sugiyama. 1986. *Japanese Women: Constraint and Fulfillment*. Honolulu: University of Hawaiʻi Press.

Lehrer, Jim. 2000. Remembering the GI Bill. Online News Hour. July 4. http://www.pbs.org/newshour/bb/military/July-dec00/gibill_7-4a.html (Accessed March 9, 2004).

Li, Jinzhao. 2002. Constructing Chinese American Identity in Hawaii: Fifty-three Years of Narcissus Queen Pageant and Festival. Unpublished paper. International Cultural Studies Certificate Capstone Project, University of Hawaiʻi.

Lieu, Nhi T. 2000. Remembering "the Nation" through Pageantry: Femininity and the Politics of Vietnamese Womanhood in the *Hoa Hau Ao Dai* Contest. *Frontiers: A Journal of Women's Studies* 21(1 – 2):127 – 151.

Lim, Shirley. 2003. Contested Beauty: Asian American Women's Cultural Citizenship during the Early Cold War Era. In Shirley Hune and Gail M. Nomura, eds. *Asian/Pacific Islander American Women: A Historical Anthology*. New York: New York University. Pp. 188 – 204.

Lind, Andrew W. 1980. *Hawaii's People*. Honolulu: University of Hawai'i Press.

Lowe, Lisa. 1996. *Immigrant Acts: On Asian American Cultural Politics*. Durham: Duke University Press.

———. 1997. Work, Immigration, Gender: Asian "American" Women. In Elaine Kim, Lilia Villanueva, and Asian Women United of California, eds. *Making More Waves: New Writing by Asian American Women*. Boston: Beacon Press. Pp. 269 – 277.

Lueras, Leonard. 1970. An Avant Garde Queen. *Honolulu Advertiser*. April 6:D6.

Mabalon, Dawn Bohulano. 2003. Beauty Queens, Bomber Pilots and Basketball Players: Filipina Americans in Stockton, 1930s – 1950s. Paper presented at annual meeting of Association for Asian American Studies, San Francisco.

Manning, Frank E. 1992. Spectacle. In Richard Bauman, ed. *Folklore, Cultural Performances, and Popular Entertainments*. New York: Oxford University Press. Pp. 291 – 299.

Marcus, George, and Michael Fischer. 1986. *Anthropology as Cultural Critique: An Experimental Moment in the Human Sciences*. Chicago: University of Chicago Press.

Marcus, Millicent. 1992. Miss Modina, Miss Sirena, Miss Farina: The Feminized Body-Politics from *Bitter Rice* to *La Voce Della Luna*. *Romance Languages Annual* 4:296 – 300.

Marling, Karal Ann. 2004. *Debutante: Rites and Regalia of American Debdom*. Lawrence: University Press of Kansas.

Marshall, P. David. 1997. *Celebrity and Power: Fame in Contemporary Culture*. Minneapolis: University of Minnesota Press.

Masuda, Koh, ed. 1974. *Kenkyusha's New Japanese-English Dictionary*. 4th ed. Tokyo: Kenkyusha.

Matsuo, Michael. 1994 [Letter]. *Honolulu Japanese Junior Chamber of Commerce Forty-Second Cherry Blossom Festival*. Honolulu: Honolulu Japanese Junior Chamber of Commerce. P. 15.

Matsuura, Patsy. 1968. First Cherry Blossom Queen Violet Oishi Is Now a Devoted Mother. *Honolulu Advertiser*. February 18:C8.

May, Elaine Tyler. 1988. *Homeward Bound: American Families in the Cold War Era*. New York: Basic Books.

McCurdy, John, Jr. 2004. http://www.asiancosmeticsurg.com/eyelids.htm/ (Accessed April 15, 2004).

McKinley High School. 1952. Campus Queens. *Black and Gold* [McKinley High School yearbook]. Honolulu: McKinley High School.

Mengel, Laurie M. 1997. *Issei* Women and Divorce in Hawai'i, 1885 – 1908. *Social*

Process in Hawaii 38:18 – 39. Special issue edited by Joyce N. Chinen, Kathleen O. Kane, and Ida Yoshinaga, *Women in Hawai'i: Sites, Identities and Voices.*

Milanese, Marisa. 2002. Focus on Inner Beauty: Miss Vietnam Tet Pageant Rewards Educated Area Women Who Honor Traditional Values. *The Mercury News.* Posted online February 15, 2002, at http://www.mercurynews.com/mld/ mercurynews/news/local/2676891.htm (Accessed February 16, 2004).

Mink, Patsy T. 1999 [Letter]. *Honolulu Japanese Junior Chamber of Commerce Forty-Seventh Cherry Blossom Festival.* Honolulu: Honolulu Japanese Junior Chamber of Commerce. P. 9.

Mishima, Kiyomaru. 1981. Japanese Archery. *Honolulu Japanese Junior Chamber of Commerce Twenty-Ninth Cherry Blossom Festival.* Honolulu: Honolulu Japanese Junior Chamber of Commerce. Pp. 77 – 79.

Mishima, Roy Y. 1980. Samurai. *Honolulu Japanese Junior Chamber of Commerce Twenty-Eighth Cherry Blossom Festival.* Honolulu: Honolulu Japanese Junior Chamber of Commerce. Pp. 77 – 79.

Miss Asian America Pageant. 2004. http://www.missasianamerica.com (Accessed February 1, 2004).

Miss Chinatown Hawaii. 2004. http://www.misschinatown.com/history (Accessed April 19, 2004).

Morita, Robert S. 1994 [Letter]. *Honolulu Japanese Junior Chamber of Commerce Forty-Second Cherry Blossom Festival.* Honolulu: Honolulu Japanese Junior Chamber of Commerce. P. 14.

———. 1995. Our Meeting with the Emperor and Empress of Japan. *Honolulu Japanese Junior Chamber of Commerce Forty-Third Cherry Blossom Festival.* Honolulu: Honolulu Japanese Junior Chamber of Commerce. Pp. 35, 55.

Moriyama, Mildred, with the assistance of Ruth Adaniya. 1981. Hui Makaala. In Ethnic Studies Oral History Project and United Okinawan Association of Hawaii, eds. *Uchinanchu: A History of Okinawans in Hawaii.* Honolulu: Ethnic Studies Program, University of Hawai'i at Mānoa. Pp. 337 – 344.

Morris, Meaghan. 1996. Banality in Cultural Studies. In John Storey, ed. *What is Cultural Studies? A Reader.* London: Arnold.

Morrison, Judith. 1977. Being Chinese in Honolulu: A Political and Social Status or a Way of Life. Unpublished Ph.D. dissertation, University of Illinois at Urbana-Champaign.

Mulvey, Laura. 1975. Visual Pleasure and Narrative Cinema. *Screen* 16(3):22.

Murayama, Lori. 2000 [Unpublished folder of guidelines for future Queens]. Honolulu.

Nakahodo, Lisa. 1985 [Queen's Letter]. *Honolulu Japanese Junior Chamber of Commerce Thirty-Third Cherry Blossom Festival.* Honolulu: Honolulu Japanese Junior Chamber of Commerce. Pp. 15 – 17.

Narayan, Kirin. 1993. How Native is a "Native" Anthropologist? *American Anthropologist* 95:671 – 686.

National Park Service. 2004. History of the Cherry Trees in Washington, D.C. http://www.nps.gov/nacc/cherry/history.htm (Accessed May 24, 2004).

Nguyen, Nhien T. 2000. My Pink *Ao Dai. Frontiers: A Journal of Women's Studies* 21(1 – 2):126.

Nishida, Merle M. 1980. The Role of the Female in Japanese Family Life: A Look at Two Real-life Families. *Honolulu Japanese Junior Chamber of Commerce Twenty-Eighth Cherry Blossom Festival.* Honolulu: Honolulu Japanese Junior Chamber of Commerce. Pp. 73 – 75.

Nishino, Janet. 1963 [Queen's Letter]. *Honolulu Japanese Junior Chamber of Commerce Eleventh Cherry Blossom Festival.* Honolulu: Honolulu Japanese Junior Chamber of Commerce. P. 72.

Nomura, Gail. 1989. Issei Working Women in Hawaii. In Asian Women United of California, ed. *Making Waves: An Anthology of Writings By and About Asian American Women.* Boston: Beacon Press. Pp. 135 – 148.

Oda, Ethel Aiko. 1984. Onna — Onnarashii (Woman — Womanly, Ladylike). *Honolulu Japanese Junior Chamber of Commerce Thirty-Second Cherry Blossom Festival.* Honolulu: Honolulu Japanese Junior Chamber of Commerce. Pp. 35, 38.

Odo, Franklin. 1984. The Rise and Fall of the Nisei. Part 4. *Hawaii Herald.* October 5:14.

Ogawa, Gotaro. 1999 [Letter]. *Honolulu Japanese Junior Chamber of Commerce Forty-Seventh Cherry Blossom Festival.* Honolulu: Honolulu Japanese Junior Chamber of Commerce. P. 5.

Ohnuki-Tierney, Emiko. 2002. *Kamikaze, Cherry Blossoms, and Nationalisms: The Militarization of Aesthetics in Japanese History.* Chicago: University of Chicago Press.

Okamura, Jonathan Y. 1980. Aloha Kanaka Me Ke Aloha 'Aina: Local Culture and Society in Hawaii. *Amerasia Journal* 7:119 – 137.

———. 1994. Why There are No Asian Americans in Hawai'i: The Continuing Significance of Local Identity. *Social Process in Hawaii* 35:161 – 178.

———. 1998. The Illusion of Paradise: Privileging Multiculturalism in Hawai'i. In Dru Gladney, ed. *Making Majorities: Constituting the Nation in Japan, Korea, China, Malaysia, Fiji, Turkey, and the United States.* Stanford: Stanford University Press. Pp. 264 – 284.

———. 2001. Race Relations in Hawai'i During World War II. In Jonathan Okamura, ed. *The Japanese American Historical Experience in Hawai'i.* Dubuque, Iowa: Kendall/Hunt Publishing Co. Pp. 67 – 89. Reprinted from *Amerasia Journal,* 2000, 26(2):117 – 141.

———. 2002. Baseball and Beauty Queens: The Political Context of Ethnic Boundary Making in the Japanese American Community in Hawai'i. *Social Process in Hawai'i* 41:122 – 146.

Okihiro, Gary. 1991. *Cane Fires: The Anti-Japanese Movement in Hawaii, 1865 – 1945.* Philadelphia: Temple University Press.

Okihiro, Michael. 1999. *AJA Baseball in Hawaii: Ethnic Pride and Tradition.* Honolulu: Hawaii Hochi, Ltd.

Okinaga, Sam. 1971 [Letter]. *Honolulu Japanese Junior Chamber of Commerce Nineteenth Cherry Blossom Festival.* Honolulu: Honolulu Japanese Junior Chamber of Commerce. P. 61.

Omi, Michael, and Harold Winant. 1994. *Racial Formation in the United States from the 1960s to the 1980s.* 2nd ed. New York: Routledge.

Oshiro, Dennis. 1980 [Letter]. *Honolulu Japanese Junior Chamber of Commerce Twenty-Eighth Cherry Blossom Festival.* Honolulu: Honolulu Japanese Junior Chamber of Commerce. P. 13.

Oshiro, Sandra. 1977. A Year of Cherry Blossom Time. *Honolulu Advertiser.* March 28:B8.

Pageantry Magazine. 2004. http://www.pageantrymagazine.com (Accessed January 30, 2004).

Palumbo-Liu, David. 1999. *Asian/American: Historical Crossings of a Racial Frontier.* Stanford: Stanford University Press.

Paradise of the Pacific. 1948. University of Hawaii Beauty Queens. 60(12):28 – 29.

Peiss, Kathy. 1998. *Hope in a Jar: The Making of America's Beauty Culture.* New York: Henry Holt and Company.

Perlmutter, Dawn. 2000. Miss America: Whose Ideal? In Peg Zeglin Brand, ed. *Beauty Matters.* Bloomington: Indiana University Press. Pp. 155 – 168.

Petersen, William. 1966. Success Story, Japanese American Style. *New York Times Magazine.* January 9:20 – 21, 33, 36, 38, 40 – 41.

Phelan, Peggy. 1993. *Unmarked: The Politics of Performance.* London and New York: Routledge.

Quinn, William F. 1958 [Letter]. *Honolulu Japanese Junior Chamber of Commerce Sixth Cherry Blossom Festival.* Honolulu: Honolulu Japanese Junior Chamber of Commerce. P. 7.

———. 1960 [Letter]. *Honolulu Japanese Junior Chamber of Commerce Eighth Cherry Blossom Festival.* Honolulu: Honolulu Japanese Junior Chamber of Commerce. P. 7.

Robertson, Jennifer. 2001. Japan's First Cyborg? Miss Nippon, Eugenics and Wartime Technologies of Beauty, Body and Blood. *Body & Society* 7(1):1 – 34.

Rogers, Terence, and Satoru Izutsu. 1980. The Japanese. In John McDermott, Jr., Wen-Shing Tseng, and Thomas Maretzki, eds. *People and Cultures of Hawaii: A Psychocultural Profile.* Honolulu: University of Hawai'i Press. Pp. 73 – 99.

Rosa, John P. 2000. Local Story: The Massie Case Narrative and the Cultural Production of Local Identity in Hawai'i. *Amerasia Journal* 26(2):93 – 115.

Saito, Carlton. 1991. The Ultimate Cherry Blossom Festival Fan. *Honolulu Japanese Junior Chamber of Commerce Fortieth Cherry Blossom Festival.* Honolulu: Honolulu Japanese Junior Chamber of Commerce. P. 51.

Sanders, Richard, and Sarah Pink. 1996. Homage to "La Cordobesa": Local Identity and Pageantry in Andalusia. In Colleen Ballerino Cohen, Richard Wilk, and Beverly Stoeltje, eds. *Beauty Queens on the Global Stage: Gender, Contests, and Power.* New York: Routledge. Pp. 47 – 60.

Sato, Marlene. 1988 [Queen's Letter]. *Honolulu Japanese Junior Chamber of Commerce Thirty-Sixth Cherry Blossom Festival.* Honolulu: Honolulu Japanese Junior Chamber of Commerce. Pp. 19 – 22.

Sato, Robert. 1975. 25 Years Ago. *Honolulu Japanese Junior Chamber of Commerce Twenty-Third Cherry Blossom Festival.* Honolulu: Honolulu Japanese Junior Chamber of Commerce. Pp. 94 – 96.

Savage, Candace. 1998. *Beauty Queens: A Playful History.* New York: Abbeville Press.

Sheard, Helen. 1969. Japanese Etiquette. *Honolulu Japanese Junior Chamber of Commerce Seventeenth Cherry Blossom Festival*. Honolulu: Honolulu Japanese Junior Chamber of Commerce. Pp. 87 – 88.

Silverman, A. 1955. Pin-ups, Hawaii. *Paradise of the Pacific* 67(7):22 – 23.

Smith, Margo L. 1973. Domestic Service as a Channel of Upward Mobility for the Lower-Class Woman: The Lima Case. In Ann Pescatello, ed. *Female and Male in Latin America: Essays*. Pittsburgh: University of Pittsburgh Press. Pp. 192 – 207.

Stacey, Jackie. 1994. *Star Gazing: Hollywood Cinema and Female Spectatorship*. London: Routledge.

Stallybrass, Peter, and Allon White. 1986. *The Politics and Poetics of Transgression*. Ithaca: Cornell University Press.

Stewart, Kathleen. 1996. *A Space on the Side of the Road: Cultural Poetics in an "Other" America*. Princeton: Princeton University Press.

Stoeltje, Beverly. 1996. The Snake Charmer Queen: Ritual, Competition, and Signification in American Festival. In Colleen Ballerino Cohen, Richard Wilk, and Beverly Stoeltje, eds. *Beauty Queens on the Global Stage: Gender, Contests, and Power*. New York: Routledge. Pp. 13 – 29.

Stone, Scott. 2001. *From a Joyful Heart: The Life and Music of R. Alexander Anderson*. Honolulu: Island Heritage Publications.

Sturm, Circe. 2002. *Blood Politics: Race, Culture, and Identity in the Cherokee Nation of Oklahoma*. Berkeley: University of California Press.

Suzuki, Bob. 1977. Education and Socialization of Asian Americans: A Revisionist Analysis of the 'Model Minority' Thesis. *Amerasia Journal* 4(2):23 – 52.

Suzuki, Genevieve A. 2002. Values Fit for a Queen. *Hawai'i Herald*. April 19:A5.

Tachiki, Amy, Eddie Wong, and Franklin Odo, eds. 1971. *Roots: An Asian American Reader*. Los Angeles: UCLA Asian American Studies Center.

Takahata, Carrie Y. 2002. Making Yonsei. In Jonathan Okamura, ed. *The Japanese American Contemporary Experience in Hawai'i*. Social Process in Hawai'i 41:73 – 74.

Takata, Dori Kiyomi. 2000 [Letter]. *Honolulu Japanese Junior Chamber of Commerce Forty-Eighth Cherry Blossom Festival*. Honolulu: Honolulu Japanese Junior Chamber of Commerce. P. 27.

Takeuchi, Floyd. 1999. Agent of Change. *Hawaii Business*. March 18:15.

Tamura, Eileen. 1994. *Americanization, Acculturation, and Ethnic Identity: The Nisei Generation in Hawaii*. Urbana: University of Illinois Press.

Tanaka, Rae. 1973. Reflections: The Grand Tour. *Honolulu Japanese Junior Chamber of Commerce Twenty-First Cherry Blossom Festival*. Honolulu: Honolulu Japanese Junior Chamber of Commerce. Pp. 30 – 32, 35 – 36, 38, 40, 42, 44.

Tasaka, Jack Y. 1985. *A Hundred Year History of Japanese Culture and Entertainment in Hawaii*. Honolulu: East-West Journal.

Teilhet-Fisk, Jehanne. 1996. The Miss Heilala Beauty Pageant: Where Beauty is More than Skin Deep. In Colleen Ballerino Cohen, Richard Wilk, and Beverly Stoeltje, eds. *Beauty Queens on the Global Stage: Gender, Contests, and Power*. New York: Routledge. Pp. 185 – 202.

Teramae, Janice. 1969 [Letter]. *Honolulu Japanese Junior Chamber of Commerce Sev-*

enteenth Cherry Blossom Festival. Honolulu: Honolulu Japanese Junior Chamber of Commerce. P. 54.

Thoma, Pamela. 1999. Of Beauty Pageants and Barbie: Theorizing Consumption in Asian American Transnational Feminism. *Genders: A Journal of the Arts, Humanities and Social Theory.* Vol. 29. Online journal at http://www.genders .org/g29/g29_thoma.html. (Accessed February 23, 2004).

Thompson, Kenneth. 1998. *Moral Panics.* London: Routledge.

Thompson, Rod. 1996. Time to Blossom? *Honolulu Star-Bulletin.* January 29:B1, B3.

Ting, Yu Shing. 2004. Fourth Try Was the Charm. *MidWeek.* July 7:34, 48.

Togami, Cynthia. 2001. War Brides. In Brian Niiya, ed. *Encyclopedia of Japanese American History: An A-to-Z Reference from 1868 to the Present.* Los Angeles: Japanese American National Museum. Pp. 408–409.

Tokairin, Bert. 1971 [Letter]. *Honolulu Japanese Junior Chamber of Commerce Nineteenth Cherry Blossom Festival.* Honolulu: Honolulu Japanese Junior Chamber of Commerce. P. 61.

Tomita, Theodore. 1971 [Letter]. *Honolulu Japanese Junior Chamber of Commerce Nineteenth Cherry Blossom Festival.* Honolulu: Honolulu Japanese Junior Chamber of Commerce. P. 59.

Tong, David. 1976. UH Team's Nontrip Is Myrah's Gain. *Honolulu Advertiser.* March 29:A5.

Toyama, Henry, and Kiyoshi Ikeda. 1950. The Okinawan-Naichi Relationship. *Social Process in Hawaii* 14:51–65.

Turner, Sarah, and John Bound. 2002. The G.I. Bill, World War II, and the Education of Black Americans. *National Bureau of Economic Research* (NBER). Synopsis by Les Picker. Available on http://www.nber.org/digest/dec02/w9044.html (Accessed March 8, 2004).

U.S. Census Bureau. 2001. Summary File 1 Hawaii.

U.S. Junior Chamber. 2004. http://www.usjaycees.org (Accessed April 18, 2004).

Van Esterik, Penny. 1996. The Politics of Beauty in Thailand. In Colleen Ballerino Cohen, Richard Wilk, and Beverly Stoeltje, eds. *Beauty Queens on the Global Stage: Gender, Contests, and Power.* New York: Routledge. Pp. 203–216.

Van Gennep, Arnold. 1960. *The Rites of Passage.* Chicago: University of Chicago Press.

Vinacke, W. Edgar. 1949. Stereotyping Among National-Racial Groups in Hawaii: A Study in Ethnocentrism. *Journal of Social Psychology* 30:265–291.

Von Adelung, Carolyn. 1954. Cherry Blossom Time in Hawaii. *Paradise of the Pacific* 66(4):13–15.

Vora, Kalindi. 2002. Miss India USA 2001: Flexible Practices, Creative Consumption, and Transnationalism in Indian America. Unpublished M.A. thesis, University of Hawai'i.

Waihee, John. 1994 [Letter]. *Honolulu Japanese Junior Chamber of Commerce Forty-Second Cherry Blossom Festival.* Honolulu: Honolulu Japanese Junior Chamber of Commerce. P. 3.

Wall, James M. 1995. Changes in Attitude: The Lost World of the 1950s. *The Christian Century.* October 18:947–948.

Waseda, Minako. 2004. Looking Both Ways: Musical Exoticism in Post-World War II Japan. *Yearbook for Traditional Music* 36:144 – 164.

Wilk, Richard. 1996. Connections and Contradictions: From the Crooked Tree Cashew Queen to Miss World Belize. In Colleen Ballerino Cohen, Richard Wilk, and Beverly Stoeltje, eds. *Beauty Queens on the Global Stage: Gender, Contests, and Power.* New York: Routledge. Pp. 217 – 232.

Wolf, Naomi. 1991. *The Beauty Myth: How Images of Beauty Are Used against Women.* New York: Doubleday.

Wu, Judy Tsu-Chun. 1997. "Loveliest Daughter of Our Ancient Cathay!" Representations of Ethnic and Gender Identity in the Miss Chinatown U.S.A. Beauty Pageant. *Journal of Social History* 31:5 – 31.

Yano, Christine R. 2002a. Cherry Blossoms on Parade [VHS videocassette]. Honolulu.

———. 2002b. Shifting Meanings of Japanese-American Identity. *50th Cherry Blossom Festival; "Reflections from the Past . . . Visions for the Future.* Souvenir Pageant Booklet. Honolulu: Honolulu Japanese Junior Chamber of Commerce.

———. 2002c. *Tears of Longing: Nostalgia and the Nation in Japanese Popular Song.* Cambridge, Mass.: Harvard University Asia Center, Harvard University Press.

Yim, Susan. 1992. Hawaii's Ethnic Rainbow: Shining Colors, Side by Side. *Honolulu Advertiser.* January 5:B1, B3.

INDEX

advertisements in souvenir books, 75–76, 82, 260n33

age: of contestants, 77, 200, 262n14, 264n5, 265n2; of HJJCC members, 80, 125; of Queens, 149

Ala Moana Center, 46, 253n16

Aloha Week, 67, 83, 85, 257n7

ambassadors, unofficial: nisei as, 43–44; Queens as, 91, 132–133, 224. *See also* bridge

American dream: and banality, 5; CBF and, 58, 74, 234; depicted in souvenir books, 75–76; Japanese American achievement of, 41, 48, 124, 197; Jaycee Creed and, 57

American way of life, 39–40; CBF role in, 58, 230; promoted by HJJCC, 53

Americanization, 30, 47, 78, 167, 252n8. *See also* assimilation; citizenship

Americanness, 66, 70, 78, 83

Anderson, R. Alex, 71, 74, 258n21

anti-Japanese sentiment, 47, 127–128, 255n28

ao dai (Vietnamese dress), 29–30, 34, 251n12

Asian American, 21–22, 26, 31; women, 250n8, 265n6

assimilation, 5, 42, 87, 198, 247; to mainstream American society, 21, 30, 49, 53, 252n8. *See also* Americanization; citizenship

Asuncion, Leo, Jr., 205–206

audience, 22, 33; for CBF, 86, 89–90, 187; waning, for CBF, 123–124, 154

authenticity of Japanese culture, 91, 145, 152

balloting, 82–84, 99, 257n12

banality, 5–7, 37; of CBF, 154, 190, 199, 206, 230, 232; and conservatism, 242; of Japanese Americans in Hawai'i, 245–246; and niceness, 234, 244; poetics of, 246–248

Banet-Weiser, Sarah, 5, 60

baseball, 43–44

beauty, 19–20, 31, 75, 263n1 (chap. 7); criteria eliminated for CBF contestants, 184, 191–192, 199, 212; Euro-American standards of, 1–2, 18–19, 31–32, 142, 185, 250n6; exotic, 19, 31; of *hapa* women, 185, 191; preferences in CBF, 2, 101, 103, 143–144. *See also* body; hair

beauty pageants, 14–16; American model of, 16–17, 66; Asian American, 21–22, 26, 30, 33, 36–37; CBF not, 178, 238; competitiveness of, 1–2, 141, 223; as cultural festivals, 24, 238–239; diasporic, 33–35; ethnic, 5, 22, 59, 232, 250n9, 255n29; feminist opposition to, 30–31, 63, 139; Filipino, 26, 34–35; in Hawai'i, 5; in Japan, 34; local, 15, 23, 24, 251n11, 255n29; pyramidal, 15, 111, 265n3; Thai, 19; Vietnamese American, 30, 33, 35

beauty queens: as celebrities, 2, 14, 98; as community representatives, 20, 22; and power, 14, 38; stereotypes of, 98, 140–141. *See also* Queens

Blaisdell, Neal S., 87, 91, 118

blood-quantum rule, 27, 89, 155, 183–184, 263n4 (chap. 7); change in, 187–199, 205, 230–231. See also *hapa*; mixed-race

body, 17–18; of beauty queens, 18, 101; CBF aesthetics of, 238–239; display of, 30, 76; height, 141–142, 262nn7–9; kimono, 144–145, 203; measurements, 1, 33

bowing lessons, 130, 145

brand, CBF Queen as, 84

bridge: CBF and HJJCC as, 69, 86–90, 133; Hawai'i as, 71. *See also* ambassadors

Burns, John A., 87, 110, 118

business, 52; CBF as, 82–85; etiquette lessons, 130

calligraphy, 130
cape, 14, 67, 256n4
Caucasian, 88, 260n36. *See also* haole
Cayetano, Benjamin, 133, 151
celebrity spotlight of CBF Queens, 17, 38, 91,
98, 146–148, 168; lack of privacy due to,
101, 108–109, 112
chanoyu (tea ceremony). *See* tea ceremony
chaperonage of CBF contestants and
Queens, 97, 100
cheongsam (Chinese dress), 29, 62, 240,
265n6. *See also* dress
Cherry Blossom Festival (CBF): compared
with Narcissus Festival, 59, 265n6;
Honolulu-centrism of, 114–115, 117;
parade, 85–86, 112; themes of, 126–127,
232, 262nn15–16; in Washington, D.C.,
249n2; Week, 65–66
"Cherry Blossoms" (Anderson), 71, 74
cherry blossoms, significance of, 74, 92
"Cherry Sisters," 235–236, 246
Chinese American, 31, 59–60. *See also* Narcissus Festival
Chinese Chamber of Commerce. *See* Honolulu Chinese Chamber of Commerce
Chong, Pono, 198, 231
Chrysanthemum Ball Queen, 255n29
citizenship: Chinese American, 59; demonstrated via beauty pageants, 24–25, 67–
68; Japanese American, 25, 41–42, 44–45,
48, 53, 252n8. *See also* Americanization;
assimilation
civil service, 266n7
class, 15–16; contestant expectations of,
75; and gender, 16, 130; of Japanese immigrants, 28; middle-, 4, 7, 25, 41, 253n8;
of Queens, 96, 110, 114, 116–117, 120, 158,
200; stereotypes of Naichi vs. Uchinanchu, 169; upper-, 48; upper-middle-, 19,
28; working-, 28. *See also* professions;
social mobility
Cold War era, 24–25, 40, 59
community: beauty pageants and, 15, 20;
CBF and the Japanese American, 69, 150,
199–200, 231; defining Japanese American, 191–193, 248; of Hawai'i, 151–152, 198,
227; imagined, 35; pan-ethnic, 124, 243
community service: CBF Queens and
Courts providing, 131–132, 212–213, 216–

218, 220, 243; HJJCC, 53–54, 58, 78–79,
232, 254n26, 264n5
conservatism: of Asian American communities, 31; of CBF and HJJCC, 124–127, 151–
152, 231; of CBF participants, 77, 138–140;
of Japanese American community, 126,
197–198, 242
contest, 249n2 (chap. 2). *See also* beauty pageants; pageant
contestant eligibility, 77, 233, 265n3
cosmetic surgery, 32–33, 142–143, 234,
262n10
"Cosmopolitan" (category in rainbow pageants), 60–61, 255n30
Creole English in Hawai'i ("pidgin"), 42
crown, 14, 66, 72, 246
"cultural ambassadors," Japanese art forms
as, 68–69, 91
cultural competence: not part of judging,
130–131, 204, 216, 233–234; of pageant
contestants, 27–28, 34–35; training in, 28,
129–130
cultural pageant. *See under* pageant

debutante, 16, 74–76, 250n4, 259n28
Democratic Revolution of 1954, 41, 241
diaspora, 37; Filipino, 35; Korean, 33–34
dress: of CBF participants, 251n14, 256n2,
258n19, 265n6; evening gown, 29, 33,
72; gendered differences in, 78, 259n31;
national costume, 23, 29, 62; wedding,
50. *See also* ao dai; cheongsam; kimono;
qipao

educational level of CBF contestants, 200,
264n6
emotion work, 110, 145, 237–238, 246
emplacement, 5, 37; of Asian women, 265n6;
and banality, 7, 242, 245; via CBF, 68,
230, 232; of nisei, 41, 44, 56, 58. *See also*
citizenship
English language: and assimilation, 54,
70, 167; name for CBF, 66; requirement
in Hawaii Chamber of Commerce, 56;
standard schools, 42, 252nn6–7, 261n4
(chap. 4)
ethnic: categories in rainbow pageants, 60–
61, 255n30, 256nn33–34; dress, 23, 29, 62;
enclave, 22–23, 25, 58; multi-, 183, 191, 196,

female members of, 125, 173, 216–217; formation of, 52–55; International Relations Division of, 133; progressiveness of, 219; purpose of, 17, 53, 55, 78, 200; as separate and equal organization, 52. *See also* Jaycees

Horio, Katherine (18th CBF Queen, 1970–1971), 138, 263n3 (chap. 6); herstory, 158–163

hostess, 237; CBF Queens as, 98, 110, 113, 145–146, 242

hybridity of Asian American pageants, 36–37

identity, 8, 27, 29, 155; "hyperlinked," 37; Japan as locus of Japanese American, 126, 152, 200–201, 206

Ige, Jody-Lee (30th CBF Queen, 1982–1983), 134, 142, 144, 147, 149, 153–154, 185–186

immigration, 21

indigenous anthropology, 9–11

Inouye, Daniel, 45

intermarriage, 21, 155; discouraged by issei and nisei, 184–185; as reason for changing blood-quantum rule, 188–189

issei (first-generation Japanese Americans), 42, 50–52; cooperation with nisei, 69–70. *See also* generational differences

jack-o'-lantern *manjū*, 175, 234–235

"JAL scepter," 67, 85. *See also* Japan Airlines

Japan: as audience for CBF, 89–90; beauty pageants in, 34, 251n15; CBF Queens as ambassadors to, 91, 132–133, 224; as idealized past, 72, 202, 206, 232; Japanese American relations to, 43, 127, 262n13; as locus of Japanese American identity, 126, 152, 200–201, 206

Japan Airlines (JAL), 34, 46; scepter, 67, 85

Japan Travel Bureau, 90, 101

Japanese: aesthetic, 145; anti-, 47, 127–128, 255n28; conflated with Japanese American, 69, 71, 256n1; immigration to Hawai'i, 127, 132; investors and tourists in Hawai'i, 127–128; model for womanhood, 261n4 (chap. 5). *See also* Japanese culture; values: Japanese

Japanese Americans, 21, 41–43; competing with Chinese Americans, 59–60; conservatism of, 126, 197–198, 242; defining community of, 27, 192–193, 248; reputed clannishness of, 252n8; women, 71–72, 129, 138, 210. *See also* stereotypes: of Japanese Americans

Japanese Americans in Hawai'i, 5, 41–42, 44–50, 76, 242, 266n7; backlash against exclusivity of, 41, 124, 187, 252n8; banality of, 5, 240, 245–246; marriage patterns of, 41, 155, 252n2; relevance of CBF to, 190, 195–196

Japanese Chamber of Commerce. *See* Honolulu Japanese Chamber of Commerce

Japanese culture: as arts, 200–201; CBF Queens connecting to, 128–129, 131–132, 145, 160, 178–179, 204, 213; classes in, 129, 199, 216, 222, 227; construction of idealized, 28, 55, 69, 90–91, 204; essay contest, 201, 264n9; as heritage, 127, 150, 200–201, 206, 232; maintained within CBF, 152, 174, 198, 203; transnational flow of popular, 43–44. *See also* values: Japanese

Japanese language: changing use of, 42–43, 70, 131, 166–167, 171, 253nn9–10, 257n11; not part of pageant training, 131, 234; use in CBF souvenir books, 70, 258n16

Japanese Photographers Society of Hawaii, 81

Japanese Women's Society, 51, 105, 110, 119, 171

Jaycees (United States Junior Chamber of Congress), 54–56; Creed, 56–58, 105; membership opened to women, 125; movement, 3–4, 40; organizations as ethnic enclaves, 24, 254n22; sister chapters in Japan, 125, 132–133, 195; Triangle, 57–58. *See also* Honolulu Japanese Junior Chamber of Commerce

judges, characteristics of, 25–26, 88, 130, 236–237, 265n5

judging criteria, 20, 90, 163, 214, 225–226, 236–237, 265n4; beauty eliminated from, 184, 191–192, 199, 212; knowledge of Japanese culture not part of, 130–131, 204, 216, 233–234

Junior Chamber International, 56, 254n25

Ka Palapala pageant, 51, 61–63, 110, 255n32, 256nn33–34

kabuki, 68, 257n10

kachikan (cultural values). *See* values:
Japanese

Kadoyama, Sharon (39th CBF Queen, 1991–
1992), 148, 183

Kamisugi, Keith, 183–185, 187–189, 198, 200,
232; interview, 190–197

kanji (Chinese characters used in writing
Japanese), use of in souvenir books, 70

kasa (Japanese parasol), 72, 258n24

Kaua'i Cherry Blossom Queen, 258n14

kendō (Japanese martial art), 130

kibei nisei (Japanese Americans born in
Hawai'i, educated in Japan, returned to
Hawai'i), 47. *See also* nisei

kimono, 251n12, 258n22, 259nn25–26; as
ethnic/national costume, 29, 62; as iconic,
69–70, 206–207; wearing by contestants,
29, 71–72, 100, 162; wearing lessons, 72–
73, 108, 130–131, 144–145, 202–203,
262n13

King, Rebecca, 27, 31

King, Samuel Wilder, 65–66, 72

Kirihira, Lorraine (7th CBF Queen, 1959–
1960), 76

Kodama, Deborah (25th CBF Queen, 1977–
1978), 134, 136, 139, 146–147

Kōhaku Uta Gassen (Red and White Song
Competition), 154, 263n19

Koide, Cheryl (45th CBF Queen, 1997–
1998): herstory, 175–181

Koike, Gayle (31st CBF Queen, 1983–1984),
132

Kondo, Francene (28th CBF Queen, 1980–
1981), 145, 241

Kotani, Roland, 197

koto playing, 69, 200

Kurashige, Lon, 53

Kuwata, Jayne (6th CBF Queen, 1958–1959),
76, 91, 261n3 (chap. 4)

Lekivetz, Lenny, 174, 263n2 (chap. 6)

Lieu, Nhi T., 29, 33, 35

Lim, Shirley, 24–25, 31

linguistic competence in Asian American
beauty pageants, 28, 34

"local" (identity in Hawai'i), 46, 124, 152,
230, 243; values, 4, 240, 246

Lowe, Lisa, 21–23

Mabalon, Dawn, 26, 34

makeup lessons, 129–130

martial arts, 68, 130

masculinity: of HJJCC men, 77–80, 82; of
speaking "pidgin," 42

Massie trials, 253n15

Matsui, Jill (21st CBF Queen, 1973–1974),
229, 237

Matsumoto, Vail (48th CBF Queen, 2000–
2001), 184; herstory, 214–219

Matsumura, Lori (37th CBF Queen, 1989–
1990), 133

McKinley High School Carnival Queen
contest, 60–61, 255n30

"melting pot" of Hawai'i, 60, 188, 194

Mink, Patsy Takemoto, 51, 198

minority, 21, 24, 36, 225

Miss America: beauty standard in, 1–2; protest against, 30; as prototype for pageants,
17–18, 33, 66, 238; as pyramidal pageant,
111, 265n3; as scholarship pageant, 20;
winners from Hawai'i, 249n1

Miss Asia Pacific, 35

Miss Asian America Pageant, 23

Miss Chinatown Hawaii Scholarship Pageant, 255n29

Miss Chinatown U.S.A., 23, 30–34, 255n29

Miss Congeniality, 1, 220

Miss Hawaii, 111, 249n1, 265n3

Miss Hawaii Filipina, 23, 35, 245, 255n29

Miss India Georgia, 23, 28, 34

Miss India U.S.A., 23, 35

Miss India WorldwidE (*sic*), 23

Miss Korea Hawaii, 23, 33, 245, 255n29

Miss Korea International, 23, 33–34, 251n11

Miss Nikkei International, 30, 173

Miss Nisei Week, 2, 25

Miss Ohina, 69, 257n12, 258n13

Miss Popularity, 84, 133

Miss Sakura, 133

Miss Simpatico, 263n1 (chap. 6)

Miss Universe, 17, 35, 250n5

Miss Vietnam Tet, 34, 36

Miss World, 35

mixed ancestry. *See* mixed-race

mixed-race: aesthetic, 31, 185; CBF contestants, 125, 127, 154–156, 183–185, 188, 204;
"Cosmopolitan" category, 61; demography
in Hawai'i, 254n18; marriage, 51, 103,

188–189; Queens, 215–216, 219, 230, 246, 263n3 (chap. 7). *See also* blood-quantum; *hapa;* race/ethnicity

Mizumoto, Lori Ann (29th CBF Queen, 1981–1982), 135–136, 140, 145, 148, 186

model minority, 67, 251n16, 257n8; and niceness, 5, 36, 234

modesty (physical), 30, 76, 143

Morita, LoriJoy (46th CBF Queen, 1998–1999), 136–137, 139–140, 144, 198

Morita, Robert S., 150, 152

mothers of contestants, 76, 106, 136–137

multiculturalism, 127, 151–152, 240, 245

multiethnic. *See* ethnic: multi-

Murayama, Lori (47th CBF Queen, 1999–2000), 184, 196, 243–244; herstory, 210–214

Naichi (Japanese from main islands), 47, 93, 116, 169; –Uchinanchu (Okinawan) relations, 92, 153

Nakahodo, Lisa (32nd CBF Queen, 1984–1985), 128, 154

Nakano, Lisa-Ann (36th CBF Queen, 1988–1989), 129, 133

Nakata, Slim, 105, 112

nakōdo (matchmaker; marital go-between), 50

names: family, 27, 93, 220, 260n37; Japanese middle, 70, 177, 258n17

Narcissus Festival, 59–60, 64; Queen appearances with CBF Queen, 23, 59, 245; Queen and Court, 83, 240, 265n6

native anthropologist, doing fieldwork as, 9–11

"nice girl": CBF participants as, 77, 112, 141, 146, 189, 231, 235; ideal of, 4, 76, 96, 135, 138, 140, 143; Japanese American community as, 240; and model minority image, 36, 112; smile of, 237

niceness, 4–5, 7, 145, 234, 238, 242; CBF as celebration of, 230–231, 246; community service as, 243–244, 266n8; Japanese American stereotype of, 45, 241, 246; and "personality," 237; public face of, 197, 244. *See also* banality

Nihon Sakura no Kai (Japanese Cherry Blossom Association), 132, 261n3 (chap. 5)

Niimi, Violet Tokie (1st CBF Queen, 1953–1954), 66, 110, 112, 146

nikkei (persons of Japanese ancestry), 88–89

nisei (second-generation Japanese Americans), 41–44, 46, 50–54, 253nn12–14, 261n4 (chap. 5); American identity of, 25, 31, 87, 90. *See also* generational differences; Japanese Americans

Nisei Week Queen Contest, 25, 58, 110, 254n23

Nishimura, Marjorie (3rd CBF Queen, 1955–1956), 80

Nishino, Janet (10th CBF Queen, 1962–1963), 92

Nishizawa, Gwen (15th CBF Queen, 1967–1968), 81–82, 88, 93, 238; herstory, 114–121

obi (wide sash for kimono), 130

ochanoyu. See tea ceremony

odori (Japanese dance), 113, 200–201

ojōsan (upper-class, refined, young Japanese woman): CBF contestants as not, 96, 103; CBF participants as, 100, 107, 116, 131,149, 234–235; raising nisei daughters as, 261n4 (chap. 5)

Okinaga, Lisa (50th CBF Queen, 2002–2003), 230

Okinawan (Japanese citizen from Okinawa), 47; American participants in CBF and HJJCC, 92–93, 114, 129, 153–154, 163, 165, 168–169, 260n39; American population in Hawai'i, 92, 260n40; ancestry determined by surname, 260n37; discrimination against, 93, 117, 153, 263n3 (chap. 7); organizations in Hawai'i, 92, 262n17; class stereotype of, 169

"one drop rule," 27, 263n4 (chap. 7). *See also* blood-quantum; mixed-race

100th Infantry Battalion, 53

"PAA crown," 66, 85. *See also* Pan American Airways

pageant, 20, 35, 249–250n2; CBF as separate and parallel, 30, 52, 64, 66; cultural, 20, 24, 238–239; ethnic, 5, 22, 59, 232, 250n9, 255n29; rainbow, 60–61, 64; scholarship, 19–20. *See also* beauty pageants

pageant training, 75, 117, 129–131, 140, 167, 222, 239

Pageantry Magazine, 37, 250n2 (chap. 1)

Palumbo-Liu, David, 32, 38, 256n37

photographers, 81; by tourist industry, 84–85

statehood, Japanese American support of Hawai'i, 44–45

stereotypes, 45, 63; of Asian Americans, 21–22; of Asians, 30, 32; of beauty queens, 140–141; of Japanese American women, 71–72, 185, 210; of Japanese Americans, 7, 21, 45, 47–48, 50, 210, 241, 243; of non-white men, 253n15; of Okinawans, 169

stewardesses, 67, 238, 256n3

subjectivity, 7–8, 37

Suzuki, Ann (13th CBF Queen, 1965–1966), 91

swimsuit portion of beauty pageants, 29–30, 33, 62, 76

taiko (Japanese drumming), 130, 199, 227

Takarazuka, 43

Takata, Dori, 239–240

talent portion of beauty pageants, 28, 33

Tanaka, Rae (20th CBF Queen, 1972–1973), 128, 139

Tasaka, Alison, 196, 212

tea ceremony, 28, 69, 129–130, 201, 251n10

Teramae, Janice (16th CBF Queen, 1968–1969), 138

tiki bar culture, 259n24

Tokumaru, Anna Keiko (2nd CBF Queen, 1954–1955), 67, 70, 106, 250n3, 261n1 (chap. 4); herstory, 96–105

Toth, Catherine (49th CBF Queen, 2001–2002), 184, 196, 230; herstory, 220–227

tourism, 5, 22, 45, 68; and CBF, 83–86, 150, 161

training for CBF pageant. *See* pageant training

travel to Asian homelands, 34, 91, 118–119, 162

Trump, Donald, 17–18, 250n5

Turner, Farrant, 53–54, 254n24

Uchinanchu. *See* Okinawan

United States Junior Chamber of Commerce. *See* Jaycees

University of Hawai'i Ka Palapala pageant. *See* Ka Palapala pageant

values, 20, 265n1; gendered, 4, 76; hegemonic American, 25–26, 138; Japanese, 4, 131, 138, 151, 200–201, 203–204, 241–242, 264n7; Japanese American, 7, 245–246; local Hawai'i, 4, 240, 246

Vietnam War, 68, 124

Wakaba Kai sorority, 51, 62

war bride, 51

weddings, 50, 75

Westernization of Asian faces, 32. *See also* cosmetic surgery

whiteness, 31–32, 62–63. *See also* haole; race/ethnicity

Women's Auxiliary and Women's Advisory Group, 77

Women's Liberation. *See* feminism

World War II: HJJCC linked to, 54–55; internment of Japanese Americans during, 25, 254–255n17; Japanese American veterans of, 41, 45, 47

Yajima, Lenny (34th CBF Queen, 1986–1987), 211, 263nn1–2 (chap. 6); herstory, 169–175

Yajima, Lillian, 51, 67, 104–105, 125, 171, 198, 234–235

Yamada, JoAnn (9th CBF Queen, 1961–1962), 72–74, 81

yonsei (fourth-generation Japanese Americans), 125, 131, 206, 231. *See also* generational differences

Yorita, Eiko, 145

Yoshioka, Ann (23rd CBF Queen, 1975–1976), 137

Young Okinawans of Hawaii, 262n17

ABOUT THE AUTHOR

Christine Yano is associate professor of anthropology at University of Hawai'i at Mānoa. She is the author of *Tears of Longing: Nostalgia and the Nation in Japanese Popular Song* (Harvard University Press, 2002). Her current research projects include a study of Japanese "pink globalization" through Hello Kitty, the fandom surrounding deceased Japanese postwar diva Misora Hibari, and contemporary Japanese media representations of Japanese Americans.

Production Notes for Yano | CROWNING THE NICE GIRL

Cover and interior design by April Leidig-Higgins in Garamond, with display type in Present and Scala Sans

Compostion by Copperline Book Services, Inc.

Printing and binding by Sheridan Books, Inc.

Printed on 60# Accent Opaque, 375 ppi.